Library & Information Services in Agricultural Education, Research & Extension

Library & Information Services in Agricultural Education, Research & Extension

P. RENUKA

AKANSHA PUBLISHING HOUSE
NEW DELHI-110002 (INDIA)

AKANSHA PUBLISHING HOUSE
4649-B/21, Ansari Road
Darya Ganj, New Delhi - 110 002
Ph.: 23263193 / 9811582579 / 09435116718
Telefax: 011-23263193
Email: ektabooks@yahoo.com
www.akanshapublishinghouse.com

Library & Information Services in Agricultural Education, Research & Extension

First Published 2009
ISBN 978-81-8370-180-8

PRINTED IN INDIA

Published by Akansha Publishing House, New Delhi and Printed at Mehra Offset Press, Delhi

Contents

Preface

Generally, all the fields of Science and Technology are being influenced by the phenomena known as 'Information Explosion'. The exponential growth of information which doubles in every decade generated as a result of research and development activity produced in the form of print and non-print materials is creating lot of problems to the users as well as information managers. There is no exception to even agricultural information. The progress of research in the field of agriculture and in turn improvement of production essentially requires timely supply of information to those involved with this field of activity. Libraries and information centers attached to different agricultural institutions including academic, research, government and extension centers have a very important role to play in this context. These centers are expected to serve the information requirement of those engaged in agricultural education, research, extension and developmental activities to enable the nation to achieve maximum self-sufficiency in the field of agricultural production.

The present study mainly examines the available information facility in Andhra Pradesh to serve the information needs of agricultural students, faculty, scientists, research scholars and extension workers. To obtain a comprehensive view of the existing information and infrastructural facilities of all the information centres and libraries is one of the aims of this study irrespective of their location and size. Its purpose is to furnish a body of knowledge and theoretical conclusions upon which future decisions on improving and modernizing of agricultural libraries or information centers can be based. Though there is dire need to automate and network the agricultural libraries located in different parts of Andhra Pradesh, the present information infrastructure scenario demands to bring many changes in the attitude of both professionals and management regarding the adoption of new technologies. Moreover the knowledge and skills of staff are equally important. The remote research stations and centres located in rural areas need more attention in terms of improved information facility with appropriate and adequate collections as well as qualified and adequate number of library staff. The same were emphatically presented in this study based on the findings of the survey.

Acknowdedgements

I express my deep sense of gratitude to Dr. C. Sasikala, Professor, Department of Library and Information Science, Andhra University, Visakhapatnam for her valuable guidance and encouragement in my writing and academic endeavours.

I wish to express my sincere thanks to Dr. B. Vijaya Lakshmi, Professor and Chairman, Board of Studies in Library and Information Science for her valuable suggestions.

My sincere thanks are due to Dr. R.S.R. Vara Lakshmi, Associate Professor and Head, Department of Library and Information Science, Andhra University. I am also thankful to the other faculty members of the Dept. of Library and Information Science. I wish to express my sincere thanks to the staff of all the agricultural institutions for their cooperation.

I am highly thankful to the University Grants Commission, New Delhi and the authorities of Andhra University, Visakhapatnam, for the award of fellowship under the Faculty Development Programme (FDP). I am especially grateful to Maharaja Alak Narayana Society for Arts and Sciences (MANSAS), the Management of the Maharaja's College, Vizianagaram, for deputing me to the Department of Library and Information Science, Andhra University, Visakhapatnam, for Ph.D. programme.

I am thankful to Dr. C. Madan Mohan Rao, former principal of M.R. College, Vizianagaram, for his valuable suggestions and to Mr. Ch. Sastry, Computer Programmer, for his invaluable work.

I wish to thank my husband Dr. P. Venkata Rao, my parents Dr. P. Rama Rao, Smt. Lalita and my children Amarendra, Narendra and other family members for their active cooperation and understanding throughout the course of this study.

Last but not the least, I am extremely thankful to Akansha Publishing House, New Delhi who have brought out this book neatly in the best format within an unbelievably short time.

P. Renuka

Abbreviations

AACR	:	Anglo American Cataloguing Rules
AALDI	:	Association of Agricultural Librarians and Documentalists of India
ADR	:	Associate Directorate of Research
AGRIS	:	Agricultural Information System for Science and Technology
AHRD	:	Agricultural Human Resource Development
AIBA	:	Agricultural Information Bank of Asia
AI&CC	:	Agricultural Information and Communication Centre
AICORPO	:	All India Coordinated Research Project on Oilseeds
AICRP	:	All India Coordinated Research Programme
AICRPDA	:	All India Coordinated Research Project for Dryland Agriculture
AICSIP	:	All India Coordinated Sorghum Improvement Project
ANGRAU	:	Acharya N.G. Ranga Agricultural University
APAU	:	Andhra Pradesh Agricultural University
ARFIS	:	Agricultural Research Finance Information System
ARIC	:	Agricultural Research Information Centre
ARIS	:	Agricultural Research Information System
ARISNET	:	Agricultural Research Information System Network
ARLIS	:	Agricultural Research and Library Information System
ARPIS	:	Agricultural Research Personnel Information System
ARS	:	Agricultural Research Station
ASLIB	:	Association of Special Libraries Information Bureau

ATIC	:	Agricultural Technology Information Centre
B.F.Sc.	:	Bachelor of Fisheries Science
B.Sc. (Ag)	:	Bachelor of Agricultural Science
B.Sc (HS)	:	Bachelor of Home Science
B.Tech. (Ag Engg)	:	Bachelor of Agricultural Engineering
B.V.Sc & A.H.	:	Bachelor of Veterinary Science and Animal Husbandry
CAB	:	Commonwealth Agricultural Bureau
CABI	:	Center for Agriculture and Biosciences International
CARIS	:	Computerized Agricultural Research Information System
CAS	:	Current Awareness Service
CEC	:	Countries of the European Committees
CIAT	:	Central Institute of Agricultural Tropics
CGIAR	:	Consultative Group on International Agricultural Research
CORD	:	Center on Rural Documentation
CRIDA	:	Central Research Institute for Dryland Agriculture
CRRI	:	Central Rice Research Institute
CSCA	:	Central Staff College for Agriculture
CSIR	:	Council of Scientific and Industrial Research
CTRI	:	Central Tobacco Research Institute
DAATTCs	:	District Agricultural Advisory and Transfer of Technology Centres
DARE	:	Department of Agricultural Research and Education
DELNET	:	Delhi Network
DOR	:	Directorate of Oilseed Research
DRDA	:	District Rural Development Agency
DRR	:	Directorate of Rice Research
EEI	:	Extension Education Institute
ERNET	:	Education Research Network

FAO	:	Food and Agricultural Organization
ha	:	Hectare
IARI	:	Indian Agricultural Research Institute
IAALD	:	International Association of Agricultural Librarians and Documentalists
IAAP	:	Intensive Agricultural Area Programme
IADP	:	Intensive Agricultural Developmental Programme
IBIDS	:	International Bibliographic Information on Dietary Supplements.
ICAF	:	International Centre for Research in Agro Forestry
ICAR	:	Indian Council of Agricultural Research
ICARD	:	International Centre for Agricultural Research in Dry areas.
ICGEB	:	International Centre for Genetic Engineering and Biotechnology
ICRISAT	:	International Crops Research Institute for Semi-arid Tropics
IDRC	:	International Development Research Council
IFPRI	:	International Food Policy Research Institute
IIMI	:	International Irrigation Management Institute
IITA	:	International Institute of Tropical Agriculture
IJALIS	:	Indian Journal of Agricultural Library and Information Science
INAL	:	Indian National Agricultural Library
INDSL	:	Indian National Dairy Science Library
INFLIBNET	:	Information Library Network
INVSL	:	Indian National Veterinary Science Library
ISNAR	:	International Science for National Agricultural Research
IVRI	:	Indian Veterinary Research Institute
MANAGE	:	National Institute of Agricultural Extension Management
MLISC	:	Master of Library and Information Science
M.Sc. (Ag)	:	Master of Agricultural Science
NAARM	:	National Academy of Agrioultural Research Management
NARP	:	National Agricultural Research Project

NBPGR	:	National Bureau of Plant Genetic Resources
NCTO	:	National Communication and Training Centre on Oilseeds
NDRI	:	National Dairy Research Institute
NICNET	:	National Information Network
NIRD	:	National Institute of Rural Development
NPPTI	:	National Plant Protection Training Institute
NRCOP	:	National Research Centre on Oil Palm
NRCS	:	National Research Centre for Sorghum
P.G.	:	Post Graduate
Ph.D.	:	Doctor of Philosophy
RARS	:	Regional Agricultural Research Station
RAWE	:	Rural Agricultural Work Experience Programme
RBD&TC	:	Regional Biogas Development & Training Centre
REAC	:	Research and Extension Advisory Council
SAMETI	:	State Agricultural Management and Extension Training Institute
SAUs	:	State Agricultural Universities
SDI	:	Selective Dissemination of Information
T&V	:	Training and Visit
TOT	:	Transfer of Technology
UGC	:	University Grants Commission
UK	:	United Kingdom
UNDP	:	United Nations Development Programme
UNESCO	:	United Nations Educational, Scientific and Cultural Organization
UNICEF	:	United Nations International Children's Education Fund
USDA	:	United States Department of Agriculture
ZREAC	:	Zonal Research and Extension Advisory Council

List of Tables

1

Introduction

For centuries before man began to study and record his findings about the natural world around him, agriculture is a practical art or craft practiced by the majority of the world's population. Agriculture began probably 8,000 to 10,000 years ago, somewhere in the area between the Nile in Egypt and the valley of Indus River in Western India (Salmon Hanson, 1964). Agriculture which has played an important part in the development of most societies, and man's attempts to provide a secure food supply are interwoven with the history of civilization on this planet.

Agriculture continues to be the main occupation of the world's population which meets all the three vital needs of the mankind viz. food, clothing and shelter in one way or the other. It is very interesting to study the evolution of agriculture during the last two hundred years. It is certain that agriculture has grown up gradually and helped the man enjoy the settled life from a nomadic one. At the beginning, man developed the methods of hunting animals in search of his food. Since it was a tedious job, naturally he preferred collecting grass, seeds, fruits, roots and nuts where they grew in abundance. Thus, man started to select and cultivate useful plants for his need.

In the Vedas and in ancient literature of Greek and French, one can notice that well developed and sound practices of agriculture were prevailing during the period before Christ and at the beginning of the Christian era. These included tillage, green manuring, crop rotation, use of lime and growth of legumes for soil improvement, observations of soil and plant interactions. The period from 500 A.D. to 1500 A.D. was a lull period and no valuable improvement in agriculture took place during this period (Perumalsamy, K and Arunachalam N, 2001). Later, the explosion of population and increased need for food production had created an urge to increase production from land.

Agriculture – Definition

In a broad definition of "Agriculture", one should now include any activity directly or indirectly involved in the production and distribution of food for the use of mankind (Blanchard, J. R. 1979). Agriculture is interpreted broadly to mean everything that goes into the production of plants and animals that make food and fabric, all the way from the time the seed is sown until it reaches the consumer. Thus, the primary aim of agriculture is, to improve and develop production of plants and animals as source of food and primary commodities of man. It is a means by which the resources of land and water are converted into those things needed by the people for food, fiber, shelter and recreation. To most people on the globe, farming is still a way of life. Agriculture is not only cultivation; it is a social and cultural phenomenon which provides a bedrock to the entire process of socio-economic development.

Agricultural Education, Research and Extension

In the last decade or so, there have been important shifts in the various approaches to Agricultural Education, Research and Extension especially in the developing world. To maintain relevance of agricultural education, institutions are now recognizing that they must play an active and locally relevant developmental role as well as educational one. They can no longer afford to have only an "academic relationship" to development (Bawden, *et al.,* 1990). The objectives of the agricultural university in particular, is to support the trio of teaching, research and extension programmes by acquiring the latest information and its dissemination to the students and researchers engaged in solving the nation's problem of food and hunger.

In research, for instance, active farmer participation and an on-farm, farming systems' perspective are believed to be indispensable to overcome the failure of traditional experimental research to solve the problems of many farmers, especially those outside the most favourable environment (Sand, 1985). Research in an agricultural university is problem oriented in nature. In other words, its aim is practical, suited to the needs of the agricultural population. Teaching and extension activities are complementary to each other and support research programme of the university (Somasekhar, K.T.1993).

In extension, thinking has moved from expert driven, Transfer of Technology (TOT) approaches to approaches where the emphasis is on "helping farmers to help themselves", that is, to develop his or her own skills and information/ knowledge acquisition systems (Rogers, 1993). Extension Education aims to extend, to spread or to disseminate useful information and ideas to rural people outside regularly organized educational system. It refers to the mechanism, which facilitates the social use of knowledge, which is already acquired and reached.

A major premise underlying these shifts is that education, research and extension need to be farmer-participatory and interactive in order to contribute to agricultural knowledge and technology that results in collective learning, enhances local capabilities and generates sustainable developmental processes and practices (Van Crowder, L. and Anderson, J.1997).

AGRICULTURAL EDUCATION

Till the middle of the 19th century, agriculture was based on age old methods in all parts of the world. The application of chemistry to soils in 1840 and the establishment of the Roth Amsted Research Station in 1843 followed by the opening of the first agriculture college in England at Circencester in 1845 can be described as landmarks in the development of Agricultural Science and education (Soma Sekhar, K. T.1993).

Agricultural Education in India

The earliest reference of Indian agriculture dates back to 3000 B.C. According to *Rigveda*, agriculture had been the chief occupation and various aspects of agriculture such as covering selection of land, tillage, seeds and sowing, irrigation, manuring, agricultural seasons, prediction of weather, management of labour, wages, harvesting, marketing of produce etc. were prescribed in the various *Vedas*.

The first proposal for a special department of agriculture in India had originated from the commission appointed after the Great Famine in Bengal and Orissa in 1866. In 1871, the Department of Revenue, Agriculture and Commerce of the Government of India began to function.

In 1868, a model farm was established at Sadiapet in Chennai (previously Madras) which was later developed into an agricultural school in the year 1884 for the purpose of training young people in different branches of agriculture. The school was under the control of the Director of Public Instructions from 1884 to 1905 and was then transferred to the Department of Agriculture. The government had shifted the agricultural school later to Coimbattore. In 1903, the Government of India approved a scheme for the establishment of Agricultural Research Institutes and under which a research station was started at Pusa in Bihar with the financial assistance of Henry Philip of Chicago. The College of Agriculture was started at Poona during the year 1879 and the Allahabad Agricultural Institute was founded in 1910 at Allahabad. The Agricultural College and Research Institute was opened by Sir Arthur Lawley on 14th July, 1909 at Coimbattore. In 1920, the college was affiliated to one of the oldest universities of India viz., Madras University. In the year 1937, there were 17 Agricultural Colleges in India with an annual enrolment of about 1500 students. As a result of Montague-Chelmsford Reforms in 1921, the need of agricultural institutes was intensely felt which led to the establishment of the Indian Council of Agricultural Research (ICAR) in 1929 for promoting and coordinating Agricultural Research and Education in India. In 1948, the Government of India set up a commission to study the educational needs of the country which suggested the establishment of rural universities in India. On the advice of Dr. Frank W. Parker, an advisor to the Ministry of Food and Agriculture appointed by the first joint Indo-American team, a team of Indian scientists were sent to the USA to study the research and educational institutions in the USA.

The two joint Indo-American teams on agricultural research and education (1954-55 and 1959-60) endorsed the suggestion and recommended the setting up of Agricultural Universities on the pattern of Land Grant Colleges of the United States of America. Accordingly, the first agricultural university came into existence at Pantnagar (Uttarakhand) in 1960 and now with the assistance of ICAR, 31 State Agricultural Universities (SAUs) have been established in the country including the Central Agricultural University at Imphal for the North-East region of the country.

Agricultural Education in Andhra Pradesh

The Andhra Pradesh Agricultural University (APAU) was established on 12th June 1964 under the APAU Act 1963.

Over the years, the Government of Andhra Pradesh has established several agricultural colleges and Agricultural Research stations under the control of Acharya N.G. Ranga Agricultural University with supportive agricultural libraries or collections. The Indian Council of Agricultural Research (ICAR) has also established several Agricultural Research Institutes on different crops at different places in Andhra Pradesh. This has been to promote the study, teaching, research and extension in Agriculture. The institutes and their libraries generate and disseminate agricultural information or knowledge to agricultural extension workers, researchers, teachers, students and farmers as well as policy makers in Government.

Acharya N.G. Ranga Agricultural University (ANGRAU), Hyderabad

The Andhra Pradesh Agricultural University (APAU) was established on 12th June 1964 under the APAU Act 1963. The Andhra Pradesh Agricultural University was renamed as Acharya N.G. Ranga Agricultural University (ANGRAU) with effect from Nov 7, 1996. The ANGRAU has institutions under three faculties. There are six agricultural colleges, 3 Veterinary Science colleges, 2 Home Science colleges, 4 Agricultural Polytechnic colleges and one Veterinary Polytechnic college and 1 college of Agricultural Engineering and one college of Fishery Science.

The University offers education programs at the undergraduate and Post-graduate level , Ph.D. in Agriculture, Horticulture, Veterinary Science and Home Science, while undergraduate programs are offered in Agricultural Engineering, Dairy Technology and Fisheries Science. In addition to the above programs, a two year diploma of Agricultural Polytechnic in Telugu medium is offered to Xth class passed rural students. As a part of regular curriculum in the faculty of agriculture final year B.Sc. (Ag) students are deputed to villages for one semester under rural agricultural work experience program. They are attached to host farmers. More than 5,000 personnel are employed in teaching, research, extension and administrative activities of the university.

Objectives of ANGRAU

- To make provision for education mainly of the peasants of the state of Andhra Pradesh in Agriculture.

- To promote research and extension programmes in agriculture to increase agricultural production.
- To provide technically trained manpower (Education) to generate the technology for increasing agricultural production (Research) and to disseminate the technology to the farmers (Extension).

Teaching campuses

The university has 13 teaching campuses with 18 colleges at Rajendra Nagar, Hyderabad (Agriculture, Veterinary, and Home Science), Bapatla (Agriculture, Agricultural Engineering and Home Science), Tirupati (Agriculture, Veterinary and Dairy Technology) and one each of Agricultural Colleges at Aswaraopet, Naira and Nandyal, including one Fisheries Science College at Muthukur and one Veterinary College at Gannavaram. In addition to these, 4 Agriculture Polytechnics are located at Palem, Jagtial, Maruteru and Anakapalli whereas one veterinary Polytechnic is located at Palamaner.

Agricultural colleges

i) College of Agriculture, Rajendra Nagar (Hyderabad)

The College of Agriculture was started in the year 1946 to meet the technical manpower needs of the Telangana region of erstwhile Nizam state by providing agricultural education. The college which was earlier under the Osmania University has become a constituent college of the A.P.Agricultural University in the year 1964. The college offers B.Sc. (Agriculture), B.Sc. (Horticulture), M.Sc. (Agriculture), M.Sc. (Horticulture) and Ph.D. Degree programmes.

ii) Agricultural College, Bapatla (Guntur District)

The college was started in 1945 initially by offering the B.Sc. (Ag) degree programme. Affiliated to Andhra University till the establishment of A.P. Agricultural University in 1945, Postgraduate programmes were started from the year 1968 and now, the college offers M.Sc.(Ag) in various disciplines. Doctoral degree programmes were introduced in the year 1992-93 in the departments of Entomology, Plant Pathology and Plant Physiology.

iii) S.V. Agricultural College, Tirupati (Chittoor District)

The college was established in the year 1961 and was earlier affiliated to Sri Venkateswara University and later became a constituent college of A.P. Agricultural University in the year 1964. The college offers B.Sc. (Ag) programme and M.Sc. (Ag) programmes in several disciplines. Ph.D. programmes are offered in the two departments viz., Agronomy and Genetics and Plant Breeding.

iv) Agricultural College, Aswaraopet (Khammam District)

The college was established in the year 1989 and it offers B.Sc. (Ag) degree programme.

v) Agricultural College, Naira (Srikakulam District)

The college was established in the year 1989. The college offers B.Sc. (Ag) degree programme.

vi) Agricultural College, Mahanandi (Kurnool District)

The college was started in the year 1991 to cater to the needs of agricultural education in the Rayalaseema region of Andhra Pradesh. The college offers B.Sc. (Ag) degree programme in agriculture.

vii) College of Agricultural Engineering, Bapatla (Guntur District)

The college which existed earlier as Department of Agricultural Engineering in the Agricultural College, Bapatla has attained the independent status since August, 1990. The college offers four year degree programme of B.Tech. (Ag Engg).

viii) College of Veterinary Science, Rajendra Nagar (Hyderabad)

The college was established in 1946 under Osmania University and later became a constituent college of the University in 1964. The college offers B.V.Sc., M.V.Sc., and Ph.D. in different disciplines of Veterinary Science.

ix) College of Veterinary Science, Tirupati (Chittoor District)

The college was established initially at Bapatla during 1955 to cater to the needs of Animal Husbandry Department of the newly formed Andhra State and later shifted to Tirupati in 1957. With the formation of the Agricultural University, the college was brought under APAU in the year 1964. The college offers a five year B.V.Sc. & A.H. and four year B. Tech. (Dairy Technology) degree programmes. The Dairy Technology programme was initiated during the year 1983 to meet the increasing manpower needs of the Dairy Development Corporation of the state. The college has 22 departments. Postgraduate programme leading to M.V.Sc. degree is offered in all the departments except Fisheries Science, Biochemistry, Livestock Production Management, Veterinary Public Health and Veterinary Epidemiology & Preventive Medicine. Dairy Technology programme of this college has been offering post graduate programme in two discplines i.e. M.Tech. (Dairying) and M.Sc. (Dairying), Ph.D. programmes are being offered in seven departments.

x) College of Veterinary Science, Gannavaram (Krishna District)

The college was started with temporary headquarters at the College of Veterinary Science, Rajendranagar since 1998. Subsequently, the college was shifted to Gannavaram. Its aim is to cater to the needs of livestock farmers of coastal region of Andhra Pradesh duly concentrating efforts on the overall development of livestock production and management. The college offers a five year B.V.Sc. & A.H. degree programme to the students of Coastal Andhra.

xi) College of Fisheries Science, Muthukur (Nellore District)

The college was started in 1992 with the objective to train technical manpower required by the fisheries sector in Andhra Pradesh. The college offers a four year B.F.Sc., degree programme in Fisheries Science.

xii) College of Home Science, Hyderabad

The college is a centre of learning and education leading towards overall development of the family as well as community. The college was initially under the Directorate of Technical Education, Government of Andhra Pradesh and later transferred to the A.P. Agricultural University in 1964. The college offers a three year degree B.H.Sc. (Rural), M.Sc. (H.Sc.) and Ph.D. programmes in the departments of Food & Nutrition, Textiles and Clothing, Human Development and Family Resource Management.

xiii) College of Home Science, Bapatla (Guntur District)

The college was started in the year 1983 in the Agricultural college campus, Bapatla with an objective to encourage rural girls to study B.Sc. (Home Science). The college was later shifted to the present new campus in 1990. The college offers a three-year degree programme in B.H.Sc. (Rural) and only girl students are admitted into the college.

xiv) Agricultural Polytechnic College, Palem (Mahabub Nagar District)

The college was started in the year 1989 at the Regional Agricultural Research Station, Palem, to provide facilities for education to rural youth in agriculture for providing opportunities of self employment and to train manpower needed to serve as a grass root level field functionaries in various development departments and agencies involved in agricultural and rural development activities. The college offers a two year diploma course in agriculture to the students drawn exclusively from rural areas of Andhra Pradesh.

xv) Agricultural Polytechnic College, Jagitial (Karimnagar District)

The college was established in 1996. The college offers a two year diploma course in agriculture after 10th class, for students belonging to the rural areas of Telangana region.

xvi) Agricultural Polytechnic College, Maruteru (West Godavari District)

The college was started at the Agricultural Research Station, Maruteru to provide facilities for education to rural youth. The college offers a 2 year diploma course in agriculture to the students drawn from the rural areas of West Godawari, Krishna and Guntur districts.

xvii) Agricultural Polytechnic College, Anakapalli (Visakhapatnam District)

The college was started in the year 2000 at the Regional Agricultural Research

Station, Anakapalli to provide facilities for education to rural youth. The college offers a two year diploma course in agriculture to the students drawn exclusively from the rural areas of the coastal districts of Srikakulam, Vizianagaram, Visakhapatnam, East & West Godavari.

xviii) Veterinary Polytechnic College, Palamaner (Chittoor District)

The college offers a 2 year diploma course in Veterinary science after 10th class, for students coming from rural areas of Andhra Pradesh, for providing self-employment and to train manpower needed to serve as grass root level field functionaries in various developmental departments and agencies involved in veterinary science.

Research

The changing agricultural scenario at the state, national and global level, national policies and the changing socio-economic structure warrant restructuring and re-orientation of research programmes.

Research, constantly improve and generate technologies for increasing production in Agriculture, Animal Husbandry, Home Science and allied sectors of the 3 major mandates of the university taken over the State Department of Agriculture during 1964 along with some infrastructure.

The major thrust of the university is research. With the implementation of National Agricultural Research Project (NARP), research has been reorganized with a strong multi-disciplinary approach to serve the location-specific research requirements more effectively.

Research Stations

Research in the University encompassing the major fields of Agriculture, Livestock, Home Science and Fisheries is conducted at 68 Research Stations spread over 7 agroclimatic zones of the A.P. state for conducting location specific and need-based research on various crops grown in the state.

Extension Services

The limited but specialized extension services based on the results of research are being rendered through Extension Education Units located at the Regional Agricultural Research Stations (RARS) as well as Krishi Vignan Kendras (KVKs), Extension Education Institute (E.E.I.), Agricultural Information and Communication Centre (AI & CC), Regional Biogas Training Centres (RBTDC) and also through the recently established District Agricultural Advisory and Transfer of Technology Centers (DAATTC) in each district.

i) Rural Agricultural Work Experience Programme

As part of the regular curriculum in the Faculty of Agriculture, final year B.Sc. (Ag) students are deputed to the villagers for one semester under Rural Agricultural Work Experience Programme. They are attached to host farmers.

This programme would help the students in acquiring better understanding of the village environment, besides giving them an insight into the major constraints that work as stumbling blocks in the dissemination and application of new agricultural technology at a faster rate. Also through gaining work experience in the application of new farm technology in rural areas, the students would be better equipped to practise farming and extension work. It is believed that it would also motivate many agricultural graduates to stay at rural and semi-rural centres in gainful self-employment.

ii) Rural Home Science Experience Programme

As a part of the regular academic curriculum, the final year B.H.Sc. students of the faculty of Home Science attend to the Rural Home Science work Experience Programme and stay in the villages for one semester.

iii) Internship Programme

In the faculty of Veterinary Science the final year B.V.Sc and A.H students of the veterinary science colleges are deputed for internship programme to district veterinary hospitals.

Extension Education

The concept of Agricultural University envisages a strong integration of teaching, research and extension through their balanced development. The major emphasis in extension education of Agricultural universities is on front line extension activities like testing and introduction of new technologies on the farmers' fields, processing of technical information, training of extension personnel of the state and other developmental departments and developing innovative extension methodologies and strategies etc.

In order to perform these activities, the University has the following Extension and Transfer of Technology Centres set up at different places of the state.

The university has excelled in the transfer of technology with its several innovative and novel programmes as follows.

i) District Agricultural Advisory and Transfer of Technology Centres (DAATTCs)

The ANGRAU has reorganized its extension services by establishing District Agricultural and Transfer of Technology Centres in all the 23 district headquarters except Hyderabad district. These centres provide technological back up and lend support to the extension agencies of the line departments and conduct regular field diagnostic visits, identify the field problems and provide scientific solutions.

ii) Krishi Vigyan Kendras (KVKs)

There are 6 Krishi Vigyan Kendras located at Amudalavalasa, Srikakulam District; Rastakuntabai, Vizianagaram District; Malyal, Warangal District; Reddipalli, Ananthapur District; Mahanandi, Kurnool District and Undi, West Godavari District working under the control of the university and organize the skill oriented, production oriented, short term training programmes for the farmers, rural youth and farm women.

iii) Agricultural Information & Communication Centre (A I & CC)

The Agricultural Information and Communication Centre processes technical information generated by the university scientists and other related agencies and disseminates for the benefit of the farming community and the extension personnel of line departments, through publications and other channels of mass media.

a) *Vyavasaya Panchangam*

Vyavasaya Panchangam – A farmers' almanac in Telugu provides valuable information on agriculture and allied subjects is published from this centre and is released on "Ugadi"(Telugu New Year) day every year.

b) *Bulletins*

This university started publishing crop-wise bulletins on insect pests, diseases and nutritional disorders both in Telugu and English on a wide variety of crops for the benefit of farmers as well as to the Extension officers.

c) *Distance Education*

Realizing the enormous potential of mass media, Distance Education through electronic media, as an outreach programme for the farmers, the university first of its kind in the agriculture and allied fields has introduced telecasts of 10-15 institutes direction at 6.30 A.M. daily through a private ETV Channel under the caption "Annadata – Velugu Bata".

d) *"Rytumitra"*

"Rytumitra" (which means 'Friend of the farmer') is a joint production of ANGRAU and Department of Agriculture, Government of Andhra Pradesh. This is a positive step to educate farmers through electronic media on Teja T.V. channel for one hour daily between 6 and 7 P.M. Rytumitra has two components, one telecast recorded programme (6 to 6-30 P.M.), second innovative component is phone-in live session where resource persons of ANGRAU offer solutions to the queries raised by farmers regarding agricultural and allied aspects.

iv) Agricultural Technology Information Centre (ATIC)

Agricultural Technology Information Centre (ATIC) is a "single window" support system linking the various units of the University with intermediary users and end users (farmers) in decision-making and problem solving exercise. This centre was established in the University on 25, July 2000.

v) Kisan Melas

'Kisan Melas' (farmers congregation) are being organized by this University in all the 77 revenue divisions of the state to disseminate the technical information.

vi) Village Adoption

Another novel programme implemented by the University is its "Village Adoption" programme and is being implemented in 50 centres all over the state of A.P. The frequent contact of the scientists with the villagers help farmers to take up remedial measures on time for the field problems and also have overall economic development and upliftment of the people.

vii) State-wide broadcast over All India Radio (Vyavasaya Suchanalu)

The University in collaboration with All India Radio, Hyderabad every day broadcasts a 10 minute bulletin at 6.50 P.M., on agriculture, horticulture, animal husbandry, fisheries, women in agriculture exclusively for the benefit of the farmers. This programme was introduced by the University in 1964, is the first of its kind in agricultural universities, aimed at quick dissemination of information.

viii) Agricultural Market Committee level Training

The University scientists in collaboration with the Department of Agriculture, Andhra Pradesh Government have been training several thousands of farmers at 286 Agricultural Market Committees every year both in *Kharif* and *Rabi* seasons. At each market committee, about 300 to 400 farmers are being trained on major crops grown in that particular area.

ix) Linkages of ANGRAU with Department of Agriculture, Government of Andhra Pradesh and other organizations

The linkages between ANGRAU and State A.P. Department of Agriculture are at two levels which include the linkage mechanism for coordination of research and extension programmes at state level and at regional as well as local levels.

AGRICULTURAL RESEARCH

Present day agricultural research does not limit itself to the techniques of farming alone; it has broadened its scope to embrace both basic and applied sciences and technologies involved in the production of food and materials for clothing and shelter. It also includes the improvement of plant and animal life and their protection and conservation. Agriculture, being one of the world's oldest practical arts, is now recognized as one of the youngest professions in the applied sciences like medicine. Scientific agriculture rests on the principles of the basic sciences. However, modern agriculture draws not only from botany, zoology, chemistry, physics and mathematics but also from geology, meteorology, economics, sociology, statistics and engineering. The profession of agriculture includes a wide diversity of practices and specializations as it is vitally linked with the production of basic necessities of man derived from plants and animals. The specializations include crop sciences, animal husbandry, fisheries and marine products, food science technology and home science. Sericulture, bee culture, lac culture etc. are also added to agriculture. Apart from the above, the aspects of civil and mechanical, electrical and chemical engineering are becoming increasingly the subjects of study in agriculture.

With the alarming rate of growth in population, results of agricultural research are being put into widespread use for maximizing the production which has always been subject to the vagaries of weather and climate.

Agricultural Research – International

Scientific studies in agriculture started in Europe around 1500 A.D. Van Helmont, after his famous experiments with a willow tree in pot (1577-1644) concluded that water was the principal ingredient for plant growth. Jethro Tull (1731) concluded that food consists of fine soil particles and tillage was necessary for plant growth and he developed a seed drill. In 1761, Wallerius developed the theory that humus was the source of plant food and many people accepted it. By 1770-1800, the idea that plants utilize atmospheric gases was developed by Prietle. In 1804 Theodore de Soussure established the phenomenon of respiration and photosynthesis. By 1834, J.B. Boussingault introduced the system of field study and quantitative determination of grain and loss of nutrients such as carbon, hydrogen, oxygen and nitrogen and mineral matter. In 1840, the Royal Charter encouraged practical farmers to use science and scientists to proceed on practical farming lines. In the same year Liebig's paper on chemistry and its application to agriculture and physiology explained the concept that carbon-dioxide from air was the source of carbon for plants and that nitrogen was taken from air or soil as ammonia. Thus he established the mineral nutrition theory. He was the first to introduce Super phosphate as manure. In 1843 Lawes and Bilbert established that legumes require a little nitrogen fertilizer and non-legumes require more of it. Later Lachmann (1858) found living micro-organisms in legume roots and the relationship between micro-organisms and nitrogen fixation in plants was established by Beijerinck in 1893.

At the same time improved ploughs, mechanical harvesters and threshers were developed in England and rapid mechanization followed in many of the civilized countries. Thus 19th century was the period of scientific development in most of the countries. In the United Kingdom, agricultural research and education was coordinated by Roth Amsted Experimental station. It was founded in 1843 at Harpenden in Hertfordshire, which was a pioneering institute made several landmarks in the development of agricultural research in the U.K. The first agricultural college in England was established at Cinensceta in the year 1845.

At present, there are 30 international agricultural research institutions established in various parts of the world. These are devoted to various crops like rice, maize, wheat etc. They have built up excellent collections in the subject area of their specialization. Some of them are publishing very good bibliographies. One of the International Research Institutes set up in India is "International Crops Research Institute for the Semi-Arid Tropics" (ICRISAT) at Hyderabad.

International Crops Research Institute for the Semi Arid Tropics (ICRISAT), Hyderabad, India

The research of ICRISAT is geographically divided into three regions: Western and Central Africa (WCA), Southern and East Africa (SEA) and Asia. It supports three research stations in each of African regions. ICRISAT facility in India also serves as its corporate headquarters. It is also active in Latin America and Caribbean (LAC) and West Asia / North Africa. It is supported by well organized library and the details are presented in Chapter 2.

The International Crops Research Institute for the Semi-Arid Tropics was founded in 1972 at Hyderabad, Andhra Pradesh, as part of an international emphasis on Sub-Southern Africa and Southern Asia.

Objectives of ICRISAT

i) Improving the six crops—finger millet, pearl millet, sorghum, groundnut, pigeon pea, and chickpea and conserving their genetic resources.

ii) Improving agriculture in the semi-arid tropics.

iii) Develop improved farming systems that will help to increase and stabilize agricultural production through more effective use of natural and human resources in the seasonally dry semi-arid tropics.

iv) Identify constraints to agricultural development in the semi-arid tropics and evaluate means of alleviating them through technological and institutional changes.

v) Assist in the development and transfer of technology to the farms through cooperation with national and regional research programs, and by sponsoring workshops and conferences, operating training programs and assisting extension activities.

In India there are two international research centers in agriculture. The International Crops Research Institute for Semi-Arid Tropics (ICRISAT) at Hyderabad, is part of the Consultative Group on International Agricultural Research (CGIAR) network and its mandated crops include sorghum, pearl millet, groundnut, chickpea and pigeon pea. The other institute is the International Centre for Genetic Engineering and Biotechnology (ICGEB). The ICGEB is sponsored by (UNIDO) and its facilities at Delhi focus on agriculture, animal and human health. India has also the regional offices of the International Plant Genetic Research Institute; International Potato Research Institute and national office of the International Rice Research Institute.

Agricultural Research System in India

Scientific farming began to receive attention in India with the establishment of the Imperial Department of Agriculture at Calcutta in 1881, followed by the emergence of the State Departments of Agriculture in Bombay, Madras, Shillong, Allahabad and Nagpur between 1883 and 1895. However, it was in the beginning of twentieth century that the Government of India recognized the need for setting up a sound system and laid the foundation for organized research in India by establishing the Imperial Institute of Agricultural Research at Delhi in 1905. After independence, it was renamed as Indian Agricultural Research Institute (IARI). Indian Council of Agricultural Research (ICAR) was established in 1929 as a registered society. Later the setting up of the Royal Commission on Agriculture (1926) greatly helped in examining the conditions of agriculture and rural economy in India. Subsequently, the central and State Governments adopted the objective of planned economic growth coupled with social development. Between 1921 and 1962 a number of central commodity committees dealing with research on specific crops were set up as semi autonomous bodies and were located in the main growing regions of the crops concerned. Further, the Government of India also established a number of research institutes under their direct administration including the Forest Research Institute and College at Dehradun (1906), National Dairy Research Institute, Karnal (1922), Central Rice Research Institute, Cuttack (1946), Central Potato Research Institute, Shimla (1949). Similarly the State Governments also set up their own Research Stations and Experimental Research Farms. There are a number of other agro-based institutions such as Tea Board, Coffee Board and Rubber Board, Central Food Technology Research Institute, Mysore and the Botanical, Zoological and Geological Surveys of India which conduct research in the areas of agricultural interest. As a result of reorganization of agricultural research in 1966, thirty three Research Institutes which are on crop varieties are now functioning under the administrative control of Indian Council of Agricultural Research. (Subbaiah, R. 1985)

In addition, there are corporate bodies dealing with rural and dairy development like National Institute of Rural Development, National Dairy Development Board, Institute of Rural Management etc., which are contributing to the agricultural development.

Role of ICAR in Science and Technology Missions

- Two Jai Vigyan National Science and Technology Missions, one on conservation of Agro-biodiversity and the other on Household Food and Nutritional Security through enhancement of production and productivity of life support enterprises of tribal, backward and hill areas was launched.
- Under the National Agricultural Technology Project (NATP), 27 mission mode projects have been operationalized for focused research on issues of critical importance.
- Twenty six teams of excellence are being supported by NATP in different parts of the country. This will create critical human resource for cutting edge science, keeping in view the needs of the future.

ICAR - Vision 2020

ICAR Vision 2020 is developed for all-round agricultural growth through:

a) Research

- Addresses food and nutritional security, poverty alleviation, natural resource management and globalization.
- Centres around people, productivity, profitability, partnership and permanency.
- Focuses on rain-fed agriculture, water management, diversification and intensification, post-harvest management, gender issues and integrated nutrient management and integrated pest management.

b) Education

- Bringing uniformity and raising quality in Agriculture education.
- Technological empowerment of women.
- Perspective manpower planning and counseling for placement.
- Shift in emphasis from information to skill-based curriculum so that agricultural graduates become job providers rather than job seekers.
- Promotion of excellence in frontiers and areas of science through centres of excellence.

- Distance education.
- Rural Agricultural Work Experience (RAWE).

c) Extension

- For giving effective research – extension – farmer linkages through technology assessment and refinement.
- Expanding Institute Village Linkage Programme (IVLP) approach.
- Rationalization and consolidation for sustainability of KVKs.
- Extension education to meet the growing requirements of agriculture.

Boost to Technology Transfer

53 Zonal Agricultural Research Stations are being strengthened in various parts of the country to take up the additional functions of Krishi Vignan Kendras (KVKs). With this, the total number of KVKs has been raised to 314. Forty Agricultural Technology Information centres are being opened at selected ICAR Institutes and State Agricultural Universities single window delivery centres for technology information, inputs and testing facilities.

International Linkages

ICAR has developed formal cooperation with 15 countries, 22 foreign organizations and 17 centres of Consultative Group of International Agricultural Research (CGIAR).

In the last two years, the cooperation agreement was signed with the Cornell University and Ohio State University of USA, International Centre on Genetic Engineering and Biotechnology (ICGEB), National Agricultural Research Organization of Uganda, National Agricultural Research Institute of Peru and Centre for Agricultural and Biosciences International (CABI).

The Indian Council of Agricultural Research has been a partner in international cooperation over a hundred years. The Imperial Bacteriological Laboratory established in 1889 at Izat Nagar (at present, IVRI) first evolved goat-adapted Rinderpest vaccine in 1927 which is in use, the world over. The continuous multilateral cooperative programmes with the United Nations Development Programme (UNDP), United Nations Educational, Scientific and Cultural Organization (UNESCO), Food and Agricultural Organization (FAO), Swedish Agency for Research Cooperation with Developing Countries (SARCD), Consultative Group on International Agricultural Research (CGIAR) and the Centre for Agriculture and Biosciences International (CABI) have helped in the exchange of information on both research and education, exchange of experts and ideas, and in equipping of ICAR laboratories with the latest equipment.

At present there are more than 120 projects in operation with collaborations offshore; majority of them with the USA, UK, Canada, Netherlands and Australia.

Memorandum Of Understandings (MOUs) and Agreements / Work plans have been signed with various countries like Brazil, Bulgaria, China, Cuba, Iran, Israel, Mauritius, Mongolia, the Philippines, Russia, USA, and Vietnam and private organizations of worked status (the Rockefeller Foundation and Food Foundation of the United States of America). Work plans are being finalized with Bangladesh, Nepal and Pakistan.

With the Rockefeller Foundation, the ICAR has signed a work plan to promote the development of rice biotechnology. The participating institutions, with a separate participating role are: the Biotechnology centre, IARI, New Delhi; Central Rice Research Institute, Cuttack; Directorate of Rice Research, Hyderabad; ICAR Research centre for North East Hill Region, Shillong; Haryana Agricultural University, Hisar; Punjab Agricultural University, Ludhiana; Tamilnadu Agricultural University, Coimbatore and Orissa University of Agricultural and Technology, Bhubaneswar. All negotiations between the Governments and multilateral agencies are carried out with the ICAR through the Department of Agricultural Research and Education (DARE), Ministry of Agriculture, Government of India.

ICAR Publications

ICAR publishes 50 titles a year on an average. Journals include, "The Indian Journal of Agricultural Sciences", and "Indian Farming" (Monthly).

Agricultural Research Information Centre

The ARIC maintains and provides information on agricultural scientists in ICAR institutes and agricultural universities. It also works as a national input centre for AGRIS and annually contributes more than 4000 inputs of Indian origin to the AGRIS.

Publicity and Public Relations unit is responsible for dissemination of information about major research findings of the Council through mass media, press releases to the newspapers, organization of press conferences, press visits, supplement and feature articles in newspapers.

- Periodical broadcasts and telecasts are arranged on subjects of importance.
- National and International exhibitions are organized on special occasions.
- For the rural masses, documentations and films are produced.

National Agricultural Research System (NARS)

Indian Council of Agricultural Research (ICAR), comprises of 48 Central Research Institutes (CRIs) that include 4 National Institutes viz., Indian Agricultural Research Institute, New Delhi; Indian Veterinary Research Institute, Izatnagar; National Dairy Research Institute, Karnal and the Central Institute of Fisheries Education, Bombay; 4

National Bureaus for plant, animal, fish genetic resources and for soils; 10 Project Directorates (PDs); 30 National Research Centres (NRCs); the National Academy of Agricultural Research Management (NAARM), Hyderabad and 86 All-India Coordinated Research Projects (AICRPs). It is also operating World Bank Projects and projects for Tribal, Scheduled Castes and other backward communities and schemes for their upliftment.

The total staff working in the Council in different categories is over 30,000 of which over 7,000 are scientists (ICAR, 1996). The State Agricultural Universities employ about 19000 scientists for teaching, research and extension education out of which over 5,000 scientists are employed in the ICAR- supported coordinated projects.

ICAR Institutes situated in Andhra Pradesh, India

1. Directorate of Rice Research (1965), Rajendra Nagar, Hyderabad.
2. Central Tobacco Research Institute (1947) – Rajahmundry.
3. Directorate of Oilseeds Research (1967) - Hyderabad
4. National Academy of Agricultural Research Management (1976) - Hyderabad.
5. Central Research Institute for Dry land Agriculture (1933) – Hyderabad.
6. National Bureau of Plant Genetic Resources (1985) – Hyderabad.
7. National Research Centre for Sorghum (1987), Hyderabad.
8. National Research Centre in Oil Palm (1995), Pedavegi, Eluru (W.G. Dt. A.P)

i) Directorate of Oilseeds Research (DOR), Hyderabad

Oilseeds research in India received a fillip with the setting up of the All India Coordinated Research Project on Oilseeds (AICORPO) in 1967. Initially, the project was headed by a full time project coordinator and had 32 research centres covering five major crops namely, groundnut, rapeseed, mustard, sesame, linseed and castor. In 1972 three more crops namely, sunflower, safflower and niges were added to the AICORPO. Each crop functioned under an Associate Coordinator.

The project was elevated to the status to Directorate of Oilseeds Research (DOR) in 1977 to strengthen the basic, strategic, applied research and coordination activities of AICORPO on sunflower, sesame, safflower, castor, linseed and niges. DOR started functioning with seven project coordinators for groundnut (Junagadh), rapeseed-mustard (Hisar), sesame/niger (Jabalpur), sunflower (Bangalore), safflower (Solapur), linseed (Kanpur) and castor (Hyderabad).

The DOR is located in the campus of Acharya N.G. Ranga Agricultural University, Rajendranagar, Hyderabad. The directorate is headed by a Project Director with scientists in various disciplines to carry out basic and strategic research in addition to coordination activities.

Management of genetic resources of mandated Crops in Basic, Strategic and Applied research to increase productivity and oil content; Research on quality of oil and oilseed cake; Socioeconomic research for assessing sustainability of technologies; Transfer of technology; Coordination of multi-location trails through AICRP and Network to develop varieties/hybrids and technologies.

ii) National Academy of Agricultural Research Management (NAARM), Hyderabad

The National Commission on Agriculture has recommended to establish an All India Institute of Agricultural Administration and Management for training of the agricultural scientists. The expert committee, appointed by the Government in 1973, endorsed the setting up of a national staff college for agriculture. Accepting this recommendation ICAR established the Central Staff College for Agriculture (CSCA) at Hyderabad, in September 1976 keeping in view the importance of its role at all India level and beyond. CSCA was renamed as National Academy of Agricultural Research Management (NAARM) in 1979.

Since its inception, the academy has taken up the responsibility of organizing training programs, workshops and seminars in the areas related to agricultural research, technology transfer and education management for the scientists of the ICAR Institutes and State Agricultural Universities (SAUs). Investigations on management problems associated with agricultural research and education formed another major activity of the Academy. The research from such research effort formed the basis for training as well as for organizing workshops and seminars. The Academy has also been functioning as a repository of ideas and information, both at the national and international levels, and acting as a clearing house for dissemination and utilization of such information and knowledge.

The Academy is contributing significantly to generate a sense of fraternity and inculcates scientific culture among the agricultural scientists in the country. This unique institution has already established its credibility in the national and international area. It is looked upon as a model by the developing countries and it is fast developing into a viable regional training centre in this part of the world to train agricultural scientists and academicians in agricultural research and education management.

iii) Central Research Institute for Dryland Agriculture (CRIDA), Hyderabad

The need for research on dry lands was recognized long before Independence. The earliest research date back to 1923 at Solapur, Bijapur, Hagari, Raichur and Rohtak by the then Imperial Council of Agricultural Research. Further improvement in the network of dryland research was made in 1970 when ICAR launched the all India coordinated research project for dryland agriculture (AICRPDA), with 23 centres spread all over the country. During 1985 further strengthening of dryland research was made by the creation of an institute viz., Central Research Institute for Dryland Agriculture by ICAR.

The CRIDA is a pioneering research institution in the country which addresses itself to all basic and applied research problems pertaining to dryland agriculture. It is a constituent of the Indian Council of Agricultural Research (ICAR), an autonomous body under the Ministry of Agriculture, Government of India.

CRIDA is organized into four divisions for undertaking research and transfer of technology programs and undertakes the development-cum-demonstration programmes. Various training programmes designed for subject-matter specialists and Department of Agriculture personnel through Trainers Training Center (TTC) and training farmers through Krishi Vigyan Kendras (KVK). The institute organizes several working group meetings, regional discussions, workshops, seminars, symposia during the year.

iv) National Bureau of Plant Genetic Resources (NBPGR), Hyderabad

Seed plays a vital role in the production of food. The need for increasing the food production rapidly has necessitated the exchange of germplasm rather more frequently with many countries. In the large scale exchange of germplasm, an inherent risk of introducing new pests, pathogens and weeds lies. Plant quarantine has therefore assumed considerable importance in the recent years, as a result of increased emphasis on the utilization of exotic genetic variability in ongoing breeding programmes all over the world.

To meet the growing germplasm requirements of Agricultural Research institutes, Agricultural Universities and other scientific institutions including ICRISAT, a Plant Quarantinal Regional Station of the National Bureau of Plant Genetic Resources was established by ICAR with head quarters at A.P.A.U. campus, Rajendranagar, Hyderabad in March, 1985. The quarantine processing of paddy material started in April 1986, whereas for ICRISAT mandate crops (pearl millet, sorghum, chickpea, pigeon pea, groundnut and minor millets) the work was started in August 1986.

The National Bureau of Plant Genetic Resources was established in 1976 with its main campus at New Delhi. It is the nodal organization in India with the national mandate to plan, conduct, promote, and coordinate all activities concerning plant exploration and collections and also for safe conservation and distributions of both indigenous and introduced genetic variability in crop plants and their wild relatives. The Bureau is also vested with the authority to issue Import Permit and Phytosanitary Certificate and conduct quarantine checks on all seed materials and plant propagules introduced from abroad or exported for research purposes.

It has strong linkages with leading crop-based institutes, National Research Centres, All India coordinated crop improvement projects, State Agricultural Universities and other stakeholders. NBPGR also works in close collaboration with several international institutes/organizations through memoranda of understanding and also implements work plans developed under bilateral/multilateral agreements. The bureau not only provides genetic resources to on-going crop improvement programmes to sustain continued advances in agricultural productivity and stabilize production, but also conserves them safely to meet the needs of future generations.

A two year M Sc course on plant genetic resources was started at NBPGR in collaboration with the post graduate school, IARI, New Delhi from the 1997 session organizing training programmes (on plant genetic research management) conducting workshops.

v) National Research Centre for Sorghum (NRCS), Hyderabad

National Research Centre for Sorghum (NRCS) was established on 16th November 1987. It is situated over an area of 70 acres adjoining the APAU, Rajendranagar, Hyderabad.

Prior to the upgradation of this centre as the present, NRCS was engaged in research on important dryland crops such as sorghum, castor, groundnut, red gram and cotton and sorghum based farming systems. It was first established in 1958 as a Project on Intensified Research on Cotton, Oilseeds and Millets (PIRCOM). From 1966, it became a regional research station of the Indian Agricultural Research Institute (IARI), New Delhi. Since January 1970, it also became the main unit of All India Coordinated Sorghum Improvement Project (AICSIP).

As the main unit of AICSIP, this centre helped in strengthening network system created for conducting applied research on sorghum improvement and testing of production technologies at national level. NRCS was established to further strengthen research on sorghum on a national mode with increased emphasis on basic research areas encompassing Rabi sorghum productivity, sustainability of productions, product utilization and profitability. A regional Rabi sorghum research centre was also established under NRCS at Solapur (Maharashtra) to conduct Rabi sorghum research under the representative habitat of western Maharashtra and Northern Karnataka.

vi) Directorate of Rice Research (DRR), Hyderabad

The All India Coordinated Rice Improvement Project (AICRIP) was established at Hyderabad in 1965 by ICAR to organize Coordinated Rice Research. The project over the years had grown to the present status as Directorate of Rice Research (DRR) from April 1985 with added mandate of organizing research on irrigated rice for strengthening and stabilizing rice production. Under AICRIP there are 51 test locations funded by

ICAR representing all states and all ecosystems. In addition, DRR is currently handling 4 major research networks on hybrid rice, germplasm evaluation and utilization, quality rices and biotechnology and 7 ICAR Cess Fund supported research projects.

The mandate of the Directorate of Rice Research (DRR) is as follows:

a) To coordinate multiplication testing at national level to identify appropriate varietal and management technologies for all ecosystems.

b) To conduct strategic and applied research on all major thrust areas with special emphasis on irrigated rice.

c) To coordinate and monitor research networks relating to problems of national and regional priority.

d) To serve as a major centre for exchange of research material and information.

e) To impart training to subject matter specialists and researchers and develop innovative extension mechanisms for transfer.

vii) Central Tobacco Research Institute (CTRI), Rajahmundry

The Government of India had set up the Indian Central Tobacco Committee (ICTC) in 1945, recognizing the importance of tobacco in the national economy. The committee established the Central Tobacco Research Institute (CTRI) at Rajahmundry in 1947 to introduce scientific system of tobacco cultivation in the country. The main objectives of the institute are to carry out fundamental and applied research on all types of tobacco grown in India with special emphasis on improving the productivity and quality of exportable types of tobacco. In the years 1965 the Institute was brought under the aegis of Indian Council of Agricultural Research (ICAR). It has a network of seven regional research stations situated in Guntur, Kandukur, Jeelugumilli (A.P); Vedasandur (TN) Hunsur (Karnataka); Pusa (Bihar) and Dinhata (WB) and a research centre at Jeddangi (A.P). These regional stations are catering to the requirements of the tobacco farmers in different agro-climatic zones by developing improved technologies of crop production.

The multilocation trails are being conducted on all types of tobacco through its AICRP centres. The all India coordinated research project on tobacco was started in Fourth Five Year plan in the 1970 with headquarters at Anand. It has six main centre and six sub-centres to carry out multi- location trails on various types of tobacco.

Agricultural Research System in Andhra Pradesh

As per the APAU Act, the Achraya N.G. Ranga Agricultural University has taken up the responsibility of Agricultural Research in 1966, Livestock Research in 1967, Home Science Research in 1974, and Fisheries and Farm Foresting Research in 1976. Since then, there has been significant expansion of Research stations and diversification of research programmes subsequently over the years (Table 1).

Table 1
Growth of Agricultural Research Stations in A.P.

Year	*Number of Research Stations*
1966	30
1970	35
1975	37
1980	46
1985	53
1988	59
1995	66
2000	68

The major thrust of the Acharya N.G. Ranga Agricultural University is agriculture research. To meet the increasing demand for location-specific research needs of the state, the number of research stations has increased from 41 in 1966 to 68 in 2000. The number of research schemes also rose from 104 in 1966 to 241 by 2000. The scientific manpower engaged in research increased from 172 to about 850 during the same period. The land area of the University for research, which was only 1100 hectares, is now 3400 hectares.

From the year 1966 to 1978, the university was planning, coordinating and monitoring research activities from the headquarters of the ANGRAU located at Rajendra Nagar, Hyderabad. With the implementation of National Agricultural Research Project (NARP Phase I) since 1979, the state is divided into 7 agro-climatic zones. Each has a multi-disciplinary Regional Agricultural Research Station (RARS) for effectively tackling the research programmes in the zone. These RARSs are headed by Associate Directors of Research (ADR) who are responsible for identifying local problems effecting agricultural productivity and generate technologies to suit local needs. The zonal headquarters and the research stations function under each RARS. Now there are 68 Research stations spread over the seven agro climatic zones of the state for conducting specific and need based research on various crops grown in the state. (Table 2).

Research programmes are carried out to tackle location specific problems of different agro-climatic zones of the state of Andhra Pradesh. The changing agricultural scenario at state, national and global level, national policies and the changing socioeconomic structure warrant restructuring and re-orientation of research programmes. The research programmes and activities are constantly and critically reviewed and each Research Station has been assigned priorities to make research user oriented and demand driven. Thus, the research activities are mainly focused on thrust areas identified.

Research, to constantly improve and generate technologies for increasing production in agriculture, animal husbandry, home science and allied sectors is one of the three major mandates of the University taken over from the A.P. State Department of Agriculture during 1964.

The research stations have been divided into seven zones based on the agro-climatic conditions:

i) Krishna - Godavari Zone
ii) North Coastal Zone
iii) Southern Zone
iv) Northern Telangana Zone
v) Southern Telangana Zone
vi) Scarce Rainfall Zone
vii) High Altitude and Tribal Area Zone.

Table 2
Agricultural Research Stations of ANGRAU

Research Station	*Main*	*Verification*
List of Research Stations in the Krishna-Godavari Zone		
Regional Agricultural Research Station, Lam -522 034 Dist. Guntur	Pulses, Cotton, Chillies, Coriander, Soybean and minor millets, Regl. Res. Units Soil Science, Physiology, Helicoverpa Management, Hybrid Cotton	Mustard, Castor, Gingelly, Mushroom spawn production, Farming systems research, Forage sorghum, Watershed Management
AICRP on Betelvine, Agricultural Research Station, Bapatla 522 101, Dist: Guntur	Betel vine	Management
Agricultural College Campus Bapatla 522 101 Dist: Guntur	——	
Rice Research Unit	Rice (Krishna western delta and NSP Black soils)	Rice based cropping systems
Post Harvest Technology Unit	PHT of Rice, pulses and groundnut, farm implements and machinery	——
Weed Control Unit	Integrated weed management	Control of weeds in rice fallows
Saline water research Unit	Research on use of saline water	——

(Contd...)

Research Station	*Main*	*Verification*
Indo-Dutch ORP on Soil Salinity	Soil salinity studies	—
Cashew Research Station, Bapatla-522 101, Dist: Guntur	Cashewnut	Cashew based cropping system-inter cropping
Bacterial Inoculants Unit, Amaravati 522 020, Dist: Guntur	Rhizobium culture production	—
Seed Production Farm, Jangamaheswarapuram 522 415, Dist: Guntur	Seed production in rice, soybean, cotton	—
Agricultural Research Station, Vuyyuru 522 165, Dist: Krishna	Sugarcane	Sugarcane based cropping systems (rice and pulses)
Agricultural Research Station, Machilipatnam 521 001 Dist: Krishna	Rice for saline soils	—
Agricultural Research Station, Endakuduru 521 001 Dist: Krishna	Agricultural Drainage for low land rice and other irrigated crops in delta lands lands	—
Agricultural Research Station, Garikapadu 521 175 Dist: Krishna	Crops and cropping systems, water management for NSP Left canal	Rice pulses, soybean
Agricultural Research Station, Ghantasala 521 133 Dist: Krishna	Rice fallow pulses (rabi and summer)	Rice in kharif
Horticultural Research Station, Nuzvid Dist: Krishna	Mango Research	—
Agricultural Research Station, Maruteru 534 122 Dist: West Godavari	Rice, Rice-based farming system, Soil & Water management for delta soils, Post-harvest technology (Rice), Rice-cum-fish farming, Summer pulses	—

(Contd...)

Research Station	Main	Verification
Agricultural Research Station, Pulla 534 401 Dist: West Godavari	Rice for deep water and flood situations	
Agricultural Research Station Kovvur 534 350 Dist: West Godavari	Banana, tuber crops other than potato	—
Seed Production Farm, Venkataramannagudem 534 108 Dist: West Godavari	Seed production (upland and light irrigated crops)	—
Agricultural Research Station Vijayarai 534 475 Dist: West Godavari	Oil palm, Water management for horticultural crops, melons, cropping systems and cropping models in fruit crops & research on vegetables including off-season vegetables, Apiculture	Pepper, clove
Agricultural Research Station, Ambajipet 533 214 Dist: East Godavari	Coconut, arecanut, coconut based multitier cropping system	Parasite breeding
Agricultural Research Station, Darsi 523 247 Dist: Prakasam	Crops and cropping systems for NSP right canal, oilseeds, millets, agro-forestry, soil and water management	Pulses

List of Agricultural Research Stations in the North Coastal Zone

Research Station	Main	Verification
Regional Agricultural Research Station, Anakapalle 531 001 Dist: Visakhapatnam	Sugarcandy and sugarcane based cropping systems Oilseeds and millets, Watershed management	Oilseeds and millets, Watershed management
Agricultural Research Station, Yelamanchili 531 005 Dist: Visakhapatnam	Sesamum Groundnut, sunflower	Groundnut, sunflower
Agricultural Research Station, Amadalavalasa 532 185	Mesta and mesta based cropping system	Oilseeds and pulses
Agricultural Research Station, Ragolu 532 484 Dist: Srikakulam	Rice and rice based cropping systems, technology for tankfed areas	Oilseeds

(Contd...)

Research Station	*Main*	*Verification*
Agricultural Research Station, Vizianagaram	Finger-millet, pearl-millet	Oilseeds and pulses
Agricultural Research Station, Peddapuram- 533 437, Dist: East Godavari	Ragi and tapioca	Pulses, oilseeds

List of Agricultural Research Stations in the Southern Zone

Research Station	Main	Verification
Regional Agricultural Research Station, Tirupati 517 502 Dist: Chittoor	Groundnut and groundnut based cropping systems, water management	Vegetables and floriculture (Dept. of Hort., SVAC), Pulses, Watershed management, Fodders
Agricultural Research Station, Perumallapalli 517 502 Dist: Chittoor	Sugarcane, millets	Rice and rice based cropping systems, fodders
Agricultural Research Station, Nellore-524 004 Dist: Nellore	Rice and rice based cropping systems, Tankfed cropping	Rice fallows, groundnut, pulses, sugarcane
Agricultural Research Station, Kavali 524 202 Dist: Nellore	Agro-forestry, Progeny orchard-cum-nursery for citrus, mango, sapota, guava	Pulses and oilseeds
Agricultural Research Station, Petlur 524 132 Dist: Nellore	Citrus	Citrus based cropping systems
Agricultural Research Station, Podalakur 524 345 Dist: Nellore	Sorghum based cropping systems, Pulses, fodder jowar	Chillies, oilseeds (castor, sunflower, soybean), soil management
Agricultural Research Station, Anantarajupeta 516 105 Dist: Cuddapah	—	—
Agricultural Research Station, Utukur 516 003 Dist: Cuddapah	Rice based cropping systems, water management, melons, gourds & cucumbers	Oilseeds and Pulses

(Contd...)

Research Station	*Main*	*Verification*
List of Agricultural Research Stations in the Northern Telangana Zone		
Regional Agricultural Research Station, Jagtial 505 327 Dist: Karimnagar	Rice, groundnut, sesamum, turmeric, water management, cropping systems	Pulses, cotton, mustard, sunflower, maize, rajmash, watershed management
Agricultural Research Station, Karimnagar 505 002 Dist: Karimnagar	Maize, on-farm research on water management	Oilseeds and pulses
Regional Sugarcane and Rice Research Station, Rudrur 503 188 Dist: Nizamabad	Sugarcane, rice, crops and cropping systems for Nizamsagar area	Oilseeds, pulses, onfarm research on turmeric
Agricultural Research Station, Jaipur (Bellampalli) 504 231 Dist: Adilabad	Arid horticulture	—
Agricultural Research Station, Adilabad 504 002 Dist: Adilabad	Cotton, jowar, rainfed rice, Arid Horticulture	Pulses
Agricultural Research Station, Mudhol 504 102 Dist: Adilabad	Rainfed cotton	Jowar, chillies
Agricultural Research Station, Warangal 506 002 Dist: Warangal	Rice, Pulses, water management	Cotton (irrigated), oilseeds
JVR Horticultural Research Station, Malyal 506 101, Dist: Warangal	Mango, chillies (irrigated), onion, garlic	Groundnut
Agricultural Research Station, Wyra 507 203 Dist: Khammam	Rice based cropping systems, seed production	Oilseeds and pulses in rice fallows
Agricultural Research Station, Madhira 507 203 Dist: Khammam	Pulses, Maghi jowar	Jowar, cotton, chillies

(Contd...)

Research Station	*Main*	*Verification*
Agricultural Research Station, Aswaraopet 507 306 Dist: Khammam	Vegetables (tubers and beans) for tribals, minor forest produce, banana	Oilseeds, pulses

List of Agricultural Research Stations in the Southern Telangana Zone

Research Station	*Main*	*Verification*
Regional Agricultural Research Station, Palem 509 216	Sorghum, bajra, castor castor, horsegram, fodder crops	Ragi, groundnut, greengram, blackgram, rainfed cotton, rice based cropping systems, research for tankfed and well irrigated areas, watershed management.
Agricultural Research Institute, Rajendranagar 500 030 Dist: Rangareddy	Tissue culture, floriculture, rice, grapes, vegetables, agro forestry, Home Science, Research	PHT of fruits and vegetables, rice and based cropping systems, Soil Science & Agril. Chemistry
Vegetable Research Scheme, ARI, Rajendranagar 500 030 Dist: Rangareddy	Vegetable Research	—
Rice Research Unit, ARI, Rajendranagar 500 030 Dist: Rangareddy	Rice Research	—
Farm Implements and Machinary Scheme, ARI, Rajendranagar 500 030 Dist: Rangareddy	Testing & development of farm implements	—
Radio Tracer & Agril. Chemistry Unit, ARI, Rajendranagar 500 030 Dist: Rangareddy	Soil and micro nutrient analysis	—
National Seed Project ARI, Rajendranagar 500 030 Dist: Rangareddy	Seed technology and production	—
Weed Control Unit College of Agriculture Rajendranagar-500 030 Dist: Rangareddy	Weed control	—

(Contd...)

Research Station	Main	Verification
College of Agriculture Rajendranagar- 500 030 Dist: Rangareddy	Residue analysis	—
AICARP Scheme College of Agriculture, Rajendranagar 500 030 Dist: Rangareddy	Cropping systems research and experiments on cultivators field	—
Biological Control Scheme College of Agriculture, Rajendranagar 500 030 Dist: Rangareddy	Biological control of crop pests	—
Grape Research Station, Rajendranagar 500 030 Dist: Rangareddy	Grape research	—
Aromatic & Medicinal Plants Scheme, Grape Research Station, Rajendranagar 500 030 Dist: Rangareddy	Aromatic & Medicinal plants	—
AICRP on Home Sci., Research Centre for Post Graduate Studies in Home Science, Rajendranagar 500 030 Dist: Rangareddy	—	—
Agricultural Research Station, Tandur 501 141 Dist: Rangareddy	Safflower, rabi sorghum	Oilseeds and pulses
Agricultural Research Station, Amberpet 500 013 Dist: Hyderabad	Maize, maize based cropping systems, fodder maize	Fodder sorghum
Agricultural Research Station, Sangareddy 504001 Dist: Medak	Mango, guava, sapota, Anona, PHT of fruits	—

(Contd...)

Research Station	*Main*	*Verification*
Agricultural Research Station, Mallepalli 508 243 Dist: Nalgonda	Dryland horticulture, cucumbers	Castor, jowar, oilseeds, pulses, sweet orange (on-farm research)

List of Agricultural Research Stations in the Scarce Rainfall Zone

Research Station	*Main*	*Verification*
Regional Agricultural Research Station, Nandyal 518 501 Dist: Kurnool	Rice and rice based cropping systems, setaria, groundnut, sunflower, bengalgram, tobacco, jowar, cotton, water management, fodders, seed production technology	Vegetables, onions, coriander,chillies, mustard, soybean, redgram, safflower, farming systems research (with sheep, goat and dairy),sericulture, watershed management
Agricultural Research Station, Anantapur 515 001 Dist: Anantapur	Dry farming, groundnut based cropping systems, arid fruits, pulses, fodders, implements, watershed management on red soils, farming systems research	Jowar, bajra, searia, horsegram, groundnut, field beans, pulses
Agricultural Research Station, Reddipalli 515 001	Watershed management, pulses, groundnut	Cropping systems for HLC of Tungabhadra, sunflower
Agricultural Research Station, Kadiri 515 591 Dist: Anantapur	Groundnut and groundnut based cropping systems	Sunflower

List of Agricultural Research Stations in the High Altitude and Tribal Area Zone

Research Station	*Main*	*Verification*
Regional Agricultural Research Station, Chintapalle 531 111 Dist. Visakhapatnam	Rice, cereals, millets, pulses, fruits, lead centre for niger for entire state, vegetables particularly rajma, lima bean, spices, and condiments, floriculture, agroforestry, watershed management, podu cultivation	Oilseeds, sericulture, white burley tobacco, farming systems, on-farm research on citrus, other fruit crops, turmeric, ginger, pine apple, cereals, millets, pulses, oilseeds for tribal areas
Agricultural Research Station, Seethampet 532 443 Dist: Srikakulam	Rice, rice based cropping systems, agro-forestry, fodders	Millets, pulses and oilseeds
Agricultural Research, Station, Pandirimamidi 533 288 Dist: East Godavari	Horticultural crops, particularly tamarind, cashew, custard apple, minor forest produce	——

In addition, a total of 241 research schemes, all India Coordinated Research Projects (ICAR) and schemes sponsored by Government of India are in operation. In addition to a score of non-plan schemes in operation, the University has been implementing a number of coordinated Research projects of ICAR as well as projects sponsored by Government of India and other agencies. Further impetus to research was given with the implementation of the 5.56 million goat, 0.74 million pigs, 31.84 million fowls and 0.52 million ducrs.

AGRICULTURAL EXTENSION SYSTEM

The term extension education was first coined in 1973 by the Cambridge University to describe a particular innovation (Farquhan, 1972). This was to carry the educational advantages of the universities to ordinary people where they lived and worked. The American extension movement started on the same lines in England, from the universities and large public libraries. The primary objective of extension work is to assist individuals in identifying and solving farm, home and community problems by utilizing research findings. FAO/UNESCO/ILO (1970) and Savile (1965), regarded extension as an educational service concerned with the teaching and practical application of information.

In India, although agricultural extension was started with a single line extension service, with the introduction of community development programmes in 1952, this was radically changed. The community development programme was followed by other agricultural development programmes such as Intensive Agricultural District Programme (IADP), Intensive Agricultural Area Programme (IAAP), High Yielding Varieties Programme (HYVP), National Development Programme (NDP), Multiple Cropping Programme (MCP), special programmes on commercial crops like tobacco, sugarcane, cotton, jute, oilseeds, fruit crops and Dryland Agricultural Development Programme (DADP). Some of these programmes are related to other allied sectors also.

However, a network of extension institutes has been created for the promotion and adoption of improved technologies among farmers. One of the major functions of agricultural universities is extension service. The research results are disseminated through the university extension officers to the departmental personnel as well as to the farmers. The ICAR has specific programs such as National Demonstration Programmes, Operational Research Projects, Krishi Vigyan Kendras, Lab to Land Program, Kisan melas, etc.

In most of the states in India, the Director of Agriculture is the Head of the Department responsible of formulating policies, programs and communicating them to the district level field staff for implementation and therefore he is also responsible for agricultural extension and development. The Director of Agriculture is assisted by an Additional Director and several Joint Directors. At the district level, the Deputy Director of Agriculture works with the assistance of two or three Assistant Directors of Agriculture (Subject Specialists). Each revenue division is headed by one Additional Director of Agriculture who in turn is assisted at the block level (Mandal level) by Agricultural Extension Officer. Village Development Officers and Field Assistants who are supposed to convey the agricultural messages to the farmers and assist the Agricultural Extension Officers. Although, theoretically the system is excellent in nature, in practice, the whole thing appears to be most effective at the grass root level.

Education is always considered as the key factor in the farm prosperity. In fact, education is a lifelong process for the farmer. Unless the farmers are exposed to an outpouring of materials on the latest developments in farming, they will have little knowledge of new seeds, new fertilizers, new weedicides, new pesticides, and new techniques. Education, therefore, serves as the kingpin in the affairs of farm prosperity. In America, the Land-Grant college system has made enormous contributions to the development of agricultural science. The institution is not only responsible for the education of its students but also for conducting research and experiments in its own laboratories and experimental fields and for the dissemination of knowledge gained in them. A communication service bridges the gap between the farmer and the scholar, between the farm and the laboratory.

Our country is backward in agricultural extension programmes. Ever since the partition of the country, our state agencies have been doing their best to educate millions of our farmers in better methods of farming to increase production. The extension workers have to fight a lot to convince a farmer to take to a new practice. Research, extension work and education in an integrated way are now used to develop methods to educate the farmers that they can easily learn and adopt new practices. In fact, the behavioral scientists of present day are very much concerned with their problems of adoption. They are also devising means and ways to bring about favourable change in the farmer's attitude to applications of innovations through various stages of mental preparation: (a) Awareness, (b) Interest, (c) Evaluation, (d) Trial, and (e) Adoption.

It has been found that adoption of improved agricultural practices depend on social and psychological variables. Caste, educational level participation in community activities, etc. are found to be important associates in communication adoption process. Among the various social agencies and institutions, the role of village extension library seems to be highly significant in the process of adoption to improved agricultural practices. The rural libraries are still functioning well and are creating a good impact on the life of the rural people residing in the university project area.

Our country is now facing various problems of which food constitutes a major one. Food is the basic need for the vast population in the country. It is no secret that in the agricultural sector our major aim at the moment is for steady increase in food production. To achieve all-round development in agriculture through a good foundation in agricultural education, agricultural universities have been established in recent years throughout the country. These universities through their multi faculty objectives are dedicated to awaken millions of our farmers and to change the face of our rural life. It is expected that the libraries attached to these agricultural universities would also stick to their appropriate role in attaining the various objectives for which the universities have come into being.

Role of Extension

Extension plays a pivotal role in the utilizations of agricultural knowledge and information systems. Extension functionaries serve as intermediaries between researchers and farmers, providing feedback to policy makers, liaise with input and other support agencies.

Indian policy on extension is undergoing basic changes. Government of India has released that extension needs to be broad based situation specific and its benefits should be evenly distributed. Since public sector extension may not be able to meet the needs of all farm families, there is need for better condition of various extension systems and sharing their responsibility of extension with NGOs and local farmers organizations. All this calls for new policy initiatives, creative management of the extension systems and an organized effort to upgrade the knowledge and skills of thousands of extension functionaries.

Extension activities

The main functions are to organize farmer's fair, exhibition and extension tours; conduct demonstration programmes on farmers field; organize training programmes on different aspects of agricultural and rural development and group discussion of scientists with farmers. Through Transfer of technology (TOT), Lab to Land programme and adult education programme, the scientists are actively involved in dissemination of latest technology to the farmers.

Agricultural Extension Activity in India

Krishi Vigyan Kendras (KVKs)

The extension-education activity is conducted through 314 Krishi Vigyan Kendras (KVKs or Farm Science Centres) and 8 Trainers Training Centres located in various parts of the country (Table 3).

Table 3

Distribution of KVKs in different States by Host Organization

Zone	*States / UTS*	*SAU*	*ICAR*	*NGO*	*Others*	*Reman-dating of ZARS under SAU*	*Total*
I	A & N Islands	-	1	-	-	-	1
	J & K	3	-	1	-	1	5
	Punjab	9	1	-	-	1	11
	Haryana	8	2	2	-	-	12
	HP	8	-	-	-	3	11
	Delhi	-	-	-	1	-	1
II	West Bengal	2	1	3	3	1	10
	Bihar	10	-	4	2	2	18
	A & N Islands	-	1	-	-	-	1
	Jharkhand	1	-	3	1	1	6
III	Assam	4	-	-	-	6	10
	Aru. Pradesh	-	1	-	-	-	1
	Meghalaya	-	1	-	-	-	1
	Mizoram	-	-	-	2	-	2
	Nagaland	-	1	-	-	-	1
	Sikkim	-	1	-	-	-	1
	Tripura	-	1	1	-	-	2
	Manipur	-	1	-	-	-	1
IV	UP	19	2	4	3	7	35
	Uttaranchal	2	-	-	-	1	3
V	Maharashtra	4	1	17	1	4	27
	Andhra Pradesh	6	2	8	-	3	19
VI	Gujarat	4	-	4	2	3	13
	Rajasthan	23	2	5	1	1	32
VII	Madhya Pradesh	12	1	3	-	4	20
	Orissa	8	4	-	-	2	14
	Chhattisgarh	4	-	-	-	-	4
VIII	Goa	-	1	-	-	-	1
	Karnataka	6	1	4	-	8	19
	Kerala	3	3	3	-	2	11
	Lakshadweep	-	-	-	1	-	1
	Pondicherry	-	-	-	2	-	2
	Tamil Nadu	5	-	9	2	3	19
	Total	139	28	73	21	53	314

I - ICAR S - SAUs N - NGOs

O -Others, includes state Govt., Central/State Public undertaking.

The KVKs are district-level institutions run by the SAUs, ICAR and select non-Government organizations. Each year, 2500 – 3000 farmers, farm women, rural youth and school dropouts are trained at the Krishi Vigyan Kendras in crop husbandry, horticulture, animal husbandry and dairying, fisheries and vocations leading to self-employment.

The Trainers Training Centres (TTCs) are subject-specific training institutions for providing what's new in dryland agriculture, horticulture farm machinery, inland fisheries, marine fisheries, hill agriculture, dairying and home science.

National Institute of Rural Development (NIRD), Hyderabad

NIRD is the country's apex body for undertaking training, research, action research, and consultancy and documentation functions in the rural development sector. It works as an autonomous organization of the Ministry of Rural Development and Government of India.

Mission of the Institute

- To examine and analyze the factors contributing to the improvement of economic and social well-being of people in rural areas on sustainable basis with focus on the rural poor and the other disadvantaged groups through research, action research, consultancy and documentation efforts.
- To facilitate the rural development efforts with particular emphasis and focus on the rural poor by improving the knowledge, skills and attitudes of the rural development officials and non-officials through organizing training, workshops and seminars.

Objectives of NIRD

The institute renders service to promote development of the rural poor and enhance their quality of life. Organize training programs, conferences, seminars and workshops for senior level development managers, elected representatives, bankers, NGOs and others:

- Undertake aid, promote and coordinate research on its own and other agencies.
- Study various aspects of the Panchayati Raj Institutions and Rural Development Programs across the states.
- Analyze and propose solutions to problems in planning and implementation of the programs for the rural development, and
- Disseminate information through periodicals, reports and other publications.

Centre on Rural Documentation

Centre On Rural Documentation (CORD) in the institute was established with a mandate to serve as resource centre for rural development information and servicing agency for development community, comprising planners, administrators, policy makers, functionaries, trainers, academics and researchers. Recent advances in Information Technology (IT) added a new dimension to the task of harnessing information for development. To keep in step with the advances in Information Technology and changing information needs of the development community, CORD geared itself to improve its information handling capabilities. Accordingly, during the period under review, CORD established Internet connectivity, worked on design and development of website of the institute and finalized the creation of computerized clearinghouse of information on rural development.

At the end of March 1998, the total stock of books including Hindi books, Children's books and bound volumes of periodicals stood at 89,157. CORD receives 405 journals out of which nearly 320 are subscribed to and the rest received gratis or on exchange.

National Institute of Agricultural Extension Management (MANAGE), Hyderabad

Mission

To facilitate the Extension Officers, managers, scientists and administrators in all sectors of agricultural economy to acquire managerial and technical skills that would enable them to provide most effective support and services to farmers and fishermen for practicing sustainable agriculture.

Mandate

a) Develop linkage between prominent state, regional, national and international institutions in Agricultural Extension Management.
b) Gain insight into Agricultural Extension Management systems and policies.
c) Forge collaborative linkage with national and international institutions for sharing faculty resource.
d) Develop and promote the applications of management tools for improving the effectiveness of agricultural extension organizations through better management of human and material resources.
e) Organize need-based training programs for senior and middle level agricultural extension functionaries.
f) Conduct problem oriented studies on Agricultural Extension Management as a sequel to the feedback from training programs.
g) Function as international documentation centre for collecting, storing, processing and disseminating information on all subjects related to agricultural management.

Information Technology Center

MANAGE recognizes the role of the Information Technology in improving the efficiency of the agricultural extension service in India. An information technology system has been installed primarily to address the needs of its own faculty and staff and also to train the officers from agricultural sector in Information Technology. The main aim of this information is:

a) To design and develop innovative training programs for extension managers and researchers on latest techniques of information and communication technology and its application to the agricultural extension.

b) To develop expert systems and multimedia software packages for training of extension functionaries.

c) To provide technical support to MANAGE faculty on software package and national and international communication for their research consultancy and training efforts.

National Plant Protection Training Institute (NPPTI), Hyderabad

The National Plant Protection Training Institute was established in the year 1966 as a training wing of the Directorate of Plant Protection, quarantining and storage under the Department of Agriculture and Cooperation, Ministry of Agriculture, Government of India with the main objectives of human resource development in Plant Protection by generating trained manpower in the field of plant protection for various States/Union Territories. The institute is engaged in organizing various training programs of long and short duration in plant protection and allied disciplines. The institute undertakes survey for pesticide residues in food commodities.

State Agricultural Management and Extension Training Institute (SAMETI), Hyderabad

State Agricultural Management and Extension Training Institute is established in the year 1966 with the name as Plant Production Training Centre at Old Malakpet, Hyderabad, to build up the required technical knowledge with latest agricultural information to the extension staff and for meeting successfully, situations of large and frequent pest outbreaks.

Objectives

- To function as agricultural Extension management institute at state level.
- To provide the consultancy in areas like project planning, appraisal and implementation, etc.
- To develop and promote the application of management tools for improving the effectiveness of agricultural extension services through better management of human and material resources.

SAMETI, Hyderabad organized 30 programmes during 2001-2002 for the Agriculture Extension officers, Agriculture officers and Assistant Directors of Agriculture of the state Agriculture department in the fields of integrated pest management, watershed management, crop production technology, quality control of seeds, fertilizers and pesticides and computers.

Under the NATP, the SAMETI, Hyderabad, facilitated the preparation of strategic Research and Extension plan for the ATMA districts namely Kurnool, Prakasham, Adilabad and Chittoor. During the year 2001-02, SAMETI organized 52 training programmes for the Block level Technology team of ATMA districts covering the officers of the Agriculture and Line Departments in the fields of Project Management skills, Training skills, IT and communication skills and Team building and participatory approaches.

Extension Education Institute (EEI), Acharya N.G. Ranga Agricultural University, Hyderabad

The Extension Education Institute is one of the four premier and pioneering training institutes financed by the Ministry of Agriculture and Cooperation, Government of India, New Delhi. The institute organizes on-campus and off-campus programs for middle level functionaries of developmental departments of Andhra Pradesh, Tamil Nadu, Karnataka, Kerala, Orissa, and Union Territories of Andaman & Nicobar Islands, Pondicherry and Lakshadweep. The institute also conducted three special programs for Animal Husbandry Officers of the State. The institute offers M.Sc. and PhD programs in extension education, apart from undertaking research, extension and village adoption.

- Regional Biogas Development and Training Centre
- Agricultural Information and Communication Centre
- Kisan Melas, The World Food Day celebrations
- Research and Extension Advisory Council Meeting.

Farmer Participation in Development – A Background

It has been said before that it is no longer necessary to argue the relevance of socioeconomic conditions in agricultural research (for example: Anderson, Dillon and Hardaker, 1985) but the heady achievements in large scale agriculture during the green revolution remain unattainable for many resource poor farmers in isolated regions (Farrington and Martin, 1987). Socioeconomic factors – Farmer's goals, level of participation in a cash economy, access to market, available resource and knowledge are among the reasons why this situation remains, but perhaps the principal reason has been the exclusion of poor farmers from the communication process involved in agricultural technology generation (Chambers, Pacey and Threpp, 1989).

In the 1950s and 1960s the practitioner may have concluded that farmers were ignorant and therefore set up an extension program based on change agents who aimed to achieve widespread adoption a recommended technology package (Chambers, 1993). In the 1970s and 1980s, the practitioner may have sought to identify and remove the farm level constraints, to try to make the environment fit the genotype. Poor farmers were unable to participate without sizable aid funds for infrastructure or research. Farming Systems Research (FSR), by the mid 1980s had contributed to understanding the complexity of many farming systems and the important role of the farmer within the system. Now, in the 1990s, the practitioner is frequently directed to access the situation and opportunities in participation with local rural people, recognizing that the process, which generates the technology, is the key activity.

Identification of Problems and Technology Options

Chambers (1983) points out that much agricultural knowledge is not fixed or static, but is frequently modified by the farmers who use it. Thus, each technology adoption is not a recipe, but is a dynamic package of ideas, experiences and principles on which to base discussion of ways to solve problem (or access an opportunity) identified in the farming system. This is a key concept in participative or on-farm research, and encourages farmer "Ownership" of the technologies developed.

Agricultural Extension in Andhra Pradesh

The extension education activities of the universities for transfer of technologies, developed at research stations and colleges are carried out through the 6 extension education units located regional agricultural research stations, 5 Krishi Vigyan Kendras, Agricultural Information and Communication Centres, Extension Education Institute and Regional Biogas Training and Development Centres. Identifying, documenting and incorporating indigenous knowledge systems into agricultural extension organizations are essential to achieve sustainable agricultural development.

Krishi Vignan Kendras

There are 16 Krishi Vignan Kendras in Andhra Pradesh. Six of the Krishi Vignan kendras working under the Acharya N G Ranga University are located in: i) Amudalavalasa, Srikakulam district; ii) Rastakuntabai, Vizianagaram district; iii) Malayal, Warangal district; iv) Reddipalli, Ananthapur district; v) Mahanandi, Kurnool district; and vi) Undi, Bheemavaram, West Godavari district. Two other Krishi Vignan Kendras working under the Indian Council of Agricultural Research are located at: i) Rajahmundry, East Godavari district and ii) Central Research Institute for Dry land Agriculture, Hayath Nagar, Rangareddy district. The remaining eight Krishi Vignan Kendras working under Non-Governmental Organizations (NGOs) are located at i) Kotha, Madhanpur, Mahboob Nagar district ii)Gadipalli, Nalgonda district, iii) Jammikunta, Karimnagar district, iv) Banaganapalli, Karnool district, v) Elamanchali, Visakhapatnam district, vi) Zaheerabad, Medhak district vii) Nandyal, MC farm, Kurnool district and viii) RASS Vanasthali, Karakanbadi, Chittoor district. The following table shows the names, addresses and the year of establishment of the KVKs.

Table 4
List of KVKs in Andhra Pradesh

S.No.	*Name & Address of KVK*	*Host Organization*	*Est. Year*
1.	Training Organiser, Krishi Vigyan Kendra, Behind M.R.O. Office, Kotha, Madanpur, Mahboobnagar (AP)	The Executive Director, Youth for Action, 1-8-702/26/1, Padma Colony, Hyderabad - 500044 (AP)	1992 N
2.	Training Organiser, Krishi Vigyan Kendra, Gadipalli - 508201, Nalgonda (AP)	Secretary, Aurobindo Institute of Rural Dev., Gaddipalli - 508201 (AP)	1983 N
3.	Training Organiser, Krishi Vigyan Kendra, Kalvacherla, Rajahmundry, East Godawari - 533105	The Director, Central Tobacco Research Instt., Rajamundry-500044 (AP)	1992 I
4.	Training Organiser, Krishi Vigyan Kendra, CRIDA, Hayatnagar, Ranga Reddy (AP)	The Director, CRIDA Complex, Saidabad P.O.- Santoshnagar, Hyderabad (AP)	1976 I
5.	Training Organiser, Krishi Vigyan Kendra, RASS Vanasthali, Vill.- Karakanbadi, Chittoor - 517501(AP)	Chairman, Rayalseema Seva Samiti, 9,Old Hazur Office Building, Tirupathi (AP)	1992 N
6.	Training Organiser, Krishi Vigyan Kendra, Jamikunta, Karimnagar - 505112 (AP)	Director, Gram Nava Nirman Samiti, H.No. 1-9-639/1, Vidyanagar, Hyderabad	1992 N
7.	Training Organiser, Krishi Vigyan Kendra, P.O. Banaganapalli, Kurnool - 508201 (AP)	Secretary, Shri Hanumantharaya Educational & Charitable Society, Rendakanti Public School, Illuru, Kothapeate	1989 N

(Contd...)

S.No.	Name & Address of KVK	Host Organization	Est. Year
8.	Training Organiser, Krishi Vigyan Kendra, C/oBhagya Tula Charitable Trust, Elamanchili, Vishakhapatanam -531005 (AP)	The Secretary, Bhagya Tula Charitable Trust, Yellamanchily, Vishakhapatanam - 531005 (AP)	1995 N
9.	Training Organiser, Krishi Vigyan Kendra, P.O. Box No. 214, Zaheerabad, Medak -502220 (AP)	Chairman, Deccan Dev. Society, A-5, Meera Apartments, Basheerbagh, Hyderabad (AP)	1992 N
10.	Training Organiser, N.G. RangaKrishi Vigyan Kendra, Vinayashram, Kavur, Guntur (AP)	Chairman, Vinayashram Kavur, Guntur (AP)	1992 N
11.	Training Organiser, Krishi Vigyan Kendra, OCMS Building, Kamlanagar, Anantpur (AP) – 515001	Vice - Chancellor, Andhra Pradesh Agril. University, Rajendra Nagar, Hyderabad – 500030	1983 S
12.	Training Organiser, Krishi Vigyan Kendra, Opp. Rama Krishnan Temple UMDI, Rayalam Bhimavaram West Godavari – 534208 (AP)	-do-	1995 S
13.	Training Organiser, Krishi Vigyan Kendra, Malyal Farm, Village Malyal, Warangal -506101 (AP)	-do-	1984 S
14.	Training Organiser, Krishi Vigyan Kendra, Agril. Research Station, Amudalavalsa, Srikakulam -532523 (AP)	do-	1984 S
15.	Training Organiser, Krishi Vigyan Kendra, Rastakuntabai, Vizianagaram - 535523 (AP)	-do-	1984 S
16.	Training Organiser, Krishi Vigyan Kendra, Nandyal, M.C. Farm, P.O. Kurnool (AP)	-do-	1992 S

The KVKs undertake vocational training on skill and production oriented short-term and long-term programs for farmers, farmwomen and rural youth. These centres organize training programs benefiting 3158 farmers, farmwomen and rural youth.

District Agricultural Advisory and Transfer Technology Centres (DAATTCs)

The extension activities of the University are focused on testing and verification of new technologies developed by scientists through on-farm trials and early demonstration, training the farmers, farm women, rural youth and personnel of the state developmental departments for updating their knowledge and skills. The University Extension System is also involved in disseminating the information through press, television, All India Radio and organizing Kisan melas.

In order to re-inforce and strengthen the transfer of technology, the university has reorganized its extension infrastructure by establishing the new centres of District Agricultural Advisory and Transfer of Technology Centers (DAATTCs) and introducing innovative methods like Distance Education and Adoption of Villages.

District Agricultural Advisory and Transfer of Technology Centres (DAATTCs) were established in 22 districts of the state barring Hyderabad district with a mandate to act as focal points for extension activities of the university in the concerned district.

Objectives of DAATTCs

a) Access and refine the technologies generated by the research scientists and their suitability to different farming situations.

b) Access to potentials of the district by developing database in order to exploit district resources and develop action plans in cooperation with line departments.

c) Conduct field diagnostic visit to identify the field problems and provide scientific solutions.

d) Organize Kisan Melas (Rytu Vigyana Sadassus) in coordination with line departments.

e) Extend scientific expertise to the line departments in the conduct of training programs to officials, farmers and input agencies.

f) Organize A & V workshops.

g) Establish linkages with research institutes and other district units located in AP.

h) Assist and implement the RAWE program, internship program and RHWE program for Agriculture and Horticulture, Veterinary and Home Science students under ANGRAU, respectively.

i) Maintain information centre at each district headquarters in cooperation with the line departments of the district.

j) Supply need-based scientific/popular information to the line departments on enterprises for their printing/multiplication and distribution to the farmers.

k) Coordinate with All India Radio, Television and Print media for transmission of needed agricultural information in the district.

Distance Education

To promote faster dissemination of improved technologies and farm information in agricultural and allied fields and to reach the unreached, the university has launched an innovative "Distance Education" program under the caption "Annadata – Velugebata" of E-TV.

Village Adoption

The novel program of "Village Adoption" has been implemented by the university in 50 villages all over the state. Under this program, the scientists/teachers visit the villages regularly and render on-the-spot advice to farmers on various aspects of agriculture, animal husbandry, horticulture, fisheries and women in agriculture, besides attending malady remedy analysis. The scientists/teachers help the target group to produce their own seed, arrange credit through banks and cooperatives, improve the literacy level, sanitation conditions and ultimately in the overall economic development uplift of the people.

Starting with definition of agriculture, agricultural education at national and state level, the objectives of the agricultural colleges, research carried out, extension services and extension education were given a brief description.

The agricultural research at international, national and state level, the mandate, ongoing activities and future plan (Vision 2020) were dealt with.

In agricultural extension system, role, activities in India specially by national institutes, Krishi Vigyan Kendras and non-governmental organisations were described.

2

Agricultural Librarianship

To understand agricultural information in the context of the world and India the available information was reviewed. The characteristics and structure of agricultural library profession at national level, agricultural research institutes, government departments, agro-based industries, bank and other trade organisations were assessed.

A library is a collection of information, transmission of materials - arranged, organized and controlled for the purpose of study and research or of general recreational information transfer (Dupuy, 1968). More simply, the library is a collection of books and other material made useful. Librarianship is the practice of collecting such material and putting them to maximum use. The user or user group for whom the reading material is collected thus form the major component of the library. The other components are the literature and the library professionals. The literature is the commodity used and the library professionals are the agency to serve the literature to users.

Librarianship is the nerve centre of information for academic, research and developmental activities of the country. Agricultural librarianship has vital role to play providing relevant and timely information sources and services to the research workers, teachers, subject specialists, students, farmers, Agribusiness organizations and others who are actively engaged in meeting the continuing challenge of human being for food and hunger.

Agriculture, the science of raising crops and animals began some 10,000 years ago in the Middle East when animals were first raised in capacity. Most agriculture information from that time until the mid-nineteenth century was passed from one farmer to another by word of mouth. Even during the early days of the Agricultural Revolution, when advances in crop rotation, animal breeding and mechanical inventions led to increased productivity and the need for fewer agricultural workers, most individuals learned of these developments from other farmers.

Fusonie (1975) noted that, at the time of American Revolution, 90 percent of the American people were farmers. During the years following the revolution, "New advances in agricultural technology and increased dissemination of knowledge through agricultural literature inclusive monography, published works of agricultural societies and the growing number of periodicals finally culminated in what became known as the first Agricultural Revolution".

Agriculture has been a part of human life for many thousands of years; the need for agricultural information is probably almost as old. Ancient Babylonian clay tablets have been found that contain agricultural information. Blanchard (1977) hypothesized that "the great library at Alexandria undoubtedly had many treatises on agriculture inscribed on papyrus". Through history, in many civilizations, there have been libraries that have included agricultural information, and separate agricultural libraries were established in Europe in the mid-eighteenth century.

AGRICULTURAL INFORMATION

Agricultural information can be incoded (documented) form or un-coded (oral) form. The dissemination of agricultural information is vital to improve agricultural production because it is a media through which people get acquainted with new and better farming methods, fertilizers, improved seedlings, modern pest control measures, pesticides, herbicides and fungicides.

Agricultural information is multidisciplinary in nature and should be regarded as a natural resource. The volume of pertinent literature in the field of agriculture exceeds the capacity of an individual scientist to cope with it. Cheote Lal (1989) estimated that over 3,00,000 primary items of agricultural literature were being published annually in 20,000 serials exclusively for agriculture and allied sciences. Stanley (1982) stated that agricultural information is needed by a wide range of users in varying degrees. Also the information needs of agricultural users are of specified nature and tailor-made information having direct bearing on local and regional conditions is of more use. (Ahsan and Mehla, 1987).

Agriculture has been given top priority in our planning and more so the transfer of technology is being considered as indispensable. Agricultural information should be an integral part of any agricultural research system and should be given the right priority and required human and financial resources. An enormous quantity of agricultural information is being produced by various organisations concerned with agricultural production and the agricultural libraries are primarily concerned with availability of this information. One of the greatest power forces for changes and development in the world today is the availability of information. Agriculture and allied subjects, the most basic concerns of man and the research which is producing new methods and techniques are already improving man's living standards and will continue to do so.

Gone are the days where the farmers have to be instructed by a village developmental officer as an Agricultural Officer, in each and every step in farming. In other words, they should themselves become research-oriented. This calls for a mighty mass communication endeavour. In this context, an understanding of what is happening in advanced countries would be very profitable. Agriculture Information flows not only from Government agencies, research institutes and universities, but also from the manufacturers of fertilizers, chemicals, agricultural, horticultural, piscicultural machinery and every other product connected with farming.

Among mass media, Newspapers and Radio are the most commonly used media. Newspapers are primarily a means of disseminating news and influencing the public on the current events. Newspaper plays an important role in the field of agricultural development by informing the farmers of new techniques in agriculture and helps interpreting agriculture to the rest of the society. It helps to narrow the gap between research results and their application by farmers in rural areas.

Farmers are the ultimate consumers of the agricultural research findings. Accordingly, such a category in the information communication process is likely to include illiterate as well as the literate strata. The extension workers and rural libraries have a significant role to play for communicating new ideas and practices to the farmers. For progressive educated farmers, the best means of communicating research results for library is through publications. Agricultural scientists may consider it as one of their primary duties to impart their knowledge to the farmers. This would be possible only if they convey their findings in popular languages.

The information needs of the agricultural scientists in developed countries are designed to up-to-date scientific and technical development in the field. The purpose of their search is for "generating new knowledge". They prefer telephone, e-mail, correspondence, conference, seminar, exchange of reports/ proposals, information contact and database use in the library, as means of obtaining information. They use more scientific journals, secondary sources, technical bulletins and database "as information sources". The barriers for obtaining information they face are: (i) obtaining required documents in sufficient number and (ii) obtaining machine-readable information. They hardly consult librarians for data collection. Lancaster and Beecher (1981) have discussed four characteristics that make agricultural information unique and different from other scientific literature (also listed by Sattar and Lancaster, 1984). These include the inter-disciplinary nature of agricultural research; the fugitive nature of the literature produced in agricultural librarianship; the universal applicability of agriculture and its literature, and the diversity of the treatment and the presentation of this literature. Each has a unique impact on agricultural information work in developing countries (Sattar and Lancaster, 1984).

World Agricultural Information Output

It is difficult to take a precise stock of world agricultural information output. Boyle and Buntrock (1973) in their "Survey of World Agricultural Documentation Services" mentioned a total of 17,69,000 items as reported in 354 secondary periodicals. However, the figure represents the multiple reporting of the same item of information in different secondary services. It was estimated by Phadnis and Sital (1974) that over 25,000 books and monographs were published each year in agro-biological sciences. In addition, reports, conference proceedings, technical and research bulletins, pamphlets and brochures add to the primary sources, which may be around 2,00,000. As regards the serials, the world's list of Scientific Periodicals cites about 60,000 titles of which 15,000 serials are of agricultural interest (Surendar Mohan, 1978). *The Directory of Indian Scientific Periodicals* brought out by INSDOC (1976) reported 308 serials of agricultural sciences published in India. Phadnis and Sital (1977) gave an estimate of 39,150; 12,300 and 55,000 theses in the fields of biological sciences, agriculture and chemistry respectively.

Indian Agricultural Information Output

It is very difficult to estimate the output of information published in India due to lack of well organized and established secondary services to act as the outlet of information. This may be done only through the world secondary services. Indian agro-biological literature is scattered in a wide variety of sources such as books, monographs, reports, conference proceedings, theses, state-of-art reports, technical bulletins, pamphlets etc. There is no national outlet as such for agro-biological information. Surendra Mohan (1978) enlisted 13 secondary services of agro biological areas brought out in India, but there is no comprehensive service covering the entire Indian agro-biological literature. Regarding books, some authors like Phadnis and Sital (1977) gave rough estimates, but it is very difficult to arrive at a correct estimate in the absence of a comprehensive National Bibliography on Indian Agriculture.

The prerequisite to any fruitful research activity is the ready availability of the existing information. This can be achieved only through an exhaustive bibliographical control of literature. Information has no regional or national boundaries for its proper utilization. India being a vast country with varied agro-climatological background, it is pertinent for the researcher to get acquainted with the progress on the research front. It also helps him identify the specific problems in agricultural research. The extent of comprehensiveness in the coverage of literature by libraries is considered inadequate. Even a very big library cannot claim adequacy in the present context of publication explosion.

AGRICULTURAL LIBRARIANSHIP

Librarianship is recognized as a noble and exalted profession in the entire world. Agricultural librarianship is one of the newly emerging professions associated with the world's agricultural research and education. Agricultural library profession in India has kept pace with the agricultural research and education. The agricultural librarians and documentalists have contributed their might to the agricultural development in this country. Agricultural library profession also exhibits a system of organization which marks a stage of development. There is a significant cadre of professionally competent and, in patches, brilliant library personnel working in different agricultural libraries in the country. Almost all agricultural universities and institutes have a developed library. There is an Association of Agricultural Librarians and Documentalists of India (AALDI); the Indian Association of Special Libraries and Information Centres (IASLIC) have a significant agricultural library component; and the Indian Library Association (ILA) has an agricultural libraries chapter. The Indian Council of Agricultural Research (ICAR) has established an Agricultural Research Communication Centre (ARIC) which acts as the National input centre to International Information System for Agricultural Sciences and Technology (AGRIS).

Kumar (1985) considers librarianship as a profession rather than vocation because:

(i) it needs a specialized knowledge imparted in various schools;

(ii) it needs intensive training and continued practices to gain mastery over the skills needed for successful librarianship;

(iii) a set of principles or professional ethics have been drawn;

(iv) a large number of organizations at various levels and of different groups are in existence; and

(v) it is service oriented.

Agricultural librarianship also possess the above characteristics and hence there is little scope for any doubt of its standing as a profession. Blanchard (1979) writes that a scholarly study of agricultural librarianship should begin with the eighteenth century with the establishment of the agricultural and horticultural society libraries of Europe and United States. The band of professionals working in Agricultural libraries form an independent group with a character of slight difference to the mainstream of library profession. The slight difference is their participation in the programmes of maximizing agricultural production.

Characteristics of Agricultural Library Profession

Foster E. Mohrahandt in the preface to the book *'Primer for Agricultural Libraries'* (Parker, 1969) writes "Under ideal conditions, it would be desirable to have a trained and experienced librarian incharge of each agricultural library throughout the world. Librarians provide in their services to library users the most efficient answers to their needs, the most effective support of their work in the highest utilization of the available printed resources. An agricultural librarian, like every librarian who serves a specific subject area, should have a deep understanding of the needs of library clients substantive knowledge of the subject training in modern library techniques, services and management".

ICAR's Report (1969) on the ICAR Institutes and Agricultural University libraries provides a set of characteristics of agricultural librarians as:

(i) they keep the administrators of their institutions informed of the librarian's responsibilities, the functions and the activities of the library;

(ii) they participate in staff meetings of the institutions (and in universities are on the curriculum committee) in order to be informed of contemplated changes so that the library will be ready to offer materials and services when the new developments occur;

(iii) they are well informed about the resources of the library, the number of libraries and those of their country and other countries;

(iv) they actively assume great responsibility and are able to make wise, independent judgments;

(v) they have a positive approach to problems. Every librarian must be convinced that each problem has a solution and that it is his obligation to find the solution; and

(vi) they are enthusiastic, possessed with the highest integrity dedication to service and are genuinely interested in people.

In general, the librarians who possess these characteristics and/or abilities, enjoy the respect of their colleagues both outside and inside the library profession and achieve the prestige which their accomplishments' merit.

Agricultural librarians are to play key role in the war against hunger. Their services to enrich the agricultural workers by providing latest information are going to bear fruits in the Nation's struggle for achieving Green Revolution. Agricultural librarian must be an expert in this field of specialization. He should develop interest in agriculture and achieve a fair acquaintance with the latest agricultural technology. He should have insight into various problems that encounter the agriculturalist. He should also identify the information requirements of the agriculturist and try to provide information. He should have a first hand knowledge of different on-going programmes of his institution and try to equip the library with resources suitable to the programmes. Every individual agricultural librarian should feel that he is participating in the Nation's agricultural programmes and the same is aimed at providing food to many starving countrymen.

Structure of the agricultural library profession in India

Agricultural library profession in India may be divided broadly into five groups. The first group is associated with educational institutions like agricultural universities and colleges, the second with central research institutes, the third with Government departments, the fourth with Agro-industries and the fifth with commercial and trade organizations like banks, marketing associations etc. The structure of the profession in a particular group determines the administrative hierarchy, job performed in different cadres, their pay scales, qualifications and training, incentives for growth and the prestige and status the professional enjoys.

Library profession associated with educational institutions

The librarians working in agricultural universities and in colleges of agriculture, veterinary and animal sciences, dairy science, agricultural engineering, horticulture, fisheries and home science form major group. 23 agricultural universities in India have bigger libraries with modern amenities and services. The staff strength of the university library is commensurate with its size and services. According to Subbaiah (1985), the university libraries may be divided into three categories on the basis of their resources. The first group comes under the category of developed libraries, the second is developing and the third is the one with the libraries in which development has just started. About 8 university libraries are in first category, 7 libraries in the second category and rest are in the third category. The first category libraries have the librarians' position on par with the professor of an university department and the second category have the position of librarian in the cadre of Associate Professor/Reader of a University Department and the rest have the librarian post on par with the Assistant Professor of a university department. The librarians in the professor's cadre are designated as University Librarians, the Librarians in the Associate Professors cadre are designated as the Deputy Librarian/Librarian and the librarians in the Assistant Professor's cadre are designated as Assistant Librarian/Librarian.

Hittangi and Kamalavijayan (1979) wrote "Profession of library and information science is the product of an amazing phenomenon called information explosion engineered by man's sudden interest and concern for research in all branches of human knowledge in an effort to alleviate mankind from the clusters of miseries and sufferings. To cope up this unmanageable deluge of information explosion, it became imperative for the librarians grabbed in the medieval outfit to walk out of it and wear a new outfit of information managers." This new look helped the profession to tide over the calamity of information explosion and consequently to attain new status in the modern society.

Recognizing the above challenges of the profession, University Grants Commission has accorded teacher's status and pay scales to Academic librarians working in the universities and colleges. The Indian Council of Agricultural Research (ICAR) has extended the same status and pay scales to the Agricultural librarians working in the Agricultural Universities and colleges in the country.

The very academic nature of the profession offers many challenging opportunities for building up professional image and also commanding respect. The agricultural librarians have many platforms to project their views and get reorganization.

Library profession associated with the Agricultural Research Institutes

The libraries of the research institutes vary greatly in the size of collections, equipments, facilities and staff. The library profession associated with the Agricultural Research Institutes under the control of Indian Council of Agricultural Research, New Delhi, forms the second largest group. The structure of the profession in agricultural research institutes has a uniform staffing pattern. The staff structure in the Agricultural Research Institute libraries functioning under the organizations other than Indian Council of Agricultural Research is not identical. The library of International Crops Research Institute for Semi-Arid Tropics (ICRISAT) has its own staff structure separately. The Institute of Rural Development has again the UGC pattern. The Forest Research Institute and Colleges of Forest Department, Government of India has a library of national importance in the subject. The library profession in ICAR and CSIR complexes has the 5 yearly assessment scheme which keeps the professionals far from stagnation and discontent.

Agricultural library profession associated with Government Departments

The Departments and Directorates of agriculture, animal husbandry and dairy, horticulture, fisheries and forestry of State and Central Governments have libraries. In general, all these libraries are run by one or two Junior Librarians. The librarians of the Government departments and organizations are generally placed in the pay scales suggested by the Government of India Library Association (GILA).

Agricultural library profession associated with Agro-based Industries in India

Agro-based industries in India include fertilizer industries, foods and food product industries, pesticides and agro-chemical industries, sugar and sugar products based industries, forest products industries, animal and animal product industries etc. The library professionals associated with these organizations are more or less specialists in documentation and information science. Their cadres are commensurate with those of the scientists of these industries.

Agricultural library professions associated with banks and other trade organizations

Many commercial banks have agricultural credit policies to finance the agricultural sector. They have libraries to feed them with the said information. The librarians working in banks have attractive position commensurate with those officials of commercial banks. The librarians working in these organizations work in junior cadres.

Professional Education and Training

The profession and its professional education and training are the inter-related factors.

The profession's success much depends on its education and training. Professional education, as described in the above statement, aims at providing highly specialized knowledge and skills required for the profession. The professional education must reflect the requirement of the profession.

Existing Pattern of Library Education in India

As in the United States, Canada and even to some extent in United Kingdom, the librarianship profession is largely a post graduate's profession. Therefore the levels of education for librarianship may be grouped as:

(i) under-graduate courses for obtaining certificate in library science

(ii) Graduate courses for obtaining Bachelor's degree in library and information science.

(iii) Post-graduate courses for obtaining Master's degree in library and information science.

(iv) Post-graduate research Courses for obtaining Master of Philosophy and Doctor of Philosophy degree in library and information science.

(v) Specialized courses in documentation and information science for obtaining Associateships of DRTC & INSDOC.

The certificate course in library science is an under- graduate course aimed at preparing semi-professionals for the profession. The first professional degree in library science is the Bachelor of Library and Information Science where more emphasis is given to produce junior professionals with a basic knowledge of library and information science. The second professional degree in library and information science is the Master of Library and Information Science, offered to the holders of the degree of Bachelor of Library and Information Science. The third professional degree in library and information science is the Master of Philosophy (M.Phil.) offered to the holders of Master of Library and Information Science. The fourth professional degree in library and information science is the Ph.D. degree offered to the holders of M.Phil. or M.L.I.S. degree by the universities where research facilities exist. Documentation Research and Training Centre (DRTC) offers a post-graduate course "Associateship of DRTC" in documentation and information science. A similar course is also offered by the Indian National Scientific Documentation Centre (INSDOC). Both these courses are aimed at providing specialists in documentation and information science.

Existing library education versus manpower requirement

Mangla (1985), while discussing about the importance of modern information science and technology in the library education writes "since the present age is rightly called an age of information explosion, the rich resources of information available in the world as a whole certainly needed to be taped and exploited for productive use merely because it is a well recognized fact that man's judgment is no better than his information. There is, therefore, a much grater need today for specialists with expertise in selecting, producing, organizing and presenting the information to the user at a time and place where he needs it in a form which would be best suit to his purpose". The existing pattern of library education in India is slowly getting changed to new technology as it is seen that the library science is now changed to library and information science incorporating both library science and information science in its curriculum. The larger library manpower produced in India is not in tune with that of her western counterparts.

Education and Training for Agricultural Librarianship in India

Agricultural librarianship is not dealt in the present education pattern of librarians in India. The existing education pattern for librarians in India train general librarians fit to be absorbed in public and academic libraries. The agricultural librarianship has two aspects. One is the literature aspect and the other is the library and information science aspect. Literature aspect is a complex factor because agricultural literature has a multi-subject base with many specializations. Librarian has to be subject matter specialist as well as library expert. It is only at the Library School of Delhi University that two optional papers are offered for the study of agricultural Libraries and Literature in Agriculture, i.e. Bibliography and Literature in Agricultural Sciences and Agricultural Library System. But because of lack of interest among the students in this area and non-availability of properly qualified teachers, the teaching of these papers becomes ineffective and the papers being optional are generally ignored by the students.

There has been a thinking developed among the agricultural librarians in India that an exercise to produce agricultural librarians may be done in few of the Agricultural Universities in India where both Agricultural faculty and library experts are available. The Seminar on Agricultural librarianship and documentation conducted at Punjab Agricultural University, Ludhiana in 1977 had been a venue for this topic for discussion. A paper presented by Prasher (1977) was discussed at length and a resolution was passed in support of this. Later, the Indian Council of Agricultural Research has endorsed the same. The essence of this approach was to go for a post graduate one year M.L.I.S. course for Agricultural sciences in the Agricultural Universities in India. This may be a good solution and it may be presumed that on some day, education and training for agricultural librarianship in India may be shaped in the Agricultural University complex.

Professional Associations and Development of Agricultural Librarianship in India

The professional associations play an important role in the development of the profession. They are formed for the propagation of a cause as well as to educate the public about the cause of the profession. The associations which play a prominent role in the development of agricultural librarianship in India are: (i) Indian Library Association (ILA), (ii) Indian Association of Special Libraries and Information Centres (IASLIC) and Association of Agricultural Librarians and Documentalists of India (AALDI). ILA has a chapter of agricultural librarianship and does pioneering work through its Annual conferences and other professional activities. IASLIC has in its membership, many Agricultural librarians whose main activities are of purely professional nature. The conferences and publications of IASLIC are of special significance to Agricultural librarianship. The AALDI is the apex body concerning with the Agricultural librarianship in India.

The AALDI came into existence on 11th November 1971 for the noble cause of the profession and since January, 1972 it is functioning for the achievement of its objectives. Over the years, the AALDI has developed into a platform for the propagation of library movement, besides acting as a clearing house of ideas on all matters connected with the organization and administration of libraries and information science. The AALDI is altogether is an young association supported by the Indian Council of Agricultural Research (ICAR).

The activities of AALDI include publications of *AALDI Bulletin* and *AALDI News*. Since 1985, the AALDI bulletin is given the journal status and is being published under the title "*Indian Journal of Agricultural Library and Information Science*". It is an yearly publication and it acts as the main organ of the association. The *AALDI News* is an non-periodical Newsletter and publishes occasional news of interest to Agricultural librarianship in India and abroad. AALDI also is taking up with the ICAR and State Governments the matters pertinent to Agricultural librarianship for ensuring the growth and overall development of agricultural libraries in India.

The IAALD was founded in 1955 to promote internationally and nationally, agricultural librarianship and documentation as well as the professional interests of agricultural librarians and documentalists, the term '*agriculture*' being interpreted in its widest sense so as to include forestry, agriculture, agricultural engineering, veterinary sciences, fisheries and food science and technology. Indian Agricultural Librarians may become members of this association to raise voice for the cause of agricultural librarianship at international level.

AGRICULTURAL LIBRARIES

In fact, 'Library' is an equally important tool as compared to laboratory in carrying out effective research. "The collection of all pertinent embodies thought" as defined by the father of library science Late Dr. Ranganathan, serves a vital link in the chain between research and practice. Libraries form one of the most important organizations for acquisition, organization and dissemination of information to users.

Several types of Agricultural libraries are found in research stations, government agencies, academic institutions, corporations and trade and professional associations.

Each type of library was developed to meet a different need and to serve a different group of users.

Agricultural Libraries – International

The Royal Veterinary and Agricultural University in Copenhagen and its library, which is called the Danish veterinary and Agricultural library, is the oldest of its sort in Scandinavia, founded as early as 1783. It is therefore not surprising, of course, that even though it is a modern library today, its collections, containing 2,50,396 volumes, are the most complete and reliable source of literature on Scandinavian agricultural history.

The principal agricultural libraries in the world are concentrated in Europe, Great Britain, Russia, and North America. Of these several great national and university libraries plus the Commonwealth Agricultural Bureau of Great Britain and their related libraries serve as the world's principal repositories for agricultural knowledge.

Agricultural Libraries in USA

In the United States, Agricultural librarians and documentalists coordinated their work before World War II through the now defunct Agricultural Libraries section of the American Library Association (ALA). They now work through the Agricultural and Biological Sciences section of the American Association of College and Research Libraries of ALA and the Special Libraries Association.

Many of the early agricultural libraries in the United States were connected with agricultural societies. In the nineteenth century, schools for the study of agriculture were established which were an outgrowth of the societies. The development of agricultural colleges was greatly expedited with the passing of the Federal Land Grant Act (The Morrill Act) in 1862. The majority of agricultural libraries presently existing in the United States are associated with these "Land grant" colleges and Universities, which are in most cases, are in general, state supported institutions providing education in all basic and professional subjects as well as agriculture. At some of these universities, the agricultural library is separate from the general universities library and primarily serves the college of agriculture and related colleges and the agricultural experiment stations.

There are also many libraries and documentation centers in the United States serving industrial concerns, societies, institutes, and laboratories which have valuable special collections, and provide incentive for their clientele. These include the Pineapple Research Institute of Hawaii Library in Honolulu; the American meat Institute foundation library in Chicago; The John Deere Company Library in Moline Illions; Central Research Laboratories Library of the General Foods Corporation in Hoboken, New York; the Boyce Thompson Institute for Plant Research Inc. Library in Yonkers, New York; and the Horticultural Society of New York Library in New York City.

National Agricultural Library (NAL), USA

One of the largest Agricultural libraries in the world is the library of the US Development of Agriculture in Washington, which was officially designated the National Agricultural Library in 1962. The Library was started in 1862 and is based on a collection dating back to 1839 which was originally in the Agricultural Division of the patent office. Howard (1994) states that over 2 million volumes and 26,000 current periodicals from all over the world is particularly strong in chemistry, botany, zoology, engineering, economics, history and other sciences related to agriculture. Although principally designed as a service agency for the various units of the Department of Agriculture, it is also a national library as its name indicates. Its services are extended through the "Bibliography of Agriculture, Pesticides Documentation Bulletin" other bibliographic publications and efficient copying service. The monthly "*Bibliography of Agriculture*" has been for some years the most comprehensive indexing service for agriculture and covers a major portion of the significant agricultural literature published throughout the world". The Dictionary catalog of the National Agricultural Library, 1862-1965, Indexes more than 1 million items by author, subject, and title its supplement, the National Agricultural Library catalog began publication on a monthly basis in 1966. Since 1970, NAL provided its bibliographic records for a computerized database called Agricultural Online Access (AGRICOLA), now available in magnetic tape, online and CD-ROM.

Agricultural Libraries in UK

The Agricultural library situation in Great Britain and the Commonwealth countries has been much influenced by the work of the Commonwealth Agricultural Bureaux. With their remarkably effective combination of research stations and libraries, these bureaus have contributed greatly to the improvement in agricultural techniques around the world and have provided many abstracting services and bibliographical publication which are basic for all agricultural library collections. One of the Bureaus, which can be used as an example, is the Commonwealth Bureau of soils located at Harpenden, England. It produces abstracts printed in the bimonthly Journal '*Soils and Fertilizers*', issues the triennial "*Bibliography of Soil Science*' and maintains a card index on soil science subjects amounting to about 40,00,000 cards. This bibliographical work is based on the excellent library of the Rothamsted Experiment Station also at Harpenden, which reported 70,000 volumes in 1959 and was founded in 1843. It uses a modified form of the UDC classification system and strong collections in soils, plant sciences, insecticides, entomology, statistics and the history of agriculture. Other libraries serving research needs of the Commonwealth bureaus include the Joint Library of the Commonwealth Forestry Bureau and the University of Oxford, Department of Forestry in Oxford, the Commonwealth Institute of Entomology Library in London, and the joint Library of the Commonwealth Bureau of Dairy Science and the National Institute for Research in Dairying at Sheffield.

The largest Agricultural Library in U.K

The largest agricultural library in Britain is the main Library of the Ministry of Agriculture in London. Consisting of about 1,50,000 volumes, it issues various bibliographical publications and maintains a few small branch libraries. Important society libraries include the Lindsey library of Royal Horticultural Society in London and the Linnaean Society of London Library which contains particularly strong collections on natural history. Some University libraries are the school of Agriculture Library at the University of Cambridge, the library of Agricultural Department of the University of Edinburgh and Oxford Universities, Department of Agricultural Library. Among the various special libraries are the Tropical Products Institute Library and the International Wool Secretariat library in London.

Important agricultural libraries in Ireland are the Library of Department of Agriculture, the Agricultural Library of the Royal Dublin Society and the Library of the Society of Agriculture, University College, and Dublin.

The majority of agricultural libraries in Europe and Britain use the Universal Decimal System of classification or in some cases, the Von Frauendor for System, whereas American libraries usually employ the Library of Congress or Dewey systems. They also place more reliance than do American Libraries on closed rather than subject-heading catalogs. Their staff often include personnel who are trained as subject specialists rather than as librarians although there are many exemptions to the rule. In European universities the agricultural book collections will often be in the libraries of faculties on departments rather than in the central library.

An especially strong library, noted for its services and collections, is the Lanbouwhoge School, Biblithek (Agricultural University Library) at Wagninger, the Netherlands. Founded in 1873, the Library has about 4,00,000 volumes and consists of a central library and about 40 special or departments libraries. An important indexing journal, the *landbouw documentatie*, is based on the Wageninger libraries collection.

International Crops Research Institute for Semi-Arid Tropics (ICRISAT) Library, Hyderabad, India

ICRISAT Library was established in 1973, with the primary purpose of serving ICRISAT scientists, also endeavors to help research workers all over the world by serving as a centre for the collection of world literature on major and related subjects of interest to ICRISAT. It has both resources and manpower capable of delivering the goods. It has the online access to LAB, VSDA, BIOSIS, AGRIS data bases and is fastly acquiring the shape of an international information centre for the literature pertinent to the Semi-Arid crops.

Objectives

i) To develop a comprehensive collection of information in various documentary forms relevant to ICRISAT's mandate crops.

ii) To provide a wide range of information storage, retrieval, dissemination and document delivery services to scientists and others working on programs involving ICRISAT's mandate crops and the semi- arid tropics.

iii) To participate in relevant national and international information networks for the exchange of information and for the sharing of information resources.

iv) To organize and index different types of documents (books, monographs, Annual Reports, Theses, Reports, pamphlets, current Periodicals, Newsletters, Micro forms, Annual reviews) differently for easy access and quick retrieval.

Services

The following services are offered by ICRISAT Library: Documentation service, Literature Search service, Document Delivery service, Weekly list of periodicals, Reprography service and The Semi-Arid Tropical Crops Information Service (SATCRIS).

The Selective Dissemination of Information (SDI) service of ICRISAT was started in 1979. The service is a monthly one. For the scientists located at ICRISAT centre, it is provided on group profile basis. For scientists located in cooperative programmes the service is provided on individual basis. Though the service is primarily meant for ICRISAT scientists, it is gradually being extended to other scientists also, but on a very selective basis. ICRISAT receives about 800 periodicals of which 500 are primary periodicals; about 100 secondary periodicals and the rest are newsletters.

Agricultural Libraries in India

Even though India is a land of villages where agriculture is the main occupation, there is no National Agricultural Library with well defined national policy of coordination and cooperation in its scope and areas of activities. The Indian agricultural libraries function independently of each other. There is no uniformity in the organization of libraries, nor of the procedures followed, no standards or norms have been adopted.

The status of art of Indian Council of Agricultural Research (ICAR) libraries has been assessed by the following survey teams:

1. Dr. M.S. Randhawa Committee (1957).
2. Dr. Ralp R. Shaw and Dr. Krishna Rao Committee (1956)
3. The Indo-American Agricultural Library Survey and Study Team (Dr. Dorothy Parker Committee) (1958).
4. Dr. Ramaiah Committee (1969).

In addition to above, ICAR sponsored regional agricultural library study teams and finally a survey was done by IARI Library during 1992-93. All important committees have stated that ICAR libraries were in poor condition in terms of proper collection, inadequate library manpower and physical facilities as well as inadequate financial resources to meet the literature/information requirements of the scientists of their respective institutions. So far as the budget was concerned, the libraries of ICAR have shared hardly 1.5% or less than that of the budget of their respective institutes. The appointed librarians were in the lower cadre at semi-professional level and they have been working under the supervision of some scientists who were non-professional. All these reasons have contributed for the slow pace of development ICAR libraries which still persist in most of the libraries in spite of the recommendations of various committees regarding the improvement in the physical facilities of ICAR libraries, strengthening of collection of books and journals, appointment of trained librarians, status of library staff equal to that of the Heads of Department and scientists as well as recommendations for a National Agricultural Library of India headed by the Director.

Libraries, being part and parcel of the education and research system, are playing a vital role in achieving their goal and objectives. They provide information support and function as nerve centre for research activities around which the progress of the country is spiraling high. Their development has been along with the growth and development of institutions in particular and country as a whole in general. These libraries have served the nation and borne many constraints during the span of 50 years of independence.

Role of Agricultural Library in Agricultural Education

Among Agricultural Universities, agricultural libraries are the basic centres for providing agricultural information. In other words, the Agricultural university library is the "Regional Agricultural Information centre". Agricultural University library possesses varied types of books, reference books, scientific, technical, abstracting and indexing journals, serials, etc. on agricultural sciences and allied subjects. Acquisition of these reading materials has been a continuous process. Availability of multifaceted collections in the library help the librarians/information scientists in dissemination of the agricultural information to the users by extending various library services such as circulation services, preparing annotated bibliographies, subject bibliographies, list of additions, circulation of current contents of journals, abstracting of theses and articles, reviewing of books, indexing, circulation of newspaper clippings, arrangement of book exhibitions, organization of specialist information days, reprographic services, etc. This should be the regular feature of the library, because majority of users would like to have such types of library services at their desks for knowing information as quickly as possible to carry out the work relating to agricultural education, research and extension. Journals are supposed to be the best source of nascent thought which provides the current information on agricultural education, research and extension carried out in the different areas of the world. Some of the agricultural university libraries do publish current contents, list of additions etc. regularly.

The report of the second Indo-American Team on Agricultural Education, Research and Extension, headed by Dr. M.S Radhawa stated: "Libraries are a necessary part of the researcher's tool without which he cannot make the most efficient use of his time and talent". In truth and effect, the quality of teaching and research work in any institution depends upon the potential of the library to respond; and in agriculture particularly, where so much literature is being published and the role of the libraries in acquiring and communicating the vast corpus of information to scientists cannot be underestimated.

Another problem is of access to information. The 15,000 agricultural periodicals alone contain more than twelve lakhs of articles every year. A scientist will need a life time to find out and read all the literature on his subjects, and then he will have no time left to apply it, which is the ultimate aim of research in agricultural science.

The problem is now global and even the Food and Agriculture Organization (FAO) has become interested. It is hoped that through AGRIS (Agricultural Information System), CARIS (Computerized Agricultural Research Information System), in which the Indian Council of Agricultural Research is also participating, and the AGLINET (Agricultural Libraries Network), maximum information would be identified and documentation will be provided.

Some libraries in India, with their limited resources and services, have also started Selective Dissemination of Information (SDI) and Current Awareness Services (CAS) to supply information of interest to scientists, so that they have more time at their disposal for practical work. The role which the Indian agricultural libraries can play, without duplicating the work being done elsewhere, in recording, retrieving and communicating information to scientists is vital for agricultural advancement.

Even as it is, many readers, including those who ought to know better, are not fully aware of the treasures of their library. Without the knowledge of the resources of the library (and also of how they are organized and how they can be used), full benefit of the library cannot be achieved.

Libraries, particularly of agricultural universities, have now become highly complex institutions, discharging a multiplicity of functions, catering to a wide clientele having divergent interests, and representing varying states of intellectual development. These libraries are no longer the old institutions charged with preservation and conservation of books; they are now saddled with the task of collecting, preserving and communicating information and knowledge of a colossal magnitude and variety.

Since the libraries of agricultural universities are to play a vital role in agricultural production by serving as effective centres of information communication, it is imperative that their organization, working and services are reviewed from time to time with a view to assess how far they are accomplishing the objectives for which they have been established.

Agricultural University Libraries in India

The ICAR Model Act described the powers and functions of the University to maintain laboratories, libraries, research stations and institutions and museums for teaching, research and extension. This statement gives a legal base to the libraries of agricultural universities. The librarian shall be a member of the Academic council and an officer of a University responsible to the Vice-Chancellor for all matters concerning the library and the purchase cataloguing and maintenance of books and journals and operation of the library. The contents of the sections 7 and 18 of the ICAR Model Act, incorporating the recommendations of Cunning's Committee Report (Dr. Ralph W Cunning as chairman) and Sultan Committee Report (Dr. TS Sultan as chairman –an advisor under USAID mission to PAU) has far reaching effects on agricultural university library organization, administration, powers and duties of the university librarians. Subsequently, these sections of ICAR Model Act were incorporated in the acts and status of almost every agricultural university in India. This provided the library a rightful place in the administrative setup of an agricultural university.

Two Indo-American teams in 1950s stressed on improving agricultural education, research and extension which have resulted in additional emphasis on the need for better libraries. The report of second team headed by Dr. M.S. Randhawa states: Libraries are necessary part of the researcher's tool. Every possible step should be taken to improve library facilities which are often inadequate. Dr. Randhawa as Vice-Chairman for ICAR appointed a committee consisting of Dr. Ralph R. Shaw and Dr. DB Krishna Rao in 1956 to conduct a study of library and bibliographic services for agricultural teaching and research in India. The recommendations of this committee created deep awareness among librarians and administrators for better agricultural libraries.

This survey team was set up as a result of the recommendations made at a meeting of the Directors of Agricultural Research Institutes (1967) and it was headed by Dr. Darothy Parker. The committee visited the then existing agricultural university libraries. Chief librarian of IARI was its member secretary. This committee gave 69 recommendations. The most important recommendations were regarding to:

- Improvement in the physical facilities to ICAR institute libraries.
- Strengthening of the collection of books and journals.
- Appointment of trained librarians in the institute libraries.
- Status of library equal to that of a Department of the institute.

- Status of Librarian on par with Head of the Department.
- Making of a National Agricultural library in India headed by a director.

The Table 5 shows the Agricultural University Libraries, location, year of establishment, collection, etc.

Council of Agricultural Research (ICAR) Library, New Delhi

The library has replaced its entire manual in house activities like circulation, procurement of documents, processing and information retrieval with computerization. It also developed databases for the ICAR publications and deputation reports of scientists visiting foreign countries. E-mail and Internet facility is also available. The ICAR library is the member of DELNET for getting information online for knowing and using the collection available in other libraries in Delhi. The library provides photocopy service to other libraries in Delhi. Also its documents are used on inter-library loan service.

Indian Agricultural Research Institute (IARI) Library, New Delhi

The Indian Agricultural Institute Library is the biggest agricultural library of Asia dealing with Agriculture, Agronomy, Plant Pathology, Plant protection and many other related subjects.

The Indian Agricultural Research Institute library which was deprived of being designated as the Indian National Agricultural Library was initially established along with its premier Institute in 1905 at Pusa Village in Bihar. For this reason they are still popularly called Pusa Institute and the Pusa library. The library started with a small collection of 5,000 volumes donated by the Department of Agriculture, Government of India. After the devastating earthquake in 1934, the Institute and the library were shifted to their present location in New Delhi where IARI was called Imperial Agricultural Research Institute and the library was named as Linlithgow Library. As early as 1993 the library had a collection of 70,000 volumes receiving 3,900 publications on exchange and was subscribing to about 340 journals.

Agricultural Libraries in Andhra Pradesh

In Andhra Pradesh there are 3 types of agricultural libraries. They are of Educational, Research and Extension Libraries. The Educational libraries are run by Acharya N.G. Ranga Agricultural University, the research libraries are run by the ICAR research institutes situated in A.P.and ANGRAU research stations and the Extension Libraries are run by the Extension Institutes of Central Government and are discussed below.

Agricultural University and College Libraries in Andhra Pradesh

With a view to cater to the library and information needs of teachers, students as well as research and extension personnel, the system was reorganized in 1980 forming a central library and four branch libraries at Hyderabad and Regional Libraries at Tirupati and Bapatla and college Libraries at other campuses (Fig 1).

Table: 5
Agricultural University Libraries in India

Sl. No.		*Name of the University*	*Place*	*Year of establish-ment*	*Books/ Collection*	*Periodicals Foreign/ Indian*	*Disserta-tions/ Thesis*	*Back volumes*	*Volumes*	*Compu-ters*	*Repro-graphic*
1	*2*	*3*	*4*	*5*	*6*	*7*	*8*	*9*	*10*	*11*	*12*
1.	ANGRAU	Acharya NG Ranga Agricultural University	Hyderabad	1964	2,00,000	150+150	400	-	20,000	Computer facility	
2.	AAU + BCKV	Assam Agricultural University Bidhan Chandra Krishi Viswavidyalayam	Jorhat Haringhata	1994 1974	90,048 79,578	174 yearly addition	1 budget 6.50 lakhs Xerox	-	Book bank	Readers attendance	20,000 photo copy
3.	BAU	Birsa Agricultural University	Ranchi -	1987		-	-	-	-	-	
4.	CAU	Central Agricultural University	Imphal	1993		152	49(Thesis)	967 (Periodicals)	8970	Libs of other about 3,800 books	
5.	CIFE	Central Institute of Fisheries Education	Bombay	1988	23,300		1,300	6,700 (period)		CR Rom facility	300 reprists
6.	CSAUA &T	Chandra Shekhar Azad University Agriculture and Technology	Kanpur	1975	1,29,528	67,519					

(Contd...)

1	2	3	4	5	6	7	8	9	10	11	12
7.	CCSHAU	Chaudhary Charan Singh Haryana Agricultural University	Hisar	1970	1,72,097	1556	5255	8,45041		Micro documents Readers capacity	4 photo copy machines
8.	Dr. PDKV	Dr. Panjabrao Deshmukh Krishi Vidyapeeth	Akola	1969	1,32,724 (including back vols)	268+356 gratis	3,500	26,000 (period)		Micro film ready	Repro-graphic series
9.	Dr. YSPU H&F	Dr. Y.S. Parmar University of Horticulture & Forestry	Nauni	1985	43,000 (books & back vols)	-	-	-	-	CDROM Databases	10 compute-rised in house databases
10.	G.B.PUA & T	G.B. Pant University of Agriculture and Technology Pant Nagar	Pant Nagar	1960	3,18,947	1200 (Subscription yearly addition (6,043)				Documental facility & Microfilm reading	Photo copy facility
11.	GAU	Gujarat Agricultural University	Dantiwada	1972	1,13,650				24,400 1,99,784		Micro care facility
12	HPKV	Himachal Pradesh Krishi Vishvavidylaya	Palampur	1978	36,398 (Total collection 61,617)	22,522	2036 (Thesis) misll doc 661	-		2CD Rom data base, Book bank facility	Repro-graphic service
13	IVRI	Indian Veterinary Research Institute	Izatnagar	1989	1,50,000	2,500 more than Journals	-	-	-	Micro films, Fax, repro-graphic	CD NET system, CD ROM search
14	IARI	Indian Agricultural Research Institute	New Delhi	1958	6,00,000	5000 receive more than from all other world	-	-	-	-	-

(Contd...)

1	2	3	4	5	6	7	8	9	10	11	12
15	IGKV	Indira Gandhi Krishi Vishwavidylaya	Raipur	1987	21,988	2389	525 (Thesis)	-	-	Documentation	Photo copying services
16	JNKV	Jawaharlal Nehru Krishi Vishwavidyalya	Jabalpur	1964	51,000	-	3,900 (Thesis)	1,15,000 (bound values of periodicals and reports)			350 micro films
17	KAU	Kerala Agricultural University	Thrissur	1972	1,00,000	1000	-	-	-	-	-
18	KKV	Konkan Krishi Vidyapeeth	Dapoli	1972	27,693	80	-	12,445 periodicals	-	Reference books 449 serial titles 21	-
19	MPKV Gandhi Phule	Mahatma Krishi Vidyapeeth	Rahuri	1968	58,964 subscription	400 Jls on	3,264	21,005		Micro film facility	Xerox
20	MKV	Marathwada Krishi Vidyapeeth	Parbhani	1972	64,688	362	-	-	-	Books used by readers 91,375 books issued 28,164	
21	NDVAT	Narendra Deva University of Agriculture and Technology	Faizabad	1975	38,560 (subscription)	120	-	5,000	-	Budget 15 lakhs	-
22.	NDRI	National Dairy Research Institute	Karnal	1955	80,000 (including back vols of Jls, Pamplets microfilm & reprints	400 subscription on gratis	-	-	-	Budget 18.25 lakhs	photo copy, cab database

(Contd...)

1	2	3	4	5	6	7	8	9	10	11	12
23.	OUART	Orissa University of Agriculture and Technology	Bhuba-neswar	1962	1,43,754	215 (current periodicals	-	-	-	67,600 books issued	
24.	PAU	Punjab Agricultural University	Ludhiana	1962	3,10,630 books, periodical bound volumes					Micro film & micro card facility	
25.	RAU (B)	Rajasthan Agricultural University	Bikaner	1987	1,00,000 more than	All constituent	College libs	With provision	20,000	50,000 books periodicals jls budget 25. 08 laksh	
26.	RAU (P)	Rajendra Agricultural University	Pusa	1970	45,637 (books & periodical	95 (subscription)	-	-	-	Documentation service and reprographic service budget 3 lakhs	
27.	SKUAST	Sher-e Kshmir University of Agricultural Sciences and Technology	Srinagar	1982							
28.	TNAU	Tamil Naidu Agricultural University	Coimbatore	1971	1,51,663 2425 addition	426 (Subscription)	-	-	-	54724 issued , readers attendance 81615 budget 2673 lakhs photocopy PC available	

(Contd...)

1	2	3	4	5	6	7	8	9	10	11	12
29.	TVASU	Tamil Naidu Veterinary and Animal Sciences University		1989		215 +177					
30.	UAS (B)	University of Agricultural Sciences	Bangalore	1964	1,62,831	811 (subscription)	-	-		Readers attendance 2,33,115 budget 45.80 lakhs microfilm, microfishe readers, Xerox CD Rom with subscription to 2 databases installed.	
31.	UAS (D)	University of Agricultural Sciences	Dharwad	1986	81,000	570	-	-	-		
32.	WBUAFS	West Bengal University of Animal & Fishery Sciences	Kolkata	1995	15,000	65 (current periodicals)	375 (Abstracting Journals)	10,000		Reports 151, students 105	

* *Source*: *Universities' Hand Book*, 28th Edition, A.I.U, New Delhi.

Fig. 1: Agricultural University and College Libraries in Andhra Pradesh

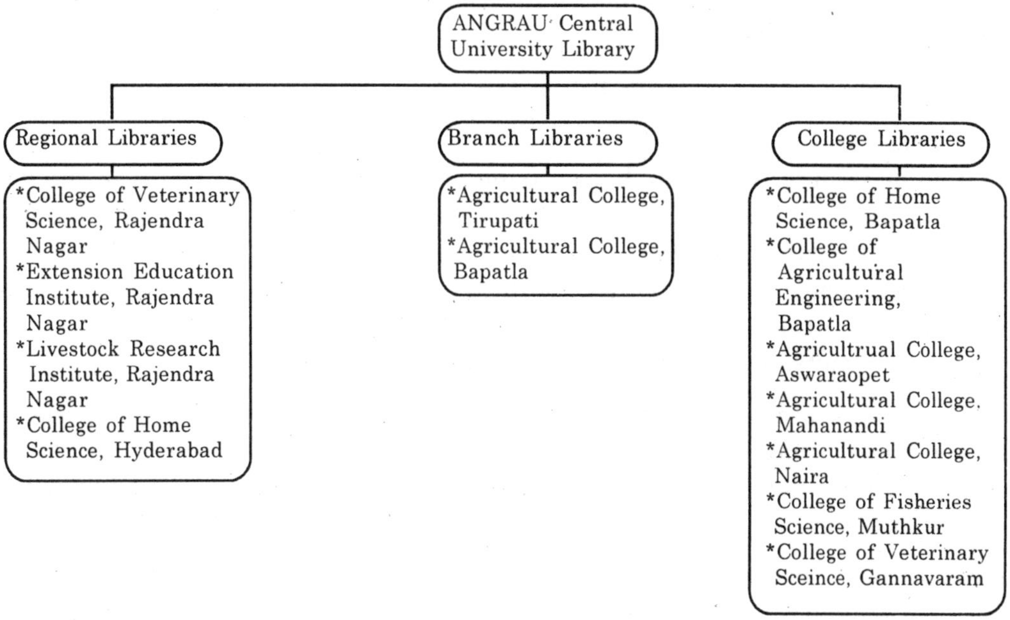

All the libraries function under the overall supervision of the university librarian. While the Central Library works under the direct control and supervision of the University Librarian, the Regional Libraries and College Libraries are run by the Assistant Librarians under the administrative control of the Principals in the respective campuses.

All the libraries together continued to receive over 600 Indian and foreign periodicals. In addition, 4,500 books and about 380 dissertations and reports were added with a view to help the SC, ST and BC students. And special text book collections have been built in each of the campuses. The photocopying facilities available in all the campuses have been put to maximum use and over 2.5 lakh copies were supplied to the library users. A monthly current awareness bulletin "*Current Agricultural Titles*" was continued and is being mailed to all the Agricultural Research Stations. The service is backed up with the supply of photo copies of articles required by the scientists at the Agricultural Research Stations. A publication under the title '*Agricultural Dissertation Abstracts*' covering Ph.D. dissertations submitted to ANGRAU was published. The central Library distributed 125 copies of *Journal of Research*, ANGRAU to various National and International institutes. On exchange the library receives foreign and Indian periodicals worth over Rs. 50,000.

The Central Library at Hyderabad and two regional libraries at Tirupati and Bapatla provided CD-ROM based database searches by subscribing to Commonwealth Agricultural

Bureau Abstracts. E-mail and internet facilities were established in the Central Library. LAN connectivity has been established in the Central Library and building up of online Public Access Catalogue using LIBSYS software is on trial.

Agricultural Research Institute Libraries

The agricultural research library may keep its researchers abreast of the latest information by issuing: 1) Research reports on various research problems in the form and language familiar with the researchers. 2) Bibliographies of latest publications on various fields of agricultural sciences. 3) Current contents of journals on various specialties of agricultural sciences. 4) A monthly and quarterly agricultural research newsletter reporting briefly various research projects at hand. 5) A quarterly research bulletin intimating the results of research conducted during that period.

Furthermore, in order to inform the researchers about the problem faced, experiences gained and observations made by the farmers in practicing the research results, the library may compile data obtained from extension workers and farmers and distribute among researchers.

Agricultural Research Institutes in India are spread in almost all the states and union territories on the basis of crop and research priorities. They are established and administered by the different agencies of central Government. Majority of them are under the administrative control of Indian Council of Agricultural Research, New Delhi. Some are under the Council of Scientific and Industrial Research (CSIR), New Delhi, and some are under different departments of Government of India. Predominant among them Indian Agricultural Research (IARI), New Delhi, being a premier institution conducting agricultural research, Post-graduate education and extension education. Indian Agricultural Research Institute's library is one of the biggest libraries in Asia and has about 4 lakh documents in its holding. It has the character of National Agricultural Library.

The libraries of Indian Agricultural Research Institute, Indian Veterinary Research Institute, National Dairy Research Institute, Central Food Technology Research Institute, and Indian Institute of Horticultural Research have the character and resources of national libraries in their respective fields. They are specialized libraries with remarkable role in the Indian Agricultural Research. These libraries have sizable collections of reading materials and offer effective library and information services.

The All India Coordinated Agricultural Research Projects functioning under the administrative control of ICAR are also dispersed in almost all the states as per their crop research priorities. Many project coordinators have established their own libraries. Apart from all these, the Coffee Board, Tea Board, Coir Board, Rubber Board, Silk Board etc. have their own libraries. The Zoological/Botanical and Geological Surveys of India also have their own libraries which are of agricultural interest. The Agricultural Research Institute libraries have rich collections of literature which form the nation's main information resources in the field of Agricultural sciences.

Directorate of Oilseeds Research (DOR) Library, Hyderabad

The library was established in the year 1988. The library and documentation unit aims at collecting, storing, organizing and disseminating information on all aspects of crop improvement, crop production, crop protection and utilization of oilseed crops. An amount of Rs. 6,31,195 was spent to acquire books and to subscribe periodicals during the period under report. A total of 122 publications were received on gratis, besides, newsletters and annual reports from different organizations. New records of books were added to the computerized library catalogue. The database of doctoral dissertations on nine oilseeds information has been developed and updated regularly. Fortnightly issues of '*Current Oilseeds Literature Alerts*' have been brought out and circulated to scientists of DOR. Two issues of '*DOR Newsletter*' have been published and distributed to ICAR institutes and agencies working on oilseeds.

Directorate of Rice Research (DRR) Library, Hyderabad

The DRR library is one of the information centres in India doing research in the field of rice literature. The library has a collection of above 16,000 books and 380 journals and a microfilming unit. It is also equipped with a learning resource laboratory with CD-ROM work databases. The directorate has strong national and international linkages with some institutions and the nodal centres for research network programmes in priority areas like hybrid rice, bio-technology, germplasm, evaluation and conservation.

National Academy of Agricultural Research Management (NAARM) Library, Hyderabad

The academy has a specialized library established in 1976, with collection focusing agricultural research management, science policy, system studies, project management, futurology, forecasting, educational technology, technology transfer system/policies, women studies, information management, research communication, computer/information technology, human resource development, administration, etc. The library has a collection of more than 16000 books and over 360 are being added every year. The library subscribes 120 foreign journals, 100 Indian journals, and gets 60 journals and newsletters on gratis/ exchange. Besides this, library has a good collection of reports and other publications of various international organizations and has also foreign tour reports submitted by the ICAR scientists.

Central Research Institute for Dryland Agriculture (CRIDA) Library, Hyderabad

The institute has established specialized library in 1972 scientists and technicians working in different research farms use the library quite extensively. At present the library holds about 6000 publications and subscribes to about 60 journals pertaining to various disciplines having relevance to dryland agriculture and allied subjects. Efforts are underway to establish an effective storage and retrieval system. Library provides photo copy facility for the benefit of the scientific and technical personnel of the institute. Library also provides current awareness service (monthly) besides bringing out necessary catalogues for reference as and when required.

Efforts are under way to bring out *'Current Content Mirror'*, *'Current Book Review'* and select bibliographies on specific topics on demand for the institute staff. The scientists are exposed to all the current scientific information on their research by gathering information from the periodicals acquired.

National Bureau of Plant Genetic Resources (NBPGR) Library, Hyderabad

The library was established in the year 1985. NBPGR library maintained its designated activities of acquisition of books and journals, exchange of literature, cataloguing and documentation. During the year, 269 new books relating to various aspects of PGR management and Hindi literature were added at headquarters and regional stations libraries through purchase. Library is procuring 166 journals including 72 foreign and 94 Indian through subscription/gifts and exchanges for the use of head quarters and different regional stations. News clipping service related to plant genetic resources and agriculture is provided to the readers regularly. The library provided reprography service to its internal as well as external users. Bureaus publications were supplied to over 500 different organizations/ institutes in India and abroad. In return 250 publications were received as gratis from various organizations. About 800 reference queries were attended to assist the scientists.

National Research Centre for Sorghum (NRCS) Library, Hyderabad

NRCS library was established in the year 1989 with an aim to provide information services in support of research activities and goals of the institute. The library holdings include popular monographs, research and technical reports and journals. Journal collection includes Indian as well as foreign journals.

Central Tobacco Research Institute (CTRI), Rajahmundry

The library of the Central Tobacco Research Institute, Rajahmundry has been established in 1950 to provide Library and Documentation services to both the research workers of the Institute and its research stations at Guntur (A.P.), Kandukur (A.P), Jeelugumilli (A.P), Vedasandur (TN), Hunsur (Karnataka), Pusa (Bihar), Dinhata (WB) in carrying out their planned research on the development of different types of tobacco.

The library has rich collection of publication on tobacco. Documents such as books, reference books, conferences and symposia proceedings, technical reports and bulletins, annual reports of ICAR Institutes, Agricultural Universities, Tobacco Research Institutes, and other institutes doing tobacco research throughout the world are being obtained regularly. The Library is also obtaining 149 newsletters of different Institutions, Agricultural universities in India and abroad regularly. It is also strong in terms of journal collections containing important foreign and Indian titles on research on tobacco.

Documentation and Information Services

Scanning of all the periodicals received in the library and indexing of articles on tobacco and other related subjects is a regular work. The indexed articles are filled in index cabinets in their respective subject headings for ready reference. On an average 400 articles per year are being indexed and filled in the card cabinets. The library is providing technical enquiry service (answers to technical questions), Current Awareness Service (CAS) and Selective Dissemination of Information (SDI) by sending user profiles, by personal intimations, preparation of annotated bibliographies on specific topics, etc. References are collected in the card form on the topics such as quality of tobacco, bi-products, smoking and health controversies, solar energy curing, production, trade and marketing in various countries, cultivars, botanical pesticides etc, for the preparation of bibliographies.

i) *Indian Tobacco Literature* (1985-1990) bibliography is under preparation. It is a continuation of series of "Indian Tobacco Literature, 1980-1983" and 1984 publications.

ii) Annotated bibliography on control of tobacco suckers for the period 1970-85 has been prepared.

Latest data on world tobacco statistics (important countries, area production and yield), production of tobacco in India (States and their production), Tobacco cultivars and other statistics are being maintained on fixograph boards as well as in the cardex system for ready reference.

Reference guides on particular topics viz. chemical constituents of tobacco, fertilizers, soils, pests and diseases, bi-products etc., are maintained in cardex cabinets.

Literature is searched either retrospective or of current periods on the topics requested by the scientists. Services in printed form, like list of additions, reference bulletin, list of periodicals, CTRI newsletter etc. are also provided.

Computerization Activities

This library is equipped with 2 computers. A database by using software package DBASE III + was developed on articles published by CTRI research workers.

Sharing of Resources of Other Institute Libraries

The Institute library has developed relations with other Agricultural Research Institutes/ Universities viz. ICRISAT, AGRIC, New Delhi and NAL, USA. The following literature searches have been obtained from their AGRICOLA data base.

1. Ridomil – Metalaxyl
2. IPM and Biological Control
3. Cultural Mechanical Weed Control
4. IPM biological control of plant pests of field crops.
5. Tissue culture.
6. Neem.

Agricultural Extension Libraries

Education of the rural people in agriculture and allied fields is one of the main functions of university extension system of an Agricultural University. Improved agricultural technology is one of the most important inputs in the present day agriculture is dynamic and challenging. Unless latest technologies are carried over to the doorsteps of the farmers, there is no possibility for rapid increase in agricultural production/ the extension services of agricultural universities and the objectives of carrying out first line extension work, which involved testing of new agricultural technology in different farming situations on the farmers' fields with a view to analyze the constraints involved in its application and adoption. Development of different strategies for technology transfer in agriculture is also one the mandates of the university extension work. The Agricultural Information and Communication Centre (AI&CC) was started in 1969 with the financial assistance from ICAR and State Government. It is located at the headquarters of ANGRAU, Rajendranagar. The centre process the latest research information generated by the university and other related agencies and disseminates it to the public in general and the farming community in particular including extension personnel through its publications, radio, press and television to support the ongoing programmes of State Agricultural department and the university.

In addition to extension services of ANGRAU the following Central Government organizations are functioning in the agricultural extension programmes.

National Institute of Rural Development (NIRD) - CORD, Hyderabad

Centre On Rural Documentation (CORD) in the institute was established with a mandate to serve as resource centre for rural development information and servicing agency for development community, comprising planners, administrators, policy-makers, functionaries, trainers, academics and researchers. Recent advances in Information Technology (IT) added a new dimension to the task of harnessing information for development. To keep in step with the advances in Information Technology and changing information needs of the development community, CORD geared itself to improve its information handling capabilities. Accordingly, during the period under review, CORD established Internet connectivity, worked on design and development of website of the institute and finalized the creation of computerized clearinghouse of information on rural development.

At the end of March 1998, the total stock of books including Hindi books, Children's books and bound volumes of periodicals stood at 89,157. CORD receives 405 journals out of which nearly 320 are subscribed to end the rest received on gratis or exchange.

National Institute of Agricultural Extension Management (MANAGE), Hyderabad

MANAGE Library was established in the year 1987, to serve as a documentation centre for disseminating information on various aspects of agricultural management. With the aid of Information Technology a wide range of facilities are provided for giving access to information to meet the requirements of institute's training, teaching, research and consultancy activities. The centre is building up a rich resource base of books, journals, videos and CD-ROMs. During the period under review, the library acquires 865 books and subscribes to 150 journals. Around 200 video cassettes on various aspects of agriculture and management make-up the video library and also subscribe to major CDROM databases such as AGRIS, AGRICOLA, TROPAG and RURAL. The library has automated most of its operations using LIBSYS software.

National Plant Protection Training Institute (NPPTI) Library, Hyderabad

The institute was established in the year 1966 and has a good collection of books and journals, which is being referred by all faculty members and officer trainees and faculty of neighbouring institutes and ANGRAU Post Graduate students.

SOURCES OF AGRICULTURAL INFORMATION

Scientists, research workers, extension specialists, teachers, planners, policy makers, practioners of agricultural area are producing a vast amount of literature, publication on many areas/subjects in the field of agriculture.

Agricultural literature is being published in various forms like books, monographs, reference books, bulletins, research and technical reports, periodicals, journals, conference proceedings, annual reports, patents, standards, abstracting periodicals and annual reviews, etc. Each has been discussed below.

Books & Monographs

In a rapidly developing field of research, the conventional sources can play only a limited role as initial medium for reporting the results of search and observation. The book may present a synthesis on a consolidation of knowledge on its topic and presents the results of search published in other forms of literature. The book also forms a source for having comprehensive information on a given topic. Hence, commercial book publication offers a vast scope for the effective communication of information. Some of the books are mentioned below:

i) Barden-Powell, H.H. *The Land Systems of British India*, 3 vols, Oxford, 1892.

ii) Irfan Habib. *The Agrarian System of Mogul India, 1556-1707*, Bombay, Asia Publishing House, 1963, 453p.

iii) Joshi,P.C. *Land Reform and Agrarian Change in India and Pakistan Since 1947*, Delhi, Asian Research Center, Institute of Economic Growth, 1970, 112p, monographed.

iv) Moreland, William Harrison. *The Agrarian System of Muslim India, A Historical Essay with Appendices*, 2nd ed, Delhi, Oriental Books Reprint Corporation, 1968, XVII, 296p.

v) Whitcombe, Elizabeth, *Agrarian Conditions in Northern India*, New Delhi, Thompson Press (India), 1971, V.1 United Provinces under British rule, 1860-1900.

Various estimates have been made about the annual output of books, etc. Twenty two countries are participating in shared cataloguing with the Library of Congress with their national bibliographies being an input in the system and the total number of publications put in system figured to more than 2,00,000 in 1909. The National Agricultural Library, Washington had collected from 1865-1965 over 12,50,000 volumes and published a catalogue of this. It has published supplementary catalogue for 1965-70 in which they have listed over 1,30,000 volumes. This indicates that over 25,000 books, etc. are published each year in agro biological subjects. *UNESCO Statistical Year Book* (1971) gives overall output of titles as 5,48,000. Indian output being 13,614. It has been further estimated that about 10,000 scientific books and monographs are produced annually.

Bulletins

Bulletins are published in series by various agricultural experiment stations, universities and research institutes in the world. At least 900-1000 series are currently being published in the world. The total retrospective output of this type of literature easily exceeds 2,00,000 publications. This is very important source of media for agricultural scientists.

Report Literature

As far as scientific report literature is concerned with agriculture, there is a large flow of this material and today they are getting much importance. The International Atomic Energy Agency has published more than 2,00,000 research reports. In USA alone, more than 75,000 unclassified reports are produced annually. There are other agencies, which bring out such reports but their figure is not known.

Scientific Papers

A huge number of scientific and technical periodicals are published in the world. The '*World List of Scientific Serials*' lists 60,000 titles. More than 35,000 scientific serials are published annually, and out of this, more than 15,000 are of agricultural interests. Various estimates have been made about the annual output of contributions made in these periodicals which range from one to three million articles. VINITI is reported to be monitoring more than one million articles annually in their abstracting periodicals.

Theses and Dissertations

Thesis form a valuable source of information for agricultural research workers. Data pertaining to various dissertations submitted in various countries is not readily available. Recently (1974), the University Microfilm Inc. has published '*A Comprehensive Dissertation Index*', in which they have indexed over 4,00,000 dissertations submitted in various universities from 1861 to 1972, in U.S.A.

Various agricultural Universities published bibliographies of the theses submitted at their universities or thesis available in their libraries. Phadnis and Sital (1977) gave an estimate of 39,150 theses in biological science, 12,300 theses in agriculture and 55,000 theses in chemistry.

Projects of Research

Various projects of research carried by research institutes get listed in their annual reports etc. Very few reports, however, are up-to-date. INSDOC has compiled and published '*Current Project of Research in CSIR Laboratories – 1972*'. This list covers 2000 current projects of research in 39 organisations under CSIR. INSDOC has also been compiling similar information about the projects of research in science and technology subjects for Indian Universities including agricultural universities. The ICAR has the research project unit which compiles and keeps profile of projects of research in the ICAR system and various agricultural universities. About 5400 projects of research have been listed by this unit.

Comprehensive Monographs, etc.

To provide comprehensive information to agricultural scientists, ICAR has published numerous monographs. These are excellent source media to scientists. Some of the titles it has covered include: '*Cotton in India*', '*Pulse Crops in India*', '*Rye, Neem, Jute in India*', '*Potato in India*', '*Indian Tobacco*', '*The Mango–A Hand book*', '*Grass Cover of India*', '*Rose India*', etc.

Indian Directories, Year Books

Directories, hand books and year books are currently being published in India which are useful sources of information to scientists, technicians, etc.

Some of the year books are mentioned below:

1. *Agricultural Year Book, New Vistas in crop yields.* New Delhi, ICAR, 1970. VIII, 689p, 160 plates.

   The first Indian year book on agriculture was published in 1970. It is a collection of contributions of scientists commanding authority on various aspects of agriculture, plant introduction, genetic improvement of crop plants, agronomic practices and contains a comprehensive bibliography of the soil science.
2. Mysore Agriculture Department: Mysore agricultural calendar and year book, Bangalore, 1960, VIII, 132p. illus, tables.
3. Year book of the Agricultural Department of Eastern Bengal and Assam, Shillong, 1911.
4. Year book of Punjab Agricultural Department. Lahore, 1913-.
5. Year book of Agriculture Department in the Southern Division. Bombay Presidency, Puna, Department of Agriculture, 1922-25.

Important Journals on Agriculture

International Journals

1. International Rice Research Notes, Philippines.
2. Biologio plantarum, Czech Republic
3. Buffalo Journal, Thailand
4. Fitoterapai, Italy
5. Cruciferal Newsletter, UK
6. Phytochemistry, U.K.
7. Journal of Agronomy and Crop Science, Germany

National Journals

1. Indian Journal of Agricultural Science
2. Environment and Ecology
3. Karnatak Journal of Agricultural Science
4. Indian Journal of Animal Sciences
5. Insect Environment
6. Indian Veterinary Journal
7. Journal of Indian Society of Soil Science

8. Indian Journal of Agronomy
9. Crop Research (Hisar)
10. Current Science
11. Indian Journal of Experimental Biology
12. Indian Forester
13. Annals of Agricultural Research
14. Madras Agricultural Journal
15. Advances in Plant Sciences
16. Journal of Maharashtra Agricultural Universities
17. Indian Phytopathology.

Newsletters

1. International Chickpea and Pigeon Pea Newsletter, India
2. International Arachis Newsletter, India
3. International Sorghum and Millets Newsletter, USA
4. MFP News, India
5. Fertilizer Marketing News, India
6. Lens Newsletter, Syria
7. Mycorrhiza News India
8. Wood News, India
9. Agrochemicals News in Brief, Thailand
10. Camel Newsletter, Syria
11. Palawija News, Indonesia
12. ILEIA Newsletter, The Netherlands
13. International Rice Commission Newsletter, Italy.

The literature on users studies reveal that students, scholars and scientists depend on various sources of information available in electronic media such as online database, CD-ROM, Multimedia and Bibliographies / Catalogues.

The requirement of the users may be recorded periodically and the much needed electronic and digital resources identified. The users should be properly oriented to and trained on the new media and the agricultural University libraries should accommodate the new features, which provide large storage and easy retrieval capacity. The collection and development process should be revised to make use of these new devices, which will be more useful to readers to save the time. Electronic media fulfills the fourth law of Ranganathan's five laws of library science.

Online Databases

CAB Abstracts, UK

AGRIS Database at Vienna (Austria) since 1975 – AGRIS Data Base collects from 117 national and international participating input centers from all over the world.

Searchable Databases on Agriculture and their links on Internet

- Ag-Info Net (http://www.aginfo.net/)
- AgEcon - Research in Agricultural Economics (http://agecon.lib.umn.edu/)
- AgKnowledge (http://info.ag.uidaho.edu/Ag Knowledge/)
- AgLinks (http://www.farmwide.com.au/links/search.asp)
- AgNews (http://agnews.tamu.edu/search.cgi)
- AgNic - Agricultural Conferences http://www.agnic.org/mtg/search.html)
- AgNIC - Agriculture Network Information Center (http://www.agnic.org/)
- Agri-Infolink (http://www.agri-infolink.com/)
- AgriBiz - (http://www.agribiz.com/agInfo/AgriBizsearch.html)
- AgriBot (http://www.agribot.com/)
- Agricola Search (http://agricola.cos.com/cgi-bin/search)
- Agricom: Les Specialistes du Commerce Agricole sur Internet (http://www.agricom.qc.ca/)
- Agricultural Communications Documentation Center (http://web.aces.uiuc.edu/agcomdb/search.html)
- Agricultural Information Modules (http://www.nzdl.org/fastcgibin/library?a=p&p=about&c=aginfo)
- Agricultural Institute of Canada (http://www.aic.ca/search/index.html)
- Agriculture and Agri-Food Canada Online (http://www.agr.gc.ca/search_e.phtml)
- Agriculture Online (http://www.agriculture.com/search/sindex.html)
- Agriculture Research Service (p://www.ars.usda.gov/search.html)

- Agriculture Research Service - National Programs (http://www.nps.ars.usda.gov/menu.htm?docid=367)
- Agriculture Search (http://www.equipmentsearch.com/categories/agriculture/)
- AgriFor (http://agrifor.ac.uk/)
- Agrigate (http://www.agrigate.edu.au/public/agrigate?form=search&Action=Query)
- AgriNet (http://agrinet.tamu.edu/search/search.htm)
- AGRINews (http://www.agrinews-pubs.com/)
- Agripedia (http://www.ca.uky.edu/agripedia/search.html)
- Agriscape (http://www.agriscape.com/)
- AgriSurf! (http://www.agrisurf.com/agrisurfscripts/agrisurf.asp?index=_25)
- Agrium (http://www.agrium.com/)
- AgriWeb Canada (http://hahtext.agr.ca/SCRIPTS/hsrun.exe/webapps/agriweb/agriweb.htx;start =HS_home_e)
- AgroLINE (http://agroline.usc.es/index_en.html)
- Agriscape (http://www.agriscape.com/)
- AgSearch (http://www.farmwide.com.au/agsearch/)
- AgView (http://www.agview.com/)
- AgWay (http://www.agway.com/search/)
- AgWeb (http://www.agweb.com/search.asp?id=19)
- American Farm Bureau (http://www.fb.com/)
- American Society of Agricultural Engineers (http://www.asae.org/search.html)
- American Society of Agricultural Engineers - Technical Documents (http://asae.frymulti.com/)
- Animal and Plant Health Inspection Service (http://www.aphis.usda.gov/)
- Board on Agriculture and Natural Resources (http://www7.nationalacademies.org/banr/search.html)
- British Society of Soil Science (http://www.soils.org.uk)
- Campocom (http://www.campocom.com/)
- Canada Agriculture Museum (http://www.agriculture.nmstc.ca/english/search/index.cfm)

- Chicago Board of Trade (http://www.cbot.com/)
- Chicago Merchantile Exchange (http://www.cme.com)
- Compendium of Pesticide Common Names (http://www.hclrss.demon.co.uk/)
- Consultative Group on International Agricultural Research (http://search.cgiar.org/search_form.asp)
- CRIS - Current Research Information System (http://cris.csrees.usda.gov/menu.html)
- Database of IPM Resources (DIR) (http://www.ipmnet.org/DIR/)
- EDIS Documents (http://edis.ifas.ufl.edu/advancedsearch/index.html)
- FAO World Agriculture Information Finder (http://www.fao.org/waicent/search/default.asp)
- FAOSTAT - Agriculture (http://apps.fao.org/page/collections?subset=agriculture)
- Farm Directory (http://www.farmdirectory.com/)
- Farm Service Agency Search (http://www.fsa.usda.gov/pas/default.asp)
- Farm Service Agency Field Office Search (http://dbweb.fsa.usda.gov/scripts/dbweb/dbwebc.dll/sitetest?getqbe)
- Farm Service Agency Phone Directory (http://dbweb.fsa.usda.gov/scripts/dbweb/dbwebc.dll/phone?getqbe)
- Farmland Industries (http://www.farmland.com/search.asp)
- Farms.com (http://www.eharvest.com/)
- FarmSource (http://www.farmsource.com/Search/Search.asp)
- Farmwide (http://www.farmwide.com.au/search/)
- Feed Industry Association - Feedsearch (http://www.afia.org/)
- FruitSearch (http://www.fruitsearch.com/)
- Grain Elevator & Processing Society (http://www.geaps.com/)
- Hay Locator (http://www.hayexchange.com/sell/search.htm)
- High Plains Journal (http://www.hpj.com/)
- InfoFarm.de (http://www.infofarm.de/search.htm)
- InfoLand - Osterreichisches Agrarinformationssystem (http://www.infoland.at/)

- Insect Images (http://www.pestweb.com/insectimages/index.cfm)
- Institute of Agricultural and Natural Resources (IANR) (http://ianrhome.unl.edu/search.shtml)
- Institute of Grassland and Environmental Research (IGER) (http://www.iger.bbsrc.ac.uk/igerweb/)
- Instituto Nacional de Tecnología Agropecuaria (http://www.inta.gov.ar/)
- Integrated Pest Management Textbook (http://ipmworld.umn.edu/ipm3/ipm3_search.htm)
- International Institute of Tropical Agriculture (http://www.iita.org/search/query.htm)
- John Deere Search (http://jdsearch.deere.com/servlet/SearchServlet?SearchID=deere)
- Journal of Extension (http://joe.org/search.html)
- Michigan State University Extension Information Management Program (http://www.msue.msu.edu/msue/imp/index.html)
- MTT Agrifood Research Finland - Experts Database (http://www.mtt.fi/tietopalvelu/database_asteri.html)
- MTT Agrifood Research Finland - Projects Database (http://www.mtt.fi/tietopalvelu/database_tuike.html)
- MTT Agrifood Research Finland - Publications Database (http://www.mtt.fi/tietopalvelu/database_jukuri.html)
- National Agricultural Library (http://www.nal.usda.gov/search.htm)
- National Agricultural Statistics Service (http://www.usda.gov/nass/search.htm)
- National Center for Farmworker Health (http://www.ncfh.org/)
- New South Wales Department of Agriculture (http://www.agric.nsw.gov.au/)
- New Zealand Institute for Crop & Food Research (http://www.crop.cri.nz/search/search.htm)
- NewCrop Search (http://www.hort.purdue.edu/newcrop/SearchEngine.html)
- NOVAGate (http://novagate.nova-university.org/cgi-bin/search.pl)
- One Globe Marketing Agriculture Business Directory (http://www.oneglobe.com/agriculture/bb_bzdir.htm)

- Open Directory: Agriculture (http://dmoz.org/Science/Agriculture/)
- Organic Pages Online North American Resource Directory (http://www.ota.com/online%20directory/Directory%20nest.htm)
- Pest Damage-Yield Web Database (http://ipmwww.ncsu.edu/napiap/search.html)
- PrairieLinks (http://www.prairielinks.com/)
- ProduceLinks (http://www.producelinks.com/main.html)
- Search Engines for Agriculture (http://www.agribiz.com/test/searchEngine/AgSea)
- Sustainable Agriculture Network (http://www.sare.org/htdocs/docs/search.html)
- Swiss Federal Research Station for Agroecology and Agriculture (http://www.admin.ch/sar/scripts/sico_search.pl?anstalt=fal&lang=e)
- U.N. Food and Agriculture Organization databases (http://www.fao.org/waicent/FAOINFO/AGRICULT/guides/resource/data.htm)
- United States Department of Agriculture USDA (http://www.usda.gov/)
- USAgNet (http://www.usagnet.com/)
- USDA Agricultural Market Service (http://www.ams.usda.gov/search/)
- USDA Economics and Statistics System (http://usda.mannlib.cornell.edu/usda/usda.html)
- USDA Online Directory of Professional Workers in Agriculture (http://www.pwd.reeusda.gov/pwd/view.asp)
- USDA Online Image Gallery & Photo Library (http://www.ars.usda.gov/is/graphics/photos/search.htm)
- Web-Agri (http://www.web-agri.com/)
- World Wide Soil Jumpstation (http://homepages.which.net/~fred.moor/soil/links/l01.htm)

Database suppliers, online hosts and CD-ROM publishers

Following is the list of database suppliers, online hosts and CD-ROM publishers:

Academic Press

24-28 Oval Road,
London CHECK POSTCODE
Tel: +44 (0)171 267 4466
Fax: +44 (0)171 485 4752
WWW: *http://www.europe.idealibrary.com*

IDEAL, the International Digital Electronic Access Library, offers access to over 170 scientific journals.

BIDS (Bath Information and Data Services)

University of Bath,
Claverton Down,
Bath BA2 7AY
Tel: +44 (0) 1225 826074
Fax: +44 (0) 1225 826176
WWW: *http://www.bids.ac.uk*

BIDS provides access to a database of electronically available material with their Journals Online service.

BIOSIS

2100 Arch Street,
Philadelphia,
PA 19103-1399, USA
Tel: +1 215 587 4847
Fax: +1 215 587 2016
WWW: *http://www.biosis.org*

BIOSIS is the world's largest abstracting and indexing service for life sciences, with bibliographic products available in hard copy, CD-ROM and magnetic tape. Their products are available from a variety of companies and online sources.

Book Data

Northumberland House,
2 King Street,
Twickenham TW1 3RZ
Tel: +44 (0) 181 892 2272
Fax: +44 (0) 181 892 9109
WWW: *http://www.bookdata.co.uk*

Book Data specializes in bibliographic information for use by libraries, publishers and booksellers. Their CD-ROM range includes BookFind-CD, BookWISE-CD and TES Bookfind.

British Library

96 Euston Road,
London NW1 2DB
Tel: +44 (0) 171 412 7111
Fax: +44 (0) 171 412 7268
WWW: *http://www.bl.uk*

The British Library offers CD-ROM products and Internet access to its library catalogues.

CAB International

Wallingford,
Oxon OX10 8DE
Tel: +44 (0) 1491 832 111
Fax: +44 (0) 1491 826 090
WWW: *http://www.cabi.org*

CAB is a leading specialist in agricultural and pest products in online, CD-ROM and Internet formats.

Cambridge Scientific Abstracts

7200 Wisconsin Avenue
Bethesda MD 20814, USA
Tel: +1 301 961 6700
Fax: +1 301 961 6720
WWW: *http://www.csa.com*

CSA provides access to over 60 major scientific medical and technology databases.

EBSCO Information Services

1 Mill Street,
St Saviour's Dock,
London SE1 2DF, UK
Tel: +44 (0)171 237 0444
Fax: +44 (0)171 231 3393
WWW: *http://www.ebsco.com*

EBSCO offers a subscription service, producer of reference databases, online host and document delivery.

Elsevier Science

PO Box 211,
1000 AE Amsterdam,
The Netherlands
Tel: +31 20 4853757
Fax: +31 20 4853432
WWW: *http://www.elsevier.nl*

Elsevier gives Internet, online and CD-ROM access to pharmacological and biomedical data.

Knight-Ridder Information

Haymarket House,
1 Oxendon Street,
London SW1Y 4EE
Tel: +44 (0) 171 930 5503
Fax: +44 (0) 171 930 2581
WWW: *http://www.corp.dialog.com*

Knight-Ridder offers information from Dialog, DataStar, KR OnDisc, KR ProBase, KR ScienceBase in online, Internet and CD-ROM formats.

Leatherhead Food RA

Randalls Road,
Leatherhead,
Surrey KT22 7RY
Tel: +44 (0)1372 376761
Fax: +44 (0)1372 386228
WWW: *http://lfra.co.uk*

Data for the food and drinks industry in CD-ROM and diskette formats.

OCLC Online Computer Library Center Inc.

6565 Frantz Road,
Dublin OH 43017-3395, USA
Tel: +1 614 764 6000
Fax: +1 614 764 6096
WWW: *http://www.oclc.org*

OCLC allows access to a wide variety of scholarly journals via the Internet.

SilverPlatter Information

10 Barley Mow Passage,
Chiswick,
London W4 4PH
Tel: +44 (0)181 995 8242
Fax: +44 (0)181 995 5159
WWW: *http://www.silverplatter.com*

SilverPlatter is a world leader in CD-ROM publishing, with over 280 databases, many available via the Internet.

UMI

The Old Hospital,
Ardingly Road, Cuckfield,
West Sussex RH17 5JR
Tel: +44 (0)1444 445000
Fax: +44 (0)1444 445050
WWW: *http://umi.com*

UMI give access to a wide variety of data on CD-ROM's published by a variety of publishers, on-demand reprints and online services.

H W Wilson Company

950 University Avenue,
Bronx,
New York NY 10452-4224,
USA
Tel: +1 718 588 8400
Fax: +1 718 590 1617
WWW: *http://www.hwwilson.com*

Provided are index, abstract and full text databases in online and CD-ROM formats.

LIBRARY INFORMATION SERVICES

The rapid development information technology has changed the routine functioning of libraries. This has emphasized the need for automation, which has made an impact on all libraries services. The Agricultural libraries provide the following information services in addition to the regular library services to its users.

a. Internet & E-mail
b. CD-ROM search services
c. Reprographic services
d. Career guidance cell
e. Book Bank service
f. Network service
g. Current Awareness service

i) Internet and E-mail facility

The internet is undoubtedly an effective medium between the information professional and information. In present times, it is an essential requirement for the information personnel to know how to access the facilities available through this new technology. The Internet has become an expert too far in searching to satisfy the users' needs. Internet is the global information infrastructure which enables the professionals to access the information and communicate the users easily and cost-effectively through a variety of media such as text, graphics, voice, etc. i.e. multimedia.

ii) CD-ROM search services

CD-ROM databases are the best, powerful and cost effective tools for information storage and retrieval. Information that can be stored and retrieved in a CD-ROM can be of different forms, viz., textual, audio, still images, digital video and animation. Some of the salient features of CD-ROM searches are:

- Search can be made quickly and efficiently in free text mode and by using field qualifiers namely author, Keyword, Journal title, Publisher, Year of publication, etc.
- Boolean operations like AND, OR, NOT can be used to broaden or limit the search.
- The search so made can be displayed, printed and even downloaded.

The agricultural libraries are considered as the service agencies to the academic and scientific community as well as to the farmers, the faculty, scholars, students and the agriculturists have been served with different services in their libraries through manual and computerized information retrieval system. Automated lending, Automated CAS, Automated translation, E-mail, Telex, Fax, CD-Net, Dial-up service, Technical communication, Electronic Bulletin Board System, CD-ROM search, On-line search, Internet browsing, Web-based OPAC, TELNET, Voice Chatting.

NORMS AND STANDARDS OF AGRICULTURAL LIBRARIES

Library standards are necessary for planning library services and subsequently for their evaluation. Standards written in one country have often influenced the form and content of standards produced in other countries and standards prepared by the International Federation of Library Associations, influenced by the existing national standards, have encouraged other countries to prepare similar standards.

Agricultural Libraries in India are following the standards and norms developed by the University Grants Commission (UGC) of India as envisaged in the Indo-American library Report (ICAR, 1969). The report reads: "It is recommended that the standards developed by the library committee of the UGC be adopted by ICAR Institute libraries and agricultural university libraries as minimum requirements and the future revisions of the UGC standards be adopted as they appear, as ICAR's minimum standards".

The UGC Library Committee Report (UGC 1965) prescribes the following library standards for college and University libraries.

Table 6

Library Standards for College and University Libraries

(i) Book Strength	*Standard*
a) University Central Library	1,00,000 to 3,00,000 Volumes
b) University departmental Library	1,000 to 5,000 Volumes
c) College Library	5,000 to 50,000 Volumes
d) Dormitory library (only if the stock of University library exceeds 3,00,000)	1,00,000 plus 50,000 n (n is the number of transformers to the Dormitory Library).
ii) Finance	
a) 6 ¼% of total budget of the Institution should be allotted to its library.	
b) Total book fund per capita	Rs.15/- per student and Rs.200/- per teacher and fellow.
c) Expenditure on staff of the total library's expenditure	50% of the library budget.
d) Expenditure on books etc. of the total library's expenditure	50% of the library budget
e) U.G.C's share	80%
f) State Governments share	20%
iii) Space Requirements	
A) Reading seats	
a) University central library	1/5 of the students and 6/10 of the teachers
b) University departmental library	10 to 20 seats
c) College library	1/5 of the students and 1/10 of the teachers
d) Dormitory library	Nil
B) Staff Room:	
a) Clear length	1.80 n plus 3.15 meters (n indicates the number of rows of book racks)
b) Clear width	3m (on the basis of one book rack plus one side gunway of 1metre) close to a longitudinal wall, or 5 meters (on the basis of 2 book racks each 2 meters long plus one side gang-way of 1metre width) close to a longitudinal wall: or 10 meters (on the basis of 4 book racks each 2 meter long plus two-side gunway or 1 meter width close to each of the longitudinal walls.
c) Clear height(Floor to ceiling)	2.35 meters.
d) Capacity of unit book-rack of 2 mts. Length	700 to 750 vols.
e) Capacity of one square meter of stack room area	150 vols.

(These standards have been laid down by the Indian Standards Institution, Delhi vide IS: 154-1960 through its sectional committee on library buildings, fittings and furniture of which Dr. S.R. Ranganathan was also the Chairman).

The above given specifications have been based on modular system (a module of 10 cm. In accordance with IS: 1233-1958).

ICAR Workshops and Seminars on Agricultural Libraries

A number of workshops, seminars and conferences for agricultural libraries were held at different places. Important among them were (i) The first library workshop at Pantnagar, (ii) All India conference on Agricultural Education relating to libraries, JNKVV, Jabalpur, (iii) Workshop on Reprography, Ludhiana, (iv) Seminar on Agricultural Librarianship and Documentation, Ludhiana, (v) National conference of Agricultural libraries, Hyderabad, and (vi) Seminar on Agricultural Librarianship and Documentation, Pantnagar, December, 1988. These workshops, seminars and conferences formulated number of recommendations for the development of agricultural libraries and their services.

With the application of some sections of the ICAR Model Act for Agricultural Universities and incorporation of some recommendations of Cummings Committee as well as Sutton Committee into the Acts and Statutes of almost of every agricultural University. The State Agricultural University (SAU) libraries went ahead of ICAR institute libraries which are still in poor state. Today, Agricultural University librarians are enjoying the status of Professor and professor's pay scale under UGC system with full administrative and financial powers for the organization and management of their libraries.

Contrary to SAU libraries, the pathology and irony of ICAR institutes libraries has been that all good recommendations of Indo-American Agricultural Library Survey and Study Team were turned down by the Ramaiah Committee and recommendations of Ramaiah Committee accepted by ICAR were never implemented by the Director of ICAR institutes.

The Standing Library Advisory Committee of ICAR remained in dormancy for the last 20 years. However, it was revived in 1995 and after a couple of meetings again paralyzed for certain reasons.

Association of Agricultural Libraries and Documentalists of India (AALDI) in 1998 at Pantnagar seminar elected new members to form a new executive committee of AALDI, which could raise the voice of librarians' grievances and suggest new measures to accelerate the pace of development of agricultural libraries. This committee of AALDI never met and since then went into long dormancy because of the lack of commitment of its members to the profession.

As early as 1957, the ICAR Library Team comprising of Dr. W. Ralph Shaw and Dr. D.B. Krishna Rao recommended to make the library of the Indian Agricultural Research Institute a Central Agricultural library because IARI is the pioneer Institute of agricultural research in India. The ICAR workshop on Agricultural libraries and Extension Services held at Pantnagar in 1967 brought together all the institute and university librarians. The results were outstanding. The recommendations emphasized the needed for cooperation among the libraries, sharing of resources, greater uniformity in library organization, standards and norms, improvement of quality and quantity of library services and the need for a national agricultural library.

The Indo-American Agricultural Library Survey and Study Team (1960) which was impressed with the widespread interest for an Indian National Agricultural Library made the following recommendations in its Final Report on the ICAR Institute and Agricultural University Libraries (1967).

- An Indian National Agricultural Library be officially established as soon as possible to give leadership and direction to the agricultural libraries in India.
- The library of the Indian Agricultural Research Institute, New Delhi considering its collection, central location and also because of the fact that it is serving in the capacity of a National library, should be designated as Indian National Agricultural Library (INAL).
- The Libraries of the Indian Veterinary Research Institute, Izatnagar and Mukteswar and the National Dairy Research Institute, Karnal be officially designated as the Indian National Veterinary Science Library (INVSL) and the Indian National Dairy Science Library (INDSL) respectively. They should become subsidiaries of INAL under the guidance and direction of the director of the INAL.
- The INAL, INVSL and INDSL should become cooperative centers for the literature in the fields of plant and animal sciences, thereby ensuring comprehensive world coverage of agricultural scientific information. They would also constitute the foundation for an Indian National Agricultural Library System (INALS).
- The position of a Deputy Director General (Library and Documentation Services) be created who will also be the Director of INAL.
- All the ICAR institute and agricultural university libraries become part of integrated and coordinated INALS.

The Ramaiah Committee (1969) which reviewed the Report and Recommendations of the Indo-American Agricultural Library Survey and Study Team opined that no useful purpose would be served by bringing the INVSL and INDSL under one administrative control by the creation of the post of Deputy Director General. The Committee felt that the libraries attached to IVRI and NDRI were to strengthen the literature collection in their respective subject areas.

The Ramaiah Committee did not also accept the recommendation for establishing an Indian National Agricultural Library and to designate the library of Indian Agricultural Research Institute as the Indian National Agricultural Library. However, the Committee recommended that the libraries of Indian Agricultural Research Institute (IARI), Indian Veterinary Research Institute (IVRI) and National repository to acquire and maintain the less commonly used materials which will be available to other libraries through photocopies or inter-library loan.

Library Budget

Budgeting is the financial aspect of planning process that is recognized as an important aspect of management in the library. If a target budget is allocated to the library i.e., if the parent organization defines the total expenditure for various budget components, such a personnel, equipment, reading materials and operating supplies, the budgeting consist of adjusting the organization's plans and objectives to the money allocated. The budgeting process is therefore assigning resources to plans, programmes, etc. usually on an annul bases.

Agricultural university libraries are generating funds from their respective state governments, Indian Council of Agricultural Research (ICAR), New Delhi and Agricultural Human Resource Development project with financial assistance from the World Bank. Budget preparation for each activity of the library, can be made in comparison with previous years. Computerized budget control will help us the future growth and requirement of the library. To put it in detail,

i) Computerized budget control will help in distributing the available resources as desired to all the areas of the library activities.

ii) It helps to monitor the expenditure effectively on various aspects.

iii) It enables efficient spending on books and other reading materials.

iv) It prevents from exceeding the prescribed limit of the budget allotted for a particular subject.

v) It helps us to understand the rise and decline of users demand and to spend accordingly.

vi) It helps us to understand the spending pattern and maintain its profile.

The statistics for the above works can be worked out fairly easily through computers which are available in libraries.

The UGC has recommended 6 percent of the working budget of the university for all-round development of libraries. Unfortunately no library perhaps, is getting its full budgetary allocation. ICAR agrees in principle for 3 percent of budgeting allocation, but there is no consistency it varies from institute to institute. As described earlier one ICAR library gets 7 percent and the other only 1.3 percent of the budget. Even the IARI library, the largest among the agricultural libraries gets about 1.5 percent of the budget. This budget allocation covers other contingencies also. The libraries have inadequate physical facilities, collection and manpower. Thus budgetary constraints do not encourage and motivate the librarians to modernize the libraries.

Users of Agricultural Information

According to Ramachandra and Kumar (1981), the scientists, the disseminators who act as two-way channel, the farmers and the policy makers, traders etc. are the users of Agricultural information.

The users of agricultural information are generally categorized as scientists, academic staff, students, research scholars, agricultural scientists, research scientists, extension workers, planners, policy-makers, industrialists, farming community and agro-industrialists, etc. (Deshpande and Deshmukh, 1985).

A classification which is a compromise among these approaches is adopted in terms of documented evidence regarding users groups, user can be conveniently classed as follows with some variations and overlaps; (1) Scientists and researchers (2) Extension scientists (3) Extension advisors (4) farmers and others – policy makers / administrators, workers in agribusiness, educators, journalists, and even consumers.

Library Staff

The agricultural (university) library is basically a service institute to the staff, students, policy makers and farmers. Quality of service depends on the quality of the staff. They should provide the right information to the right readers at the right time. Agricultural library professional who is employed as a librarian, scholar and administrator, should be made responsible to plan and frame policies, organize service and to create resources. The goal of agricultural libraries is to give enough support for the research and teaching mission of the organization. The most important task for the Agricultural library professional is to understand the function and objectives of the organization.

The Agricultural library professionals should be proactive and customer service-minded in nature. They should not wait for the users to come to the library; instead they should reach out patrons and assist them in CD-ROM searching, online searching or internet use etc. The librarian should have the responsibilities of identifying, locating, collecting, organizing, handling, managing, storing and presenting information to the user community in the manner they like. For this the agricultural library professional should be given adequate training in the field to help him attain expertise in information technology, analytical skill, managerial skill, knowledge of subject etc., which can only provide conformity to the requirements of the user in the fast growing 21st century.

Table 7
Library Standards for College and University Libraries-Staff

	Library Staff	
a)	Book selection	1 person for every 6,000 volumes added in a year.
b)	Periodicals publications section	1 person for every 500 current periodicals taken.
c)	Documentation section	1 person for every 1,000 entries prepared in a year.
d)	Technical section	1 person for every 2,000 volumes added in a year.
e)	Reference section	1 person for every 50 readers (other than the users of the text book collection) in a day.
f)	Circulation section	1 person for every 1,500 hours for which one wicket gate of the library has to be kept in a year.
g)	Maintenance section	1 person for every 6,000 volumes added in a year, 1 person for every 500 volumes to be replaced in a day and 1 person for every 1,00,000 volumes in the library.
h)	Administrative section	Minimum of 1 library Accountant, 1 steno-Typist and correspondence Clerk.
i)	Supervisory Staff	1 Librarian and Assistant or Deputy Librarian.
j)	Unskilled staff	One cleaner for every 30,000 volumes in the library, 1 Attendant each for every 6,000 volumes added in a year for each of the shifts in the circulation section, besides unskilled and the semiskilled workers normal to any institution.

Qualifications prescribed by the U G C

The UGC Library Committee (1965) headed by Dr. Ranganathan, laid down the following qualifications:

(a) *Professional Senior (Librarian/University Professor and Deputy Librarian/Associate Professor/Reader)*:

(i) Minimum qualifications : Master of Library Science, second class; and Master of Arts or Science, Second class, and Diploma in Library Science or Bachelor in Library Science, first class; a prescribed minimum experience in a research or a university library;

(ii) Desirable qualifications; doctorate in Library Science or any other subject.

(b) *Professional Junior (Assistant Librarian/ Assistant Professor/ Lecturer)*

(i) Minimum Qualifications: Diploma in Library Science or B.Lib.Sc. First Class; B.A or B.Sc. or B.Com, second class.

UGCs Qualifications (1968)

The UGC prescribed the following qualifications for librarians (1968).

a) *Professional Senior (Librarian/University Professor and Deputy Librarian/Associate Professor/Reader)*:

(i) Ist or IInd Class M.A/M.Sc/M.Com plus a first or second class B.Lib.Sc or Diploma in Library Science. The degree of M.Lib.Sc is a preferential qualification. The Librarian is required to possess 10 years experience, and a Deputy Librarian 7 years experience.

b) *Professional Junior (Assistant Librarian/Assistant Professor/Lecturer):*

(i) Ist or IInd Class B.A/B.Sc/B.Com degree, plus a first or second class M.Lib.Sc degree ; Ist or IInd class M.A/M.Sc/M.Com degree, plus a Ist or IInd class B.Lib. Sc., or Diploma in Lib.Sc.

From Professional to Non-Professional qualifications

The qualifications prescribed by the UGC in 1965 laid more emphasis on M.Lib.Sc, or Ph.D in Library Science. The alternative qualifications, M.A plus B.Lib.Sc, were only a secondary measure, meant to protect the interests of the then working professionals not having M.Lib.Sc degree. In 1968 the UGC shifted the emphasis from M.Lib.Sc to M.A/M.Com., and the M.Lib.Sc. Degree was prescribed as a preferred qualification only. Still more fantastic was to keep the M.Lib.Sc Degree as an essential qualification for an Assistant Librarian but only a preferential qualification for a librarian and a deputy librarian. It is illogical that the Masters Degree in Library Science should be essential for junior position and preferential for the senior one. This amounts to downgrading a degree in Library Science by the UGC. However, this was not an end. In 1977, the UGC further re-affirmed its above attitude towards the degree in Library Science, and prescribed that the University Librarians need not possess Library Science qualifications at all.

UGC's qualification (1977)

The following qualifications were prescribed by the UGC in 1977 for a University Librarian:

(a) Good academic record with Ist or high IInd Class Master's degree in a subject other than Library Science with a Doctorate or equivalent degree, published work of high standard and preferably with knowledge/ experience of Library Science and Management.

(b) At least 10 years experience of teaching post-graduate classes and research or research in an independent capacity in an organization of higher learning and research, or in a responsible post in Library for advance students and research workers.

Qualifications prescribed by ICAR

The following qualifications have been prescribed by the ICAR in 1978.

(a) Librarian: M.A./M.Sc/M.Com Ist or IInd Class, plus M.Lib.Sc., Ist or IInd Class: and 10 years experience in a responsible capacity in a University or research library.

(b) Deputy Librarian: Same qualifications as for Librarian, but experience of 7 years only.

(c) Assistant Librarian: Same qualifications as for Librarian, but experience of 2 years only.

(d) Candidates possessing Ph.D. degree either in Library Science or any other subject get two years of concession in experience for every cadre.

As compared to the qualifications prescribed by the UGC in 1977, the above qualifications prescribed by the ICAR are both logical and rational. M.A. / M.Sc/ M.Com and M.Lib.Sc. Degrees have been prescribed as essential qualifications for the posts of Assistant Librarian, Deputy Librarian, and University Librarian; only the extent of experience varies. In the case of a Ph.D. degree, the doctorate in Library Science has been given the same weight as the Doctorate in any other subject. These qualifications can still be improved if the Ph.D. degree in Library Science is made an alternative qualification in addition to what has already been stipulated. This will mean that the person who is holding Ph.D. degree in Library Science may not hold M.A/M.Sc./M.Com degree in addition concession of two years experience to the holders of Ph.D. degrees can still be retained. A word may be added in defense of Doctorate in Library Science. A Ph.D. degree in Library Science may help a librarian to bring in new innovations in solving library problems or in improving reader's services. A Doctorate in any other subject cannot be of much use in a library. If the efficiency of library profession is to be enhanced, degrees in library science should be given preference and due weight.

ICAR library staff norms prepared by Banerjee and others (1983)

Shri S.R. Banerjee prepared norms for the I.C.A.R. library by consulting the Standards of Indian Universities (S.I.U) norms. The following is the comparative statement given by him.

Table 8

Comparative Statement for Library Norms

(Time to be spent on a unit of work)

S.I.U Library Jobs	*S.I.U. Time*	*I.C.A.R. Library Time*
1	2	3
Job No.1		
Routine Operations for placing orders purchase of publications.	8 mts. per book purchased 4 mts. per book selected on approved but rejected.	15-18mts. For preliminary selection per book for filling in proforma for approval with comments 4-5 mts. per order cards and placing order. 3-5 mts. for sending letter for rejected book. 3-4 mts. for evaluation or selection per book from reviews and announcements, etc.
Job No.2		
Passing of bill for books	8mts per bill plus 1 min. per book	10-13mts per bill and on average 1 ½ to 2 ½ minutes per book.
Job No. 3		
Accessing of books	20 mts. per 10 books accessioned	3-4 mts. per book.
Job No.4		
Classification of publications	5 mts. per book	13 to 22 mts. per book (INSDOC Recommend-ations 15 to 25 min).
Job No.5		
Cataloguing of books	5mts. per book 1 minute per card prepared for main entry in addition to each main plus entry. Typing. 4 ½ mts. per main entry and 1 ½ meters per additions to main card.entry plus 1 min. per card for filling.	5-6 mts. per main entry 2 ½ to 3 ½ mts. per added entry. ½ to 3 mts. for typing each card. 125 mts. per 100 cards alphabetical (Primary). 225 mts. per 100 cards classified. Filling in the main catalogue 1 min. per (alphabetical sequence). 2mts per card (Classified sequence) (Time for typing of cards and

(Contd...)

1	2	3
	(Time for typing of bookcard & inscribing cal Nos. are inclusive of these timings above)	inscribing call nos are excluded):
Job No.6: Registration of numbers	90 mts. for 20 members	8-10mts. per application
Job No.7: Issue of No demand certificate	8 mts. per application	10-12mts. per application.
Job No.8 Issue of publications to readers and their receipt back	60mts. for 100 60mts. publications for 100 publications issued.received back.	4to 5 ½ mts. per issue plus 2 mts. per issue to record it in loan registers. 2 minutes. To 3.5 meters per book received back.
Job No.9 Issue of reminders to borrowers for return of publications	40 mts. per 10 reminders	5 to 8 mts. per reminder.
Job No. 10 Receipt and recording of periodicals	6mts. per issue for maintaining record in both Kardex card and check card 5 meters. per issue for one kardex Card recording.	5-6 mts. per receipt in Kardex card 2 ½ to 3 mts. for preparation of week arrivals. Recording for new subscription 6-7 ½ mts.
Job No.10A (Not in SIU) Issuing of reminder for periodicals		4-5 mts. by card (routine) while 10-15 mts. by letter special per reminder.
Job N0.11 Circulation of periodicals to offices/ branches	150 mts. for 100 calculations	21-03 mts. per issues per circular. Reminder issued 2 to 3 mts. per issue/per circular.

(Contd...)

1	2	3
Job No.12. Shelving of books	3 hrs. 100 books	2-3 mts. per books
Job No.13 Taking of books and periodicals from the shelves	125 mts. for 100 books	2-3 mts. per books
Job No.14 Binding/Repair of library books	135 mts. for 100 books	15 to 20mts. per periodical title including writing of slips. 13 to 15 mts. per book for check up and writing instructions and slips etc.
Job No.15. Passing of bills received from to binders	15 mts. Per bill book	10 to 12 mts. to check up each volume of periodical. 13 to 15 mts. to check up each old book. 14 to 16 mts. per bill after observing all formalities.
Job No.16 Complication of bulletin from source materials	10mts per entry in the bulletin for selection and indexing	35 to 40 mts. for study and scanning an article (5 to 7pp.)
	4 mts. per entry for arranging and stenciling	19 to 23 mts. per entry for classification without arrangement. 2 ½ mts. per entry for stenciling with arrangement.
Job no.17 Preparation of detailed subject bibliographies	6hrs. per bibliography for study, selection & planning, etc. 10 mts. per entry.	7-9 hrs. for study and planning etc.
		35 to 40 mts. for study and scanning each article for indexing 19-23 mts. for classification of each entry (main) 125 mts. per 100 cards for alphabetical arrangement.
		225 mts. per 100 cards for classified entries for filling in main catalogue.
		1 to 2 mts. for filling alphabetically and classified sequences respectively.

(Contd...)

1	2	3
Job No. 18 Physical verifications of books.	200 mts. per 100 books	1-3mts per book for two persons for verification 1-2 mts. for recording missing publications by one person.
Job No.19 Posting of correction . slips in codes and manuals, etc	150mts for 100 correction slips	1.5 to 13 mts. per correction slip.
Job No.20 Tidying of books and providing messengeering, etc	One unskilled person per 25,000 volumes in stock.	At least 3 persons for 70,000 publications. Besides one person as peon.
Job No.21 (Not by SIU) Documentation on bioenergy information		35-40mts for search study and scrutiny from the source material for obstracting 57-76mts per abstract (studying and preparing)
Job No.22 (Not of SIU) Indexing of parliament questions and answers		5-12 mts. for indexing each answer of parliament questions.

Library Building

A librarian who administers the library services knows his needs. He can very well communicate to the architect, the requirement of space and the workflow, in terms of what is required and where. Mutual regard and cordial working relations between a librarian and an architect are necessary for satisfactory designing of a library building.

The university library is the geographical centre of the campus. The basic approach towards the planning of the library building has been that of diversity in functions, flexibility in design and harmony in construction. The planning must be on a functional basis i.e., it should have the best arrangement in terms of location, various sections of the library etc., so as to ensure their efficient functioning. Layout and space are the two important constituents in the planning of the modern library buildings. The plan of a library building should be based on sound principles, the most important being "Library is a growing organization".

A modular library building of reinforced concrete structure is always preferable for modern days' requirement. The following features are important to make the building a success in its physical sense.

- Efficiency of the ventilation system.
- Lighting and air conditioning
- Sound absorption quality to the walls and ceiling.
- Ease with which the students can find their books for assigned reading and obtain them.

Interior Design of a University Library

Dr. Ranganathan, the father of Library Science in India has pointed out that the library should have a pleasing interior environment which may include:

- The interior of a library should be soothing to the physiology of the eye and a motivating phenomenon to the mind of the readers.
- It should put the reader's mind at ease.
- Reading is a psychological activity which needs an environmental comfort.
- Reading hall with decorations promotes long time reading.
- An aesthetic decoration reduces monotony in fatigue.

These facts emphatically explain how an aesthetically and physically comfortable interior is a must for a library to draw the readers and prolong their stay in the library.

At the entrance, the issue counter should be provided with the computer bar- coding machine, scanner, printer and other necessary equipment. All the data about the available books and reading material should easily be accessible to the readers. Reading chairs and tables should be made strong and sturdy and of good quality material.

Audio-visual library should be well furnished with air conditioning and sound proofing. Online searching and internet browsing in a separate cabin is to be provided with each user. A library with a good collection, but not maintained tidily and efficiently will be of no use.

AGRICULTURAL INFORMATION SYSTEMS

The ever growing population, depletion of natural resources and the constraints in food production have become major problems in many developing countries. These problems in many of the developing countries can be overcome by means of developing sustainable agriculture leading to adoption of new agro-technologies by farmers in rural areas. The major facts concerning information management in agricultural sector is complex in nature involving whole process of information generation, publication, organization and dissemination to the wide range of users.

Developments in science and technology are playing vital role in achieving social, political and socio-economic goals of every country. In the context of ever growing social importance of the relevance of information has been highlighted in a number of studies (Housey, D.F). The era of modern information handling activities started in the fields of aerospace, defense and medical research where computerized information storage and retrieval techniques were exploited. The emergence of Lockheeds DIOLOG, the major online host offering the access to more than 300 databases in a wide variety of disciplines is an example of modern technological development. As such, there are over 2000 online databases publicity available covering more than 80 million records with annual growth rate at 8 million records. Besides these there have been numerous systems created in wide range of disciplines covering various types of information mainly developed by government, industry and professional societies which all together emphasize collection on primary documents, ongoing research, all emerged as a result of intensive research, training and development in a myriad of disciplines. In this context, the agricultural universities, research institutes and agro-based industries play vital role in flow of information.

There are three systems that emerged in the recent past on international scene are AGRICOLA, AGRIS and CABI, which all together cater information needs of researchers, agribusiness industry and farmers.

Agricultural Databases

To begin with, databases were created capturing all relevant information. These are organized collection of different subject areas, which could be bibliographic or full text. Bibliographic databases consist of citations or references of documents. Enhanced by computer capabilities, databases provide more access points than printed abstracting or indexing Journals. Most of the databases are accessible through commercial vendors that load the databases in their large computers and provide software to retrieve information held by them (Parta, M.A). There were about 428 agricultural databases in the Agricultural databases directory in mid 1980s (Frank, R.C), of which 302 are word oriented including bibliographic, referral or natural language text and remaining 126 are numeric databases that provide statistical data. The three international cooperative databases are briefed below.

AGRICOLA (Agricultural online Access)

This database is produced by National Agricultural library (NAL) of United States department of Agriculture which focuses more on information generated on agriculture in USA, containing more than 3 million records. It is the best source for tracking publications by USDA, land grant universities and other associated agencies. The coverage in database includes references to journal articles, government publications, technical reports, theses, etc. It corresponds to printed products like: Bibliography of Agriculture; NAL library catalogue and Food Nutrition quarterly. It started in 1970 as CAIN (cataloguing and Indexing of NAL). Since 1984, NAL has expanded its scope of AGRICOLA to include information not held by it in its collection and about 5000 serials are scanned for indexing. It is available in magnetic tape since 1970 and online access is possible through DIALOG and BRS (Frank, R.C).

AGRICOLA is now available on CD-ROM covering from 1970 containing 3 million records in 3 CDs and about 1,00,000 records are added annually. Indexing is done using AGROVOC. Word list of Agricultural serials which is stored with NAL - USDA with support of CABI and FAO and other cooperating agencies is published by Silver plates covering about 54,000 titles indicating which of the three major databases index titles eliminating likely duplication in each database.

Current Research Information System (CRIS)

Besides access to AGRICOLA for conventional / non-conventional literature, access to current agricultural research projects is ensured through USDA's CRIS, which contains over 27,000 items of current publicity supported agricultural and forestry research projects of USDA agencies, State agricultural Experiment stations and other cooperating institutions. (Reid, J.N.A).

It gives information on what is being done by the personnel undertaking the project, organizations affiliations, place, year of commencement, progress of project and publication emanating from the Project. Over 1,00,000 citations are included and many of them are not covered in any other database. CRIS is available in machine readable form since 1969 and is accessible through DIALOG. There is no prescribed version of this database.

International Information system for Agricultural Sciences and Technology (AGRIS)

It is an international system working under Food and Agricultural Organization (FAO) of United Nations, providing access to world information in the field of agricultural and related fields to researchers, planners, extension workers and farmers. It is a cooperative and decentralized system covering both conventional and grey literature wherein 171 countries and 24 regional and international research centres participate. Annual input is about 1,30,000 items.

Activities of AGRIS

Each participating country / institute prepare an input sheet collecting a wide-range of information on scientific and socioeconomic information in the form of journals, articles, books, reports, etc. and provide in different media like magnetic tapes, floppy diskettes or input sheets to AGRIS processing unit located in IAEA, Vienna, Austria, where data is merged into main database. Such data so received is processed and bare copy in the form of AGRINDEX is produced for sale/distribution. In turn, each participating country/institute receives AGRIS tapes thereby generating SDI service, Current Awareness Service or bringing out National Agricultural Bibliography, facilitating retrospective search, equipped with database management system such as Micro CDS/ISIS.

AGRIS was conceived to function in two levels, i.e. AGRIS level-I and AGRIS level-II, which are briefly described as follows.

AGRIS level- I

In this level, AGRIS functions to have comprehensive coverage in providing documentation service and current awareness in all fields of FAO mandate.

It became operational in 1975 and main outputs are:

* AGRINDEX, a monthly printed bibliography arranged by categories
* AGRIS database on magnetic tapes.

AGRIS Publications

The main publications of AGRIS are:

AGRINDEX/AGRIS Database on Magnetic tapes:

AGROVOC – a multilingual thesaurus for standardized indexing;

Various reference manuals and guides.

Online Access to AGRIS Database

AGRIS database is accessible online through number of hosts viz:

Direct dialing telex, public packet switching networks;

Through telecommunication networks such as ESANET; ESA/IRS and EVRONET.

On DIMDI in Cologn, Germany or DIALOG, USA.

AGRIS on CD-ROM

AGRIS is available on CD-ROM published by silver platter. The records from 1975-1991 are available on a set of 5 CDs and current discs are updated quarterly.

AGRIS Input Centers

In regard to input to AGRIS, there are 171 countries and 24 regional/International organizations of which regional organizations coordinate AGRIS activities at regional level. Some of them are:

Agricultural Information Bank of Asia (AIBA), Philippines, covers ASEAN countries, Bangladesh and the Republic of Korea;

Centro Interanmericano de Documentatione Informationy communication Agricola (CIDIA) in Costa Rica covering Latin America and Caribbean (except Brazil and Cuba).

The Commission of European Communities (CEC) in Brussels covers CEC countries and Portugal.

OMVS in Senegal, Africa. At present Malis Mauritanice and Senegal are participating in the programme.

Agricultural Information Systems in India

The Food and Agricultural Organization of United Nations in the early seventies came up with two global information's system – AGRIS and CARIS and requested the member countries to cooperate in their venture. The Government of India took a decision in 1974 to participate in the global systems through a National Input centre under the Indian Council of Agricultural Research the apex body for agricultural research and development in the country.

This was the beginning of information system and services in India using computer technology. With the help of magnetic tapes, a SDI service was started as early as in 1978 and India became an active partner in the world wide system. A number of computer-aided products were MARC available to the scientific community.

It has now been possible to link the ICAR Research Institutes, State Agricultural Universities, Zonal Research stations and Project Directorates with the help of the communication satellite of the National Informatics Centre (NICNET) of Planning Commission, Government of India by providing them with LAN server and PC workstations and e-mail connectivity.

Nowadays libraries are playing a very important role in providing information to the users by building good collections of books, monographs, and serials. Several ICAR institutes and State Agricultural Universities have good libraries. It is interesting to note that the library of the Indian Agricultural Research Institute (IARI 1905) has over a million entries in the catalogue. The computerization of catalogue in most of the libraries is yet to be done due to the non-availability of trained manpower in the field of agricultural library and information systems and services. There is no organization which gives training to agricultural librarians and information scientists; as a result the development of proper Agricultural Research Information System has not reached the desired level.

To exploit the potential of modern computing power in planning and management of agricultural research and scientific communication, ICAR started an Agricultural Research Information System (ARIS). Basic guidelines to implement this project were provided by a team of experts from ICAR and International Service for National Agricultural Research (ISNAR). In its report, a phased implementation was recommended to create infrastructure for ARISNET, a national wide area Network for agricultural research.

Agricultural Research Personnel Information System (ARPIS)

To maintain computerized Biodata and service history of scientific, technical and administrative staff working at all ICAR institutions, a personnel information system has been planned at ICAR headquarters so as to provide easy access on different types of information like cadre strength, number of scientists in position, type of trained manpower available, distribution of scientists in position, type of trained manpower available, distribution of scientists according to sex, caste, state, institute and discipline, etc. The information on awards won by different scientists has also been included. This will help the management in planning the personnel policies, manpower planning, recruitment, identification of subject matter specialists in various fields, research work being undertaken on different commodities with respect to agro-climatic zones and resources used, etc. The software and database of all ICAR scientists numbering about 4,500 has already been created. It also generates 36 types of predefined reports and any number of queries. This will further be expanded for all staff at KVKs and scientists working at SAUs.

Agricultural Research Financial Information Systems (ARFIS)

It will maintain computerized monthly accounts of all ICAR institutes and ICAR headquarters. Grants of SAUs, All India Coordinated Research Projects (AICRP), AP Cess Fund Research projects, Revolving Fund Schemes and General Provident Fund (GPF) Schemes are all ICAR institutes. In consultation with selected SAUs, a financial information system will also be developed for SAUs after examining the financial information systems already in-place at some of the SAUs.

A software package (ARFIS) has already been developed to computerize the monthly accounts of ICAR institutes and has been successfully implemented in most of the institutes. Its use has been made mandatory from April 1, 1997. More than 300 personnel from account sections of these institutes have been trained on use of this package. Codification of all accounting heads (institutes, regional stations, schemes, etc.) has also been carried out.

Agricultural Research & Library Information System (ARLIS)

All libraries of ICAR and SAUs will be computerized and linked to IARI Library which has been identified as National Agricultural Library. This will provide scientists an opportunity to access information in India or abroad electronically. Thus, library automation and their networking will form a significant part of the ARIS.

Besides modernization and networking of libraries of ICAR institutes and SAUs, the creation of databases and CDs on both national and international agricultural research contents will be a major work under ARLIS. Agricultural Research Information Centre (ARIC), New Delhi is involved in compilation of information on AP Cess Fund schemes and other research projects funded by ICAR. Also ARIC is serving as National Input Centre for International Information System (AGRIS) for the Agricultural Science and Technology, Current Agricultural Research Information Systems (CARIS) Projects of Food and Agricultural organization (FAO) and SAARC Agricultural Information Centre (SAIC).

AGRICULTURAL INFORMATION NETWORKS

An Information network is "a systematic organization of separate units, interconnected for the purpose of achieving some goal that is more than any one of the units can achieve individually." (Duchesne, 1982, p.i) More specially, an information network refers to: "a formal association among libraries, Documentation centers, archives and global on regional information systems created with the aim of coordinating their efforts and sharing resources to satisfy information needs of users in a subject area and or geographic region of mutual concern to network members.

Today, in fact, there is no national or regional network of agricultural libraries. However, ICAR, New Delhi has taken initiatives in this direction. First of all, IARI library made a beginning of computer based activities in 1993 and had computer connectivity with DELNET through a modem-Telephone line. In 1995, IARI management started a project of campus networking through CMC Ltd, and in just one year, a powerful network having 100MB fiber optic backbone was installed and commissioned in February 1996. This electronic information Network of star topology on IARI campus connects over 50 computers housed in 17 buildings remotely located within the radius of two kilometers. It is further being strengthened speedily and it will have more than 100 connections.

IARI library has installed a 28 drive CD - Net consisting of 11 Networking terminals providing simultaneous access to different CD - Rom databases Search and retrival, downloading and Printing facility. This is in addition to stand alone single drive CD - Rom search facilities.

The CD-Net housed in the library has also been made accessible from various divisions of the institute on this network. Agricultural libraries can join INFLIBNET of UGC as well as ERNET of NICNET for global access to information to serve their users. The IARI network has its V-SAT based main hub housed in the library and library thus, has access to global information for library catalogues, full text journal databases, magazines, newspapers etc. through World Wide Web. ICAR has a plan to connect all agricultural universities and ICAR institutes through modems and V-SATs, with IARI network as early as possible. Thus libraries of SAUs and ICAR and work of computer network is progressing fast under the expert technical leadership of CMC Ltd.

Under the ARIS programme most of the ICAR & SAUs were provided with suitable servers and nodes. Six institutes are already having VSAT connectivity for more than two years and 11 more have been provided with VSATS during March 1997. The E-mail connectivity has been established to 73 ICAR institutes (47 institutes 9 PDS and 17 NRCS) out of 86 by linking these institutes through dial-up, including 17 institutes with VSAT connectivity, to the nearest National Information Centers (NIC), a Government owned national service provider. It was expected that all of the ICAR institutes and SAUs will have Local Area Network and access to the Internet either by VSAT or by dial-up facility by the end of 1998 to provide effective satellite connectivity 1401 will be added to the network during next three years.

AGLINET

This network was established in 1974 based on statutes formulated at a joint FAO/IAALD (International Association of Agricultural Librarians and Documentalists) symposium in 1971. The goal of this international cooperative network was efficient document delivery through flexible and effective cooperation among the large agricultural libraries of the world and regional decentralization of responsibilities. (Stone, 1990).

The Agricultural Network Information Centre (AgNIC)

The Agricultural Network Information centre (AgNIC) is a source of agricultural information in electronic form over an international Network of networks. Agricultural information includes basic, applied, and developmental research, extension, and teaching activities in the food, agricultural, renewable natural resources, forestry and physical and social sciences, AgNIC will provide scamless access to distributed sources of agricultural information, subject area experts and other resources in a manner in which the physical location of these resources is transparent to the user.

Agricultural Information Network Models Suggested for Andhra Pradesh

Review of literature reports good number of effects made by both institutions and individuals to purpose models for developing National Agricultural information Network and National Information system for Agriculture. The network modal initiated by ICAR , is already taking shape to connect all libraries of ICAR and State Agricultural Universities with IARI Library, New Delhi named has ARISNET. It is expected that this network will be completed in a phase-wise manner covering libraries and institutes involved with generation and communication of agricultural research findings at each level of agricultural information infrastructure in the country. One more network modal was suggested by Subbaiah (1985), which facilitate resource sharing at national level.

Models also have been suggested even at the state level for developing an inter-related agricultural information system to facilitate proper flow of information and data required by uses of agricultural information. One such network model was suggested by Veeranjaneyulu (1997) with the name AP-AGRINET which connects the libraries of Agricultural colleges and research stations in the state of Andhra Pradesh with seven objectives, aiming at developing a better information facility in the field of agriculture in the state. He suggested both hardware and software requirements to be fulfilled by the libraries that are willing to participate in the statewide network activities. The number of terminals to be connected AP-AGRINET include:

1. Agricultural libraries in Hyderabad
2. Agricultural college libraries in Andhra Pradesh
3. Regional Agricultural Research Stations
4. Agricultural Research Institutes
5. Agricultural Research Stations.

The international and national agricultural libraries, the sources of information, information services, agricultural information systems and the networks were briefly dealt in the present chapter.

3

Review of Literature and Methodology

A comprehensive review of literature has become an essential part of any investigation as it identifies the problems and gaps in the area of research and also provides a basis for theoretical framework of the study and interpretation of the findings. In this chapter, an attempt is made to review briefly the available literature on the information facility for agricultural education, research and extension in general, and in India in particular. The review doesn't claim to be comprehensive since it was not possible to trace all works on the subject published throughout the world.

This chapter reviewed literature on Agricultural Education, Research and Extension, Agricultural Libraries Management, Services, Online services, Information systems, Networks etc.

There has been many studies on use of Agricultural Libraries at International level, and very few studies are made in India on different aspects of Agricultural libraries and its users. They were made with different scope and objectives.

Review of literature indicates various studies made at doctoral level in India on Agricultural libraries. There are four such studies having varied scope and objectives. A study by Subbaiah (1985), deals with the agricultural information facility in India at the national level whereas the remaining three studies focused on some or other aspects of agricultural users and libraries in Andhra Pradesh. The main objective of two of these studies is, to survey the information needs of extension workers in Andhra Pradesh. The third study done by Veeranjaneyulu (1997) mainly deals with the existing infrastructure facilities and their suitability for creating a state-wide agricultural network to meet the information requirements of agricultural scientists and academicians. None of these studies are found to be covering all categories of agricultural libraries and the information seeking behavior and the needs of all types of users to make them more comprehensive to offer suggestions which are more scientific and universal in nature. Majority of the studies covered are of other countries. The scope ranges from surveys of agricultural libraries and their services to end users of Agricultural Information systems.

In addition, frequent deficiencies in the two-way communication linkages between researchers, administrators, Extension agents, and farmers occur. Further, he suggests ways for improving the situation, emphasizing the high priority which must be attached to the bibliographic control of the grey literature, produced within the country itself.

Mbwana (1987) discusses the importance of agricultural research and training in the overall development of a country. He explains the need for the free flow of agricultural information to agricultural scientists in their research and training activities. He also discusses the existing situation and gives suggestions to improve the dissemination of agricultural information in Tanzania.

Harris (1990) focuses on some issues or assumptions that information specialists in industrialized countries may find useful to examine before looking at the problems of the developing world and solutions that have worked there. It also covers problems associated with isolation—political, organizational and cultural. The article looks at the economic situation of agricultural research and information. Finally, the article discusses solutions for a variety of libraries and information centers especially networking and technology based solutions. Many of the sources identified in the references are non-conventional and not retrievable through bibliographic databases.

Boraiyan (1992) deals with the information resources on agricultural users or agricultural literature. He narrates the collection development and transfer of the agricultural research information. He also identifies the centres and services of agricultural research information in India.

Bankapur and Kumbar (1993) opine that the management of technology transfers; research and development policy studies and planning require qualitative and quantitative data to ensure perfect productivity in any discipline. The data originated by the scientists are scattered in different sources and a thorough investigation of such data and its impact could easily be determined by using 'Bibliometrics' and 'Scientiometrics' tools for measuring the productivity in any discipline. This will help the policy-makers to make suitable decisions. Such tools and sources have been discussed; Agricultural Research has been taken a theme study.

Sanjeev (1994) analyzed the topics of theses available in the College of Agriculture library, Vellayani using the schedule for Agriculture in Colon Classification. The details about different facts occurring in the topics of the theses and the context in which they occur were studied. Using the "bond theory" formulated by Dr. S.R. Ranganathan, the nature of specialization in agriculture, the bond connecting the main class and other isolates are examined.

Goldberg (1996) discusses in his paper about the findings based on the analysis of international databases which shows inadequate coverage of the diverse information sources on natural resource management. Further more, these databases are not readily available to regional researchers, extensionists, producers, policymakers and information personnel. There are languages, financial and training barriers that limit or prohibit access. It presents a project that challenges information providers, producers and intermediaries in six Latin American countries to work in partnership to ensure recovery of and access to key sources through a range of communication channels.

Russell (1997) explains with evidence from the literature that indicates the various ways of use of information in Agriculture and Scientific research. Coverage includes the contributions information makes in creativity, technology transfer, the diffusion of innovation, paradigm shifts, regular revisions of national guidelines on nutrition and other subjects, and in solving national and regional cries relating to agriculture and food safety. In addition, reference is made to the value of information in reducing duplication of effort and in helping scientists redirect their research into new areas.

Agricultural Extension

Aina (1985) reports the findings of the survey of the agricultural information needs of farmers in six villages in Nigeria. Most of the farmers are aged 36 years or older and most were part-time farmers. They required information on a wide range of subjects, but all were concerned with ways of increasing production. Information on fertilizers and pest and disease control was particularly important. The farmers made little effort on their own to obtain the required information and very few visited agricultural institutions in search of information. It was decided that libraries should be established in rural areas so as to meet the needs of farmers.

Aina (1991) discusses about the agricultural information needs of extension officers in Africa. The needs are identified as control of major pests, credit and cooperatives, proper handling of wise articles, marketing of agricultural products, etc. The information needs of farmers are identified to be in areas of the supply of fertilizers, pest and disease control, planting materials and credits and loans. To obtain information specialists' training and education should be re-oriented to include courses on agricultural sciences, rural sociology, adult education, and computer sciences.

Isahak (1991) states that the mid term revive of the fifth Malaysia Plan (1986-1990) has stated that emphasis will be placed on accelerating transfer of technology to small holders to improve their productivity and efficiency. Technology transfer can be achieved through publications, newspapers, radio and television networks and interpersonal methods as exemplified by the Agricultural Information Dissemination Programme launched in 1983 by the Ministry of Agriculture which has contributed to increased farmer awareness of new agricultural technologies. This approach to publication is not only more cost effective but faster.

Prasher (1993) opines that India has made good progress in agricultural production. But the yield over hectare is considerably low and the cropping area is also diminishing rapidly due to industrialization and urbanization. Despite these constraints, in order to meet the food requirement of ever growing population effective research and transfer of technology to the farmers is needed. To support the scientists engaged in these activities an effective library service is essential. The library must become a partner in agricultural production not meant only for the scientists but for the farmers also through rural library services. For this, the government should support the libraries with liberal grants, enactment of library legislation and formulating a national policy on information.

Beraho; Sheahan and Reeves (1996) discuss the aspects of rural extension from the perspective of experience gained in Uganda between 1989 and 1992, insight into the operation of land care groups in Australia 1993, as well as observations and survey recently carried out in the Mukono district during 1994. The paper highlights strengths and weaknesses in the current extension system based on the Training and visit (T & V) model, points out challenges an extension agency has to face in rural change, do best in enhancing communication, and utilization of agricultural information in rural places.

It also discusses the need for developing and strengthening grass root institutions, in order to develop a local capacity to sustain development and break the dependency syndrome is highlighted.

Landon-Lane (1996) observes that in an agricultural extension project in a number of locations in Sumatra, Indonesia, a participatory approach was taken to the analysis of individual farming systems and to the process of formulating agricultural advice.

Crowder and Anderson (1997) reviewed the weak linkages among research, education and extension (REE) institutions resulting in systematic "bottlenecks" in national agricultural technology systems and limit their effectiveness to contribute to development (ISNAR, 1989; Roling, 1990, Kaimowitz, 1990). The advantages of strong linkages are well known. Evidence shows that integrating research, education & extension can improve the overall performance of agricultural technology systems (Engel, 1990; Ortiz, 1990). This paper discusses some of problems and opportunities related to integrating and linking research, extension and education institutions and incorporating the active participation of farmers in technological innovation. At the end it makes some general suggestions for approaches that might be useful in attaching the "linkages problem".

Agricultural Librarianship

Agricultural information professionals include librarians, documentalists, information scientists etc., and perform the jobs in a way that is very similar that of agricultural extension workers. Agricultural Information Professionals work in a variety of institutions, either as 'one-man-bands' or with dozens of colleagues, with various levels of subject specialization in centres dealing with one commodity only or embracing most aspects of sophisticated systems and technologies, according to the level of development reached by their country, region or institution.

Kotei (1983) expressed the opinion that it is hard to make distinction between the special, as appose to general, training programmes. Factors that can be considered special are the specific purposes of trend, e.g. pest control and the geography (both physical and human) of the area. There is another sense in which special can be defined, namely the different categories of the users of agricultural information to whom user training is offered, special training should be coordinated with other specialties, programme outline should relate to normal agriculture operations and methods, innovative methods should be adopted, consistent with the complex, unique, ecosystem and other environmental conditions. Training programmes and policies should take cognizance of appropriate technology equipment, rather than non-operational ones, in that particular area. Modifications should be made between simple traditional modes of operation and scientific modes. Traditional methods should be introduced. More recent operations research findings should be studied before practical lessons being offered. Role and function of national and international organizations concerned with agricultural production, both trainer and trainee should understand finance, research, marketing, distribution, education and training, together with other "non- productive" promotional activities. Agricultural information programmes must lead to results that can be assessed quantitatively and qualitatively. Educational programmes and packages should be designed specially for each of the following categories: researchers, administrators, students and teachers, extension officers, writers and editors and non-literate traditional farmers. Each of these has their own peculiar problems of communication with library/information centres on the one hand, and with large scale and small-scale agricultural workers on the other.

Martinelli (1983) in his article summed-up remarks at the International Conference on Education and Training for Agricultural Library and Information work held in Nairobi from 7th to 12th March 1983. The paper surveys all the subjects discussed at the conference. A profile of the agricultural information, professional and their educational requirements are identified. Currently available education and training programmes in agricultural information work are described and discussed. Proposals for future action reflecting the views of conference and participants are discussed.

Teresa (1983) reviews and analyses all subjects discussed at the International Conference on Education and Training for Agricultural Information Work, organized by IAALD in Nairobi, 7th–12th March 1983. Over 100 participants attended the conference. That survey tried to identify the profile of the Agricultural Information Professionals (AIP) as it emerged from the 42 papers contributed to the conference, his/her educational and training requirements, comparing these with currently available programmes as reported at the conference. The review highlights the findings of the Conference extracting most of the relevant sections from that paper. It also provides some personal views that are the outcome of numerous conversations and discussions with colleagues of the ETWG, of IAALD and with other educations after that meeting.

Aina (1989) discusses the need for curriculum designed for the education of libraries for the provision of agricultural information to research scientists, extension officers, farmers, managers and policy-makers. The study recommends that the program should be at the masters' degree level and normally it should last 18 months. According to the paper, the curriculum includes courses in agriculture, rural development, agricultural extension, library studies, information sciences, computer science and archives in appropriate proportion. The paper also states that on graduation, trainees will be able to function effectively in the provision of information to agricultural information user population, thereby contributing to the accelerated growth of agricultural production in Africa.

Lenggang; Sirdi; Chan and Powell (1989) discuss about in 1981, the University of Kentucky that became involved in a ten-year project to improve agricultural education in the Western Islands of Indonesia. Part of this project was library improvement. This article details the methods used for constructing and teaching a management short course in the local environment.

Rajasekharan (1989) comment on the seniority based promotion which still continues to be in vogue in many academic libraries in India, and states that it is detrimental to profession and library development as a whole. Here, an attempt is made to work out the details of a meaningful selection procedure for the position of librarian in an Agricultural college, duly emphasizing the advantages of merit-based promotion system. Its implication on the professional status, the educational qualification and qualities required for the aspirant, a proposal for selection test etc, are delineated. Finally, the paper concludes that fixation of a rational criterion for selection of librarian in Agricultural education and consequent Agricultural development of our country.

Deshmukh and Deshpande (1991) opined that the object of the library is effective communication of information to the students, teachers and scientists. For this, the libraries have adopted various information technology techniques for developing bibliographic database and for retrieval of information. In order to make best use of libraries by the clientele, it is necessary to acquaint them with these techniques by the use of User Education Programme and Reader Instruction Programme.

Morton (1991) discusses the need to maintain and update the skills of professional staff in a changing technological environment and presents special training problems in an agricultural library system that are widely spread geographically. The development of in-house training standards and schedules for both searching and for local computer application is outlined. The resolution of questions on shared funding with host establishments is described, as is the training of end users to access and exploit network information services in the absence of intermediaries. The use of electronic mail to hasten document deliveries and the introduction of CD-ROM facilities to end-users is discussed.

Boraiyan (1992) defines the agricultural librarianship, describes the goals and objectives, and organizational responsibility of agricultural libraries; states the ethical relation with the users, administrators and suppliers of information; and sketches the, pressure for more services and the application of computers and communications in its activities.

Lal (1994) discusses the concept of staffing and its role in agricultural library. He traces the history of RAU library and its staff position since the day of its inception. His paper compares the staff with eight leading agricultural universities in India. It also studies the present strength in the light of UGC/ICAR staff formula. And it proposes the minimum required staff for an agricultural university library.

Boraiyan (1995) deals with the management functions in an Agricultural University Library, depicts the factors influencing the decision-making of the Library. He states various personal, administrative, organizational and managerial abilities with librarian like a manager in a larger service/organization.

Haendalor and Powell (1995) described the history and activities of the International Association of Agriculture Information Specialist (IAAIS) from its beginnings in Belgium in 1955. A primer for agricultural libraries was published by IAAIS in 2 editions. IAAIS also focuses on training the dissemination of agricultural information.

Ramarao; Muralidhar and Kalla (1996) present brief profile of scientific staff in the State Agricultural Universities (SAU) in India. The data collected through a survey sketches the scientific staff background, age, gender, education, mobility, career details and time spent on various activities.

Kaur (1998) discusses about the requisite knowledge and skills for the agricultural information professionals and suggests for reorienting the existing syllabi of library and information science schools to train agricultural information professionals for the changing role of libraries and information centres.

Somasekhar (1980) opined that the cooperation will be of much importance to the agricultural libraries in our country because the agricultural universities have been and are being established with the main intention of improving agricultural technology, and thereby, agricultural production. Suggests for setting up of National Agricultural Library (NAL) as a central body for chalking out the details is the need of the hour. This central body can coordinate between the cooperating agencies and suggests organizational pattern and policy for any agricultural university to prompt this activity.

Mohan (1977) surveys the world output of agricultural literature, describing the important indexing and abstracting services in the subject area. A brief account is given on the publications of the Commonwealth Agricultural Bureaux. The paper traces the development of the International Information System for Agricultural Sciences and Technology (AGRIS), and discusses AGLINET, ICARIS and the operation of AGRINDEX and AGRIS.

John (1978) describes the objectives and activities of Commonwealth Agricultural Bureaux. The Commonwealth Agricultural Bureaux was founded to meet the need among commonwealth countries for a world agricultural information service. The structure and development of the organization are discussed, as are the journals.

Goyal (1979) points out the need for theses and abstracts in the field of agriculture and allied subjects in India which resulted in a quarterly *Thesis-Abstracts* published by the Haryana Agricultural University, Hisar. He examines the coverage of Thesis-Abstracts and depicts the subject-wise trends in the disciplines covered. He also suggests the improvements for better coverage and prompt service of Thesis-Abstracts to scientists.

Vashishth (1979) defines 'Information' and describes the factors that have led to increase in cooperation among various nations in the management of information leading to multinational global information systems.

It explains the structure to handle the information effectively. It also discusses in detail, the organizational and operational aspect of INIS and AGRIS and their products. It mentions the procedure and mode of communicating input data by India. It makes a case for 'Online' availability of information to the Indian scientists.

Kumar and Dutta (1982) evaluated the SDI service of ICRISAT. They observe that it is restricted to 5 crop improvement programmes. ICRISAT's mandate also includes farming systems and social economics. A thesaurus is being developed and the information collected will be computerized in future in order to provide a more pinpointed SDI service to a wider range of clientele. However, the feedback received indicates that the system has been successful.

Deshmukh (1983) reports the results of a user survey counted to evaluate the library resources of the Central Soil and Water Conservation Research and Training Institute, Dehra Dun, through a questionnaire. The data has been analyzed and the results are presented in this paper. Such surveys can be helpful in future developments of the library.

Eswar Reddy (1985) has conducted a study for the assessment of a range of library and information services offered for agricultural extension officers. His study confirmed that the agricultural extension officers require effective library and information services as his respondent had been using the libraries available to them frequently. Further, he outlined the basic information requirements of agricultural extension officers as: (i) traditional information used in education and training it covers, for example, basic agricultural knowledge, agricultural practices, farm skills, etc. (ii) innovative information resulting generally in research and development works, (iii) timely information required at a particular time for a specific purpose. It is the question-answer or problem solving type of information. It is further established from the study that the agricultural extension officers would like to have free photo copying service followed by bibliographical information and study of information and specific problems. It is evident from this study that the extension works also require bibliographic information apart from processed information and data.

Harris (1985) traces out the unique characteristics of agricultural information especially, tropical agricultural information and calls for special kinds of current awareness services. The current awareness services of the Centre International de Agricultural Tropical (CIAT) are discussed in the light of these needs.

Hemasundar Naidu and Gunjal (1985) discuss the importance of newspaper clippings in agricultural information, and stress the need for newspaper clipping service. Describes various problems connected with the organization of newspaper clippings to storage and retrieval of these clippings in agricultural libraries. The paper traces out newspaper clipping and indexing services provided by agricultural libraries and emphasizes the need to make effective use of their vast information resource. It suggests more newspaper-clipping units in specialized areas in agriculture for wider coverage.

Palmer (1986) states that since the late 1970's mounting concern about farming practices and agricultural policy has coincided with as steady decrease in funds available for policy funded research.

Rajasekharan (1986) states that the subject agriculture is covered with numerous abstracting and indexing services encompassing all interrelated specific subjects. Studies show that agriculture is not confined to journals exclusively dealing with agriculture alone. He opined that online services offer efficiency in dissemination of agricultural information with more speed and accuracy.

Livingston and Narisimha Raju (1989) studied through a questionnaire, the nature of information requirement, opinion on library services and collection and assessed the need for a union catalogue of Andhra Pradesh Agricultural University. Circulation of reprints, organization of SDI information services and the implementation of latest information technology into the libraries/information centres are recommended.

Walton (1989) describes the efforts made to document information on plant protection. A regional plant protection information system will insure that the non-conventional documents that are so valuable to agricultural researchers are not inadvertently lost. The regional plant protection information service will enhance national capabilities through training in database manipulation, ultimately to improve plant protection within the region.

Bird and Smith (1990) reviewed the literature on agriculture and its related fields. The authors discussed major issues and trends in agricultural information, agricultural libraries and in doing so, have relied upon the diverse and expanding literature on agricultural information. This review provide a framework for understanding the current and future status of agricultural information and agricultural libraries.

Fisher and Kinch (1990) stress the need for reference service in the agricultural libraries. Reference service provides the mechanism by which the user of agricultural information can interface with the larger body of knowledge to secure what is desired. Technological advancements have greatly improved the accessibility of the broad range of information relevant for the achievement of successful reference.

Gessesse and Mbwna (1990) describe the Tanzanian Literature Service (TALIS), established by the Ministry of Agriculture as a joint project between the governments of Ireland and Tanzania, and types of information services it offers to research scientists engaged in various agricultural and veterinary establishments in Tanzania. The paper highlights the requirements of funds for continuation of the service.

Aina (1991) discusses about the agricultural information needs of extension officers in Africa. The needs are identified as control of major pests, credit and cooperatives, proper handling of wise articles, marketing of agricultural products, etc. The information needs of farmers are identified to be in areas of the supply of fertilizers, pest and disease control, planting materials and credits and loans.

Raju (1991) describes in detail, about the three major abstracting services - Rural Development Abstracts, International Development Abstracts of the UK and Abstracts of Rural Development in the Tropics of the Netherlands to examine their scope, coverage, pattern of citation and indexing together with the services offered. This paper suggested that the publishers of these abstracting services make an effort to augment the coverage for better bibliographic control of gray literature. This can be done in cooperation with regional organizations and international donor agencies.

Thomas (1991) discusses about a detailed, comprehensive, multilingual agricultural thesaurus which would provide enhanced access to indexed agricultural literature. Out of this discussion has come a proposal for a feasibility study which would suggest effective solutions to the international problem of thesaurus based access information.

Hemasundar Naidu and Gunjal (1992) stressed the importance of inter-library loan service. Inter-library loan relations of the agricultural libraries is studied. The type and number of documents borrowed and lent is discussed including the response. Certain steps for effective inter-library loans are suggested.

Livingston and Narasimha Raju's (1992) reported the results of a survey of the library and information resources and services for agriculture in the district of Guntur in Andhra Pradesh of India. It points out the inadequacies of library facilities, proposes effective utilization of information resources through library cooperation and networking to support research and education in agriculture.

Suryanaryana and Raman (1992) discussed in detail, the objectives and activities of the library and documentation services at Central Tobacco Research Institute, Rajahmundry. Some of the areas such as collection development, documentation and various information services, computerization activities, sharing of resources of other institute libraries, and institute's research publication and distribution.

Lal (1993) defines the purpose of a book-bank in a university/college library. He narrates the operation of this scheme at Rajendra Agricultural University, Pusa, its rules, year-wise growth in collection, the expenditure incurred and the services rendered. His paper offers suggestions for its further development.

Entsua-Mensah (1995) discusses about an inefficient system in Ghana that prevents the peasant farmer from receiving the correct type of information at the right time. He says that this has led to the decline in food crop production in Ghana. It is necessary to bridge the gap between available knowledge on improved technologies and actual practice and effective information delivery service which is the missing link between the research-extension interfaces on one hand, and practical application of the result by the peasant farmers on the other. Available options like efficient extension service throughout search and demonstration programmes, agricultural shows, use of the opinion of leaders, news media, audiovisual materials and posters are discussed.

Singh and Mehla (1995) discusses about the issues involved in establishing a CD-ROM station which include assessment of users' requirements, selection of databases, networking decisions, hardware selection, staff and user education and service policies. Products available on CD are described including CAB abstracts and AGRICOLA as well as Toxline. The paper includes a discussion of using CD-ROM versus online databases on the paper products in providing information services as well as the cost effectiveness and the impact of space in a facility. The conclusions are that CD-ROM holds promise for developing countries and CD-ROM will remain the medium of choice for the publishing industry.

Srinivas and Venketasan (1997) describe the growth and development of Semi-Arid Tropical Crops Information Services (SATCRIS), its objectives and its products and services. Their paper also describes the process through which the SATCRIS services and products are promoted. It explains the change from a manual system to an automated system of the SDI services and the process of getting feed back from the users of this service.

Aguolu (2000) reports the findings of a study of a studies a random sample of ten agricultural libraries and their collection to determine their role in dissemination of agricultural information to agricultural information seekers in Nigeria. An assessment of the collection and services offered revealed that agricultural libraries in Nigeria disseminated information through document loan and reference services. Provision of photocopy and modern computer-assisted information services, which would facilitate information dissemination, remains a rarity.

Agricultural Information Sources and Collection Development

Sources of Agricultural information are of different types. Agricultural Information is now available in various formats. Books and journals, both popular and scholarly, undoubtedly will continue to be the principal means of providing agricultural information. Theses, dissertations and conference proceedings are included in this category. Another familiar form is the research report or technical bulletins published by experiment stations, government agencies or other research organizations.

Singhvi (1964) presents in his paper the findings of a field study of Division of Bibliography of United States Department of Agricultural Library. It describes the development of bibliographic work and coming into existence as 'Bibliography of Agriculture'. The 'Biological Abstracts' is fully analysed with respect to its subject matter, coverage and scope, arrangement and overlappings. Lastly, it concludes with its usefulness and drawbacks and with a suggestion for reviewing again the subject index for each issue brought out and for providing the cumulative indexes.

Singhvi (1964) explains the importance of the reference tools of general nature which were useful for the subject fields, general as well as special intended tools to deal with the sources that can serve the basic needs of research workers in the specialized field i.e. Agriculture.

Bremnen (1974) conducted a survey of 51 cooperating libraries located at land grant universities and the National Agricultural Library to evaluate the periodical collections on tropical and sub-tropical agriculture. The six-month study showed wide ranges in coverage of serial literature in the subject field among the cooperating libraries. The results of the study present a strong case in favour of the division of subject fields among libraries within regional areas in the United States.

Phadnis and Sital (1974) presented the results of a general survey of literature in the field of Agriculture. The coverage of secondary periodicals, the organization having important collections a complete picture of Agricultural research in India and an account of the information facilities available to an agricultural scientist in India are presented and assessed. Suggestions for new services in the future are also made.

Metcalfe and Cooper (1982) critically examined the reasons behind the CAB's policy regarding non-conventional literature. CAB is a business operation, and meeting user needs is the key to its survival. Efficient use of staff expertise, development in computer technology, reducing overheads and improving marketing by CAB are helping to reduce costs. The options for handling non-conventional literature are outlined: CAB favors each country handling its own and only inputing to AGRIS and CAB a selected, internationally relevant subset. The inclusion of extension literature in AGRIS would not be cost effective.

Rolls' (1982) paper is based on his experience as a user professionally interested in how information, especially innovation in agriculture, is communicated to the farmer; it is limited to experience at the Agricultural Extension and Rural Development Centre (AERDC).

Subbaiah (1982) outlines Indian agro-biological literature and stresses the necessity for making this literature available at one place. Important International and Indian documentation agencies are described. An attempt made at the Marthwada Agricultural University Library, Parbhani (Maharashtra) towards the biological control of Indo agro-biological literature is explained. A bibliographic research cell was set up at this library in collaboration with the scientists and the library's professional staff prepared an information file and also published seven documentation projects on various aspects of agriculture.

Musib (1984) makes an attempt to find out the countries publishing maximum number of journals in the field of agriculture, agricultural economics and economics. Attempts to analyze the frequency and agency of publications of journals show that USA published maximum number of journals in all the three fields. Points out that only ten countries are sufficient to cover 70% of journals production. Mention that the most popular frequency of publications is 'monthly' followed by 'quarterly' in the three fields in the most popular agency of publication in business firms in economics, 'government' in agriculture economics and 'associations' in agriculture.

Aina (1988) conducted an analytical study of 3 source journals used by researchers in agricultural economics and agricultural extension in Nigeria to determine the reliance on government documents by researchers. The result shows that government publications constitute about 20% of the literature cited by researchers in agricultural economics and agricultural extension. The government documents cited were predominantly technical reports, statistical reports and annual reports. It appears that agricultural libraries should endeavor to acquire government publications and disseminate information there in to researchers.

An attempt has been made by Lal (1988) to identify the most important source of citation, its geographical and chronological distribution in the field of agronomic research in Bihar. The most important journals identified through the technique of citation analysis as indicted by their frequency of citation were *Indian Journal of Agronomy, Indian Journal of Agricultural Science, Indian farming, Fertilizer News, Agronomy Journal, Madras Agricultural Journal, Field Crop abstract and Plant and Soil.* Among the cited journals India occupied the first rank as a country of publication followed by USA and UK. The chronological distribution of citation to journals suggests that the researchers in agricultural cite from current journals and seldom refer to back number.

Lal (1989) makes an attempt to identify the main sources of citations and prepare a list of the most important journals in various branches of agricultural science. In addition to it, a list of 59 most citied primary journals in order of their merit has been prepared. The geographical and chronological scattering of citations has also been included. The information inferred in the paper may be of help to agricultural university libraries to arrive at a need-based consideration in the selection and acquisition of journals within the limited resources.

Jones (1990) reviews the concept of agriculture today which embraces not only the traditional areas of food and fibre production, but also an increasingly broad spectrum of related subjects and concerns, which have become important to this evolving field. This article will provide an over view of the types of agricultural information, the formats now being utilized for its storage and distribution, the organizations which play a role in its creation and dissemination and finally where it may be found or how it may be accessed.

Kabir (1990) reports the results of a citation analysis study, involving citation from the PhD theses in the field of agriculture from 1981 to 1988, to determine the Indian periodicals most frequently used by the researchers in the field of agriculture. A total of 7049 citations were collected, compiled, analysed. Identifies and lists the most important Indian periodicals.

Pichappan (1990) reports the use of citation analysis to determine how information is transmitted in formal information communication by use of citation data generated from a study of Indian agricultural scientific periodicals, involving citation frequency, impact factor and discipline influence score.

Thomas (1990) opines that bibliographic control of agricultural publications is a complex and costly process. There is also no single source in which to locate all citations to particular topic in agriculture. AGRICOLA, AGRIS and CAB Abstracts are three major databases that provide journal article-level analysis of agricultural topics, the overlap in relationships among these databases and their unique features are described. Points out that new technologies have also brought significant gains in the area of bibliographic control and developments in automated indexing could make the process of providing bibliographic access and control more productive in the future.

Manjunatha (1991) identifies the key concepts in literature published in Agricultural Sciences. Varieties of information resources, variations in the subjects, conventional, primary, secondary and tertiary literatures are identified are described. Computer-based bibliographic services are analyzed.

Olsen and Olsan-Jan (1991) discusses about the efforts made at the Mann library at Cornell University to identify and list the core literature of the agricultural sciences in CD form appropriate for education and research in Third World countries.

Thomas (1991) explains how a detailed, comprehensive, multilingual agricultural thesaurus would provide enhanced access to indexed agricultural literature suggests that access to agricultural publications would be simplified if a unified agricultural thesaurus were employed for assigning descriptors. Indexers could select varying levels of specificity when analyzing documents. Alternately, database searchers could invoke a gateway to navigate the various levels of thesaurus application in particular databases. The gateway could accommodate the use of multiple languages for effective retrieval.

Boriyan (1992) explains about various the activities and services of Tamil Nadu Agricultural University Libraries.

Garg (1992) analyzed the papers published by Indian agricultural scientists in Indian and non-Indian journals were analysed to find the areas of agricultural research, institutions involved in agricultural research and the papers published by them.

Lal (1993) defines the purpose of a book bank in a university/college library; narrates the operation of this scheme at Rajendra Agricultural University, Pusa, its rules, year-wise growth in collection, the expenditure incurred and the services rendered; Offers suggestions for its further development.

Bharati and Stanley (1993) advocate that the scientific periodicals occupy most vital and important position for the quick and better communication as they report recent developments and trench out the publication trench in the field of agriculture by Indian authors.

Apurba Baruah (1994) reviews the types of annual reports and their importance as sources of information in agricultural sciences and described. Boraiyan (1994) discusses the use, coverage etc., of atlases and maps relevant to agriculture and allied fields; Lists various kinds of maps and atlases with their uses particularly to Indian agriculture.

Suryanarayana (1995) reported the results of bibliometric analysis of publications of CTRI and its Research Stations from 1949 to 1997. Analysis is done on the authorship pattern, yearly distribution of literature; publication pattern in broad disciplines at the main institute and at the stations before and after implementation of UGC scales to the scientists; publication in regional language periodicals and foreign language journals; concludes that there is reduction of publication of articles after UGC scales in foreign journals.

Besemer and Verman (1995) outline the ways in which information can be located on the internet, through the use of internet resource guides, subject trees in gopher, listings and subject trees on the world wide web, researchable indexes on the world wide web, Usenet postings and electronic mail discussion groups. Describes 3 case studies from the field of Agriculture in which information was sought on specific topics using these methods.

Clark (1996) provided an annotated listing of Internet resources for agriculture and agriculture related information including: government sites; library resources; databases; agricultural statistics; agricultural organizations; electronic journals and magazines; lists and news groups; weather; major guides to agricultural resources; clip art and agricultural image sites; and other interesting sites.

Peres and others (1996) described about the objectives of their developing an index of citations in agricultural science (IBCC Ag) similar to Science Citation of Index (SCI) published by the Institute of Scientific Information. The IBCC Ag will be complementary to SCI. the additional database is necessary due to the locational characteristics of the agricultural sciences especially in its applied part. Thomas (1996) assesses the coverage, of Indian agro biology journals in Biological Abstracts (BA), Agri index, current advances in Biological Sciences (CABS) and current contents (CC) was done based on subject specialization, periodicity and multiple coverage.

Hemasundar Naidu (1998) outlined the importance and the components of the agricultural literature. Stresses need for exchange of publications. Discusses exchange relations among the agricultural libraries in India and the type of documents exchanged.

Sharma (1998) described about the modern agricultural journalism which was born in India with the advent of printing when three books on modern methods were got translated by Sir Syed Ahemad Khan. Now ICAR publishes four journals and two newsletters in English and three in Hindi. Overall, about 250 periodicals in India are devoted to agriculture. The paper also describes the Agricultural Research Information Centre (ARIC) at Indian Council of Agricultural Research Headquarters, India, the databases available, publications brought out and services rendered by the centre.

Arunachalam, S (2000) presents an assessment of India's contribution to research in agriculture and related fields based on an analysis of publications indexed in CAB Abstracts published during 1990-1994.

It attempts to map agricultural research, in which journals of Indian research works get published, in what sub-fields is India strong, and so on. It aims not only to inventory agricultural research in India but also to provide an appreciation of endogenous research capacity in this crucial field.

Biradar (2000) studied the existing rural libraries in Karnataka and collected the opinion of farmers of the region. One thousand farmers were interviewed for determining the sources of information used in various stages of farming activities. Also suggests strategy to develop the collection of rural libraries and to make use of them.

Boraiyan's (2000) paper deals with the concept of information. It delineates the nature of information sources, and draws the attention of consumer of information (user) towards the information (storage) systems and its services. It depicts the significance of information provider (librarian). It also explains the importance of information dissemination in an Agricultural Research and Development Institute. It illustrates the mode of linkages such as the current services and other dissemination of information services available for agricultural scientists.

Impact of Technology on Agricultural Libraries and Information Sources

Information plays an important role in agricultural research and development. It helps in keeping the research workers abreast of what is going on the fields of specific interest in the minimum possible time. In this information age tremendous flow of information is emerging particularly in the field of Agro-Biology, Biotechnology, Tissue culture, Agro-forestry etc. As such, the problem of providing information in time is not due to lack of information. Existing information is not capable of providing the services as expected. Increasing the efficiency of the existing system is one of the solutions to the problem. To improve efficiency, a computer-based information system at local level with participation in a network service has to be developed in all the agricultural libraries in the country as it is more convenient, more flexible and more comprehensive and in the long run more economical.

Demas; Chiang; Ochs and Curtis (1985) justified the reasons for establishing a collection of computer-readable information and a microcomputer facility in an agricultural research library. It provides an overview of the considerations for selecting microcomputer software and data files for both microcomputers and mainframe computers. Recent developments in standardizing cataloging practices and policies governing loan procedures are also outlined.

Bankapur and Vardaraj (1989) while summing up the entire gamut of the situation analyzed the strategic issues in information technology making a reference to developing countries have pointed out that although there is plenty of 'know-how' available in agricultural sciences at the global level, it is rarely useful to developing countries because of local conditions prevailing with them. The basic strategy should be to develop indigenous database in the literature produced in their respective countries. The existing manual or conventional methods also play vital role in the diffusion and utilization of knowledge, which needs to be continued. Information packages are the need of the hour.

Bose (1989) states that computer based catalogue system can save the time and efforts involved in producing the information products and sparing the library staff for important functions like reference services to the users. With the availability of microcomputers and related software at comparatively reasonable cost Agriculture libraries should come forward to implement the software applications and can give a new look to the entire gamut of library house- keeping operations.

Attaulbah and Johnson (1991) described about the activities of the North-West Frontier Province (NWFP) Agricultural University in Peshawar, Pakistan which was recently combined with the Ministry of Agriculture Research station in NWFP to upgrade both the research and training capabilities for agricultural scientists in the province. Various steps and stages of the modernization of the information storage and retrieval systems and implementation of services for faculty, students and provincial agricultural scientists are outlined.

Chottey Lal and Bhatia (1993) opined that it is "better late than never" in the case of Indian Agricultural Libraries. Since published literature is increasingly made available on CDs, Floppies/Diskettes etc., the agricultural libraries cannot afford to lag behind in their procurement and use. Suggested that to solve many problems faced by the Indian libraries latest technologies can be incorporated into library operations.

Kaur (1996) analyzed the use of computer and CD-ROM in the libraries of Agricultural Universities and Research Institutes in the states of Punjab, Haryana and Himachal Pradesh and offers brief suggestions for the efficient use of computer and CD-ROM for improving the working of these libraries.

Impact of Information Technology on Agricultural Information

Bose (1976) proposed a model for evolution of information system for national development and explains the necessary steps to be taken. India participates in both AGRIS and CARIS, and the projected aims and services of CARTS. The Research Project Unit of Indian Council of Agricultural Research (ICAR) handles both these FAO projects in India until a fully-fledged computerised Agricultural Research Information and documentation centre is established at ICAR.

Quibo (1989) study traces out from seven subject samples; average overlapping between the three major agricultural databases (AGRICOLA, CAB, AGRIS) and proposes thus for better coverage of any given subject, searching all three databases where financial and communication conditions allow.

Stone (1990) reviewed present day information networks and how they evolved as a result of new information technologies. The needs of end user and how they influence the design of information networks: as well as how the increased demand for technology transfer and the evolving role of information systems, in this transfer process have influenced the structure of national, regional and international agricultural information networks are discussed.

Attaulbah and Johnson (1991) described the activities of the North-West Frontier Province (NWFP) Agricultural University in Peshawar, Pakistan. Various steps and stages of the modernization of the information storage and retrieval systems and implementation of services for faculty, students and provincial agricultural scientists are outlined.

Beecher (1991) describes about the United States Agricultural Information Network (USAIN) is the first organization developed specifically to provide a national forum through which U.S agricultural librarians might address many issues associated with the collection, access and delivery of agricultural information.

Van Hartevelt (1991), explained the activities of Royal Tropical Institutes (KIT). The projects consisted of the supply of workstations including hardware, software; agricultural databases on CD-ROM; and the training in basic PC skills, word processing and literature retrieval.

Zhang (1991) reviewed the design of a cooperative Acquisition programme (CAP) for a regional network- ZALINET- in China. The model is presented both descriptively and quantitatively for the purpose of design and planning. The types of participating libraries and potential network users are identified in the following sectors: research, education, production, government department and marketing. A descriptive model has been worked out for the distribution of information resources.

Krieger and Schmiol (1993) explained the retrieval mechanism for AGRIS. The databases available on CD-ROM. A special searching feature, AGROVOC, is a multilingual thesaurus of Agriculture terminology, in English, French, Spanish, Italian and German and is AGRIS's attempt to respond to demands for multilingual access the database. The thesaurus is divided into two main sections: a list of permuted terms providing access to online thesaurus via descriptors and cross references; and a term detail selection providing information about relationships between descriptors.

Monaterios (1993) described about AGRISEARCH, a CD-ROM database, produced by Silver Platter information institution, aiming to coordinate current agricultural research projects in Africa, Australia, Canada, Europe and the USA. Concludes that, considering this is the first attempt to harmonize agricultural research project information, the database has much to offer those involved in the development, planning and coordination of agricultural research.

Zhang (1994) observed that the development of agriculture and the reform to the rural economy in China in the last decade has brought about great changes, which have raised increased demand for information and high lighted in inadequate performance of existing agricultural library and information systems. A critical overview of China's agricultural library and information system is given, with particular emphasis on the future importance of networking.

Bellamy (1995), based on the literature and on the experience of CAP International and others of assessing the needs and advising appropriate systems in a wide range of developing countries, provide a draft Plan for a sustainable agricultural information system for a hypothetical country whose circumstances match those found in many Anglophone African countries, but which may be more widely applicable. It develops a five-year scenario which allows for changes in both needs and technology, but which incorporate essential elements of the original structure and resources, the ultimate goal being a system which is demand-driven, not technologies-led.

Besmer and Irene (1995) gave a detailed description about the use of Internet to access and download information from various available on Internet. That information on the internet can be stored as document in an FTP server, Gopher server or World Wide Web (WWW) server, as a record in WAIS indexed database, or appear as a posting to a mailing list or a use net news group. Each information unit has unique address (now mostly represented by a Uniform Resource Locator (URL)). Veronica server can do searching gopher space but indexing for the WWW is being developed. Internet resource guides are available in printed form as well as documents that can be downloaded. The clearinghouse for Subject-Oriented Internet Resource Guides is maintained by the university of Michigan's University Library and school of Information and Library Studies and is available over the Internet. Various gopher sites also maintain subject-trees in gophers. Searching on the Internet is limited but browsing the Internet with the help of gopher and WWW will lead to expected sources of information. Currently indexes to WWW are available free of charge but commercial enterprises such as Info seek are charging a fee for the use of their indexes.

Britton (1995) discussed about the role of the Ohio Agricultural Research and Development Center which became an agriculture information provider on the Cleveland Free-Net, the first community based computer system.

Perera (1995) traced out the development of Agricultural Information Network in Sri Lanka from its beginning in 1982 with 24 member librarians attached to research institutes and universities. The system presently serves the information needs of agricultural sector with 26 member libraries to nearly 1000 agricultural scientists scattered around the country using modern information processing and dissemination technologies.

Singh and Mehla (1995) explained about the issues involved in establishing a CD-ROM station which include assessment of users' requirements: selection of databases; networking decisions: hardware selection: staff and user education and services policies. Products available on CD are described including CAB abstracts and AGRICOLA as well as Toxline. The conclusions are that CD-ROM holds promise for developing countries and CD-ROM will remain the medium of choice for the publishing industry.

Addison and Cullen (1996) discussed about the Natural Resources Institute (NRI) disseminates information on research and new techniques in natural resources management to developing countries. The paper reviews existing services in Africa, discussing the networks available, the technologies used and the organizations involved. The impacts, real and potential, of networks on the way people work, the human feedback factor perceivable at NRI and implication for information management are examined.

Andre (1996) discusses about the issue of communicating critical information resources to remote places in US using many new technologies available for information dissemination and access. Example from a wide range of institutions will show how the information community is responding to this opportunity and how we, in the agricultural information community, can play leadership role in this exciting transition.

Chris and Cullen (1996) discussed about the activities and role of the Natural Resources Institute (NRI) disseminate to the information on research and new techniques in natural resources management to developing countries. For four years, NRI has been involved in the use of e-mail for the dissemination and communication of agricultural information, specifically in Africa. The paper reviews existing services in Africa, discussing the networks available, the technologies used and the organizations involved. NRIs own use of the systems will be presented. The impacts, real and potential, of networks on the way people work, the human feedback factor perceivable at NRI and implication for information management are examined.

Lopez-Perez and Roste-Vela (1996) in his paper critically points out that despite progress in both the public and private sectors, a National Agricultural Information system for Mexico has not yet been developed. They observed that current agricultural information centres in Mexico function independently and informally without a formal organization for coordinating services and activities for its users. As such, the present document attempts to identify the key factors in developing a National Agricultural Information System, analyzing general theories and proposing a model for implementation.

Ogbourne and Ison (1996) reviews some of the partnerships in which CAB international is participating in support of the dissemination of scientific and technical information in the agricultural sector of the developing world. It indicates the main thrusts for strengthening collaborative activities in the information domain, so as to build on the global response to agenda 21 recommendations.

Gajendra Singh and Kushal Pal (1998) reviewed the development of Indian National Agricultural Research System (NARS) with its nationwide network of educational and research institutions consisting of State Agricultural Universities, Zonal research institutions, ICAR institutes with regional station established Agricultural Research Information System in 1995 to strengthen its research information base with funds from National Agricultural Research Project. It has two main components: creation of infrastructure for providing electronic connectivity and creation of MIS and computerised/ electronic databases of Indian research findings of NARS in various fields of agriculture and allied fields.

Patil and Kumar's (1998) study deals with information transfer chain from generation to potential users through various international cooperative efforts in the field of agricultural sciences and technology. The international information system like

AGRICOLA, AGRIS and CAB are briefed keeping in view their products, services and how to access them using modern tools so that sustainable information is provided for better agricultural production.

Kannappanavar, B.V and Vijaya Kumar (2001) describe the use of hardware and software facilities in the University of Agricultural Science Libraries in Karnataka state. A survey conducted in agricultural universities in Karnataka at Dharwar and Bangalore, found that neither institutions was making much use of databases nor implementing information technology in their libraries.

Automated Agricultural Information Services

Burton (1978) explained about a cooperative programme undertaken by Agricultural Research Service & National Agricultural Library to provide selective dissemination of information service to three groups of land-grant university scientists working in the area of sorghum researchers was undertaken by the Agricultural Research Service and the National Agricultural Library. Analysis of user feedback indicated that BIOSIS previews and the Commonwealth Agricultural Bureaus file were the most productive databases.

Rajasekharan (1986) observed that information on agriculture can be provided with numerous abstracting and indexing services encompassing all interrelated specific subjects. Online services offer efficiency in dissemination of agricultural information with more speed and accuracy describes various information services that might be of interest to agriculture scientists and librarians and concludes that automated information services are expected to become widespread in the near future in the field of agriculture.

Bankapur and Vardaraj (1989) summing up the entire gamut of the situation analyzing the strategic issues in information technology making a reference to developing countries, it may be pointed out that although there is plenty of 'know-how' available in agricultural sciences at the global level, it is rarely useful to developing countries because of local conditions prevailing with them. The basic strategy should be to develop indigenous database in the literature produced in their respective countries.

Subbaiah (1989) strongly advocates that it is now inevitable for agricultural libraries to switch over to automation. The librarians and the authorities of institutions should now realize the trends of modernization and adopt the technology for effective dissemination of agricultural information. He suggests for the involvement of both ICAR and State Governments in this regard.

Thomas (1989) reviewed the developments in networking in United States. Information networking has been a tradition in the agricultural information community. NAL's efforts for the five years have led to the formation of the United States Agricultural Information Network (USAIN), an asson whose goal is to provide a forum for discussion of agricultural information issues.

Ditzler, Veronica and Thompson (1990) provided a broad overview of how document delivery and inter-library loan have changed dramatically in recent decades moving from providing the patron with original materials to providing a photo copy, telefacsimile, and even electronically formatted material. This article discusses ongoing new technology projects, which may influence document delivery. CD-ROM online catalogs and databases OCLC, AGRICOLA, ADONIS, Group IV telefacsimile, high speed digital communication networks, text digitizing, expert systems and hyper-media are all part of continuing research and development in document delivery.

Andre (1991) described the activities of National Agricultural Text Digitizing Project. The project was designed to test the premise that optical imaging with distribution on CD-ROM held the greatest potential for information delivery. A variety of issues have been raised regarding the effectiveness of these technologies for developing and disseminating full text databases including the need for a basic low-cost retrieval work station, standards for image material, a standard user interface and the capability to provide long-term archival storage for electronic media. These issues are discussed from the end users viewpoint.

Inger (1991) described the origin and growth of the Danish Veterinary and Agricultural Documentation Centre. The centre has the following objectives: to function as the Danish AGRIS input centre, to supply qualified online searching in international agricultural and related databases for private agricultural clients, research institutions and students, to teach online searching techniques and to supply document delivery for search customers. The Danish Veterinary and Agricultural Library supplies close to 50% of the literature ordered based on the online searches. The remainder is obtained through AGLINET.

Jones (1991) explained the advantages of online services especially for scientists. Librarians are now in a position to take advantage of the opportunities presented by relatively low cost computers, CD-ROM databases available for a fixed annual fee and the reduced online services available on evenings and weaken from vendors such as BRS and DIALOG. By establishing end user search programmes, the librarians moves away the role of directly providing information to users and towards the role of managing or facilitating direct access to information by the user.

Ochs (1991) opined that telefacsimile; computer networks and optical scanning hold great potential for rapid document delivery. Several projects are now underway in the US to combine optical scanning and network transmission for document delivery. The United States National Agricultural Library and the Research Libraries Group are both conducting tests on document transmission via the Internet. These projects are discussed briefly. Some of the barriers to the use of scanning, network transmission and fax in the developing countries, such as high costs and dependence on high-speed telecommunications, will be discussed.

Xinanfu; Likaiyang and Shuchen (1991) discussed about the results of the project of Chinese Agricultural Information Services and evaluated against the pre-defined goals. The evaluation was positive and the service has reached or exceeded its goals. It has played a key role in promoting the establishment of an agricultural scientific information system at the national level in China.

Boraiyan (1993) defined a database and its types in detail. He outlined the producer of databases and described the features major databases available for Agriculture like AGRICOLA, AGRIS, BIOSIS, CAB Abstracts, TROP-AG and RURAL.

Bankapur and Tukaram (1995) made an attempt to predict the strategic issues in agricultural information in relation to developing countries and opined that much depend upon the socioeconomic consequences and limit of exact information needs of countries concerned.

Singh and Mehla (1995) described about the issues involved in establishing a CD-ROM station. The paper also includes a discussion of using CD-ROM versus online databases on the paper products in providing information service as well as the cost effectiveness and the impact on space in a facility. The conclusions are that CD-ROM holds promise for developing countries and CD-ROM will remain the medium of choice for the publishing industry.

Sittler (1995) discussed about the Texas Agricultural Extension Service (TAEX) that has been experimenting with electronic information services and the World Wide Web (WWW) as an adjunct to traditional information distribution methods. It presents a brief analysis of current use and cost savings achieved; Presents some guidelines for online information providers. Internet information servers allow access to a broader audience at lower cost than traditional distribution.

Aw, Samba (1996) presents the findings of their study on agricultural information provision in Africa. It shows that in the Sahel region which poorest region in Africa, agricultural databases an data banks are often created without preliminary analysis, and some times without responding to clearly defined and expressed needs. The study reveals that 80% of these databases are under utilized or difficult to get access to and that the agricultural CD-ROM databases available in the region are not often consulted. Recommendations were made to improve the existing position.

Haavisto and Ofversten (1996) in their paper described about the Agro net. By technical nature, the typical services may be classified as electronic mail, information dissemination, information management as well as responding to adhoc service requests. Classified by their contents, these services comprise real time advisory services, price information, product information, library services, farm business management, bank transaction and so forth. The users include farmers, extension service, research institutes administration, industry, entrepreneurs and consumers. The author predicts that by 1995 Agro net will be commercially profitable.

Lal and Panda (1998) traced the history and growth of plant pathology literature and measures the dimensions of its systematic development in India.

Patil and Kumar's (1998) study deals with information transfer chain from generation to potential users through various international cooperative efforts in the field of agricultural sciences and technology. The international information system like AGRICOLA, AGRIS and CAB are briefed keeping in view their products, services and how to access them using modern tools so that sustainable information is provided for better agricultural production.

Surendra Kumar and Kumar, S. (2000) in their paper have discussed about Agricultural Research Information System (ARIS) in India and its various modules like Agricultural Research Personnel Information System (ARPIS), Agricultural Research Financial Information System (ARFIS), Agricultural Research Management Information System (ARMIS) and Agricultural Research Library Information System (ARLIS). It also describes the Information System Development (ISD) and ARIS Cells, their funding and computer equipment availability.

Arun Kumar Chakraborty (1991) stressed the need for building up a network of documentation and information services in the field of agriculture and allied areas. It delineates an information base for agricultural policy and enumerates categories of information and data requirements, information collecting agencies, important documents as sources of information relating to agriculture. It also mentions briefly about what should be a national policy for agriculture.

Agricultural Libraries

Shrimali (1978) expressed the view that the agricultural library is a vital link between research and practice. To control the increasing amount of technical literature, the library must be well administrated, well organized and well developed. The librarian should aim to acquire selectively, books and non-book materials on a wide range of agricultural related topics; provide a good service with both potential and actual in mind, and gain good knowledge of agriculture, related to sciences and languages. They should have the same status and pay scales as the teachers and researchers in the agricultural universities.

Gillian (1980) opined that quantity of existing agricultural information is so large and the variety so diffuse as much research and actions are required to ensure the Aglists know about the available information relevant to their work and can obtain it easily. In addition agriculturalists, particularly those working in applied area of agriculture, need more review articles, which select, collate and evaluate information on specific topics? Periodic reviews evaluating research and development results relevant to practicle agriculture would improve the transfer of information from researchers to agriculturists to require information to be adapted to use on farms.

Deutsch (1981) explains the role of agricultural librarians in assisting weed scientist through appreciating the extent and seriousness of the threat and taking several steps to provide and organize literature that bear the problem.

Thomas (1981) expressed the opinion that Agricultural Research in Nepal is under pressure to help increase food production. Libraries to support this research are found at Khumaltar, Kirtipur, Katmandu and Teral. Descriptions of these libraries are given.

Ranganath, et al. (1981) analyzed the examined information published in the area of Food Science and Technology from India. The experience gained in sending the Indian input to international food information service has also been analysed and the usefulness of such collaboration has been delineated. This analysis also pointed out the areas of most active research in food field based on the information available in published articles.

Rajasekharan (1984) described the situation regarding Kerala Agricultural University Library system, mentioning collection, technical processing, finance and kinds of users served, proposes a structure of Library system contributing network of libraries at three levels with central Library at the apex-suggests the services, staff and teaching processing to be provided by such a network.

Deshpande and Deshmukh (1985) mention the significance of agricultural libraries and their treatment as special libraries. Refers to the number of indexing and bibliographic services in the field of agriculture giving their details. Suggests the coordination of existing indexing and abstracting services and the need for special training in agricultural documentation.

Thomas (1985) reviews the adoption of the CAB (Commonwealth Agricultural Bureaux) thesaurus by the US National Agricultural Library (NAL) in order to standardize the indexing process and facilitate the retrieval of information from the AGRICOLA database.

Mangla (1988) traces the development in the field of agriculture, particularly after the country achieved the Independence. It also examines the developments in the field of agricultural education and establishment of various universities and institutions. Suggestions were given in areas such as: financial resources; National Information System in Agricultural services; Declaration of IARI library as National Agricultural Library; Application of computer in library operations and services.

Rajasekharan, K. (1988) points out the present position in Kerala Agricultural University, inadequacy of library facilities and suggests that centralized system for procurement of foreign agricultural journals can also be evolved for agricultural libraries in the state with a view to minimize cost and avoiding duplication of work.

Gregoric and Sison (1989) state that much progress has been made in the past two decades in agricultural information provision in Southeast Asia. There is now a need to draw finer distinctions when referring to the problems of information transfer in the region. Urban users are now relatively well served, but their rural counterparts at the village/farmer level remain neglected. The use of new information technologies ought to be marshaled for use in developing countries, through these have to be worked into programs using natural development strategies and approaches which have proven to be successful.

Hemasundar Naidu and Gunjal (1989) review the importance of Agricultural library and information services in India. The growth and development of agricultural university libraries are explained. The existing library and information services for agriculture in India are examined.

Shuchum's (1989) paper discusses about various aspects of the Library of the Chinese Academy of Agricultural sciences established in 1957.

Paskoff (1990) emphasized the importance of Agriculture and says that the need for agricultural information has existed for thousands of years. In this paper he traces out the development of various libraries and agencies during different stages of historical development of America.

Hauzner and Janoves (1992) describe about the services provided including access to a wide range of information sources such as special journals and daily newspapers, literature searchers carried out on the polTox III and AGRIS databases on CD-ROM and SDIs which can be set up on current contents. Results of searches are presented either in printed format or on disks. The audiovisual section produces educational and promotional video programmes while the graphics section is responsible for the production of exhibitions, maps and diplomas.

Hemasundar Naidu and Gunjal (1992) report the findings of a comparative study of collections among three categories of Agricultural libraries in India. They observed that books and periodicals available in the National Research Institute Libraries were found to be very high when compared to other categories.

Prasher (1993) describes the importance of agricultural information facility in India for effective research and transfer of technology to the farmers. The library must become a partner in agricultural production not meant only for the scientists but for the farmers also through rural library services. For this, the government should support the libraries with liberal grants, enactment of library legislation and formulating a national policy on information.

Singh and Singh (1993) presented the state of art report on Agricultural college libraries in the Bihar state in terms of collection, usage, finance, staff, services, etc. whereas Stanley (1993) emphasizes the importance of Agricultural Libraries and traces the history of the endeavors to establish a National Agricultural Library in India.

Lal and Singh (1995) trace the history and development of agricultural universities in India and discuss the importance of the libraries of these institutions in acquiring and communicating information to scientists. Their paper describes the different aspects of the Nehru Library at Haryana Agricultural University.

Chottey Lal (1998) traced out the origin and development of agricultural libraries in India beginning with the creation of Department of Agriculture in 1873. The recommendation of various committees having bearing on library matters are also discussed and listed the pathos of agricultural libraries, studies the impact of information technology in the storage and retrieval of agricultural information. The author sees a bright future for agricultural libraries in the growing network of information networks.

Agricultural Information Management

Oviss Oruma (1984) discussed in his article about three basic problems that contribute to the existing complexities in Agricultural Information. One problem is the two levels of operation in agriculture: there exist at present a dichotomy in agriculture largely due to governmental participation in institutionalized agricultural research while traditional agricultural practices remain largely unsubsidized. Another problem is the imprecision of the term "Agriculture". Agriculture has grown so broad that at now includes every remotely related area in addition to what is traditionally known as agriculture. As a result of this the term "Agricultural literature" has acquired an indefinite and imprecise meaning, which creates another problem.

Thorpe (1985) observed that weak information management is a feature of many agricultural research systems in the developed world. Problems identified include lack of coordination, deficiency in communication or research findings, lack of linkages with various other institutions at national and international level and so on. He suggests for improving the situation, emphasizing the high priority, which must be attached to the bibliographic control of the grey literature, produced within the country itself.

Hemasundar Naidu and Gunjal (1989) surveyed all the agricultural university libraries and ICAR institute libraries following the DDC for classification of documents and adopting the second edition of AACR for cataloguing the documents. The author suggests that acquired documents should endeavour to complete the necessary formalities and make the documents available to the users, for avoiding the backlog of technical processing work should immediately update the same using the DDC 20th edition and AACR-II.

Kennedy (1990) reviewed in a broad way, agricultural library trends of 1990s. Although a number of trends could have been selected, those included here were chosen for their deep and permanent impact on Agricultural Libraries.

Olsen and Kennedy-Olsen (1991) describe the efforts made by Mann library at Cornell University to develop electronic collections. The Mann library at Cornell University has received a $550,000 grant from the Rockefeller Foundation to identify the core literature of the agricultural sciences appropriate for education and research in Third World countries.

Samuel (1991) discusses using the A.R. Mann Library as a case study, principles applied instructing a local presentation program and a model for preservation decision-making. Emphasis is on evaluating preservation policies; selection for preservation and administrative considerations in planning, implementing and operating a preservation program. Several representative approaches to this process and a summary of actual preservation policies are presented. Consideration of scale, the relationship of preservation selection to ongoing collection management and development and cooperative preservation are discussed. Methods of integrating preservation decision-making into library process, staff training and a cost analysis of basic preservation treatments are presented.

Bankapur and Kumbar (1993) discuss about the management of technology transfer; research and development policy studies and planning that require qualitative and quantitative data to ensure perfect productivity in any discipline suggest the use of 'Bibliometrics' and 'scientiometrics' tools for measuring the productivity in any discipline. To help in collection development policy. Agricultural Research has been taken as a theme study.

Agricultural Library Building

Deshmukh (1993) discusses about the guidelines for planning a library building and emphasizes the need for healthy collaboration between librarian and architect. He also gives norms for the selection of a site and provides guidelines for planning exterior and interior of the library building, ventilation, air-conditioning and lightning.

Hemasundar Naidu and Gunjal (1993) emphasize the role of the library building in rendering effective service. The study reveals that nearly 40% of agricultural libraries studied possessed independent buildings. It works out the area utilized various library functions. The paper stresses that quite a large number of agricultural libraries need additional floor area to meet its immediate and future requirements. It also suggests that library housed in non-functional buildings should plan for new library buildings on functional lines.

Aswath, L. (1998) traces the development of agricultural education in the Indian state of Karnataka, and founding of University of Agricultural Sciences Library. It describes the planning and various aspects of the new building, which was opened in 1976, and critically evaluates how space is utilized as different functional points.

User Needs and User Studies

Phadnis and Shoiab (1977) outline the present work of Indian agricultural scientists, and their need for published and non-published information. They describe the complexities of some secondary source publications and the problems of information retrieval there from. Suggests the user of computers for providing better services to scientists stresses the need for user training programmes in agricultural libraries.

Yaikava (1981) describes about the importance and activation the Central Scientific Agricultural Library of USSR.

Ranmanna and Gopinath (1982) explained the emphasis given assessing user need by NICFOS before planning and implementing systems and services. NICFOS has always tended to abide by the concept of user orientation for which information is collected by various methods like observation, contact and questionnaire. Besides, a feedback system also has been in corporate to assess the effectiveness of the services and to alter or improve the services.

Deshmukh (1983) presents the results of a survey conducted to evaluate the library resources of the Central Soil and Water Conservation Research and Training Institute, Dehra Dun, through a questionnaire. Survey results, according to him are helpful in improving the quality of existing library facility.

Aina (1985) reports the findings of the survey of the agricultural information needs of farmers in six villages in Nigeria. The important aspects of agricultural information they required and how these requirements are met are explored to make suggestions. It was suggested that libraries should be established in rural areas so as to meet the specific needs of farmers.

Maheswarappa and Trivedi (1986) surveyed the information needs of food scientists and evaluate the services provided to them at CFTRI, Mysore. Results of the study are expected to be of help to those involved in planning and execution of effective information services with field of food science and technology.

Malhotra (1990) studied the relationship between the adequacy of library collections and the amount of daily library use by postgraduate students. Results did not support the hypothesis, that the use of library is directly proportional to the relevance of the library resources to the contemporary needs of the student community.

Sengupta (1990) describes the effects of the information revolution brought about by development of computer and ancillary techniques and equipment for the modification and processing of stored information places the information scientists in an agricultural institute.

Andre (1991) explains the objectives of the National Agricultural Text Digitizing Project. The purpose of this project was to test the feasibility, cost and effectiveness of newly emerging technologies for capturing page images, providing access to their content and disseminating them via CD-ROM.

A variety of issues have been raised regarding the effectiveness of these technologies for developing and disseminating full text databases including the need for a basic low-cost retrieval work station, standards for image material, a standard user interface and the capability to provide long-term archival storage for electronic media. These issues are discussed from the end users viewpoint.

Barile-Frias (1991) explained the role of Agricultural Libraries Association of Philippines (ALAP) to facilitate the transfer of required agricultural information to the extension workers and farmers. As professional organizations are the ALAP brings together not only the librarians but also the resources of the libraries of private and government institutions. A regional approach on information awareness and information delivery is adopted to make information more accessible to the end users.

Frierson and Panline (1991) reported about a major market study was conducted by the CGIAR secretariat and Digital publications to assess the information needs in agriculture in the developing and developed countries and to relate these needs to the potential for CD-ROM products. The survey covered twelve hundred libraries and research centers worldwide.

Isahak (1991) in his paper discussed about the revived Fifth Malaysia Plan (1986-1990) which placed more emphasis on accelerating transfer of technology to increase the awareness about the new agricultural technologies. The use of various mass media technologies for this purpose is also described.

Livingston and Narasimha Raju (1991) explained the importance of agricultural information and its needs to agricultural researchers outlined. The nature of agricultural information required, research facilities and the library and information services available to agricultural researchers in Guntur district of Andhra Pradesh described. Based on the results, a set of conclusions was drawn to enhance the library and information services for the region.

Pozdnjakov (1991) studied the features and functioning of USSR agro-industrial complex. The data obtained are used to improve the libraries acquisition policy, to optimize its collections that will allow us to satisfy the information requests of agricultural scientists and specialists in a more complete and a prompt way. This study allows the creation of an optimal model of collections in a scientific agricultural library.

Kaur (1993) studies the relationship of academic achievement of the postgraduate students (regarded as the independent variable) and the quantum of daily library use (regarded as the dependent variable). Two independent samples of post-graduate students, one each from Haryana Agricultural University, Hisar and Punjab Agricultural University, Ludhiana has been taken. The Spearman's Rank Correlation coefficient has been calculated for the two different sample groups and their results compared.

Monspart (1993) presents the results of a survey of 617 rural agricultural specialists concerning their information needs and their ease of obtaining suitable information. Recommends that a reference system be established for small farms via the agency of public libraries, and that the telecasting movement, widespread in Scandinavian countries, may help the disadvantaged small settlements to join the reference system.

Darko (1995) presents results of a survey of the information needs of research scientists at the Cocao Research Institute of Ghana and the Coca Research Institute at Nigeria, along with the library facilities available to them. Express the hope that the respective libraries will use the surveys to improve their services to the research scientists.

Ozowa (1995) deals with the identification of the nature of small scale farming agricultural input and diffusion of Agricultural Information Technology through extension education. Explores marketing of information needs of farmers and analyses the medium of information dissemination in use. Points out the limiting factors and apart constraints in agricultural information dissemination in Nigeria and suggests to satisfy the needs of farmers with emphasis on traditional media.

Bay-Petersen (1996) discussed about marketing for small-scale farms in Asia and traces out the problems in providing regular timely and relevant information to geographically remote users. What farmers in remote areas need is information about the local centres is by low-cost methods such as display boards in villages. The paper discusses current programmes of this kind in several Asian countries including Indonesia, Taiwan and Japan.

Beavers, Russell and Sibia (1996) provided a systematic review of research studies related to the delivery of information services to agricultural scientists working at remote laboratories in fields. The paper concludes with the discussion of strategies for improving access to information for scientists at remote locations, and with suggestions for future research on this topic.

Ramarao; Muralidhar and Kalla (1996), presented a brief profile of scientific staff in the State Agricultural Universities in India. Interesting differences were found in the activities of scientific staff of different grades. The findings show certain positive and negative features.

Swarnalata and Lahiri (1997) discussed about the purposes for collection of agricultural information in basic area of research conducted by the scientists, various sources and medium used by the scientists for dissemination of research results and their views about the accessibility of agricultural information in the state.

Veeranjaneyelu and Seshagiri Rao reported the findings of the survey the S.C farmers of in their paper. Based on them they have suggested the organisation of different awareness programmes and establishment of rural agricultural information centers in the state of Andhra Pradesh.

User Education

Deshmukh and Deshpande (1991) explains the role of the library in creating awareness and literacy skills among the students, teachers and scientists. In order to make best use of libraries by the clientele, it is necessary to acquaint them with these techniques by way use of User Education Programme / Reader Instruction Programme. There is also need for restructuring of course curricula for library science education to meet the challenges in for the profession.

Stewart (1995) describes the stages in the development of a master plan for user education at the NAL of the US Department of Agriculture (USDA). The purpose of the plan is to enable NAL users to become independent and successful in their use of the library's vast information resources..

Siva Prasad and Gaddigamath (1996) described user education programme organised for Agricultural scientists of NAARM stated about the meaning, objective, course content, faculty resource persons, teaching methodology, evaluation, and future plans of user education programmes.

Agricultural Information

Guha Roy, K. K. (1940) traces out the growth and history of research in agriculture. He mentions about some old and classic books on Agriculture. Further, he suggests preparing a union catalogue of scientific periodicals and books available in India and the cooperation among the libraries in India.

Blanchard, J. (1967) traces the concepts of agriculture, Agricultural Information availability in the library of the Food and Agriculture Organization of the U.N in Rome, National Agricultural Library, Central Scientific Agricultural Library, Moscow. The paper describes sources of Agricultural Information and different branches of Agriculture i.e. Botany, Horticulture and Agronomy, Plant Breeding, Plant Pathology, Animal Sciences, Physical sciences related to agriculture, food and nutrition, Agricultural economics and Rural Sociology.

Phadnis and Rajpal (1974) conducted a general survey of output of literature in the field of Agriculture, to give a complete picture of agricultural research in India. The information facilities available to an agricultural scientist in India are also presented and assessed. Suggestions for new services in the future are also made.

Vashishth (1979) highlights the role played by UNISIST and various other world bodies and commercial concerns in providing technical help and guidelines for the creation and maintenance of necessary infrastructure to handle the information effectively. Discusses in detail the organizational and operational aspect of INIS and AGRIS and their products. Mentions the procedure and mode of communicating input data by India. Makes a case for 'online' availability of information to the Indian scientists.

Chillag (1982) described briefly the value of grey literature and summarizes detailed studies, some relating to the development of AGRIS, carried out by a number of authors during the past 15 years.

Subbaiah (1985) pointed out in his paper that the users play a vital role in an information storage and retrieval system and explains the need to consider users opinions in this regard.

Joshi (1985) analyzed the citations taken from research articles sent to various journals by the staff of the Central Plantation Crops Research Institute during 1983 and 1984. A total 1,114 papers yielded 990 references. The analysis covered different forms of cited documents and cited journals and their frequencies. The citation data was matched with library's journal subscription list. This matching showed that 40% of the subscribed journals were not cited and 50% of the cited journals were not subscribed to. Journals accounted for 70% of the citations. Out of the 213 journals cited, 6.6% earned 38% of the citations. Matching of staff-strength in various subject disciplines with journal subscriptions showed that Animal Sciences and Engineering ranked second and third respectively in the number of journals being subscribed to in these disciplines those formed only 1.7 and 3.1% of the total staff-strength. It suggested that the library's acquisitions policy should take into account these two criteria, i.e., journal use as shown by citations and relative manpower in different subjects.

Samuel; Chiang and Howard (1985) reviewed the reasons for establishing a collection of computer-readable information and a microcomputer facility in an agricultural research library. Their analysis provides an overview of the considerations for selecting microcomputer software and data files for both microcomputers and mainframe computers. Recent developments in standardizing cataloging practices and policies governing loan procedures are also outlined.

Rajasekharan (1989) attempts to work out the seniority based promotion which still continues to be in vogue in many academic libraries in India, and states that it is detrimental to profession and library development as a whole. Here, an attempt is made to work out the details of a meaningful selection procedure for the position of librarian in an Agricultural college, duly emphasizing the advantages of merit-based promotion system. Its implication on the professional status, the educational qualification and qualities required for the aspirant, a proposal for selection test etc, are delineated. Finally, the paper concludes that fixation of a rational criterion for selection of librarian in Agricultural education and consequent Agricultural development of our country.

Udo (1989) gave a description of the situation, in the field of food and agricultural information is given, based on the historical development with special reference to financial development. The relationship between information in industrialized countries is emphasized and examples are given that demonstrate the possibility to improve the exchange of scientific information.

Olsen and Kennedy-Olsen (1991) describe the efforts made by Mann library at Cornell University to develop electronic collections. The Mann library at Cornell University has received a $550,000 grant from the Rockefeller Foundation to identify the core literature of the agricultural sciences appropriate for education and research in Third World countries. The literature identified through this project will be put in full text onto compact disks and made available as core libraries. The core literature will be determined by citation analysis and other bibliometric techniques, including review by scholars in eight subject disciplines. The lists will be published in eight volumes: Agricultural Economics and Rural Sociology, Agricultural engineering, Plant sciences—Basic, Plant Sciences-Applied, Animal Science, Economic Entomology, Forestry and Silviculture and Soil Sciences. Details of the programs, purposes and schedule, subject areas to be included and progress on the compact disk (CD) effort are provided. The bibliometric methods used in determining the core literature in each of the eight subject categories are outlined. The methods for choosing reviewers, determining balance in the lists weighting of reviewer's decisions and threshold levels for removal of titles are covered. The project includes the selection of core literature not only for the Third World, but also for the developed world, and the relationship between these two points-of-view is noted.

Hemasundar Naidu and Gunjal (1992) report the findings of a comparative study of collections by the division of Agricultural libraries in India into three categories. They mention that books and periodicals procured by these libraries have been considered as the core collection and the collection tendencies are studied on the basis of the activities of parent institution. They observes that books and periodicals available in the National Research Institute Libraries were found to be very high when compared to other categories.

Sharma and Murthy (1995) emphasised need for the full use of the wealth of agricultural information generated in India, by processing it into consumer oriented and user friendly forms. They considered the steps required for this, including the diagnosis of user needs, information formats, collection and delivery agencies and management of training programmes, as well as the development of new research programmes to predict future information needs.

Gachie (1996) describes about a survey carried out by BPDA-SCETAGRI, a French consulting company, and its Russian partner, covering private and collective agricultural producers within 3 Russian regions. It was found that producing that disseminating extension documents is needed because there is a shortage of this type of document in the various CIS republics. This survey also showed that the procedures prefer both printed media and direct contacts with the information provider. The experience, both in Central Europe and in Western Europe, indicates the need to setup new information/training services that would be accessible and useful to the Russian and Ukrainian agricultural producers.

Niang (1996) in his paper reviewed the developmental settings of the African, Caribbean and Pacific (ACP) countries and the challenge of agricultural information as well as the role of the Technical Centre for Agricultural and Rural cooperation (CYA) in facilitating the availability and accessibility of information to support agricultural development in the ACP countries.

Damodaran, T and Sambashiva Rao, V. (1998) in their paper, have presented the analysis of the compiled *Bibliography on Doctoral Dissertations in Oilseeds in India* in terms of year wise, crop wise and discipline wise growth of doctoral dissertations during the period 1986 – 96. It examines the bibliographical control of doctoral dissertations.

Hemasundar Naidu and Gunjal (1998) outlined the importance and the components of the agricultural literature. They stressed the need for exchange of publications and discussed exchange relations among the agricultural libraries in India and the type of documents exchanged.

Agricultural Library Networks

Hillary (1978) reviewed a cooperative programme that aimed at providing selective dissemination of information service to three groups of land-grant university scientists working in the area of sorghum researchers undertaken by the Agricultural Research Service and the National Agricultural Library. After one year, analysis of the retrieved citations and user feed back shows that no single database is sufficiently comprehensive in courage in terms of maximum information yield and retrieve ease of effective profile construction. BIOSIS previews and the common wealth Agricultural Bureaus file were the most productive databases.

Stone (1990) reviews the present day information networks, and how they have evolved as result of new information technologies. There is recognition that information networks are not ends in themselves, but rather are critical tools to ensure the exchange, transfer and utilization of information, which will facilitate the increase quality quantity of agricultural production.

Beecher (1991) described the United States Agricultural Information Network (USAIN) is the first organization developed specifically to provide a national forum through which US agricultural librarians might address many issues associated with the collection, access and delivery of agricultural information. USAIN strives to ensure the fullest possible sharing of information and library materials in the most cost effective manner. The success of these efforts will help to ensure equality of access and availability of resources for agricultural information users throughout United States.

Jean-Francois, et al. (1991) describes about a center established to facilitate the establishment and operation of national networks, a reference manual for national bibliography databases, named as BABINAT (Bases de Donnes Bibliographiques Nationales), has been produced by a consortium of French organizations which currently develop information systems in the less developed countries. It is anticipated that the use of BABINAT will spread whole the format itself will be improved and expanded as a result of experience with its utilization.

Smith and Martin (1993) reports the findings of a study done at Pennsylvania State University to survey agricultural extension personnel in terms of their use of university library resources. Describes the procedure and notes that Pennsylvania State University is looking at this system as a prototype for future document delivery services.

Howard (1994) refers to the National Agricultural Library (NAL), Washington, DC, as the world's foremost Agricultural Library. He mentions the libraries holdings the largest collection of agricultural sciences. He describes its collection; automated management access to the collection and Caricola highlights the application of expert systems, hypermedia technology, text digiting, image transmission and other projects and programmes. His research points out search programmes through 14 information centres.

Addison and Cullen (1996) explains about the Natural Resources Institute (NRI) disseminates information on research and new techniques in natural resources management to developing countries.

Haavisto and Ofversten (1996) describes the features and activities of that the Agro net. In Agro net, the conceptual idea of networking is taken further to a practical level. This real network connects the main suppliers and users of information services in Finnish Agri-business. It is based on the integration of the latest information technology.

Thomas (1989) opined that informal networking has been a tradition in the agricultural information community. In the last five years, however the National Agricultural Library has worked assiduously to bring a formal organization into being. National Agricultural Library's efforts have led to the formation of the United States Agricultural Information Network (USAIN), an association whose goal is to provide a forum for discussion of agricultural information issues.

FINDINGS OF EARLIER STUDIES

From a review of the previous studies presented in this chapter, the following conclusions may be drawn:

- Most of the previous studies are descriptive in nature which only described and analyzed information resources in agricultural institutions.
- The areas covered in the studies include history and development of the library, management, resources and staff, physical facilities, finances, user, application of modern technology, proposals for agricultural information systems and networks and user education programmes.

- User surveys dealt with mainly the information seeking behaviour needs and demands of various user groups such as scientists, faculty and extension workers in agricultural institutions, government departments, research and development centres and societies.
- Some of the surveys on library use are also concerned with effects of factors like nature of the user's job, experience, qualifications, type of institution, number of subordinates, the user work place, access to the library collection and use of other channels on the use of the agricultural library.

The gaps identified in previous research on agricultural libraries include: exclusion of students from user surveys; study about fee based service, links with other organisations etc; partial coverage of the agricultural libraries in India and Andhra Pradesh; Users opinion on library staff and use of computers, Internet, E-mail & CD-ROMS etc.

As can be seen from the review of literature, most of the studies on the use of agricultural information are confined to western countries. Not much research has been conducted at the doctoral level on the services and facilities of agricultural libraries and information centres in India.

Of the few research studies, Subbaiah (1985) surveyed the information needs and information seeking behaviour of users i.e. scientists from eleven universities connected with teaching, research and extension in the agricultural field. He also made a study of 41 agricultural libraries out of a total of one hundred seventeen in the country and framed a model for Indian National Agricultural Information System (INAGRIS). The remaining three studies confined themselves geographically to the state of Andhra Pradesh. Veeranjaneyulu (1997) made a comparative study of facilities of the existing agricultural information system in Andhra Pradesh and explained a model for a comprehensive network of these systems and libraries. His study covered only scientists and libraries from sixteen institutions related to agriculture and of a total of seventy five. On the other hand Sugunavathi (1997) surveyed the Subject Matter Specialists (SMS) working in the Training and Visit (T&V) system of the Department of Agriculture, Government of Andhra Pradesh functioning in all the 23 districts of A.P. in order to identify their information requirement and to develop suitable strategies to meet them. The fourth study by Eswar Reddy (1982) also covers Agricultural extension workers of Department of Agriculture , Government of Andhra Pradesh.

THE PRESENT STUDY

1. The present study is not a simple descriptive study but, aims at evaluating the existing facilities and services in the agricultural libraries using parameters like extent of their use, usefulness to users, users' preferences for them, degree of

dependency on them for various purposes and users assessment of these facilities in terms of their adequacy coverage, currency and convenience.

2. Besides collecting the basic details about various aspects about the library the present study tries to assess the readiness and suitability of the present library environment to incorporate new methods, procedures and services.

3. Previous studies have not focused on the aspect of charging the library services and facilities and the users' attitudes towards paid services. This study focuses on this crucial aspect of modern library management.

4. The present study also attempts to review the impact of technology on the agricultural libraries in Andhra Pradesh, which aspect has not been covered by previous studies.

5. It also focuses light on other sources outside the library in meeting the information needs of users. It also attempts to find out alternative sources of information outside the Insititutions library that would be of use in meeting user requirements.

METHODOLOGY

India is essentially an agrarian society and basically depends on agricultural outputs. It is therefore essential that the technology thrust should lay greater emphasis on the transfer of scientific and technological information from the research institutes to its actual users, who constitute to a large extent the farmers in rural areas. Libraries and Information Centers are playing a very important role in providing information to the users by building print and electronic collections. In India, however, direct application of computerized, information systems to the farmers is not feasible in the present setup.

Andhra Pradesh, the fifth largest state in the country with a total gross cropped area of 39.44 lakh hectares is one of the most progressive states in agricultural development. Appreciable work has been carried out in agricultural development through agricultural education, research and extension activities of the institutions, centres and research schemes established in various districts. The agricultural researchers in all these wings need to be provided with proper and timely information in their respective fields. Production in the state depend extensively on their skill and knowledge in developing techniques for its enhancement.

The present study covers agricultural scientists, faculty, research students and post graduate and under graduate students of various agricultural institutions and organisations. The term agricultural-scientists cover administrators, research scientists and extension workers who strive to develop the economy of the state. Even though agricultural research and developmental activities have been carried out since quite a long time in Andhra Pradesh, a comprehensive study surveying all the users and all the aspects of agricultural information facility has not been done so far. The present study attempts to review the information services provided to agricultural information users in

Andhra Pradesh and to suggest certain steps for the betterment of such services.

The purpose of the study is to investigate through a survey, the organization of agricultural libraries and information facilities in Andhra Pradesh and to evaluate them keeping in view the findings made through user surveys.

Objectives of the Study

The main objectives of the present study are:

1) To survey the existing agricultural libraries and their infrastructure facilities.
2) To identify the various types of information facilities catering to the needs of agricultural education, research and extension activities in Andhra Pradesh.
3) To study the infrastructure, management, staff, services and resources of these information centers and libraries.
4) To study the existing facilities if any for resource sharing and cooperation among the various centers and to examine the possibility and modeling for setting up a cooperative network.
5) To study the information needs of various user groups concerned with the agricultural field and the type of services required to meet them.

Methodology and Data Collection

The study covers two major areas:

a) Organisational and administrative aspects of Agricultural libraries in Andhra Pradesh, including an evaluation of their infrastructure resource and facilities.
b) Information needs and requirements of two levels of users viz., Students of Agricultural Colleges and Faculty / Scientists / Research students of agricultural university, ICAR Institutes, Central Government Institutes, International Agricultural agency, ANGRAU and its Research stations (RARS and ARSs), Krishi Vignan Kendra and of their use of agricultural library and information facility.

The Institutions selected in this survey are related to Agricultural Education, Research and Extension which have specific objectives towards contributing to the universe of knowledge in agriculture.

Survey of Libraries

The survey of agricultural libraries is based mainly on data collected from the forty six agricultural librarians through a questionnaire schedule. The researcher made visits to these forty-six agricultural libraries and observed the prevailing conditions.

Data regarding the various aspects of the library including material and physical resources, manpower, links with other libraries and data bases etc. were gathered through a data sheet. Information on other areas like fields of interest, budget, origin, clientele, librarian's qualifications, their experience, scale, publications, and knowledge of foreign languages, details of library staff, physical facilities, collection, dependency on other libraries for additional information, information services, Computer applications, professional training programmes, further plans, problems encountered in the management of libraries as identified by the librarians, opinions and suggestions for improving the existing libraries has been collected through a detailed questionnaire-I.

Survey of Users

The data for the present study was mainly obtained by circulating two types of questionnaires II and III to users.

The questionnaire-II war meant for students of Agricultural University and Colleges. The purpose of this questionnaire was to obtain information concerning the purpose and frequency of visits to the library; average number of hours spent in the library per week.

Use of other libraries; ranking of library material according to their usefulness, opinion regarding the collection and existing services and frequency of use of the available services, means and ways of finding required information; opinion regarding the library rules and regulations; borrowing privileges, etc.

Questionnaire-III was administered to Scientists / Faculty/ Research students of Acharya N.G. Ranga Agricultural University (ANGRAU) and its colleges, Indian Council of Agricultural Research (ICAR) Institutes, Central Government Institutes, Agricultural Research Stations of ANGRAU, Krishi Vignan Kendras (KVKs) and District Agricultural Advisory and Transfer of Technologies Centres (DAATTCs).

The purpose of this questionnaire was to obtain information regarding:

Purpose and frequency of visits to the library made by the faculty, Research students and Scientists; Number of publications / contributions of Faculty, Research students and Scientists; User dependency on the library for publishing purpose; Extent of users' dependency on other sources; Opinions on various aspects of the library, such as physical facilities, rules etc.; Maintenance and usefulness of library catalogue; Methods used to find required material in the library; opinions on borrowing privileges and the existing issuing system; library staff and library timings; Computer knowledge skills and need for user training in the use of computers; Access to Websites; Availability and extent of use of computer, Internet and E-mail facility out side the library; Users' Suggestions regarding all aspects of the information facility.

Personal visits were also made to all the above centers/stations to gather, verify and obtain clarification regarding the responses to the questionnaires.

Sample Selection

The two issues related to the sample selection for this study are:

i) Selection of the Agricultural Institutions like University, Colleges and Research Institutions situated in Andhra Pradesh.

ii) Selection of the users (Scientists, Faculty, Research students, P.G. and U.G Students) within these Institutions/Agricultural University and its Colleges.

The criterion adopted for selecting the Agricultural Institutions was that, they were first sent data sheets and latter on those institutions that did not respond to them were eliminated from this study. The Selected Institutions in the study includes Acharya N.G.Ranga Agricultural University and its Agricultural Colleges, Regional Agricultural Research Stations and Agricultural Research Stations, District Agricultural Advisory and Transfer of Technology Centers (DAATTCs), ICAR Institutes, Central Government Institutes, Krishi Vignan Kendras of ICAR, Agricultural University and NGOs located in Andhra Pradesh.

Initially 89 Institutions were requested to furnish brief particulars of existing library facilities. Out of the 89 institutions only 46 responded. The sample of 46 libraries surveyed includes libraries of Agricultural University, Agricultural Colleges, Regional Agricultural Research Stations, Agricultural Research Stations, ICAR Institutions and Central Government Institutions located in Andhra Pradesh (Table-9)

Table 9
Sample of Libraries

S. No.	*Category of Agricultural Libraries*	*Total Number of Libraries*	*Distributed sample*	*Response*
1.	International agency, Central Government Institutions, State Government	5	5 (100%)	5 (100%)
2.	ICAR Institutes	9	9 (100%)	9 (100%)
3.	Agricultural University & Colleges	7	7 (100%)	7 (100%)
4.	Regional Agricultural Research Stations (ANGRAU)	7	7 (100%)	5 (100%)
5.	Agricultural Research Stations (ANGRAU)	61	61 (100%)	20 (100%)
	Total	89	89 (100%)	46 (100%)

The study is concerned with two types of populations namely libraries and users. There are 89 libraries associated with agricultural institutions excluding those dealing with veterinary sciences, fisheries and home science. The organisations associated with agro-based industries, banks and other trade organisations related to agriculture and allied subjects are also not included in the sample.

The agricultural institutions have 920 scientists, 298 faculty members, 94 research students, 347 Post Graduate students, 1850 Undergraduate students at the time of present survey. Each of these groups were taken as unit, in attempting to ascertain details about their information seeking behavior.

Using the stratified random sample technique with proportional allocation, a 25 percent sample is collected for the survey of post graduate and undergraduate students. Regarding faculty a sample of 50 percent is choosen since the faculty is involved in both teaching and research. Regarding Research students, cent percent enumeration is carried out since the population size is small. The sampling distribution and their response rates are shown in Table-10.

Table 10
Sample of Users

S. No.	*Users*	*Total strength*	*Distributed sample*	*Response*
1.	Scientists	920	230 (25%)	184 (20%)
2.	Faculty (7 Agricultural Colleges)	298	149 (50%)	133 (45%)
3.	Research Students	94	94 (100%)	94 (100%)
4.	Post Graduate Students	347	87 (25%)	69 (20%)
5.	Under Graduate Students	1850	463 (25%)	400 (22%)

The data collected from users was analyzed with the aid of a computer, while the data collected from the 46 librarians was analyzed both manually and with the aid of computer. Further the data collected through questionnaires was supplemented with information obtained through personal visits and observation. After the analysis of data suitable tables were drawn and the percentages were calculated. Classification of data into different groups was done where ever appropriate. Chi-square technique is applied to test the statistical validity of the findings wherever applicable.

4

Analysis of Data

A detailed study of agricultural information facility in Andhra Pradesh assures great significance. The analysis and presentation of data was done under two major heads i.e. 1. Libraries survey, 2. User Survey consisting of i) Students Survey and ii) Scientists, Faculty and Research Students survey.

The data for the present study was mainly obtained through 3 questionnaires distributed to 1) Agricultural libraries of the Acharya N.G. Ranga Agricultural University and its colleges; Research institutes / Stations libraries of ANGRAU, ICAR and Central Government; 2) Under- graduate and Post graduate students of ANAGRAU and 3) Scientist, Faculty and Research students of ANGRAU; ICAR Research Institutes and State & Central Government Research Institutes situated in Andhra Pradesh.

LIBRARIES SURVEY

This part of the chapter deals with the analysis of the data collected from the librarians of the agricultural libraries situated in Andhra Pradesh. The areas mainly covered in this section are origin and growth of libraries, organizational structure of library systems, administrative arrangement, location and type of personnel served, library staff, budget and expenditure, area, building and equipment, library access, issuing systems, average number of regular users, subjects covered and other aspects like links with other libraries, problems encountered, future plans of librarians etc.

Categories of Agricultural Libraries

Several categories of Agricultural libraries are working in different government and non-governmental agencies at different levels. Each one of these libraries has a set of distinctive objectives and scope to meet the information requirements of the specified group of users.

Table 11
Categories of Libraries

Category of Agricultural Libraries in A.P.	*Total No.of Libraries*	*Libraries surveyed (N=46)*
International Agricultural library Agencies	1	1 (2.17%)
State & Central Government Institute Libraries	4	4 (8.69%)
ICAR Institutes libraries	9	9 (19.57%)
Agricultural University & College libraries	7	7 (15.22%)
Regional Agricultural Research Station libraries	7	5 (10.87%)
Agricultural Research Station libraries	61	20 (43.48%)
Total	89	46 (100%)

As shown in Table-11, the majority of libraries (43%) are located in Agricultural Research stations. The next highest percentage is libraries of ICAR Institute (nearly 20%). Only one library covered in the survey is having the library of international scope. i.e. International Crops Research Institute for Semi-Arid Tropics (ICRISAT), located at Hyderabad.

Field of Interest

a) *Major Divisions*

As seen in the above table, there are different libraries and information centers working at different levels with varied objectives and scope in Andhra Pradesh. In order to know the thrust area of coverage by these libraries, information has been gathered. The details about the thrust areas of these libraries are provided in the Table 12.

Table 12
Major Divisions (more than one)

Major Divisions	*No. of. Libraries (N=46)*
Agriculture	46 (100%)
Home Science	2 (4.35%)
Veterinary	2 4.35%)
Ag. Research Management	1 (2.17%)
Crop Production, Protection, improvement	1 (2.17%)
Agricultural Extension	2 (4.35%)

It is observed from the table that majority of the libraries are concentrating on agriculture as major thrust area. In addition to agriculture, very few of these libraries are also maintaining collections on the allied subjects of agriculture.

b) *Major Subjects*

Having agricultural science as the main thrust area, libraries are concentrating on building collections to support education and research on more specialized aspects of agriculture. The table below shows specialized areas of agriculture covered by the libraries surveyed.

Agronomy (35%) and plant breeding (33%) are the specialized areas on which majority of the libraries are concentrating. Next to these two specializations, Horticulture is found to be the area of interest. In addition to this, 21 percent of the libraries are focusing mainly on Entomology and Plant Pathology each. These findings generally reflect major areas of research going on in agricultural sciences at various centers of agricultural education, research and extension Andhra Pradesh.

Table 13
Major Subjects (more than one)

Major subjects	*No. of libraries (N=46)*
Plant breeding	15 (32.61%)
Genetics	9 (19.57%
Agronomy	16 (34.78%)
Entomology	10 (21.74%)
Agricultural Extension	3 (6.52%)
Tobacco Research	2 (4.35%)
Soil Science	9 (19.57%)
Agricultural Economics	3 (6.52%)
Tobacco Research	2 (4.35%)
Soil Science	9 (19.57%)
Agricultural Economics	3 (6.52%)
Agricultural Statistics	2 (4.35%)
Plant Pathology	10 (21.74%)
Plant Physiology	4 (8.70%)
Horticulture	12 (26.09%)
Agricultural Engineering	3 (6.52%)
Veterinary Science	2 (4.35%)

Budget for the Institution

Libraries, big or small, need adequate finance to provide efficient user services. Financial allocation may be made basing on the estimates prepared by the librarian, keeping in view of the previous year's expenditure. Budget is the major deciding factor in deciding the efficiency of overall library functioning and its services. To assess the financial status of the libraries surveyed relevant data about the budget of the parent institutions has been collected. Out of 46 libraries surveyed, only 32 libraries responded for this question, hence 'N' varies in this table. The Table 14 reveals the amount allocated to the institution every year.

Table 14
Budget for Institution

Budget in lakhs	*No. of Institutions (N=32)*
0-10	13 (40.63%
10-20	5 (15.63%)
20-30	5 (15.63%)
30-40	0 (0%)
40-50	1 (3.13%)
50 and above	8 (25.00%)
Total	32 (100%)

Majority of institutions (41%) to which libraries are attached are allocated below Rs.10 lakhs. Twenty five percent of the institutions have more than Rs.50 lakhs allocation of funds. An equal percent of libraries (15%) are receiving Rs.10 to 20 lakhs and 20 to 30 lakhs.

Organization and Administration of Agricultural Libraries

The areas covered in this section include origin and growth of libraries, structure of library, systems, administrative arrangement, location and type of persons served, library staff, library budget and expenditure, area, building and equipment, library access, issuing systems, user and issue statistics and linkages with professional associations etc.

Origin & Growth of the Libraries

The emergence of agricultural libraries on the horizon of special libraries is comparatively of recent origin, compared to other special libraries. Majority of the agricultural libraries (33%) surveyed were established between 1981 and 1990. The second highest percentage of libraries (22%) were established before 1960s. Of the 46 libraries, only 6 libraries (17%) were founded during 1971-80 (Fig.2). The oldest library covered in the survey is the Regional Agricultural Research Station (RARS), Lam, Guntur, established in 1906 and the library of the most recent origin is Agricultural Research Station, (ARS), Petlur., established in 1996.

Among the ICAR institute libraries in Andhra Pradesh, the oldest one covered in the survey is the Central Tobacco Research Institute (CTRI), Guntur, established in 1936 and the library of the most the recent origin is the National Research Center for Oil-Palm, Pedavegi.

Among the libraries of Agricultural University and colleges in Andhra Pradesh, the oldest library is Agricultural college Library at Bapatla., established in 1945 and the most recent one is that of Agricultural Engineering College, Bapatla, established in 1994. A.P. Agricultural University library was established in 1964.

Thirty-six libraries responded to this question hence 'N' varies in this table. Table-15 indicates the distribution of libraries decade wise based on their origin or the year of establishment.

Table 15
Year of Establishment of Libraries

Year of establishment	*No. of Libraries (N = 36)*
Before 1960	8 (22.22%)
1960-70	5 (13.89%)
1971-80	6 (16.67%)
1981-90	12 (33.33%)
After 1990	5 (13.89%)
Total	36 (100%)

Among the libraries serving at Regional Agricultural Research Stations, the oldest Library is RARS, Lam, Guntur, established in 1906 and the most recent one is RARS, Jagityal, established in 1985.

Among the libraries of Agricultural Research Stations (ARS) of APAU., the oldest one is, Agricultural Research Station, Vizianagaram, established in 1954 and the most recent one is ARS of Petlur., established in 1996.

Library Users

'Users' are the most important components of a library. Any facility planned or activity taken up will be decided basing on the user composition and their nature. With this aim in mind, the data has been gathered regarding the type of users and their number in different libraries. The N (total) in the Table 16 i.e. 7 represents only the libraries attached to the University and colleges consisting students and research students as users.

Table 16
Number of Users (Students and Research Students)

No. of Libraries	*No.of Users*		
	UG (N=7)	*PG (N=4)*	*Research Students (N = 6)*
Below 100	3 (42.86%)	2 (50%)	4 (66.67%)
101-200	1 (14.29%)	0 (0%)	2 (33.33%)
201 & above	3 (42.86%)	2 (50%)	0 (0%)
Total	7 (100%)	4 (100%)	6 (100%)

Data analysis from Table16 shows that an equal percentage of the libraries (43%) have users below 100 and above 200 Under Graduate (UG) students. Likewise, an equal percentage of the libraries (50%) below 100 and above 200 Post graduate students (PG) 67% of the libraries are found to be serving the research students below 100 in number.

Table 17
Number of users served (Faculty, Scientists & others)

	No. of Libraries		
Users	*Faculty (N=7)*	*Scientists (N=33)*	*Others (N=11)*
Below 25	5 (71.43%)	27 (81.82%)	8 (72.73%)
26 and above	2 (28.57%)	6 (18.18%)	3 (27.27%)
Total	7 (100%)	33 (100%)	11 (100%)

Among the libraries surveyed, only 7 of them have users comprising of teachers (faculty) and 33 have users comprising of research scientists and are serving other than Agricultural University and college students, Research associates/fellows etc, Trainees from State/central government and Tobacco officials.

Seventy one percent of the libraries are serving faculty below 25 in number. Only forty percent have more than 25 faculties to be served. Among the libraries serving, scientists eighty two percent of the libraries (80%) have only below 25 Research students.

Library Staff

The reputation of a library very much rests on the activities like quality of services offered to readers, building the collections keeping in view, the requirements of its users, processing and organizing the acquired documents and information to facilitate easy access.

However good its physical sources are, library will be able to function as an effective information dissemination centre of an organization, only if it has adequate and qualified library personnel. Details of the library staff are given below.

Table 18
Total Staff of the Library

Library staff	*No. of libraries (N=46)*
1-10	42 (91.30%)
11-20	2 (4.35%)
21 and above	2 (4.35%)
Total	46 (100%)

Highest percentage of the libraries are found to be having less than ten staff members. Only two libraries are served by 10-20 staff. Another two have above 20 library staff.

Academic Qualifications of the Librarians

Information on educational background of librarians has been presented to know whether the persons managing the libraries have the required professional qualifications or not. Twelve of the forty six librarians are professionally qualified in Library and Information Sciences (Table-19).

Table: 19
Qualifications of the Librarians

Qualifications	*No. of. Libraries (N=46)*
BLISc	4 (8.70%)
MLISc	7 (15.22%)
ADIS	1 (2.17%)
Other Qualifications	34 (73.91%)
Total	46 (100%)

Analysis of data reveals that 74 percent of the in-charge librarians are non-professionals. Only 24 percent of the librarians are having professional qualifications

Among them, four (9%) have Bachelor of Library & Information Science (BLISc) degree and seven (15%) hold Master of Library & Information Science (MLISc) degree. Out of the seven librarians having MLISc., four have post graduate qualifications in another subject and one has post graduate Diploma in Library and Automation Networking and one M.Phill at Agricultural College, Bapatla. Out of the four librarians having BLISc, two have Post-Graduate Degrees in another subject. One of the librarians (2%) with ADIS also has a Post-graduate degree.

The librarian should have professional qualifications as per UGC standards. He or she must be assisted by a group of semi and non-technical staff. Sometimes the library staff may include supporting staff having some technical documentation and reprographic skills. Table-19 shows the qualifications of library staff surveyed.

Knowledge in the use of Computers

Out of the forty-six librarians reported, only two stated that they have knowledge in computer applications. Only one of them has a professional qualification in LIS.

Experience of Librarians

The experience of the librarian in the organization has also been considered as one of the factors, which may affect his job performance. Following table presents data on years of experience of the librarians surveyed.

Table 20
Experience of Librarians

Experience in years	*No. of Librarians (N=46)*
Below 5 years	12 (26.09%)
6-10 years	4 (8.70%)
11-15 years	9 (19.57%)
16-20 years	8 (17.39%)
21 and above	13 (28.26%)
Total	46 (100%)

Data analysis indicates that most of the librarians (nearly 28%) have an experience of more than 21 years. The next highest percentage (26%) is of those who have less than 5 years. Only 9 percent of them have an experience of 10 years.

Publications of the Librarians

Professional activities of the libraries reveal how far they are active and involved in their profession. One of such activity is communicating their professional experience in the form of publications to other fellow professionals. Table-21 and Table-22 reveal details regarding this aspect of librarians surveyed.

Table 21
Publications of the Librarians

Publication	*Librarians (N = 46)*
Yes	15 (32.61%)
No	31 (67.39%)
Total	46 (100%)

Only 33 percent of the librarians stated that they have publications to their credit. Majority of them (67%) do not have any kind of publications to their credit. Following table shows number of publications the librarians have.

Table 22
Number of Publications by the Librarians

No. of Publications	*Librarians (N=15)*
Less than 5	7 (46.67%)
6-10	3 (20%)
11-15	1 (6.67%)
15-20	3 (20%)
21 and above	1 (6.67%)
Total	15 (100%)

Forty seven percent of the librarians have less than 5 publications to their credit. An equal percentage (20%) of librarians have 6–10 and 15-20 publications respectively. An equal percentage (7%) of the librarians have between 11-15 and above 20 publications respectively.

Knowledge of Foreign Languages

The international nature of knowledge makes it available in various languages. For the user not well versed with all the languages or at least some of the languages, language becomes a barrier. It is the responsibility of the librarian to help the user in this context. As a professional, it is expected from a librarian, he should know at least one or two foreign languages other than English. The following table provides details of librarians having foreign language skills.

Table 23
Knowledge of Foreign Language-Librarians

Knowledge of Foreign language	*No. of Librarians (N=46)*
Yes	2 (4.35%)
No	44 (95.65%)
Total	46 (100%)

Data in the Table-23 indicates that out of forty-six librarians, only two librarians have knowledge in foreign languages. Out of the two librarians with knowledge in foreign language, one knows French and the other German. However, these two are not professional librarians.

Categories of Library Staff

The library staff has been divided into four main categories. They are—i) Professionals, ii) semi-professionals, iii) Supporting staff; and iv) Non-technical staff.

Professional staff are normally called as subject specialists. They have professional qualifications in the field of Library and Information Science. They are involved in planning and control activities. They identify the library and user needs, analyze the problems, set goals, plan activities to satisfy the information needs of the users and objectives of the library. Librarian, Deputy Librarians, Assistant Librarians will come under the category of professional staff. Semi professional staff will have only certificate in library science qualification.

Table 24
Categories of Library Staff (more than one)

	No. of libraries having			
No. of Library Staff	*Professional staff (N= 12)*	*Semi Professional staff (N=14)*	*Supporting staff (N=9)*	*Non-technical staff (N=12)*
1.	4 (33.33%)	7 (50.00%)	6 (66.67%)	5 (41.67%)
2.	2 (16.67%)	3 (21.43%)	3 (33.33%)	2 (16.67%)
3.	2 (16.67%)	1 (7.14%)	0 (0%)	1 (8.33%)
4 and above	4 (33.33%)	3 (21.43%)	0 (0%)	4 (33.33%)
Total	12 (100%)	14 (100%)	9 (100%)	12 (100%)

Data analysis in Table-24 indicates that highest percentage of libraries (33%) have only one professional staff. An equal percentage of libraries (16%) are run by two or three professional staff. Fifty percent of libraries have one semiprofessional staff. Among the libraries having supporting staff, majority (66%) have one non-technical staff. However, 33 percent have 4 and above non technical staff.

Professional staff of the library are identified with designations like Librarians, Deputy Librarians and Assistant Librarians. Designation for semi-professional staff includes Technical Assistant, Senior Library Assistant, Senior Library Assistant and Junior Library Assistant. Support staff includes staff assistant, Xerox operator and binder. Attenders and sweepers will come under non-technical staff.

Scale of pay of the library staff

The University Librarian is equal in status to a university professor and is in the same pay scale. There is no Deputy Librarian, but his grade is equal to that of an Associate Professor. Similarly, Assistant Librarians are in the same pay scale as that of Assistant Professors.

The findings of the survey revel that out of 46 agricultural libraries, only one librarian is in a rank equal to a University Professor.

i) Scale of Professional Staff:

University Librarian : 16,400-450-20,900-500-22,400

Deputy Librarian : 12,000-420-18,300

Assistant Librarian/ College Librarian : 8,000-275-13,500

(ii) Semi Professional Staff:

Technical Assistant : 5000-150-5300-170-6150-200-7150-250-8400-300-9600

Senior Library Assistant : 4190-120-4550-150-5300-170-6150-200-7150-200-8400- 300-8700

Junior Library Assistant : 3290-80-3450-100-3950-120-4550-150-5300-170-6150- 200-6550

(iii) Supporting Staff:

Xerox operator and Binder : 2780-60-3050-80-3450-100-3950-120-4550-150-5300-170 5470

(iv)Non-technical Staff

Attender, Sweeper : 2780-60-3050-80-3450-100-3950-120-4550-150-5300-170 5470

Physical Facilities

Physical facilities like area, seating capacity, building, location and internal facilities will influence the image and reputation of library. They also play a crucial role in making the library exterior and interior comfortable, functional and attractive. The following sections will describe various facilities available in the libraries surveyed.

Area of the library

Allocation of adequate space for the library plays an important role in serving the users effectively. All the details are not furnished by all libraries. Information about floor area was given by 19 libraries about stack area by 7 librarians, about work area for staff by 5 libraries, about reading room facility by 5 libraries and about the area for other facilities by only 2 librarians. Data collected in respect of the plinth area of the libraries surveyed is given in the Table-25.

The plinth area occupied by eleven of the libraries is less than 150 Sq.mts. The other eight libraries are located in a plinth area of more than 150 sq.mts.

Five libraries had provision of separate rooms for library. The stack area occupied by four of the libraries is below 5 sq.mts. Among the others, three libraries have stock area of more than 50 sq.mts.

Five libraries have the provision of separate rooms for library staff. Two libraries mentioned that they are equipped with other facilities i.e. Air Conditioning, Photocopying facility and Library Automation.

Table 25

Physical Facilities of the libraries (area in sq.mts) Number of Libraries

Sq. Mts.	*(i) Floor area (N-19)*	*(ii) Stack area (N=7)*	*(iii) Area for staff (N=5)*	*(iv) Other facilities (N=2)*	*(v) Reading Room (N=5)*
Below 50	5 (26.32%)	4 (57.14%)	05 (100%)	2 (100%)	4 (80%)
51-100	3 (15.79%)	2 (28.57%)	0 (0%)	0 (0%)	0 (0%)
101-150	3 (15.79%)	1 (14.29%)	0 (0%)	0 (0%)	0 (0%)
151-200	1 (5.26%)	0 (0%)	0 (0%)	0 (0%)	1 (20%)
201 and above	7 (36.84%)	0 (0%)	0 (0%)	0 (0%)	0 (0%)
Total	19 (100%)	7 (100%)	5 (100%)	2 (100%)	5 (100%)

Analysis of data in Table-25 indicates that five libraries gave details about reading room facility. Four of the five libraries have reading facility of less than 50 Sq.mts. in area. Only one library has an area between 151 and 200sq.mts for reading room. MANAGE library has an Air-conditioned reading room.

There are published standards and guidelines for space planning in special libraries in general and in particular for Agricultural libraries which provide separate space requirement for different purposes. The details about space allotted for different purposes in the eight libraries are not available. Chapter-2 covers details about various standards suggested by different committees.

Seating Capacity

Provision of reading room space is one of the primary features of any library. Data regarding this aspect in forty six libraries is given in table-26.

Table 26
Distribution of Libraries by Seating Capacity of reading space

No. of Seats in the Library	*No. of Libraries (N=46)*
1-15	32 (69.57%)
16-30	5 (10.87%)
31-45	4 (8.69%)
46 and above	5 (10.87%)
Total	46 (100%)

Data analysis in the above table indicates that nearly 70 percent of the libraries have seating capacity to accommodate users ranging from 1 to 15. The highest capacity to accommodate 46 and above is found in only 5% of the libraries surveyed. Another 10 percent stated that they have the capacity to accommodate 16 to 30 users at a time.

Library building

Library Building plays a vital role in meeting the overall objectives of the library in an efficient manner. Especially provision of separate or exclusive space or accommodation will have lot of implications on the functioning of libraries.

Table 27
Library building

Building	*No. of. Libraries (N=46)*
Separate building	4 (8.69%)
Part of the other building	42 (91.31%)
Total	46 (100%)

Above table shows that only 9 percent (nearly) of the libraries have separate building and 91 percent of the libraries are situated in other buildings.

Location of the library

Extent of the use of a library facility is closely associated with its location. Frequent visits to the library by users are made if it is located in a convenient and approachable location.

Table 28
Location of the Libraries

Location	*No. of. Libraries (N=46)*
Centrally located	26 (56.52%)
Not centrally located	20 (43.48%)
Total	46 (100%)

Analysis of data in the Table 28 shows that 56 percent of the libraries surveyed are centrally located. However, 43 percent libraries are not located in a central place causing inconvenience to users.

Future Plans Regarding the Library Building

Library, as a growing, needs some future planning, especially in terms of physical facilities like library building. It requires provision for expansion and modifications. The following table explains future plans of librarians regarding the building.

Table 29
Future Plans Regarding the Library Building

Future Plans	*No. of. Libraries (N=21)*
Increase floor area	3 (14.28%)
Separate building	4 (19.05%)
Computerisation & Networking	6 (28.57%)
A.V. Material	5 (23.81%)
Air Conditioning	3 (14.28%)
Total	21 (100%)

Twenty one of the libraries indicated their future plans regarding different aspects. Among them, 6 (29%) of the librarians have plans to introduce Networking &

computerization of library with LAN. Twenty four percent of the librarians (24%) have plans to introduce audio visual reading room. Another 19 percent are planning to have a separate building for library. 14 percent of the librarians have plans to air-condition the library and to increase the floor area of the library.

Library Budget and Expenditure

Libraries, big or small, need adequate finances to provide minimum facilities and efficient user services. Financial allocation may be done based on estimates prepared by the librarians or based on Institution's turnover or adhoc allocations with or without demand.

Library Budget

In order to know the financial position of the libraries surveyed, data regarding library budget has been gathered.

Table 30
Total Budget for the Library

Amount Rs.	*No. of Libraries (N= 46)*
Upto 1 lakh	27 (58.70%)
1-25 lakh	16 (34.78%)
25 lakh and above	3 (6.52%)
Total	46 (100%)

Analysis of data shows varying trends in the budget allocation to the libraries surveyed. Majority of the libraries getting up to 1lakh budget allocation every year. However, majority of libraries are found to be receiving upto Rs.25,000 per year only as budget allocation. Nearly 35 percent of the libraries are yearly provided with the amount ranging between 1 lakh and 25 lakh. Very few (7%) have allocations of more than 25 lakh per year.

In spite of ICAR's recommendations, the situation about the actual expenditure on the agricultural libraries is as bad as in the case of general university libraries. There does not seem to be any reason why the library budget cannot be provided to the extent accepted by ICAR.

The Indo-American Agricultural Library Survey and Team recommended that at least 6% of the total operating budget of each institute or university be allocated to the library for its annual operation. Ramaiah committee which reviewed the recommendations of the Survey Study Team have changed the words 'at least' to about. The recommendations, as accepted by ICAR now read as follows; "It is recommended that about 6 percent of the total annual recurring budget of each institute or university be allocated to the library for its annual operation."

Table 31
Percentage of Library Budget in Total Budget

% of library budget in total budget	*No. of libraries (N=11)*
Below 0.5	6 (54.55%)
0.5 – 1	2 (18.18%)
1 and above	3 (27.27%)
Total	11 (100%)

Analysis of data in the Table shows that more than half of the libraries (55%) indicated that the percentage of library budget in total budget is below 0.5 percent. Above one quarter (27%) of libraries indicated 1 and above percent. Only 18% of libraries indicated that the percentage of library budget in total budget is between 0.5 and 1.

Libraries, big or small, need adequate finances to provide efficient user services. Financial allocation may be alone based on estimates prepared by the librarians or based on institution allocation with or without demand. Budget allocation may be item-wise or lump sum.

Table 32
Allocation of Library Budget

Budget	*No. of libraries (N=46)*
Item-wise	13 (28.26%)
Lumpsum	33 (71.74%)
Total	46 (100%)

Analysis of data in Table-32 shows that large number of libraries (72%) have lump sum budget. 28 percent of the libraries indicated that they have item wise budget.

Expenditure

Expenditure of allocated amounts is always dependent on proposals prepared and also on the amount sanctioned. Most of the libraries have not responded to this question. Percentages are calculated only for the number of libraries responded. Expenditure made on books, periodicals, A V materials, information services etc. by different libraries has been presented in Table 33.

Table: 33
Amount Spent per year on an Average

	No. of Libraries						
Amount (Rs).	*Books (N=13)*	*Periodicals (N=10)*	*AV material (N=2)*	*Electronic Equipment (N-1)*	*Inf. Service (N=3)*	*Binding (N=4)*	*Any other (N=6)*
Upto 10,000	3 (23.08%)	2 (20%)	1 (50%)	0 (0%)	2 (66.67%)	4 (100%)	4 (66.67%)
10,001- 1,00,000	7 (53.85%)	3 (30%)	1 (50%)	1 (100%)	1 (33.33%)	0 (0%)	2 (33.33%)
1,00,001 –5,00,000	2 (15.38%)	1 (10%)	0 (0%)	0 (0%)	0 (0%)	0 (0%)	0 (0%)
5,00,001 – 10,00,000	0 (0%)	2 (20%)	0 (0%)	0 (0%)	0 (0%)	0 (0%)	0 (0%)
above 10,00,000	1 (7.69%)	2 (20%)	0 (0%)	0 (0%)	0 (0%)	0 (0%)	0 (0%)
Total	13 (100%)	10 (100%)	2 (100%)	1 (100%)	3 (100%)	4 (100%)	6 (100%)

Books: Only thirteen libraries responded for this questionnaire. Among these libraries nearly 54 percent of libraries spent Rs.10,000 to 1,00,000 amount on books. Only one library (nearly 8 percent) spent above Rs.10,00,000.

Periodicals: Only ten libraries responded to this questionnaire. 30 percent of the libraries allocated an amount of Rs.10,001 to 1,00,000 on periodicals.

AV Material: Only two libraries spent for AV material. Among those 50 percent of libraries spent in between Rs.10,000 to Rs.1 Lakh.

Electronic equipment: Only one Agricultural college library (Bapatla) spent an amount between Rs.10,001 to 1,00,000.

Information services: Only three libraries spent on information service. Nearly 67% the libraries spent unto Rs.10,000 and 33 percent of the libraries, between Rs.10,001 to 1,00,000.

Binding: All the libraries have spent an amount below Rs.10,000 on binding.

Any other: Six libraries spent an amount for other miscellaneous expenditure. Nearly 67% of the libraries stated that they have spent up to Rs.10,000 for office maintenance and servicing. 33 percent of the libraries spent an amount upto Rs.10,000 for photocopying service.

Library Collection

Collection development is one of the primary functions of Agricultural libraries. The range of subjects covered is determined by the objectives of the Physically, the collection of Agricultural libraries may include a variety of materials, all of which may not be available in an agricultural library. The collection comprises books, dissertations and theses, periodicals, indexing, abstracting and other services, year books, reports, directories, external and internal technical reports, research and archival materials, patents, specifications, audio-visual material and special collections like maps, manuscripts, catalogues etc.

The present study covered the resources of the library both printed and non-printed materials. Data regarding these sources is analysed item wise and group wise where feasible. Information provided by the librarian regarding major categories of information services is given below.

Books

The collection of books in the forty six libraries surveyed has been classified under three groups. The number of libraries are distributed among these groups, depending on the total book strength of each library.

Table 34
Distribution of Libraries by No. of Books

No of Books	*No of libraries (N=46)*
Below 25,000	42 (91.30%)
25,000 – 50,000	3 (6.52%)
Above 50,000	1 (2.17%)
Total	46 (100%)

The Table-34 indicates that most of the libraries (91%) have below 25,000 books. 6.52 percent of the libraries have between 25,000-50,00 books and only 2.17 percent of libraries have above 50,000 books.

Periodicals and CD ROM databases

Periodicals, as sources of latest information assume much significance in institutions where research is the major activity. Details of the number of current periodical are grouped into three categories.

Table: 35
Distribution of Libraries by No. of Periodicals and CD-ROMs

Number of Periodicals / CD -ROM databases	*No. of libraries (N=46)*	
	Periodicals	*CD - ROM*
Below 25	34 (73.91%)	5 (10.87%)
Above 25	12 (26.09%)	2 (4.35%)
Not available	0 (0%)	39 (84.78%)
Total	46 (100%)	46 (100%)

Table-35 indicates that 74 percent of the libraries have about 25 periodicals and 26 percent of the libraries have above 25 periodicals. Majority of the libraries (85%) are not having CD-ROM data bases. Eleven percent of libraries have below 25 CD-ROM databases. Four percent of libraries have above 25 CD-ROM databases.

Table 36
Distribution of Libraries by Number of Pamphlets, Microforms, Theses/ Dissertations, AV Material and Other Items

	No. of Libraries (N=46)				
	(v) Pamphlets (N=20)	*(vi) Micro forms (N=3)*	*(vii) Thesis/ dissertation (N=10)*	*(viii) AV Materials (N=6)*	*(ix) Other (N=16)*
Below 500	19 (95%)	2 (66.67%)	7 (70%)	6 (100%)	11 (68.75%)
Above 500	1 (5%)	1 (33.33%)	3 (30%)	0 (0%)	5 (31.25%)
Total	20 (100%)	3 (100%)	10 (100%)	6 (100%)	16 (100%)

It is evident from the Table 36 that only 20 libraries have pamphlets, 3 microforms, 10 thesis/dissertations and 16 other items as part of their collection. The table also indicates that 95% of libraries out of 20 have below 500 pamphlets only 5% of the libraries have above 500 pamphlets. Among libraries having other collection, 31 percent have above 500 annual reports and news letters.

Microforms

Microfilming of reports and back issues of periodicals in particular, was undertaken mainly for convenient storage, maintenance of file integrity, cheapness of reproduction and ease of transmission. Only three of the libraries have microforms in their collection, ranging from 1 to above 500 microforms. Nearly 67% of the libraries have below 500 microforms. Thirty three percent of the libraries have above 500 microforms.

Theses/dissertations

Theses and dissertations are primary sources of information containing the findings of original research work. The thesis and dissertations pertinent to Agrobiological subjects are of importance to agricultural scientists. Only seven libraries reported that they have thesis and dissertations. Analysis of data in the table-31 shows that majority (70%) of the libraries have less than 500 thesis and dissertations and only 30% of the libraries are having more than 500 thesis and dissertations.

Audio-visual materials

Besides printed forms of information, non-book materials i.e., audio visual materials also became effective source of information in the last three decades. Only six libraries reported of having audio-visual materials like video cassettes, films, audio-cassettes and slides as part of their collection. Only six of the libraries reported of having audio and visual material. All the six libraries have below 500 Audio and Visual material.

Annual acquisition

Annual additions of different types of materials to the existing collections will indicate the growth of the collection quantitatively year wise.

Books, Pamphlets, Monographs

On an average, the collection of books, pamphlets and monographs per year in the forty six libraries surveyed has been classified under four groups. The number of libraries is distributed among the groups, depending on the total collection of each library.

Table 37

Annual Acquisition of Library Collection on an Average of Books, Pamphlets and Monographs

Acquisition of Books, pamphlets and monographs	*No. of libraries (N=13)*
Below 100	5 (38.46%)
101 – 200	1 (7.69%)
201-300	3 (23.08%)
301 and above	4 (30.77%)
Total	13 (100%)

Only 13 librarians have responded to this question out of which nearly 38 percent of libraries are annually on an average acquiring below 100 books, pamphlets and monographs whereas 30 percent of the libraries have indicated the annual acquisition of above 300 books, pamphlets and monographs. Varying quantity of books, pamphlets and monographs are added annually to the existing collection by different libraries surveyed depending on their yearly budget allocation.

Library collection also increases in the form of various other information sources like periodicals (general), Indexing and abstracting periodicals, microforms, CD-ROM collections etc. Usually any periodical, whether primary or secondary, is acquired through annual subscription only. All the issues of the periodical will be acquired by the library. It is natural that the number of back issues /volumes will be automatically added to the reference collection. Though other collections may not grow on par with books, one can observe significant additions in the form of modern electronic information sources. Regarding the annual acquisition of periodicals, indexing/Abstracting, Review periodicals, microforms, CD -ROM and other material in the forty six libraries surveyed has been classified under three groups.

Table 38
Annual acquisitions of Library Material Periodicals, Indexing/Abstracting Review Periodicals, Microforms, CD - ROMs and others

	Number of libraries				
Annual acquisition	*(iv) Primary Periodicals (N-23)*	*(v) Indexing/ Abstracting/ review Periodicals (N=10)*	*(vi) Microforms (N=1)*	*(vii) CD -ROMS (N=8)*	*(viii) others (N=4)*
1-10	6 (26.09%)	7 (70%)	1 (100%)	7 (87.50%)	2 (50%)
11-20	4 (17.39%)	1 (10%)	0 (0%)	0 (0%)	0 (0%)
21 and above	13 (56.58%)	2 (20%)	0 (0%)	1 (12.50%)	2 (50%)
Total	23 (100%)	10 (100%)	1 (100%)	8 (100%)	4 (100%)

Periodicals

Nearly 57 percent of the libraries have above 20 of the annual acquisition of primary periodicals. Twenty six percent of the libraries have upto 10 periodicals. Seventeen percent of the libraries are subscribing on an average of 11 to 20 periodicals.

Indexing / Abstracting / Review periodicals

Seventy percent of libraries have indicated the annual acquisition of 10 indexing/ Abstracting/Review periodicals. Twenty percent of the libraries have indicated above 20

Indexing/ abstracting/Review periodicals. Ten percent of libraries have indicated between 11-20 Indexing/Abstracting/Review periodicals.

Microforms

Only one library is found to be having less than 10 of the annual acquisition of microforms.

CD-ROMS

Among total number of libraries only eight libraries indicated that they are having CD-ROM collections. Majority of them have only below 10 of the annual acquisition of CD-ROMS. One library is found to be having 21 and above CD- ROMS.

Others

Others represented collection in the form of annual reports, trade catalogues, reprints, newsletters and house bulletins. Fifty percent of the libraries have up to 10 annual reports, bulletins and Trade catalogues where as another fifty percent are having more than 20 of these materials in numbers.

Methods of acquisition

Books

Books are procured by libraries through various channels. Procurement may be through local booksellers, or directly from publishers, exchange or through as gifts. Sometimes a combination of more than one of these methods may be followed for procuring books.

Table-39 indicates the prominent ways of acquiring of books in the agricultural libraries surveyed.

Table 39
Acquisition Methods of Books (more than one)

Method	*No. of libraries (N=46)*
Local Booksellers	24 (52.17%)
Directly from publishers	25 (54.35%)
Exchange	12 (26.09%)
Gift	19 (41.30%)

Analysis of data shows that 54 percent of the libraries are acquiring books by directly placing order to publishers. Fifty two percent of the libraries have also stated that they are depending on local book sellers. Forty one percent of the libraries have also required books as gifts. Only 26 percent are found to be getting books through exchange. Libraries are depending equally on both local book sellers and the publishers for the purchase of required books and other materials.

Periodicals

Methods of acquiring vary from library to library. There are different modes of acquisition—subscription, membership, gift or exchange. Usually libraries acquire different journals through a combination of more than one of these methods. The following table indicates prominent mode of acquisition of periodicals among the libraries surveyed.

Table 40
Method of Acquisition of Periodicals
(more than one)

Acquisition Method	*No. of libraries (N=46)*
Subscription	22 (47.83%)
Membership	13 (28.26%)
Gift	16 (34.78%)
Exchange	7 (15.22%)

Analysis of data shows that nearly 48 percent of the libraries are acquiring periodicals by subscription. 28 percent of the libraries are having membership in various National and International organisations and enjoy the privileges. Nearly 35 percent of the libraries are also found to be acquiring them in the form of gifts.

Dependency on Other Library Resources

It is a known fact that at any time one single library cannot be self sufficient to satisfy all the requirements of all the users. Due to various factors it is not possible and at the same time need not be expected from a library. Whenever there is a demand for some information on information source not available in the local library, it is responsibility of the concerned library, some how to make it available to the user. Maintaining information about and contact with other libraries is a prerequisite for providing such services. There are various mechanisms to offer such a facility. For example, Inter Library Loan services, Online access to other library resources, etc. Details regarding the extent of dependency on other libraries for satisfying the requirements of users are presented in the following table for further analysis.

Table 41
Dependency on Other Library Resources
(more than one)

Other libraries	*No of libraries (N=46)*
a) Other university libraries	19 (41.30%)
b) Public libraries	2 (4.35%)
c) Government libraries	7 (15.22%)
d) Agricultural libraries outside the state	14 (30.43%)
e) Other Agricultural university libraries	16 (34.78%)
f) ICAR libraries	24 (52.17%)
g) Others	6 (13.04%)

As per the analysis of data, majority of libraries (52%) depend on ICAR libraries within the state, followed by 41 percent of the libraries depending on other university libraries. Thirty five percent of the libraries depend on other Agricultural University libraries. Thirty percent of the libraries depend on other agricultural libraries other than Agricultural University libraries outside the state. Dependency on libraries of State and Central Government departmental libraries were seen only among fifteen percent of of the libraries. 'Others' category includes NGO libraries, virtual libraries on internet and British Council Library.

Links with other Libraries

As already discussed in the previous section, libraries which are responsive to their user demands, naturally will make efforts to get the information from any other source. In order to be effective in these efforts, they have to maintain contacts with other libraries and sources and cooperate with them for mutual benefit.

Table 42
Links with other Libraries

Links with other libraries	*No of libraries (N=46)*
Yes	26 (56.52%)
No	20 (43.48%)
Total	46 (100%)

Analysis of data in the Table-42 shows that 56 percent of the libraries have links with other libraries. However, significant percentage i.e., 43 percent of the libraries exhibited passive attitude in maintaining contacts with other libraries.

Table 43
Details about the Links

Details about the links	*No of libraries (N=26)*
Mentioned	20 (76.92%)
Not mentioned	6 (23.08%)
Total	26 (100%)

Seventy seven percent of the libraries mentioned the details about the links. Those libraries stated to be having links with other libraries, have clearly mentioned the names of other libraries and centers. They include ICAR institute libraries, ICRISAT, HYLIBNET, British library; ANGRAU libraries, Palm-Oil Research Institute of Malaysia (PORIM), CCMB and INSDOC. Majority of the libraries surveyed are found to be utilizing sources and services of the above institutions through conventional methods.

Services offered by the libraries

Libraries are service oriented institutions, the resources of which are utilized and exploited to provide best possible services to users. Some of the services are provided in anticipation of the users requirements and some on demand from the users. All libraries may not offer all types of services.

Table 44
Information Services Offered by Libraries
(More than one)

Name of the services	*No. of libraries (N=46)*
Reference service	26 (56.52%)
Bibliographic service	23 (50%)
Photocopying service	14 (30.43%)
Indexing / Abstracting service	9 (19.57%)
Translation service	1 (2.17%)
Referral service	11 (23.91%)
Inter Library lending service	10 (21.74%)
Any other	6 (13.02)

Regarding the services offered by the libraries surveyed, much variation is seen among the libraries except in terms of reference service. The reference service is found to be a common service offered by all the libraries surveyed. Besides reference service, half of the libraries are offering bibliographic service. Photocopying services are provided by 30 percent of the libraries. It is found that only one library (2 percent) is offering translation service.

Reference Service

Reference service is transforming into the shape of information service. In simplest terms, the reference service is the personal assistance rendered by the librarian to individual readers in pursuit of knowledge of information. Reference work broadly includes the identification, location and supply of information demanded by the users. It may be in the form of long range service or short range service or both.

Table 45
Types of Reference Services offered by the Libraries

Types of reference service	*No of libraries (N=26)*
Long Range	10 (38.46%)
Short Range	11 (42.31%)
Both	5 (19.23%)
Total	26 (100%)

Analysis of data in the Table 45 shows that majority of them (42%) stated that they are offering short range reference service. However, 38 percent of the libraries also are providing long range reference service. Only 19 percent of the libraries are offering both short range and long range reference service.

Bibliographic service

Provision of bibliographic services includes the preparation of bibliographies on specific subjects or simple lists of references or lists of references with abstracts or combination of more than one of the above items. Usually, such types of services are offered on demand.

Table 46
Types of Bibliographic Services offered by the Libraries

Service	*No. of Libraries (N=23)*
On Demand	13 (56.52%)
In anticipation	10 (43.48%)
Total	23 (100%)

Bibliographic service is offered by 23 of the libraries surveyed. Almost 57 percent of the libraries are found to be developing bibliographies only on demand from users whereas 43 percent are preparing bibliographies in anticipation and keeping them ready for the sake of users. As a part of this service, bibliographies and documentation lists on specific subject are compiled based on the literature available in the library.

Bibliographies

Out of the 46 libraries, 23 libraries are found to be involved in preparing bibliographies.

Table 47
Number of Bibliographic prepared by Libraries Per Year

No. of. Bibliographies prepared by libraries	*No. of Libraries (N=23)*
1-50	19 (82.61%)
51 and above	3 13.04%)
Total	23 (100%)

Out of 23 libraries, majority (83%) are preparing below 50 bibliographies per year on an average. However, 13 percent of libraries are preparing more than 50 bibliographies on an average in a year.

Documentation List

Table: 48
Frequency of Documentation list

Documentation list	*No. of Libraries (N=15)*
Regular	9 (60%)
Occasional	6 (40%)
Total	15 (100%)

Among those libraries preparing documentation lists (15 libraries out of 46%), 60 percent are found to be preparing documentation lists on a regular basis with three types of frequencies fortnightly, monthly and yearly. 40 percent of the libraries are offering documentation lists occasionally.

Periodicity of Documentation Lists

As mentioned above, only 9 libraries stated that they are preparing documentation lists on regular basis.

Table 49
Periodicity of Documentation List

Periodicity	*No. of. Libraries (N=9)*
Fortnightly	3 (33.33%)
Monthly	2 (22.22%)
Yearly	4 (44.44%)
Total	9 (100%)

Majority of the libraries are found to be preparing documentation lists on an yearly basis. 33 percent are compiling the lists for every 15 days and monthly compilations are noticed only by 22 percent of the libraries.

Contents of Documentation Lists

Table 50
Contents of Documentation Lists

Contents	*No. of Libraries (N=15)*
Only reference	10 (66.7%)
Reference with abstract	3 (20%)
Only title	2 (13.33%)
Total	15 (100%)

The Table 50 gives details regarding the contents included in the documentation list. It is found that majority (67%) of them are preparing only simple lists of reference where as 20 percent are providing even reference with abstract. Still 13 percent are only listing the titles of articles as documentation lists.

Photocopying Service and Translation Service

Photocopying service and translation service are offered by only 30 percent and 2 percent of the libraries respectively. Charges for photocopying for one exposure ranged from p.0.50 to Rs.1.00. 43 percent of the libraries are charging p.0.50 per exposure for both students and research scholars.

Table 51
Charges for Photocopying Service

Rates charged	*No. of libraries (N = 14)*		
	Students (N=12)	*Research Students(N-12)*	*Faculty / Scientists (N=14)*
0.50p	6 (50%)	6 (50%)	9 (64.29%)
0.75p	3 (25%)	3 (25%)	1 (7.14%)
Re.1 and above	3 (25%)	3 (25%)	2 (14.29%)
Free service	0 (0%)	0 (0%)	2 (14.29%)

An amount of Rs. 0.50 is charged for teachers and scientists by 64 percent of the libraries. 25 percent and 7 percent of the libraries are charging Rs. 0.75 to students and scholars and teachers and scientists respectively. Even some of the libraries (25%) are charging Rs.1.00 and more. None of the libraries having photocopying facility are found to be offering free service to students and scholars. But only 14 percent of them are providing this service free of cost to the teachers and scientists. It is also noticed that some libraries (7%) charging Rs.0.75ps per exposure for non book materials like reports articles, patents etc. otherwise it is only Rs.0.50ps per copy.

Indexing and Abstracting Service

Services in the form of indexing / abstracting are offered by only 20 percent of the libraries though they are maintaining reasonable collection of periodicals.

Referral Services

Referral services are found to be offered by 24 percent of the libraries.

Inter-Library Loan Service

Since no library can acquire every thing published which is of interest to the users, a well organised inter-library loan service is a must in every agricultural library. Exchange of publications of interest, developing contacts with other libraries for receiving publications of interest gratis, developing contacts with other librarians and information centers for receiving reprints and photocopying copies of articles of inter-library lending services and publication exchange programmes should be done properly.

Table 52
Inter-Library Loan Service

ILL Service		*No. of Libraries (N=10)*
Average no. of documents received	1 – 25	5 (50%)
	Above 25	5 (50%)
Average no. of documents supplied	1 -25	6 (60%)
	Above 25	4 (40%)

Nearly 22 percent of the libraries are offering inter-library loan service. An equal number of (50%) libraries received below 25 and above 25 documents per year through Inter library loan service. A large number (60%) of libraries supplied below 25 documents per year. 40 percent of the libraries are supplied above 25 documents per year through Inter library loan service.

Utilization of Union Catalogue for Inter-Library Loan Service

To satisfy the information requirements which could not be met with locally available resources, libraries can make arrangements to procure required document or information from other libraries. Libraries participating in such a programme are required to use a catalogue representing the collection of all the participating libraries. Only 10 out of 46 libraries are offering Inter-library loan service.

Table 53
Utilization of Union Catalogue for ILL

Utilization of Union catalogue	*No. of Libraries (N=10)*
Yes	5 (50%)
No	5 (50%)
Total	10 (100%)

Among the libraries offering inter library loan facility, 50 percent are using union catalogues to identify the availability of specific items in other libraries. Others are either enquiring informally about the availability of items over phone or sending the requests directly to the libraries without any kind of enquiry.

Number of Libraries covered under Inter-library Loan

Table 54
Number of Libraries covered under ILL

ILL	*No. of Libraries (N=10)*
1-10	6 (60%)
10 and above	4 (40%)
Total	10 (100%)

Analysis of data in the table-54 shows that majority of libraries (60%) are covering 10 or less number of libraries for inter library lending service. The remaining 40 percent of the libraries are found to be contacting more than 10 libraries for this purpose.

Publication brought by the Libraries

Publishing of in-house-bulletins, library newsletter and journals is not a new phenomenon in libraries. Their publications communicate various activities of the library to the members of the organisation. Some libraries may publish them in regular intervals or some may not follow any specific periodicity.

Table 55

Publications brought by the Libraries

No. of Publications	*No of libraries (N -=12)*
1-5	11 (91.67%)
6 and above	1 (8.33%)
Total	12 (100%)

Only 12 libraries have responded to this question. Majority of them are found to be bringing out publications of some type, ranging one to five. They include library brochures, pamphlets, newsletter and bulletins. Only one library is found to be publishing more than six publications.

Binding Facility in the Library

Binding is one of the important activities to be taken up by the libraries for maintaining stock for longer periods of use. Maintaining a separate Binding section is expensive and small libraries cannot afford it. Instead, outsourcing the binding works is considered to be more economical for them. However, libraries with large collections, and having provision to procure hundreds of books every year, need a separate binding section for the reason that it is more cost benefit and effective than outsourcing.

The necessity for binding of reading material arises in every agricultural library because: (i) to avoid damage from miscellaneous handling, (ii) to fight against wear and tear, (iii) to avoid shabbiness, (iv) to preserve perishable and frail material, and (v) to tie the issues of a volume of the journal together. Details about availability of this facility are given in the Table 56.

Table 56

Binding Facility in the Library

Binding facility	*No of libraries (N -=46)*
Yes	8 (17.39%)
No	38 (82.61%)
Total	46 (100%)

Analysis of data in the above table shows that very few (17 percent) of the libraries have their own binding facility. The remaining 83% of the libraries are sending their library materials to private binders for binding, whenever there is a need.

Stock Verification

Periodic verification and rectification of stock is a must for libraries to identify mutilated, missed and unused items in the collection and to keep the collection up to date and in a proper helpful sequence. The items which need binding and chemical treatment are also identified for necessary further action. Obsolete and less used items can be separated from the collection in demand and may be organized as dormitory collections.

Table 57
Number of Libraries doing Stock Verification

Stock Verification	*No of libraries (N =46)*
Yes	29 (63.04%)
No	17 (36.96%)
Total	46 (100%)

Analysis of data in the Table-57 indicates that majority of the libraries (63%) are found to be doing stock verification. However, nearly 37% have so far not done stock verification.

Table 58
Frequency of Stock verification

Frequency	*No. of libraries (N=29)*
Annually	13 (44.83%)
Occasionally	16 (55.17%)
Total	29 (100%)

Among those libraries stated to be verifying the stock, nearly 45% are doing it annually and the remaining (55%) are doing the stock verification occasionally.

Processing of Materials and Procedures Followed

Cataloguing of books

Cataloguing of books and preparation of entries, filing of entries in catalogues cabinet, are all part of processing activity. The findings of the survey revealed that majority of the libraries (76%) are not doing cataloguing of books. Only 24% are cataloguing books systematically using standard codes. Among them, 91% are preparing dictionary catalogue using Anglo American Cataloguing and Classified Catalogue Code (CCC). Remaining libraries are maintaining accession wise list of books in the form of registers (72%). Alphabetical listing of books noted down in the register is also in practice in 16% of the libraries. The collection in the form of non book materials is mostly shown as alphabetical lists in all the libraries surveyed.

Table 59

Catalogue Code used for Books

Catalogue Code	*No. of Libraries (N=11)*
AACR II	10 (90.91%)
CCC	1 (9.09%)
Total	11 (100%)

Only 11 libraries are cataloguing their collection. The remaining libraries are not maintaining any catalogue. Among them, nearly 91 percent of the libraries are following AACR II for cataloguing the books. Only 9 percent of libraries followed CCC for this purpose.

Table 60

Physical Form of the Catalogue for Books

Physical form	*No. of Libraries (N=35)*
Card form	2 (5.71%)
Register / Book form	33 (94.29%)
Total	35 (100%)

Register or book form of catalogue is found to be most prevalent form of catalogue followed by majority of the libraries (nearly 94%) surveyed.

Scheme of Classification

Classification of books assists in the arrangement of books on shelves of libraries. Libraries may follow any type of classification scheme for this purpose. Some may not follow the classified sequence for the shelf arrangement. Alternate methods like accession number wise arrangement, alphabetical sequence, subject wise arrangement or combination of one or more of these methods may be used.

Table 61

Classification Scheme followed by the Libraries

Classification scheme	*No. of Libraries (N=13)*
DDC	7 (53.85%)
UDC	6 (46.15%)
Total	13 (100%)

Only 13 libraries are using classification schemes. Among the libraries, 54% are following DDC for classification of books and 54% are following UDC. Remaining libraries are found to be following different other methods for shelf arrangement. Only 2% of the libraries are arranging the books accession number wise whereas 3% libraries are following subject wise arrangement.

Table 62

Method of Organising Books on Shelves

Method	*No. of Libraries (N=33)*
Accession Number	15 (45.45%)
Subject-wise	18 (54.54%)
Total	33 (100%)

Subject-wise shelf arrangement of books is followed by majority of the libraries that are not classifying the collections according to a scheme. However, 45.45 percent are adopting accession number wise arrangement of books on shelves.

Indexing of Periodicals and Serials

Only 17 libraries are responded to this question.

Tables 63

Indexing of Periodicals and Serials

Indexing	*No. of Libraries (N=17)*
Periodical as whole just like book	13 (76.47%)
Indexing of articles	4 (23.53%)
Total	17 (100%)

Analysis of data in Table 58 shows that only 76 percent of the libraries are classifying back volumes of just like books periodicals; 24 percent of libraries are creating indexes for the contents of the periodicals.

Computerization

Using computers for performing library operations has become an order of the day in modern society. They enable them to provide better services with added quality and efficiency. To know the impact of computers on the existing agricultural information facility, pertinent information is gathered and analyzed in the following Tables.

Use of computers in Libraries

All the 46 libraries have responded to this question. But the response is not encouraging.

Table 64
Use of Computer in Libraries

Using computer	*No. of Libraries (N=46)*
Yes	13 (28.26%)
No	33 (71.74%)
Total	46 (100%)

The responses show that majority (72%) are still following the manual methods and are not using computers.

Areas of Computerization

Computers can be employed for various operations in libraries and literature shows evidences of its benefits enjoyed by libraries over manual methods.

They may cover the entire house keeping operations and information services or some of them. The following table indicates the areas of computer application in those libraries using computers.

Table 65
Areas of Computerization (more than one)

Areas	*No. of Libraries for Books (N=13)*
a) Acquisition	6 (46.15%)
b) Circulation	5 (38.46%)
c) Serial control	4 (30.77%)
d) Database creations	10 (76.92%)
e) Information services	8 (61.54%)
f) Library Publication	4 (30.76%)

Highest percent of libraries (77%) are using computers and other technologies for database creation for information storage and retrieval followed by usage for providing information services (61%). Computers are also used for acquisition, circulation and serial control by 46 percent, 38 percent and 30 percent of the libraries respectively.

Details about computer software and hardware used

Majority of the libraries are using Windows-98 as the software part; and Pentium-2, 386 and 486 processor and Pentium-pro 200 MHz processor and the Celeron 400 MHz processor as the hardware part in the automation of the libraries.

Advanced facilities like Internet, E-mail and Networking

Besides automating their routine housekeeping activities, libraries can also take advantage of modern computer and telecommunication technologies like Internet, E-mail and networking facilities for providing wide access to information and facilitating better communication and exchange of information. The details about provision of these facilities by the libraries surveyed have been presented in the following table:

Table 66
E-mail, Internet and Network

	No. of libraries having		
Advanced facility	*E-mail (N=46)*	*Internet (N=46)*	*Network (N=46)*
Yes	13 (28.09%)	13 (28.26%)	7 (15.22%)
No	33 (71.91%)	33 (71.91%)	39 (84.78%)
Total	46 (100%)	46 (100%)	46 (100%)

The analysis shows that majority of the libraries surveyed did not have Internet connectivity. Only 28 percent of the libraries have Internet connectivity, though 28 percent are offering E-mail facility. Separate E-mail facility is not provided by any of the libraries. Almost 85 percent of the libraries are not being connected in the local area network. Online contacts are maintained by 15 percent of the libraries via Internet.

Charging for the Services offered by the Libraries

Revenue generation is also considered to be one of the important responsibilities of library management. As an alternative source of income, some of the services may be charged by the libraries. Details of libraries charging their services are given in Table 67.

Table 67
Charging for the services

Charging the services	*No. of libraries (N=46)*
Yes	5 (10.87%)
No	41 (89.13%)
Total	46 (100%)

Only 11 percent of libraries are charging for subject bibliographies, reprography, library bulletins, literature search, CD-ROM search, Internet and E-mail services.

However, 89 percent of the libraries are not charging for any services. Though Internet connectivity is there in 13 libraries, only 5 libraries are found to be charging for browsing the Internet and using E-mail facility.

User Education/ Training/ Orientation Programmes

Besides maintaining collections and offering services, it is the responsibility of the library to orient, educate and train the users to create awareness about and develop skills in the use of latest information sources and facilities available in the library. Otherwise, optimal use of library resources and services may not be possible. Table –68 shows the efforts made by the libraries in this regard.

Table 68
Conduction of User Education Programmes

Conduction of user education programmes	*No. of libraries(N=46)*
Yes	13 (28.26%)
No	25 (54.35%)
No response	8 (17.39%)
Total	46 (100%)

It is observed that only 28% of libraries are organizing user education/ training/ orientation programmes for their users. 54% of the libraries stated that they have not conducted any such programmes. Moreover, 17% of the libraries have not responded to this question. The reason may be, librarians or library in charges of these 17% may not be aware of such programmes.

Table 69
Conduction of User Education/Training/Programme – User Levels (more than one)

Programme offered to:	*No. of libraries (N=13)*
Students	7_(53.85%)
Research students	4 (30.77%)
Faculty	4 (30.77%)
Scientists	7 (53.85%)

Only 13 of the 46 libraries are providing conduction/ organizing/ training/ orientation programmes. 54 percent of the libraries are reported to have conducted training programmes on internet, CD search for scientists. 54 percent of the libraries are conducting orientation to fresh students on Internet for agricultural information communication. Equal percent of libraries (31%) are conducting orientation and training on CD-searches to the research scholars and teachers respectively.

Conducting User Surveys

Before planning or offering any service or facility, it is always better to know and understand what actually the library user wants and demands. There are different direct and indirect methods of assessing the needs of users. Survey method is one type of direct method which collects the opinions, ideas and attitudes of users directly.

Table 70
Conducting of User Surveys by Libraries

User surveys	*No. of libraries (N=46)*
Yes	15 (32.61%)
No	25 (54.35%)
No response	6 (13.04%)
Total	46 (100%)

Majority of the libraries (54%) are not conducting any survey to study the information needs of their users. 33 percent of the libraries have stated that they are conducting user surveys occasionally whenever there is a need. 13% of the libraries have not responded to this question may be due to ignorance of the importance of conducting such surveys or not having interest in them or lack of infrastructure to conduct such surveys.

Future Plans

Every prospective library and librarian will have some vision for improving the existing library services. This involves long term planning considering the past, present and future of different aspects of the library. Planning for optional utilization or available resource and identifying the ways and means of trapping alternate source is also an important aspect of future planning.

Table 71
Future Plans about the Libraries

Future Plans	*No. of libraries (N=46)*
Yes	23 (50%)
No	12 (26.09%)
No response	11 (23.91%)
Total	46 (100%)

Half of the libraries surveyed have positively responded to the question of future plans for improving the existing library facilities and services. However, 26 percent of libraries have stated that they do not have future plans. It is also observed that 24 percent of the libraries have no idea about their future plans.

Libraries which are active and optimistic about the future development of their libraries have also pointed out the areas where the plans were made for improvement and change.

Table: 72
Future Plans of the Libraries (more than one)

Future plans	*No. of Libraries (N=23)*
Automation	12 (52.17%)
E-mail, Internet	3 (13.04%)
Creation of database	1 (4.35%)
Air Conditioning	1 (4.35%)
New building, Furniture and equipment	3 (13.04%)
To subscribe more journals	6 (26.09%)
Computerized books	1 (4.35%)
Software	1 (4.35%)
Local Area Network	4 (17.39%)
CD Net	1 (4.35%)
Reprographic service	1 (4.35%)
No funds	1 (4.35%)

Analysis of data on future plans of different libraries surveyed reveals some interesting findings. Majority of them (52%) are planning to go for library automation, which is a positive sign for the overall development of the existing information facility. The second highest percentage of the libraries are interested in subscribing to more number of journals. In addition to these, 17 percent are thinking of developing LAN environment, 13 percent for introducing Interest and e-mail facilities, another 13 percent making plans for new building, building expansion, furniture and other equipments.

Problems Encountered

Any library will have the privilege of experiencing some facilitating factors and some obstructing factors. Knowing the weak points and problems is equally important for effective management. Libraries were asked to identity and present their problems. The responses are analyzed in the following table.

Table 73
Problems Encountered

Problems encountered	*No. of Libraries (N=46)*
Yes	17 (36.96%)
No	29 (66.04%)
Total	46 (100%)

Most of the libraries have stated that they are not facing any problems. But nearly 37 percent have accepted that they had encountered certain problem.

Table 74
Problem Areas

Problem area	*No. of Libraries (N=17)*
1. Professional staff is inadequate / lack of supporting semi professionals (Less staff/No librarian)	8 (47.06%)
2. Economic and financial problems lack of sufficient funds/Low budget	9 (52.94%)
Total	17 (100%)

Among the libraries experienced problems in managing the libraries, nearly 53 percent of the libraries have pointed out the economic and financial problems, whereas 47 percent of the libraries are facing problems with inadequate professional staff, lack of supporting semiprofessional staff. They have also pointed out lack of qualified librarian as the head of the library as one of the significant problems.

Opinions and Suggestions

In addition to regular proposals and plans made as part of official responsibility, librarians may have constructive ideas and suggestions to give for improving the existing library services. Following two tables describe the details regarding the opinions and suggestions made by the librarians.

Table 75
Opinions & Suggestions by the Librarians

Opinions & Suggestions	*No. of Libraries (N=46)*
Yes	25 (54.35%)
No	21 (45.65%)
Total	46 (100%)

More than half of the libraries (54%) offered their opinions and suggestions for improving the existing library services. The remaining have not made any suggestions in this regard. Suggestions were made pertaining to different aspects of the library facility and services based on librarians past and present experience as well as their vision about future. Table-76 presents the descriptive account of the areas highlighted by librarians for enhancing the existing facilities.

Table 76
Suggestions of the Librarians (more than one)

Areas		*No. of Libraries (N=25)*
a)	Computerization/Hardware/Software	15 (60%)
b)	Required trained staff/ existing staff ; requires training in computer and I.T.; Supporting staff should be provided	16 (64%)
c)	Information need survey is necessary	1 (4%)
d)	Networking with all ICAR / Agriculture University, and its college libraries.	14 (56%)
e)	E-mail, Internet, LAN, CD-ROM facility	11 (44%)
f)	Inter Library Loan facility	5 (20%)
g)	Current Awareness Service	10 (40%)
h)	Selective Dissemination Service	9 (36%)
i)	Abstracting service	4 (16%)
j)	Awards for good library professionals and best library awards etc.	4 (16 %)
h)	Library should be independent with separate library building; with good furniture and separate reading room facility	12 (48%)

The suggestions made by the library professionals are reflecting their understanding about the basic requirements on one hand and modernizing the library activities on the other. Majority of them (64%) suggested improvements regarding various aspects of library staff. They pointed out the need for trained library staff and suggested to provide exclusive training in the use of computers for libraries to the existing library staff. Moreover, they advocated the need to have more number of supporting staff in order to relieve the librarian to do more professional work and offer personal services to users.

The second highest percent of librarians advocated computerization of all the activities of their libraries with proper and efficient hardware and software facilities. In addition, 48% suggested networking of all agricultural information centers and libraries for the purpose of individual libraries becoming strong in terms of collections and services by cooperation and resource sharing among libraries. Nearly 50 percent of the librarians who made suggestions, requested for providing all kinds of modern information access facilities like Internet, E-mail, CD-ROM Databases etc. Half of the librarians also expressed the need to have an independent accommodation or building for the library with good furniture and reading room facility. In terms of information services, 20 percent, 40 percent and 36 percent of the librarians suggested to offer ILL, CAS, SDI services respectively on regular basis.

USER SURVEY OF UNDERGRADUATE AND POST- GRADUATE STUDENTS

This part of the chapter deals with the analysis of the data collected from users through two different questionnaires. Section-1 covers the responses from students whereas Section-2 explains the response from user group consisting of scientists faculty and research students.

Frequency of Visits

The major objective of a library or information center is to satisfy the information needs of users. With this aim, library acquires, processes, stores and disseminates the information and information sources. User community consists of various individuals with varied information needs and information seeking behavior. To satisfy their information needs, users interact with the information facility in different ways. The personal visits made to the library are part of this interaction. In order to find out the extent of use made of the library, users were asked to indicate their frequency of visiting the institutional library. The data regarding frequency of visits made by both Under graduate (UG) and Post Graduate (PG) students of Agricultural University Colleges is presented in the Table 77.

Table 77
Frequency of Visits - Students

Frequency	*U.G. Students (N=469)*	*P.G. Students (N=400)*	*Total (N=69)*
Daily	146 (36.50%)	47 (68.12%)	193 (41.15%)
Once or Twice a week	182 (45.50%)	18 (26.09%)	200 (42.64%)
Once in a month	14 (3.50%)	0 (0%)	14 (2.99%)
Several times a month	39 (9.75%)	3 (4.35%)	42 (8.96%)
Seldom	19 (4.75%)	1 (1.45%)	20 (4.26%)
Total	400 (100%)	69 (100%)	469 (100%)

Analysis of data in Table 77 shows that significant variations exist between UG and PG students in terms of their visits to the library. Visiting the library once or twice a week is found to be common among highest percent (46%) of UG students where as, highest percent (68%) of PG students are visiting the library daily. Nearly 37 percent of

UG Students and 27 percent of PG students are found to be visiting daily and once or twice a week respectively. Visiting the library seldom is found to be very insignificant feature among PG students. Even in the case of UG students it is found that only 5 percent of them have never visited the library.

In general, analysis shows that most of the students (43%) are found to be visiting the library once or twice a week.

A χ^2-test revealed that the level of study has an impact on frequency of visits to the library by both UG an PG students at 5% level of significances (Calculated χ^2 24.903, Table $c^2_{(2)}$ at 5% level of significance = 5.99)

Average Number of Hours (Used)

Extent of time spent in the library by the users indicates how their use of library facilities is influenced by factors like existing physical environment, availability and relevance of the collection and hospitality extended by the staff. It is also closely linked with the nature of use or purpose with which users are visiting the library.

The data regarding average number of hours spent in the library by both Under Graduate (UG) and Post Graduate (PG) students of Agricultural University Colleges is presented in the Table 48.

Table 78
Average Number of Hours Used

No. of Hours per Week	*Students*		*Total*
	(N=469)	*UG (N=400)*	*PG (N=69)*
less than 5 hrs	173 (43.25%)	21 (30.43%)	194 (41.37%)
6-10 hrs	162 (40.50%)	24 (34.78%)	186 (39.66%)
11-20 hrs	42 (10.50%)	16 (23.19%)	58 (12.37%)
21-30 hrs	17 (4.25%)	6 (8.70%)	23 (4.90%)
31-40 hrs	6 (1.50%)	1 (1.45%)	7 (1.49%)
Over 40 hrs	0 (0%)	1 (1.45%)	1 (0.21%)
Total	400 (100%)	69 (100%)	469 (100%)

From the above Table 78 it may be seen that highest percentage (43%) of UG students is using the library for 5 or less hours. In addition to that, highest percentage (35%) of PG students uses the library for 6 to 10 hours. Nearly 11 percent of UG students and 23 percent of PG students are found using the library for 11 to 20 hours. Nearly 4 percent of UG students and 9 percent of PG students are using the library from 21 to 30 hours.

Using the library for 31 to 40 hours and over 40 hours is found to be a very insignificant feature among PG students. Even in the case of UG students it is found that they have never used the library over 40 hours.

The analysis shows that most of the students (41%) used the library for 5 or fewer hours and 40% of the students used it for 6 to 10 hours. In addition, only 1 percent of the students use the library material between 30 and 40 hours. The UG students never use the library above 40 hours and only 1 percent of PG Students use the library for above 40 hours.

From a Chi-square-Test, it is observed that the level of the course has an impact on No.of hours visiting the library (Calculated χ^2 =13.524, Table value at 5% level of significance χ^2= 9.49.

Reasons

Users may need different kinds of information from different sources. Their purpose of visiting the library to a greater extent is shaped by their information needs. Knowing the reason behind the purpose of their visit to the library assists in planning and designing the facilities. With this aim, users were requested to indicate reason(s) for making visits to the library. The Table 79 presents a list of reasons mentioned by users.

Table 79
Reasons for Visiting the Library (More than one)

Reasons	*Students*		*Total*
	(N=469)	*UG (N=400)*	*PG (N=69)*
To borrow books / Journals	228 (57%)	38 (55.07%)	266 (56.72%)
To read library books / Journals	250 (62.50%)	63 (91.30%)	313 (66.74%)
To read for University and Competitive Exams	104 (26%)	17 (24.64%)	121 (25.80%)
To use reference material	141 (35.25%)	23 (33.33%)	164 (34.97%)
To receive help from library staff	19 (4.75%)	2 (2.90%)	21 (4.48%)
To use photo copying facility	150 (37.50%)	34 (49.28%)	184 (39.23%)
To study own books or notes	54 (13.50%)	6 (8.70%)	60 (12.79%)
To use inter-library loan facility	11 (2.75%)	5 (7.25%)	16 (3.41%)

Among various reasons pointed out by UG students, visiting the library to read the library materials is found to be significant. Half of the UG students are visiting the library to borrow library materials. Significant percent (37%) of UG students are also coming to the library to use photocopying facility. The same trend is noticed even among the PG students. A significant percent (nearly 35%) of students are personally visiting the library to use the reference collections in the library.

Formal Instruction

Providing some sort of guidance to the users in the use of library collections and other facilities is not a new service in the libraries. But the libraries may or may not be offering formal user instruction or training programs to train their users in the better utilization of library resource. Sometimes in academic institutions, the teaching departments may take the initiative in this regard.

The data regarding user instructions made by both Under Graduate (UG) and Post Graduate (PG) students of Agricultural University colleges is presented in the following Table 80.

Table 80
Library Instruction / Orientation

Formal Instruction	*U.G (N=400)*	*P.G (N=69)*	*Total (N=469)*
Department	130 (32.50%)	35 (50.72%)	165 (35.18%)
Library	87 (21.75%)	6 (8.70%)	93 (19.83%)
No response	183 (45.75%)	28 (40.58%)	211 (44.99%)
Total	400 (100%)	69 (100%)	469 (100%)

Departments in the academic institutions are found to be taking more interest rather than the library, in providing instruction and guidance to the students in the use of library resources. Significant percent of the students are seen to be not having any idea about such kind of guidance or assistance in the use of the library.

To know how to use the library for various purposes (more than one)

Depending upon his or her requirement for any information or information sources, the users may utilize the library services in different ways. While getting the required information for a book or any other information source in the library, the users may take the help of different people around him or her. In order to know the users' ways of getting required material from the library, information regarding various channels he/she is using has been ascertained. The corresponding data in this regard is presented in the following table.

Table 81
Ways of Learning in Using the Library
(more than one)

Ways of learning	*Students*		*Total*
	(N=469)	*UG (N=400)*	*PG (N=69)*
On your own	130 (32.50%)	31 (44.93%)	161 (34.33%)
With the help of library staff	77 (19.25%)	21 (30.44%)	98 (20.90%)
With the help of teacher	59 (14.75%)	12 (17.39%)	71 (15.14%)
With the help of friend	102 (25.50%)	25 (36.23%)	127 (27.08%)
By reading library brochure	18 (4.50%)	4 (5.80%)	22 (4.69%)
By following library signs and guide books	39 (9.75%)	5 (7.25%)	44 (9.38%)
Previous knowledge & Experience	70 (17.50%)	12 (17.39%)	82 (17.48%)

Analysis of data from the above table shows that significant variations does not exist between UG and PG students in terms of the way they have accessed the library materials. Majority of PG students (nearly 45%) and UG students (32%) use the library on their own. Second highest percent of them have taken the help of a friend. Third highest percent (nearly 21%) have acknowledged the help taken form the library staff.

Very few said that they have taken the help from teachers (15%), followed the signs and boards in the library (9%) and guidance from the published brochures of the libraries (5%).

Using Other Libraries

Besides the institutional library, always, there is a probability that the users may try to satisfy their information needs using other sources or alternative information sources in and around their area. The importance given to their sources by the user indicates the relative status given to the institutional library among various libraries in the locality. The data collected regarding the use made of other sources is indicated in the following table.

Table 82
Use of Other Sources of Information

Using other libraries	*Students*		*Total*
	(N=469)	*UG (N=400)*	*PG (N=69)*
Yes	77 (19.25%)	21 (30.44%)	98 (20.90%)
No	323 (80.75%)	48 (69.56%)	371 (79.10%)
Total	400 (100%)	69 (100%)	469 (100%)

It may be seen from the above table that a high percentage (79%) of both Under Graduate and Post Graduate students do not make use of other libraries. Nearly 81 percent of the UG students and nearly 70 percent of the PG students do not make use of other libraries. This means that students generally depend on their own college libraries.

In addition to the Agricultural university and college libraries, the UG and PG students are using District libraries, University libraries i.e., S.V. University library, ICAR libraries, British libraries, DRR, DOR, NIRD, MANAGE, CRIDA, ICRISAT, NAARM libraries etc.

Extent of Dependency on other Libraries

User dependency on other libraries relies on some of the inadequacies of the institutional library and users' dissatisfaction about the available facilities. Degree of dependency on other libraries is shown on a three point scale. The details are provided in the following table.

Table 83
Extent of Dependency on Other Libraries

Extent	*Students*		*Total*
	(N=98)	*UG (N=77)*	*PG (N=21)*
Greatly	8 (10.39%)	0 (0%)	8 (8.16%)
Moderately	48 (62.34%)	15 (71.43%)	63 (64.29%)
Scarcely	21 (27.27%)	6 (28.57%)	27 (27.55%)
Total	77 (100%)	21 (100%)	98 (100%)

The data in the table shows the extent of dependency on other libraries in respect of the majority of PG students (71%) who are using the libraries moderately. The next highest percentage of (29%) of them uses scarcely and considerably none of them used greatly.

The highest percentage (nearly 62%) of UG students using other libraries is moderately. Next highest percentage (27%) scarcely and 10 percent of them are greatly using other libraries.

In general, majority of the students moderately (64%) depend on other libraries. Further 27 percent of them are scarcely dependent on other libraries. Very few of them (8%) are dependent greatly on other libraries.

Reasons for Using Other Libraries

Majority of the students, both under graduation and post graduation are visiting other libraries for referring journals, newspapers and latest information for preparing seminar topics which are not available in their libraries. Others reasons mentioned for visiting other libraries include borrowing novels, books for competitive examinations and other reference books on subjects other than agriculture.

Table 84
Reasons for Using Other Libraries

Reasons	*Students*		*Total*
	(N=98)	*UG (N=77)*	*PG (N=21)*
To read Journals /Newspapers	48 (62.37%)	102 (57.14%)	60 (61.22%)
Preparing for seminars	20 (25.97%)	5 (23.81%)	25 (25.5%)
Reading Competitive books	7 (9.09%)	3 (14.29%)	8 (8.16%)
Borrowing novels	2 (2.60%)	1 (4.76%)	3 (3.06%)
Total	77 (100%)	21 (100%)	98 (100%)

Analysis of data shows in the Table 84 majority of the UG students (62%) and PG students (57%) gave the reason "More Journals & News papers are available in other libraries. Both UG (25%) and PG (24%) students gave the reason "for preparing seminars". Further (4%) of the PG students and (9%) of the UG students gave the reason "competitive books", very few of them gave the reason borrowing novels for using other libraries.

Usefulness of Library Materials

Library is a resource of sources. Different types of materials stored in the library collection carry information on different subjects in different forms organized in different ways.

Each source has some value and helps the reader in many ways. Depending on the purpose, library users make use of the library materials. Some of them may be highly relevant for their purpose and some may have a little value to them. To ascertain information on the usefulness and relevancy of library materials for users, users were asked to rank the listed items, keeping in view their usefulness to them. For ranking purpose, users were asked to use a scale of 0 to 9 where '0' indicates least useful items and '9' indicates most useful library materials.

Table 85
Usefulness of Library Materials –UG (N=400)

	1	*2*	*3*	*4,5 &6*	*7,8&9*
Books	207 (51.75%)	58 (14.5%)	15 (3.75%)	25 (6.25%)	30 (7.50%)
Periodicals	21 (5.25%)	50 (12.5%)	72 (18%)	82 (20.5%)	74 (18.50%)
Dissertation	8 (2%0)	3 (0.75%)	14 (3.5%)	97 (24.25%)	149 (37.25%)
Newsletters and communications	14 (3.5%)	14 (3.5%)	37 (9.25%)	136 (34%)	58 (14.50%)
Standards	3 (0.75%)	2 (0.5%)	27 (6.75%)	130 (32.50%)	72 (18.00%)
Patents	1 (0.25%)	8 (2%)	17 (4.25%)	84 (21%)	116 (29.00%)
News Papers	92 (23%)	124 (31%)	36 (9%)	38 (9.50%)	30 (7.50%)
Reports	6 (1.5%)	11 (2.75%)	46 (11.5%)	111 (27.75%)	67 (16.75%)
Others	11 (2.75%)	1 (0.25%)	4 (1%)	6 (1.5%)	50 (12.50%)

More than half of the UG students considered the books as most useful sources of information for them. Second and third highest ranks were given to periodicals by majority of them. 4th, 5th and 6th ranks were given to news letters and 7th, 8th and 9th ranks were given to dissertations.

Analysis of data shows that books, followed by news papers and periodicals are the most useful type of library materials for under graduate students.

Table 86

Usefulness of Library Materials Ranks –P.G(N=69)

	1	*2*	*3*	*4,5 & 6*	*7, 8 & 9*
Books	23 (33.33%)	8 (11.59%)	5 (7.25%)	7 (10.15%)	11 (15.94%)
Periodicals	6 (8.70%)	14 (20.29%)	4 (5.80%)	15 (21.75%)	12 (17.39%)
Dissertation	0 (0%)	2 (2.90%)	1 (1.45%)	28 (40.60%)	13 (18.84%)
Newsletters & communications	0 (0%)	1 (1.45%)	8 (11.59%)	25 (36.23%)	17 (24.64%)
Standards	2 (2.90%)	0 (0%)	13 (18.84%)	13 (18.84%)	17 (24.64%)
Patents	0 (0%)	12 (17.39%)	2 (2.90%)	6 (8.70%)	21 (30.45%)
News Papers	4 (5.80%)	7 (10.15%)	9 (13.04%)	17 (24.64%)	17 (24.64%)
Reports	2 (2.90%)	5 (7.25%)	6 (8.70%)	27 (39.13%)	10 (14.49%)
Others	1 (1.45%)	1 (1.45%)	2 (2.90%)	9 (0%)	6 (8.70%)

Thirty three percent of the PG students considered the books as most useful sources of information for them. They considered periodicals as 2nd highest rank of materials useful to them. Majority of the PG students gave 3rd rank to standards, 4th, 5th and 6th ranks to dissertations and 7th, 8th and 9th to patents.

Finding the Required Item

Users make effort always to find or get required information or material from the library when they approach the library with a demand for required information. But they may / may not succeed always in their efforts. How far they have succeeded in getting the need information or library material depends on various factors like accessibility provided to the collection, availability of the materials, the approach of the users and efforts made by the user. The success rate in getting the required information from the library has been indicated in the form of a scale as shown in the following table.

Table 87

Finding the Required Item

Possibility	*Students*		*Total*
	(N=469)	*UG (N=400)*	*PG (N=69)*
Always	99 (24.75%)	13 (18.84%)	112 (23.88%)
Sometimes	279 (69.75%)	54 (78.26%)	333 (71%)
Never	22 (5.50%)	2 (2.90%)	24 (5.12%)
Total	400 (100%)	69 (100%)	469 (100%)

From the above table it may be seen that highest percentage, both UG (70%) and PG (78%) have stated that some times they could manage to get the required item. Nearly 25 percent of UG students and 19 percent of PG students found to be always finding the required item in the library respectively. Very few PG (5%) and UG (3%) students have stated that they never found the required item in the library.

Making Suggestions

In order to get the feed back from the users about the overall performance of the library, it is always required to invite suggestions from the users. Such efforts will help the library to act as a responsive organization which evaluates its performance regularly with an aim to be more and more effective. Constructive suggestions are of real value for library planners. Users should be encouraged to offer their suggestions by organizing suggestion box / book inviting them to review meetings and discussions. The students were asked whether at any point of time they thought of suggesting any thing about the library to the management.

Table 88

Making Suggestions Regarding the Collections in the Library

Making suggestions	*Students*		*Total*
	(N=469)	*UG (N=400)*	*PG (N=69)*
Yes	149 (37.25%)	39 (56.52%)	188 (40.09%)
No	251 (62.75%)	30 (43.48%)	281 (59.91%)
Total	400 (100%)	69 (100%)	469 (100%)

Analysis of data in the Table 88 shows that highest percentage (nearly 57%) of PG students are making suggestions regarding the collection in the library. And the highest percentages (nearly 63%) of UG students don't make any suggestions to the library. In general, analysis reveals that variations exist between UG and PG students. Most of the students, both UG and PG (60%) are not making suggestions regarding any aspect of the library.

A Chi-square on significance of level of study over making suggestion is performed and found the level on course has an impact on suggestions (Calculated $\chi^2_{(2)} = 9.100$ and table value $\chi^2_{(2)}$ at 5% level significance = 5.99).

Frequency of Making Suggestions

Being humans, library users exhibit different personalities. Some of them may be shy, some maybe arrogant and some may be over smart and so on. Some of them though have complaints may feel shy to express them. Instead, they prefer to continue facing the problem in the library. Some may come forward to express their problem after long suffering. Some may not take the problems seriously and prefer to leave them to their dissolve. To assess the readiness of users to come out with suggestions and the frequency with which they are making suggestions, a question is asked to indicate the frequency of making suggestions.

The data regarding frequency at which suggestions are made to the library by both Under Graduate (UG) and Post Graduate (PG) students is presented in the following table.

Table 89
Frequency of Making Suggestions

Frequency Making suggestions	*Students*		*Total*
	(N=188)	*UG (N=149)*	*PG (N=39)*
Frequently	21 (14.09%)	6 (15.39%)	27 (14.36%)
Occasionally	128 (85.91%)	33 (84.62%)	161 (85.64%)
Total	149 (100%)	39 (100%)	188 (100%)

Analysis of data in the above table shows that significant variations do not exist between UG and PG students in terms of their frequency of making suggestions to the library. Frequency of making suggestions to the library occasionally is found to be common among highest percent of both PG students (85%) and UG students (86%). Making suggestions to the library frequently is found (15%) among UG students and nearly 14% among PG students.

In general, analysis shows that most of the students, both UG and PG (nearly 86%) are found to be making suggestions occasionally to the library. Very few of them (14%) are making suggestions frequently to the library.

Response from the Library

Modern libraries, being responsive organisations need to invite suggestions from users, analyse and filter them. The suggestions and comments which are constructive in nature are to be documented. While making decisions regarding library services and facilities, documented suggestions have to be given due considerations. Giving weightage to the suggestions offered by users and trying to respond to them is a healthy sign for a library to prosper.

In general, the response from the library to the suggestions /criticisms /comments was positive and encouraging. But significant percentages (33%) of libraries have not reacted either positively or negatively.

The data regarding response to the suggestions from the library received by the students are shown in the following table.

Table 90
Response from the Library to the Suggestions of Students

Response	*Students*		*Total*
	N = 333	*UG (N=290)*	*PG (N=43)*
Positive	143 (49.31%)	20 (46.51%)	163 (48.94%)
Negative	46 (15.86%)	14 (32.56%)	60 (18.03%)
No response	101 (34.83%)	9 (20.93%)	110 (33.03%)
Total	290 (100%)	43 (100%)	333 (100%)

The analysis of data reveals some encouraging findings. The response to the suggestions / criticisms received by majority of both UG (49%) and PG (nearly 47%) students is positive, as expressed by the students. However nearly 35 percent of UG students stated their library was silent in response to their suggestions/complaints, where as nearly 33% of P.G. students receive negative response.

Ways of Finding Specific Information or Document

Libraries are considered to be complex stores of different types of materials. Very often ordinary users will be facing the problems in locating the item of their interest due to the artificiality of the representation and organisation of the collection in the store. User as a layman may not be in a position to understand the classified arrangement on shelves or to use the catalogue. They indeed, need some sort of assistance from somebody who can guide them in getting the required information or item available in the library. Different ways followed and persons relied upon by the users for this purpose is stated in the following Table-91.

Table 91
Ways of Finding Information or Book
(more than one)

Ways of finding the information	*Students*		*Total*
	UG (N=400)	*PG (N=69)*	*(N = 469)*
Using the library catalogue	158 (39.50%)	60 (86.96%)	218 (46.48%)
Taking the help of library staff	217 (54.25%)	43 (62.32%)	260 (55.44%)
Taking the help of other students	177 (44.25%)	35 (50.72%)	212 (45.20%)
Browsing the stacks	74 (18.50%)	25 (36.23%)	99 (21.11%)
Taking the help of teacher	98 (24.50%)	15 (21.74%)	113 (24.09%)

The analysis data in the above table shows that majority of PG students (87%) used the library catalogue to find information or book. Only 22 percent have taken help of the teacher to find the information or book. Sixty two percent have taken the help of library staff. Fifty one percent are taking the help of other students. Thirty six percent browsed the stacks.

Among the UG students, as many as nearly 55 percent have taken the help of library staff. Nearly 45 percent have taken the help of other students to find the information. Nearly 40 percent of them used the library catalogue to find the information or book. Twenty five percent of UG students have taken the help of the teacher to find the information or book. Only 19 percent of them browsed the library stack to find the information.

In general, the analysis shows that Majority of students (55%) has taken the help of the library staff, 46 percent used the library catalogue, 45 percent have taken the help of other students and 24 percent browsed the stacks.

Usefulness of Library Catalogue

While searching for a book in the library, Library catalogue is the first tool to be consulted by the user to know about the availability of an item in the collection. Catalogue reflects the total collection in the library. Extent of use of catalogue depends on its simplicity, accessibility format of entries, ease of use and up-to-date-ness. Students' opinions on the usefulness of their Library catalogue were ascertained and presented in the Table 92.

Analysis of data in the Table 92 shows that majority of PG students (nearly 89%) considered library catalogue as useful, where as 57% of UG students also expressed the same opinion. Only 12 percent of PG students expressed that the Library catalogue is not useful. Further, 43 percent of UG students also feel that the library catalogue is not useful. In general, 61 percent of both U.G. and PG students stated the library catalogue useful.

Table 92
Usefulness of Library Catalogue

Usefulness	*Students*		*Total*
	UG (N=400)	*PG (N=69)*	*(N = 469)*
Yes	226 (56.50%)	61 (88.41%)	287 (61.19%)
No	174 (43.50%)	8 (11.59%)	182 (38.81%)
Total	400 (100%)	69 (100%)	469 (100%)

They may be consulting catalogue to know: (i) The place of the required book on the shelves; or (ii) The bibliographical details of the book; or (iii) the relative strength of a subject in the library collection; or (iv) what books by a particular author are available in the library.

Suggested Areas of Improvement in Catalogue

Previous table shows the feelings of students about the usefulness of library catalogue. Majority of UG students are not satisfied with the catalogue. For the purpose of improving the usefulness of the catalogue, students were asked to suggest the areas where there is a need for improvement. The details are given in the Table 93.

Table 93
Suggested Areas of Improvement in Catalogue

Areas of Catalogue	*Students*		*Total*
	UG (N=174)	*PG (N=8)*	*(N = 182)*
Author	47 (27.01%)	1 (12.5%)	48 (26.37%)
Subject	65 (37.36%)	6 (75%)	71 (39.01%)
Title	62 (35.63%)	1 (12.5%)	63 (34.62%)
Total	174 (100%)	8 (100%)	182 (100%)

Analysis of data shows that the subject part of the catalogue was suggested for improvement by both UG (nearly 37%) and PG (75%) students. Further, 36% of UG students and 13% of PG students suggested improving the title catalogue. The least percentage of both UG (27%) and PG (13%) students expressed the need to improve the Author catalogue.

In general both UG and PG students in majority (39%), expressed the need to improve the subject catalogue of their library. Nearly 35 percent suggested changes and improvements in the title catalogue. Further, nearly 26 percent of the students demanded for improvement in the author catalogue.

Awareness about Library Rules

Every library will formulate certain rules and regulations for the systematic execution of its functions and provision of services to users. All the users are expected to follow these norms to maintain smooth running of the library. Usually the information about rules and regulation are communicated through library broachers supplied to the students at the time of admission of the students.

To know whether the users are aware of the rules of library or not, information is gathered and displayed in the Table 94.

Table 94
Awareness about Library Rules

Awareness	*Students*		*Total*
	UG (N=400)	*PG (N=69)*	*(N = 469)*
Yes	292 (73%)	58 (84.06%)	350 (74.63%)
No	108 (27%)	11 (15.94%)	119 (25.37%)
Total	400 (100%)	69 (100%)	469 (100%)

Analysis of data shows that the majority of students, both PG and UG (75%) were aware of the existence of library rules and regulations. Seventy three percent of the UG students were aware of the existence of library rules. Only 16 percent of PG students were not much aware of library rules.

In general, majority of students (75%) were aware of the existence of library rules and 25 percent of students were not aware of the existence of the library rules.

Opinion regarding the library rules and regulations

Majority of the PG and UG students expressed their opinion regarding the library rules, about issue system and present issue timings, number of books issued by library, renewal period of books are not enough and need to be increased. Some have expressed silence should be maintained in the library.

Awareness about Borrowing Privileges

Library users once becoming as registered borrowers can enjoy different privileges given to them by the library. Unless the user knows the available facilities for a registered borrower, he cannot fully utilize the services.

The data regarding awareness among students about borrowing privileges is presented in the Table 95.

Table 95
Awareness about Borrowing Privileges

Borrowing privileges	*Students*		*Total*
	UG (N=400)	*PG (N=69)*	*(N = 469)*
Yes	328 (82%)	50 (72.46%)	378 (80.60%)
No	72 (18%)	19 (27.54%)	91 (19.40%)
Total	400 (100%)	69 (100%)	469 (100%)

Analysis of data shows that significant variations do not exist between UG and PG students in terms of the awareness about borrowing privileges of library. The majority of UG students (82%) were aware of borrowing privileges 72 percent of PG students were aware of borrowing privileges. Only 18 percent of UG students and 28 percent of PG students were not aware of borrowing privileges.

In general majority of students (81%) were aware of borrowing privileges. Only 19 percent of the students were not aware of borrowing privileges.

Satisfaction

To ascertain the opinion regarding the existing privileges, users were asked to indicate whether they are satisfied with them or not.

The data regarding users' satisfaction about borrowing privileges is presented in the Table 96.

Table 96
Satisfaction

Satisfction	*Students*		*Total*
	UG (N=400)	*PG (N=69)*	*(N = 469)*
Yes	277 (69.25%)	43 (62.32%)	320 (68.23%)
No	123 (30.75%)	26 (37.68%)	149 (31.77%)
Total	400 (100%)	69 (100%)	469 (100%)

Analysis of data shows that significant variations exist between UG and PG students in terms of their satisfaction about borrowing privileges of the library. The majority of UG students (69%) were satisfied with the borrowing privileges of the library. Sixty two percent of PG students were satisfied with the borrowing privileges of the library. Nearly 31 percent of UG students and 38 percent of PG students were not satisfied with the borrowing privileges of the library.

In general, majority of students (68%) were satisfied with borrowing privileges of the library, 32 percent of students were not satisfied with the borrowing privileges of the library.

A Chi-square test has shown that the level of study has no inference on satisfaction levels of the students i.e both PG and U.G are having statically same satisfaction levels regarding library facilities (calculated $\chi^2_{(1)}$=1.304; table value $\chi^2_{(1)}$=3.84)

Reasons for Dissatisfaction on Borrowing Privileges

Thirty one percent of the UG students, 38 percent PG students were not satisfied

Table: 97
Frequency use of Library Services

Library Services	*Frequently*			*Occasionally*			*Seldom*		
	UG (N=400)	*PG (N=69)*	*Total (N=469)*	*UG (N=400)*	*PG (N=69)*	*Total (N=469)*	*UG (N=400)*	*PG (N=69)*	*Total (N=469)*
Reference service	235 (58.75%)	45 (65.22%)	280 (59.70%)	114 (28.50%)	16 (23.19%)	130 (27.72%)	51 (12.75%)	8 (11.59%)	59 (12.58%)
Bibliographic service	25 (6.25%)	13 (18.84%)	38 (8.10%)	71 (17.75%)	15 (21.74%)	86 (18.34%)	304 (76%)	41 (53.42%)	345 (73.56%)
Current Awareness service (CAS)	132 (33%)	21 (30.43%)	153 (32.62%)	157 (39.25%)	25 (36.23%)	182 (38.81%)	111 (27.75%)	23 (33.33%)	134 (28.57%)
Translation Service	22 (5.5%)	2 (2.90%)	24 (5.12%)	49 (12.25%)	10 (14.49%)	59 (12.58%)	329 (82.25%)	57 (82.61%)	386 (82.30%)
Indexing / Abstracting Service	34 (8.5%)	11 (15.94%)	45 (9.59%)	80 (20%)	22 (31.88%)	102 (21.75%)	286 (71.5%)	36 (52.17%)	322 (68.66%)
Inter-Library Loan service	18 (4.5%)	3 (4.35%)	21 (4.48%)	39 (9.75%)	9 (13.04%)	48 (10.24%)	343 (85.75%)	57 (82.61%)	400 (85.29%)
Literature Search Service	52 (13%)	12 (17.39%)	64 (13.65%)	93 (23.25%)	11 (15.94%)	104 (22.18%)	255 (63.75%)	46 (66.67%)	301 (64.18%)
Selective Dissemination of Information (SDI)	43 (10.75%)	12 (17.39%)	55 (11.73%)	84 (21%)	16 (23.19%)	100 (21.32%)	273 (68.25%)	41 (59.42%)	314 (66.95%)
Photo copying service	112 (28%)	24 (34.78%)	136 (29%)	149 (37.25%)	14 (20.29%)	163 (34.76%)	139 (34.75%)	31 (44.93%)	70 (36.25%)

with the borrowing privileges. They have stated the following reasons for their dissatisfaction: (i) number of issue books are not sufficient and need to be increased; (ii) Renewal time is not enough and need to be extended; (iii) Penalty is high; and (iv)Relevant books are not available.

Frequency Use of Library Services

Different approaches of users towards information are often influenced by various factors like level of the user, nature of job on hand, phase of research in which he is involved and so on. The same user may interact with the library differently on different occasions with varied information needs and the extent of use of information services usually depend on the approach of the user towards information he may be in need of current information. He wants to be abreast of latest development in the field of interest. In such a situation, he regularly prefers to use current awareness service. Occasionally, when he is in need of a book not available in his library, he may try inter library loan facility to get the item from other libraries. The relevance and usefulness of the information services are also critical in deciding the frequently of use of these services by users. Following table shows frequency of use of the information services by the students.

Many variations were not noticed between UG and PG students in terms of frequency of use of information services. Among various services offered, reference service is found to be the most popular service and used frequently by both UG and PG students. Next to the reference service, majority of the UG students frequently use current awareness service. Photo copying service is the service used frequently by PG students next to reference service.

Among the services used occasionally, current awareness service occupies the first place in the case of both UG & PG students (39% & 36%) respectively. Second highest percent of UG students (28%) found to be using reference service occasionally. Next to current awareness service, the second highest percent of PG students (31%) are occasional users of Indexing & Abstracting service.

Majority of both UG & PG students have stated that they never used inter library loan services (86% and 83%) respectively. Translation service was also not used by significant percent (82%) of UG students. Other services specified by UG students are question papers, reference service and catalogue available in the library.

Opinion about the Library Services

Information services provided by the library will have varied implications for the users. Depending on their usefulness, coverage, currency of content, regularity mode of presentation and ease of use, users evaluate the value of each of these services. Based on their evaluation, users will be in a position to state whether they are satisfied or not. Opinions of users about information with the services are presented in table (Table 98.)

Table 98

Opinion about the Library Services

Opinion on Services	*Satisfactory*			*Not Satisfactory*			*Can not Say*		
	UG (N=400)	*PG (N=69)*	*Total (N=469)*	*UG (N=400)*	*PG (N=69)*	*Total (N=469)*	*UG (N=400)*	*PG (N=69)*	*Total (N=469*
Reference Service	309 (77.25%)	42 (60.87%)	351 (74.84%)	50 (12.50%)	19 (27.53%)	69 (14.71%)	41 (10.25%)	8 (11.59%)	49 (10.45%)
Bibliographies	74 (18.50%)	20 (28.99%)	94 (20.04%)	41 (10.25%)	11 (15.94%)	52 (11.09%)	285 (71.25%)	38 (55.07%)	323 (68.87%)
Current Awareness Service	197 (49.25%)	31 (44.93%)	228 (48.61%)	78 (19.50%)	11 (15.94%)	89 (18.98%)	125 (31.25%)	27 (39.13%)	152 (32.41%)
Translation Service	43 (10.75%)	3 (4.35%)	46 (9.81%)	42 (10.50%)	6 (8.70%)	48 (10.23%)	315 (78.75%)	60 (86.96%)	375 (79.96%)
Indexing / Abstracting Service	82 (20.50%)	28 (40.58%)	110 (23.45%)	57 (14.25%)	6 (8.70%)	63 (13.43%)	261 (65.25%)	35 (50.72%)	296 (63.11%)
Inter-Library Loan	28 (7%)	6 (8.70%)	34 (7.25%)	47 (11.75%)	5 (7.25%)	52 (11.09%)	325 (81.25%)	58 (84.06%)	383 (81.66%)
Literature Search Service	91 (22.75%)	16 (23.19%)	107 (22.81%)	64 (16%)	19 (27.54%)	83 (17.70%)	245 (61.25%)	34 (49.28%)	279 (59.49%)
Selective Dissemination of Information (SDI)	57 (14.25%)	10 (14.49%)	67 (14.29%)	39 (9.75%)	16 23.20%)	55 (11.72%)	304 (76%)	43 (62.32%)	347 (73.99%)
Photo copying service	192 (48%)	16 (23.19%)	208 (44.35%)	101 (25.25%)	33 (47.83%)	134 (28.57%)	107 (26.75%)	20 (28.99%)	127 (27.08%)

Reference Service

Analysis of data shows that significant variations did not exist between UG and PG students in terms of their opinions about reference service. Majority of both UG and PG students are satisfied with the reference services offered by their library.

In general, analysis shows that most of the students (75%) are found to be satisfied with the reference service. Nearly 15 percent of the students felt unsatisfactory. Only 10 percent of them could not express their opinion about the reference service.

Bibliographic Service

Majority of the UG as well as PG students (69%) expressed their inability to state their opinion about this service. This may be due to the fact that most of them are neither aware of this service nor used it. However, nearly 16 percent of PG students and 10 percent of UG students are not satisfied with the service. General trend also reveals that though majority of the students could not express their opinion, compared to users (11%) not satisfied, the percentage of users satisfied (20%) is more.

Current Awareness Service

Majority of the students are found to be satisfied with the current awareness service. However, nearly 20 percent of UG students and 16 percent of PG students have expressed their opinion about this service.

Translation Service

Analysis of data shows that the large number of UG students (nearly 79%) and PG students (87%) have not expressed any opinion about translation service. Nearly 11 percent of UG students and 9 percent of PG students are not satisfied with the service. Only 10 percent of UG and 4 percent of PG students expressed their satisfaction regarding the translation service.

Indexing and Abstracting Service

Analysis of data shows that majority of PG students (nearly 41%) are satisfied with this service, whereas majority of UG students (65%) could not give any opinion about indexing and abstracting service. Majority of students (63%) stated that they can not give any opinion about this service. But from the remaining, 22 percent of students are found satisfied and 13 percent are not satisfied with service.

Inter-Library Loan Service

Majority of the UG (nearly 81%) and PG (86%) of the students could not express their opinion for Inter Library loan. Further 11.75 percent of UG students and 7.25 percent of PG students felt not satisfactory. Very few of them (UG 7% and PG 9%) felt satisfactory.

Literature Search Service

An equal percentage (23%) of both UG and PG students felt satisfactory for literature search service. Further 16 percent of UG and 27 percent of PG students felt not satisfactory and 61 percent of the UG and 49 percent of the PG students could not express their opinion.

Selective Dissemination of Information (SDI)

Majority of UG students (76%) and PG students (nearly 62%) could not give any opinion about selective Dissemination of Information. An equal percent (14%) of UG and students considered the service as satisfactory.

Photocopying Service

Forty eight percent of UG students and nearly 23 percent of PG students felt satisfactory for photocopying service. Further 25 percent of UG and nearly 48 percent of PG students are not satisfied with photocopying service. 27 percent of UG students and PG students (29%) could not express their opinion.

Suggestions for Improving the Services

UG and PG students have suggested that reference service, bibliographic service, CAS, ILL, literature search services along with trained professional library staff should be provided where it is not available at present.

Willingness to Pay for the Services

Pricing the services is not new to the libraries charging for photocopies and membership subscriptions are common practices in libraries. Pricing is a management policy aimed at improving quality of services, developing value added service, generating revenue and the meeting the challenges posed by competitive environment. While fixing the price for a service factors like demand for the service user capacity to pay the quality of the service, competitors' product/service and so on willingness to pay, besides buying capability and interest in the service, is crucial for service to users following are the showing details about users' willingness to pay for the service.

Table 99

Willingness to Pay for the Services

Willingness	*Students*		*Total*
	UG (N=400)	*PG (N=69)*	*(N = 469)*
Yes	302 (75.50%)	48 (69.57%)	350 (74.63%)
No	98 (24.50%)	21 (30.43%)	119 (25.37%)
Total	400 (100%)	69 (100%)	469 (100%)

Analysis of data shows that majority of UG students (76%) are willing to pay for some of the services if they are charged. Nearly 70 percent of PG students were also showed their willingness to pay for the services.

Opinion about Book Issuing

Among different library routines, charging and discharging function is most important function since majority of the users especially students, regularly interact with the library with this purpose. Data is also gathered on the opinion of users about issuing procedures and is analyzed in the following table 100.

Reasons for Inconvenience in Book Issue

Nearly 12 percent of the students, both UG and PG, have expressed their inconvenience in book issue system. They have stated the following reasons for their inconvenience: (i) issue time is very slow (ii) book renewal period is not enough (iii) reference books not offered for loan (iv) most of the books are not available in the collection (v) Insufficiency of books for loan.

Table 100
Opinion about Book Issuing

Opinion	*Students*		*Total*
	UG (N=400)	*PG (N=69)*	*(N = 469)*
Convenient	322 (80.50%)	54 (78.26%)	376 (80.17%)
Non-convenient	47 (11.75%)	9 (13.04%)	56 (11.94%)
No opinion	31 (7.75%)	6 (8.70%)	37 (7.89%)
Total	400 (100%)	69 (100%)	469 (100%)

Analysis of data shows that majority of UG students (81%) and PG students (78%) found the book issue system at their library convenient. Only 12 percent of UG students and 13 percent of PG students felt that the book issue system at their library was not convenient. In addition, very few students gave no answer.

Finding a Place for Reading in Libraries

Besides browsing and borrowing, the library material users also prefer to read many items sitting in the library. Hence provision for reading area is also the responsibility of the library. But allocation of reading area adequately is a big problem for libraries. So, user may not find the place for reading every time. Details were gathered on the availability and use of reading space and presented in Table 101.

Table 101
Finding a Place for Reading in Libraries

Finding place	*Students*		*Total*
	UG (N=400)	*PG (N=69)*	*(N = 469)*
Always	174 (43.50%)	39 (56.52%)	213 (45.42%)
Sometimes	198 (49.50%)	23 (33.33%)	221 (47.12%)
Never	28 (7%)	7 (10.14%)	35 (7.46%)
Total	400 (100%)	69 (100%)	469 (100%)

Analysis of data shows 57 percent of PG students felt always finding a place for reading in library, 50 percent of UG students felt sometimes finding a place for reading in libraries, 44 percent of UG students felt that they always finding a place for reading in libraries. Thirty three percent of PG students felt that they are some times finding a place for reading in libraries only 7 percent of UG students and 10% of PG students were felt that they never find a place for reading in libraries. In general 47 percent of students felt that they are some times finding a place for reading in libraries, 45 percent of them felt always finding a place for reading in libraries. Only 7 percent of them were felt never finding a place for reading in libraries.

Majority of the UG students (50%) stated that they could manage to get the reading space only sometimes whereas highest percent (56%) of PG students are always availing the reading room facility. Very few students stated that they never got for the reading room facility in the library. The variation between the percentages in terms of finding place for reading may be attributed to the fact that the number of students at PG level is comparatively less.

Opinion about Physical Facilities

Sufficient ventilation, cool and pleasant atmosphere, attractive interiors, drinking water and vehicle parking facilities are the factors which influence the users visits to the library and they stay in the library. Users were asked to express their opinion on the available physical facilities in the library and indicated in the tables below.

Location of Library

Extent of use of the library is always influenced by the factors like easy of access, use and the relevance of the collection and services and so on. Location of the library in a place which is central to all user departments always attracts more number of users. Users opinions were gathered about the convenience of the location of the library and interpreted in Table 102.

Table 102
Location of Library

Opinion	*Students*		*Total*
	UG (N=400)	*PG (N=69)*	*(N = 469)*
Easy to reach	290 (72.50%)	53 (76.81%)	343 (73.13%)
Out of the way	30 (7.50%)	4 (5.80%)	34 (7.25%)
Centrally located	58 (14.50%)	6 (8.70%)	64 (13.65%)
Far away	22 (5.50%)	6 (8.70%)	28 (5.97%)
Total	400 (100%)	69 (100%)	469 (100%)

Analysis of data shows a significant variation do not exist between UG and PG students. Majority of PG students (77%), UG students (73%) were of the opinion that the library was located at a place easy to reach. Nearly 15 percent of UG students and 9 percent of PG students were of the opinion that the library was located at a central place. But 8 percent of UG students and 9 percent of PG students also felt that the library was situated in a location out of the way.

In general, 73 percent students were of the opinion that the library is located at a place easy to reach. Fourteen percent of them were of the opinion that the library is located centrally. Six percent also stated that it is located in a far off place.

There is no difference in opinion regarding location of library for both P.G. and U.G students. This is evident from a Chi square test of signification. (calculated $\chi^2_{(2)}$=1.702, table value $\chi^2_{(2)}$ at 5% level of signification = 5.99).

Furniture

Furniture in the library includes different types of tables and chairs procured for both office and users' purposes. For users spending longer time in the library, the furniture should be comfortable and convenient to use. Opinions of users on the existing furniture facility, especially in the reading room area were sought and presented in Table 103.

Table 103
Furniture

Opinion	*Students*		*Total*
	UG (N=400)	*PG (N=69)*	*(N = 469)*
Comfortable	261 (65.25%)	44 (63.77%)	305 (65.03%)
Uncomfortable	125 (31.25%)	22 (31.88%)	147 (31.34%)
No idea	14 (3.50%)	3 (4.35%)	17 (3.62%)
Total	400 (100%)	69 (100%)	469 (100%)

Many variations are not seen in the opinions of UG and PG students regarding the utility aspect of furniture. Majority of the UG students (65%) and PG students (nearly 64%) thought that existing furniture is comfortable. However, 31 percent of UG as well as PG students are found to be not satisfied with the library furniture in use.

Lighting and Ventilation

Physical environment in the library, especially lighting, ventilation, acoustics and appearance are the factors making the users stay in the library comfortable, pleasant and interesting. Proper lighting arrangement is a must for comfortable reading and browsing. Natural lighting combined with the artificial lighting helps in providing comfortable reading atmosphere for users. User's feelings about the existing lighting facility are shown in Table 104.

Table 104
Lighting and Ventilation

Opinion	*Students*		*Total*
	UG (N=400)	*PG (N=69)*	*(N = 469)*
Adequate	236 (59%)	38 (55.07%)	274 (58.43%)
Inadequate	142 (35.50%)	24 (34.78%)	166 (35.39%)
No idea	22 (5.50%)	7 (10.14%)	29 (6.18%)
Total	400 (100%)	69 (100%)	469 (100%)

Analysis of data shows that 59 percent of UG students and 55 percent of PG students were of the opinion that the library had sufficient ventilation and lighting arrangement. But 36 percent of UG students and 35 percent of PG students were of the opinion that some of the work areas in the library do not have adequate lighting, (for example Stack area).

Internal Design

Internal arrangement of different sections in general and within the sections in specific is considered to be an important factor helping not only the smooth and efficient functioning of the library, but also its use by the user community. It is an internal part of planning of the library building. Users' access to different departments/ sections especially the service areas like stack area, reference, text book collection, periodical section, photocopying facilities may be either limited or facilitated by the interral structural and functional arrangements of library Ergono – followed also have its own effect on the extent of use of the library. Data is gathered about the feelings of users regarding the utilization point of internal arrangement.

Table 105
Internal Design

Opinion	Students		Total
	UG (N=400)	PG (N=69)	(N = 469)
Helpful	211 (52.75%)	51 (73.92%)	262 (55.86%)
Unhelpful	99 (24.75%)	11 (15.94%)	110 (23.45%)
No idea	90 (22.50%)	7 (10.14%)	97 (20.69%)
Total	400 (100%)	69 (100%)	469 (100%)

Majority of the PG (74%) as well as UG (56%) students were of the view that the internal design of the library is helpful and convenient as far as the use of the library is concerned. Nearly one quarter of students are not satisfied with the arrangement. Interestingly, significant percent of users so far have not given any thought to this aspect and are very casual.

Suggestions Regarding the Physical Facilities

UG and PG students have suggested the following regarding the physical facilities: (i) The library building may be located adjacent to the main building; (ii) They wanted the library to be nearer to the hostel; (iii) Present library building is not sufficient and wants to be extended; (iv) They want comfortable and more furniture; (v) Sufficient lighting, air conditioning and continuous power supply should be arranged; (vi) Cubicles are being requested for individual study; and (vii) Drinking water and toilet facilities are requested.

Opinion about Library Staff

Libraries are considered to be service institutions working through direct or indirect contact with the users. User satisfaction is crucial for adjudicating these institutions as successful. Besides the physical facilities and good collection, the role of staff is central for building up of an image among the users and in the view of management. Staffs' helpful attitude and behavior with users influence the extent of use of the library. Especially, staff has important role to play in the service areas whereas users will have regular interaction with library staff and need their help assistance and guidance in the use of resources of the library. Areas where users will have regular contact with the staff are identified. Users were asked to rate the behavior of staff keeping in view their attitude, helpful nature and knowledge in guiding them (Table 106).

Circulation Desk

Analysis of data in the Table-106. show that 34% of students considered library staff at the circulation desk as good. Very few (10%) of them rated the staff as poor.

Reference desk

Majority (41%) of students have rated the library staff at the reference desk as good. In addition, 33 percent of them considered library staff at the reference desk as fair in extending help to the users.

Periodical Section

The services of staff working in the periodical section were considered to be 'good' by 27% of the students both at UG and PG level. They have considered them as good. Twenty percent of them felt as fair. Nearly 9 percent of them considered as excellent. Majority of the students (34%) have not responded.

Photocopying Service

Majority of the students (33%) have rated the library staff at the photocopying service fair. In addition, 26 percent of them considered library staff at photo copying service as good. Nearly 22 percent of them felt poor. Very few of them (nearly 7%) express their opinion excellent for the staff at photocopying service.

Loan Section (Stacks)

Very few of the students have rated the library staff at the loan section fair (16%), good (13%) and excellent (only 3%). In addition, 15% of them express their opinion as 'poor' for the staff at stacks. Majority of them have not given any response to this question.

Textbook Section

Majority of the students (38.59%) have rated the library staff at the Textbook section as good. In addition 23.24 percent of them considered library staff at Textbook section as fair and 15.35 percent of them felt that the library staff at Textbook section as excellent.

Newspapers Section

Nearly 38 percent of the students felt the newspapers section as good. Next highest percentage (nearly 22%) felt them as excellent. Further, 19 percent of them considered as fair and very few of them (9%) felt as poor. Only 2 percent of them could not express their opinion.

Reading Room

Nearly 32 percent of the students considered the staff of the Reading Room as good. Twenty percent of them felt as fair. Fifteen percent of them felt it excellent. Further 14 percent of them felt as poor and only 4 percent of them could not express their opinion.

Availability of Computerized Services

Computerization is the current trend of the modern libraries and is fast acquiring

Table: 106
Opinion about Library Staff (More than one)

Opinion on	Excellent			Good			Fair			Poor			No Response		
	UG (N=400)	*PG (N=69)*	*Total (N=469)*	*UG (N=400)*	*PG (N=69)*	*Total (N=469)*	*UG (N=400)*	*PG (N=69)*	*Total (N=469)*	*UG (N=400)*	*PG (N=69)*	*Total (N=469)*	*UG (N=400)*	*PG (N=69)*	*Total (N=469)*
a)Circulation desk	39 (9.75%)	5 (7.25%)	44 (9.38%)	131 (32.75%)	29 (42.03%)	160 (34.12%)	87 (21.75%)	13 (18.84%)	100 (21.32%)	39 (9.75%)	9 (13.04%)	48 (10.23%)	111 (27.75%)	6 (8.70%)	117 (24.95%)
b) Reference desk	37 (9.25%)	7 (10.14%)	44 (9.38%)	156 (39%)	34 (49.28%)	190 (40.51%)	142 (35.50%)	15 (21.74%)	157 (33.48%)	21 (5.25%)	7 (10.14%)	28 (5.97%)	46 (11.50%)	4 (5.80%)	50 (10.66%)
c) Periodical section	38 (9.50%)	4 (5.80%)	42 (8.96%)	102 (25.50%)	23 (33.33%)	125 (26.65%)	77 (19.25%)	18 (26.09%)	95 (20.26%)	36 (9.00%)	16 (14.49%)	46 (9.81%)	158 (39.5%)	3 (4.35%)	161 (34.32%)
d) Photo-copying service	31 (7.75%0	0 (0%)	31 (6.61%)	112 (23%)	12 (17.39%)	124 (26.44%)	136 (34%)	19 (27.54%)	155 (33.05%)	70 (17.50%)	32 (46.38%)	102 (21.75%)	57 (14.25%)	0 (0%)	57 (12.15%)
e) Loan section (stacks)	10 (2.50%)	2 (2.90%)	12 (2.56%)	56 (14%)	5 (7.25%)	61 (13.01%)	59 (14.75%)	14 (20.29%)	73 (15.57%)	53 (13.25%)	15 (21.74%)	68 (14.50%)	237 (59.25%)	18 (26.09%)	355 (54.36%)
f) Text book section	66 (16.50%)	6 (8.70%)	72 (15.35%)	146 (36.50%)	35 (50.72%)	181 (38.59%)	96 (24%)	13 (18.84%)	109 (23.24%)	21 (5.25%)	6 (8.70%)	27 (5.76%)	78 (19.50%)	2 (2.90%)	80 (17.06%)
g) News papers section	84 (21%)	18 (26.09%)	102 (21.75%)	155 (38.75%)	23 (33.33%)	178 (37.95%)	73 (18.25%)	15 (21.75%)	88 (18.76%)	38 (9.50%)	5 (7.25%)	43 (9.17%)	56 (14.94%)	2 (2.90%)	58 (12.37%)
h) Reading Room	65 (16.25%)	7 (10.14%)	72 (15.35%)	109 (27.25%)	41 (59.42%)	150 (31.98%)	86 (21.50%)	7 (10.14%)	93 (19.83%)	60 (15%)	5 (7.25%)	65 (13.86%)	75 (18.75%)	14 (20.29%)	89 (18.98%)

popularity among the library users owing to its ease of use and ready information on the books available in the library. Keeping this in view, users were asked about computerization in their libraries and their responses were tabulated as under.

Table 107
Availability of Computerized Services

Availability	*Students*		*Total*
	UG (N=400)	*PG (N=69)*	*(N = 469)*
Yes	192 (48%)	46 (66.67%)	238 (50.75%)
No	208 (52%)	23 (33.33%)	231 (49.25%)
Total	400 (100%)	69 (100%)	469 (100%)

Analysis of data in the Table 107. shows majority (67%) of PG students' state that they have the availability of computerized services in their libraries. But majority of UG students (52%) stated that computerized services are not available in their library.

Access to Modern Facilities

Impact of Information Technology is seen in every walk of human life. Libraries are not exception to this. Provision of E-mail, Internet services, CD-ROM search and access to on-line databases in addition to conventional services are the remarkable features of modern libraries. Users in order to exploit the advanced IT facilities must be first made aware of these services. Following set of tables show the availability of these modern facilities to be in the libraries surveyed.

Table 108
Access to E-mail Facilities

E-mail	*Students*		*Total*
	UG (N=400)	*PG (N=69)*	*N = 469*
Yes	89 (22.25%)	7 (10.14%)	96 (20.47%)
No	311 (77.75%)	62 (89.86%)	373 (79.53%)
Total	400 (100%)	69 (100%)	469 (100%)

Analysis of data in the Table 108 shows that majority of PG (nearly 90%) and UG (nearly 78%) students have no access to E-mail facility. In general only 20 percent stated that they have access to E-mail facility.

Table: 109
Access to Internet Facility

Internet	*Students*		*Total*
	UG (N=400)	*PG (N=69)*	*N = 469*
Yes	91 (22.75%)	6 (8.70%)	97 (20.68%)
No	309 (77.25%)	63 (91.30%)	372 (79.32%)
Total	400 (100%)	69 (100%)	469 (100%)

Majority of both PG (91%) and UG (77%) students have no access to Internet facility. In general, Internet facility is available to 20 percent of students.

Table 110
Access to CD-ROM Database

CD – ROM	*Students*		*Total*
Database	*UG (N=400)*	*PG (N=69)*	*N = 469*
Yes	49 (12.25%)	21 (30.43%)	70 (14.93%)
No	351 (87.75%)	48 (69.57%)	399 (85.07%)
Total	400 (100%)	69 (100%)	469 (100%)

Even access to CD-ROM databases is not available to majority of the students (85%). Only 30 percent of PG and 12 percent of UG students are found to be having access to CD-ROM databases.

Table 111
Access to Library Database

Library Database	*Students*		*Total*
	UG (N=400)	*PG (N=69)*	*(N = 469)*
Yes	42 (10.5%)	5 (7.25%)	47 (10.02%)
No	358 (89.5%)	64 (92.75%)	422 (89.98%)
Total	400 (100%)	69 (100%)	469 (100%)

Analysis of data in Table 111 shows that majority of PG (nearly 93%) and UG (90%) students do not have access to library database. Only 10 percent of UG students and 7 percent of PG students state that they have access to library database.

Table 112
Frequency of Use of Internet

Internet	*Students*		*Total*
	UG (N=91)	*PG (N=6)*	*(N = 97)*
Frequently	21 (23.08%)	2 (33.33)	24 (24.74%)
Occasionally	32 (35.16%)	4 (66.66)	36 (37.11%)
Never	38 (41.76%)	3 (50%)	41 (42.27%)
Total	91 (100%)	6 (100%)	97 (100%)

Thirty seven percent of the students occasionally used Internet in the libraries. Further, nearly 25 percent of them made use of it frequently. Majority (42%) of them have never used Internet.

Table 113
Frequency Use of E-mail

E- mail	*Students*		*Total*
	UG (N=89)	*PG (N=7)*	*(N = 96)*
Frequently	24 (26.97%)	1 (14.28%)	25 (26.04%)
Occasionally	30 (33.71%)	2 (28.57%)	32 (33.33%)
Never	35 (39.32%)	4 (57.14%)	39 (40.62%)
Total	89 (100%)	7 (100%)	96 (100%)

Thirty three percent of the students made use of E-mail occasionally. Further, 26 percent of them made use of it frequently. Nearly 41 percent of them have not used E-mail.

Table 114
Frequency Use of CD-ROM Databases

C.D. ROM Database	*Students*		*Total*
	UG (N=49)	*PG (N=21)*	*(N = 70)*
Frequently	8 (16.33%)	5 (23.81%)	13 (18.57%)
Occasionally	21 (42.86%)	11 (52.38%)	32 (45.71%)
Never	10 (20.41%)	5 (23.81%)	15 (21.43%)
Total	49 (100%)	21 (100%)	70 (100%)

Majority of the students made use of CD-ROM databases occasionally. Twenty one percent of them have never used CD-ROM databases. Nineteen percent of them frequently use the CD-ROM Databases.

Table 115

Frequency Use of Library Database

E- mail	*Students*		*Total*
	UG (N=42)	*PG (N=5)*	*(N = 47)*
Frequently	3 (7.14%)	0 (0%)	3 (6.38%)
Occasionally	10 (23.81%)	2 (40%)	12 (25.53%)
Never	29 (69.05%)	3 (60%)	32 (68.08%)
Total	42 (100%)	5 (100%)	47 (100%)

Majority of the students (68%) do not use the library databases. Twenty six percent of them use the databases occasionally. Very few of them (6%) are using library databases frequenly.

Usefulness of Internet

Table 116

Usefulness of Internet

Useful	*Students*		*Total*
	UG (N=91)	*PG (N=6)*	*(N = 97)*
Yes	83 (91.21%)	5 (83.33%)	88 (90.72%)
No	8 (8.79%)	1 (16.66%)	10 (10.30%)
Total	91 (100%)	6 (100%)	97 (100%)

Analysis of data shows that for majority of UG (91%) and PG (83%) students, Internet is a useful source of information. Only 9 percent of the UG students and nearly 17 percent of PG students considered that it is not useful.

Reasons for Using Internet

Table 117

Reasons for using Internet (more than one)

Reasons	*Students*		*Total*
	UG (N=91)	*PG (N=6)*	*(N = 97)*
To find subject information	89 (97.80%)	6 (100%)	95 (97.93%)
For Job information	68 (74.72%)	5 (83.33%)	73 (75.26%)
For information on further studies	90 (98.90%)	5 (83.33%)	95 (97.94%)
To chat with student / teacher in the same field	42 (46.15%)	5 (83.33%)	47 (48.45%)
For entertainment	64 (70.32%)	4 (66.66%)	68 (70.10%)
Other, please specify	8 (8.79%)	0 (0%)	8 (8.25%)

From Table-117, 100 percent of the PG students are found to be using Internet to find subject information. Nearly 99 percent UG students are found to be using Internet for gathering information for further studies for the sake of information on relevant subjects. Seventy five percent are found searching for jobs related information. For entertainment purpose, also 70 percent of the UG students are having access to Internet. Equal percentages (83%) of the PG students are found using internet for further studies, job information and to chat with students and teachers in the same field. The other reasons specified for using internet are e-mail, chatting, online news and net phones.

Need for User Training for Automated Services

Unless users are fully aware of techniques of using a particular service, they will not come forward to use the service confidently. At the same time, all the users might not have background knowledge about the new facility available in the library. In order to make the users to use the new services offered to the maximum extent possible, library should take initiative for offering user-training programmes in their use. Following set of tables indicate the need for offering training programmes as mentioned by students.

Table 118

Need for User Training in the Use of Automated Library Catalogue

Need for user training	*Students*		*Total*
	UG (N=400)	*PG (N=69)*	*N = (469)*
Yes	178 (44.50%)	34 (49.28%)	212 (45.20%)
No	125 (31.25%)	8 (11.59%)	133 (28.36%)
No response	97 (24.25%)	27 (39.13%)	124 (26.44%)
Total	400 (100%)	69 (100%)	469 (100%)

Analysis of data in Table-118. shows that majority of PG (49%) and UG (44%) students expressed the need for the use of automated catalogue. Only 31 percent of UG students and nearly 12 percent of PG students felt that there is no need for user training in automated library catalogue. Remaining, both UG (24%) and PG (39%) students have not responded.

Forty five percent of the both UG and PG students expressed the need for the use of automated catalogue and 28 percent of them felt that there is no need for user training in the automated catalogue. Remaining percentage (26%) of the students have not responded.

Table 119

Need for User Training in Internet Use

Internet	*Students*		*Total*
	UG (N=400)	*PG (N=69)*	*N = (469)*
Yes	183 (45.75%)	39 (56.52%)	222 (47.33%)
No	115 (28.75%)	10 (14.49%)	125 (26.65%)
No response	102 (25.50%)	20 (28.98%)	122 (26.01%)
Total	400 (100%)	69 (100%)	469 (100%)

Analysis of data shows that majority of the students, both PG (56%) and UG (46%) felt the need for user training in the use of Internet. In general, analysis of data shows that 47% of both UG and PG students have pointed out the need for offering user training in the Internet. Only 27 percent of them felt that there is no need for offering user training in the Internet. Remaining (26%) of the students have not responded.

Table 120
Need for User Training in Use of E-mail

E- mail	*Students*		*Total*
	UG (N=400)	*PG (N=69)*	*N = (469)*
Yes	156 (39%)	40 (57.97%)	196 (41.79%)
No	132 (33%)	9 (13.04%)	141 (30.06%)
No response	112 (28%)	20 (28.98%)	132 (28.14%)
Total	400 (100%)	69 (100%)	469 (100%)

Analysis of data in Table 120 shows that majority of PG students (58%) and 39 percent of UG students recognized the need for training in the use of E-mail. However, 33 percent of UG students and only 13 percent of PG students felt that there is no need for user training in the use of E-mail. In general, analysis of data shows that total (both UG and PG) students (42%) recognized the need for user training in E-mail. Thirty percent of them felt there is no need for user training in E-mail. Remaining (28%) have not responded.

Table 121
Need for User Training in the Use of CD-ROM Databases

CD-ROM's search	*Students*		*Total*
	UG (N=400)	*PG (N=69)*	*N = (469)*
Yes	148 (37%)	34 (49.28%)	182 (38.81%)
No	116 (29%)	10 (14.49%)	126 (26.87%)
No response	136 (34%)	25 (36.23%)	161 (34.33%)
Total	400 (100%)	69 (100%)	469 (100%)

Same trend is noticed in the case of CD-ROM database search. The majority of PG students (49%) agreed with the fact that there is a dire need for user training in CD-ROM Database search. Only 29 percent of UG students and 14 percent of PG students opinioned that there is no need for user training in CD-ROM Database search (Table-121).

In general, analysis shows that most of the students (both UG and PG) felt that there is a need for user training in CD-ROM Database search. Twenty seven percent of them felt that there is no need for user training in CD-ROM Database search. Remaining (34%) have not responded.

Willingness to Pay for Computerized Services

Provision of computerized services, especially with modern and advanced equipment involves a lot of expenditure, on the part of library. Moreover, besides over head costs, regular maintenance and updating of existing facility requires extra finances. One of the alternatives available before the library management for generating revenue is charging the services. To implement such a policy, there is a need to study the minds of users in terms of their willingness to pay for the services and costs of the priced services. Table-122 indicates the details about the willingness of users to pay for the service.

Table 122
Willingness to Pay for Computerized Services

Opinion	*Students*		*Total*
	UG (N=400)	*PG (N=69)*	*N = (469)*
Yes	280 (70%)	46 (66.67%)	326 (69.51%)
No	120 (30%)	23 (33.33%)	143 (30.49%)
Total	400 (100%)	69 (100%)	469 (100%)

The response to this question is encouraging. Majority of UG (70%) students and PG (nearly 67%) students are willing to pay for computerized services. Only 33 percent of PG students and 30 percent of UG students are not willing to pay computerized services.

Suggestions for Library Improvement

The following suggestions received from 400 Undergraduate and 69 Postgraduate students:

a) Suggestions regarding services are 1) more number of reference books to be procured i.e., Dictionaries, Competitive books etc. 2) to provide current awareness service related to social sciences. 3) Current publications of books, National and international journals should be procured and displayed. 3) Translation service should be provided. 4) To provide inter library loan facility and issue more number of books. 5) Literature search service should be provided. 6) Photocopying service to be improved, long process should be avoided; working hours are not enough and should be increased.

b) Suggestions regarding the staff are 1) Staff should be cooperative 2) Should be punctual, honest and user friendly. 3) Existing library staff needs training using modern facilities like internet, E-mail, data search etc.

c) Suggestions regarding physical facilities are 1) Drinking water facility, toilets.

2) Sound absorbing walls. 3) Proper ventilation. 4) Comfortable furniture. 5) Air-conditioning. 6) Continuous power supply should be provided.

d) Suggestions regarding modern facilities are 1) Free access of Internet, E-mail facilities.2) Online contacts with other libraries. 4) Access to CD-ROM data bases.

USER SURVEY-SCIENTISTS, FACULTY AND RESEARCH STUDENTS

Frequency of Visits to the Library

To know whether there exists any variation in the frequency of use of the library among Scientists, Faculty, and Research students, respondents were asked to indicate their pattern of use of the library. Frequency of visits has been classified into seven categories. Responses of the three categories of users indicating their usual frequency of visits to the library are presented in Table 123.

Table 123
Frequency of Visits

Frequency of Visits	*Scientists (N=184)*	*Faculty (N=133)*	*Research students (N=94)*	*Total (N=411)*
a) Daily	36 (19.57%)	27 (20.30%)	33 (35.11%)	96 (23.36%)
b) Twice a week	53 (28.80%)	54 (40.60%)	38 (40.43%)	145 (35.28%)
c) Once in a week	31 (16.85%)	22 (16.54%)	13 (13.83%)	66 (16.06%)
d) Once in a fortnight	19 (10.33%)	9 (6.77%)	2 (2.13%)	30 (7.30%)
e) Once in a month	8 (4.35%)	7 (5.26%)	1 (1.06%)	16 (3.89%)
f) Occasionally	31 (16.85%)	14 (10.53%)	5 (5.32%)	50 (12.17%)
g) Seldom	6 (3.26%)	0 (0%)	2 (2.13%)	8 (1.95%)
Total	184 (100%)	133 (100%)	94 (100%)	411 (100%)

The analysis of data in Table 123 shows that the majority of faculty members (nearly 41%) visited the library "twice a week", followed by those who visited the library daily (20%). The percent of faculty visiting the library once in a month is found to be very less

(5%). Like faculty, a large number of the research students (40%) visited the library twice a week and 35 percent visited the library daily. Same trend is seen among scientists. As many as 29 percent of scientists visited library twice in a week, followed by nearly 20% who visited the library daily.

In general, largest number of users (35%) visited the library twice a week, followed by daily visits (23%). The overall percent of the users who had never visited the library is significantly low i.e nearly 2 percent out of the total sample.

Analysis of frequency of visits indicates that among daily visitors, research students are more in percentage compared to other two categories.

Categories of users has an impact on the frequency of visit to the library. A Chi-square test also supported the finding at 5% level of significance. (Calculated $\chi^2_{(6)}$=26.481, table value $\chi^2_{(6)}$=12.59).

To facilitate statistical analysis, all the six frequencies are grouped as 'frequent visits' (including daily, twice in a week and once in a week); 'less frequent visits' (once in a fortnight and once in a month) and 'seldom visits' (occasionally and seldom).

Table 124
Percentage Distribution of Three Groups (Scientists, Faculty and Research Students) by Nature of Frequency of Visits

Nature of frequency of visits	*Scientists (N=184)*	*Faculty (N=133)*	*Research students (N=94)*	*Total (N=411)*
Frequently	120 (65.22%)	103 (77.44%)	84 (89.37%)	307 (74.70%)
Less frequently	58 (31.52%)	30 (22.56%)	8 (8.51%)	96 (23.36%)
Seldom	6 (3.26%)	0 (0%)	2 (2.13%)	8 (1.95%)
Total	184 (100%)	133 (100%)	94 (100%)	411 (100%)

The Table 124 shows the three kinds of frequencies of visits to the library by the three groups of users. There is a much difference in terms of frequency of visits among them. Highest percent of scientist (65%), faculty (77%) and research students (89%) are visiting the library frequently. None of the faculty stated that they never used the library, whereas very few scientists and research students are found to be non users of the library services (2 to 3%).

Purpose of Visiting the Library

The purpose of visiting the library may vary depending on the users' information needs. They may visit the library to read current journals and latest books etc. They may also visit the library to borrow the items like: books, journals, standards, specifications, etc. or for obtaining a specific piece of information either from the documents or from the library staff or to consult reference sources on a specific subject of individual interest or in support of their research work or with combination of more than one purpose stated above. Accordingly, the purposes of visit to the library were made into six categories and the users were asked to indicate the purpose for which they usually visit the library. The following table indicates the percentage distribution of the three groups (scientists, faculty and research students) by purpose of their visit to the library.

From the above table, it is evident that the highest percentage (81%) of users among the three groups (scientists 82%, research students 81% and faculty members 79%) was reported to be visiting the library to refer and read the material in the library. Second highest percentage (nearly 54%) of users among the three groups (faculty 69%, research students 50%; scientists 45%) is found to be visiting the library for borrowing books. Third highest percentage (nearly 33%) of them (scientists 36%; faculty 32%; research students 27%) is visiting the library for borrowing journals. Very few of them are visiting the library for using internet (8%), E-mail (4%), and for other reasons like to read newspapers.

Table 125
Purpose of Visiting the Library (more than one)

Purpose	*Scientists N=184*	*Faculty N=133*	*Research students N=94*	*Total N=411*
Borrowing books	83 (45.11%)	92 (69.17%)	47 (50%)	222 (54.01%)
Borrowing journals	67 (36.41%)	43 (32.33%)	25 (26.60%)	135 (32.85%)
Reading library materials	151 (82.07%)	105 (78.95%)	76 (80.85%)	332 (80.78%)
Using Internet	13 (7.07%)	15 (11.28%)	7 (7.45%)	35 (8.52%)
Using E-mail	1 (0.54%)	11 (8.27%)	5 (5.32%)	17 (4.14%)
Any other	3 (1.63%)	5 (3.76%)	2 (2.13%)	10 (2.43%)

Category-wise differences in the purpose of visiting the library are not noticed among the users. Irrespective of their category, majority of them are visiting the library for reading and borrowing books and journals.

Purpose of Seeking Information

Information sought by scientists, faculty members and research students from different sources, may be used for different purposes. All possible intentions with which scientists, faculty members and research students who seek information are categorized into nine types. Scientists, faculty members and research students were asked to answer whether they visit to library for more than one purpose, if necessary. Responses are sought from all the three levels of users to find out whether any differences exist regarding their information use pattern. The following table gives the motives behind seeking information among the scientists, faculty members and research students.

Table 126

Purpose of Seeking Information from the Library (more than one)

Purpose of seeking information	*Scientists (N=184)*	*Faculty (N=133)*	*Research students (N=94)*	*Total (N=411)*
For teaching	21 (11.41%)	110 (82.71%)	6 (6.38%)	137 (33.33%)
Guiding scholars	18 (9.78%)	61 (45.86%)	2 (2.13%)	81 (19.71%)
For writing research reports	106 (57.61%)	43 (32.33%)	30 (31.92%)	179 (43.55%)
Writing an article	96 (52.17%)	67 (50.38%)	34 (36.17%)	197 (47.93%)
Research study	49 (26.63%)	47 (35.34%)	64 (68.09%)	160 (38.93%)
Writing exam	6 (3.26%)	3 (2.26%)	25 (26.60%)	34 (8.27%)
For writing Research proposals	62 (33.70%)	36 (27.07%)	17 (18.09%)	115 (27.98%)
To be abreast of latest information	102 (55.43%)	69 (51.88%)	43 (45.74%)	214 (52.07%)
Any other	2 (1.09%)	5 (3.76%)	4 (4.26%)	11 (2.68%)

Analysis of data reveals that majority of the scientists are seeking the information for writing research reports (58%) followed by the need to be abreast of latest developments in their field of interest (55%).

Majority of the research students (68%) indicated that they sought the information for the purpose of research study. Nearly 46 percent of them also stated that they seek information to know the current developments in their field of study.

Among the teaching faculty, majority (83%) sought information for teaching and instructional purposes. More than half of them (51%) are using information to know the latest developments in the concerned subject fields.

In general, majority of the users (52%) surveyed are seeking information from the library to keep themselves up-to-date in the areas of their interest. Second highest percent of the users (48%) stated that they have utilized information from the library for writing articles for publication in journals. Significant percent (44%) of users sought information from the library for the sake of writing research reports. Nearly 3 percent of the users responded for 'any other'. They have indicated that they are using information to guide the farmers.

Category-wise analysis shows significant differences in the purpose of seeking information among the user groups. In-fact, these variations reflect the nature of job with which the user is involved with. Four percent of the research students indicated their purpose to be preparing for competitive examinations. One percent of the scientists stated that their purpose of seeking information is to guide the farmers, and four percent of the faculty indicated the reason to guide research students.

Other Sources of Information

Scientists, faculty and research students may approach different sources like personal books, journals etc.; colleagues, other libraries, research students/scientists working in other institutions/organizations and also internet to ascertain relevant information and exchange of ideas. To assess the dependency of the three categories of users on the above mentioned sources other than the library to get required information, data was gathered. The following table shows the response from the three groups of users (scientists, faculty and research students) using other sources.

Table 127
Response from Three Groups of Users Using Other Sources of Information

Using other sources	*Scientists (N=184)*	*Faculty (N=133)*	*Research Students (N=94)*	*Total (N=411)*
Response	177 (96.20%)	130 (97.74%)	92 (97.87%)	399 (97.08%)
No response	7 (3.80%)	3 (2.26%)	2 (2.13%)	12 (2.92%)
Total	184 (100%)	133 (100%)	94 (100%)	411 (100%)

Response to this question is very much encouraging. Majority of the three groups have responded. Sometimes the users may gather information from more than one source. Hence, multiple responses are allowed and totals are not additive. From the above table, it is evident that majority of the three groups of users are trying other sources before visiting the library. Further, data showing the use of more than one kind of other sources by the three groups of users. Hence, 'N' changes for all the three groups of users.

Table 128

Categories of Other Sources of Information (more than one)

Categories of other sources	*Scientists (N=177)*	*Faculty (N=130)*	*Research students (N=92)*	*Total (N=399)*
Personal Collections	105 (59.32%)	102 (78.46%)	42 (45.65%)	249 (62.41%)
Colleagues	94 (53.11%)	68 (52.31%)	37 (40.22%)	199 (49.87%)
Other libraries	81 (45.76%)	62 (47.69%)	61 (66.30%)	204 (51.13%)
Scientists working in other Agricultural institutions	105 (59.32%)	80 (61.54%)	43 (46.74%)	228 (57.14%)
Other institutions/ organizations	79 (44.64%)	47 (36.15%)	37 (40.22%)	163 (40.85%)
Internet	71 (40.11%)	60 (46.15%)	41 (44.57%)	172 (43.11%)
Any other	3 (1.70%)	4 (3.08%)	2 (2.17%)	9 (2.26%)

Among the research students, highest percent (66%) are depending on other libraries, and followed by those using the services of research students and scientists in other agricultural institutions (47%) are found to be depending. Nearly 46 percent of the research students are found to be depending on their personal collection. Dependency on Internet was seen among 44% of research students. An equal percent (40%) of the research students are also consulting their colleagues and other institutions / organizations for necessary information.

It may seen from Table-128. that majority of the faculty members are depending on their personal collection (78%) followed by those depending on fellow researchers / scientists (62%) in other organisations and colleagues (52%). Dependency on other libraries nearly (48%) and Internet (46%) was also noticed among significant percent of faculty. Thirty one percent of the faculty members are also found to be consulting other institutions/ organizations.

In case of scientists, an equal percent (59%) are depending on personal collection and fellow researchers / scientists in other organisations. Colleagues are considered as sources of information by 53 percent of the scientists. Regarding other libraries and institutions, 46 percent and 45 percent respectively are utilizing them as sources of information. Interestingly, Internet was indicated as reliable source of required information by 46 percent of faculty, 45 percent of research students and 40 percent of scientists.

Dependency on personal collection was greater in the case of faculty under 'any other source' members than in scientists and research students. Research students' dependency on other libraries for required information was greater than faculty members and scientists.

Two percent of the scientists, research students and teaching faculty reported that they are attending workshops, conferences and seminars to acquire latest knowledge and information in their field of interest.

Extent of Dependency on Other Sources

Table 129
Degree of Dependence on Other Sources (more than one)

Dependence	*Scientists (N=177)*	*Faculty (N=130)*	*Research students (N=92)*	*Total (N=399)*
Greatly	30 (16.95%)	18 (13.85%)	22 (23.65%)	72 (18.04%)
Moderately	103 (58.19%)	90 (69.23%)	52 (56.52%)	245 (61.40%)
Scarcely	44 (24.86%)	22 (16.54%)	18 (19.57%)	82 (20.55%)
Not at all	7 (3.95%)	3 (2.31%)	2 (2.17%)	12 (3.01%)
Total	184 (100%)	133 (100%)	94 (100%)	411 (100%)

Analysis of data on the degree of dependency on other sources of information in Table-129 shows that much difference is not seen among the three groups in this regard.

Majority of the scientists (58%), research students (57%) and faculty (69%) are moderately depending on other sources of information. Second highest percent of scientists (25%) is found to be scarcely dependent on other sources. Twenty four percent of research students are dependent on other sources greatly, where as nearly 25 percent of faculty are scarcely dependent on other sources. Small percentage of scientists, faculty and research students (4%, 2% and 2% respectively) are found to be seldom used the other sources of information.

Reasons for Using Other Sources

There are different reasons to use other sources from which scientists, faculty and research students get the required information. Inadequate, obsolete and irrelevant collections; problems of access and non availability of Internet may be some of the reasons for consulting other sources. The Table 130, gives details of the reasons for using other sources.

It may be seen from Table 130 that both scientists and faculty stated the same reasons for using other sources. Inadequate collections in the library was the main reason quoted by majority of the scientists (64%) and faculty (62%). The second highest percent (36%

scientists, 42% faculty) of them pointed out non coverage of foreign publications in library collection as a reason. It may be seen. that the reason 'library does not have adequate collection' was greater in the case of scientists rather than in faculty and research students.

Among the research students, also highest percent (60%) stated the reason to be 'Library does not have adequate collection'. Second highest percent (38%) has given the reason to be 'Library does not have Internet facility' followed by 'collection does not cover foreign publication' (37%), and 'collection is outdated (33%).

Table 130
Reasons for Using Other Sources (more than one)

Reasons	*Scientists (N = 177)*	*Faculty (N = 130)*	*Research Students (N = 92)*	*Total (N = 411)*
a) Library does not have adequate collection	114 (64.41%)	80 (61.54%)	55 (59.78%)	249 (62.41%)
b) Library collection is outdated	29 (16.38%)	29 (22.31%)	30 (32.61%)	88 (22.06%)
c) Collection is not relevant	21 (11.86%)	14 (10.77%)	15 (16.30%)	50 (12.53%)
d) Collection is not in good condition	17 (9.60%)	14 (10.77%)	15 (16.30%)	46 (11.53%)
e) Collection does not cover foreign publications	63 (35.59%)	54 (41.54%)	34 (36.96%)	151 (37.84%)
f) Library does not have internet facility publications	46 (25.99%)	43 (33.08%)	35 (38.04%)	124 (31.08%)
g) Do not know about the availability of the required item in the library	15 (8.47%)	14 (10.77%)	10 (10.87%)	39 (9.77%)
h) Don't find time to visit the library	16 (9.04%)	18 (13.85%)	7 (7.61%)	41 (10.28%)
i) Library is located distant place	13 (7.34%)	12 (9.23%)	14 (15.22%)	39 (9.77%)
j) It is more convenient to use them	11 (6.21%)	25 (19.23%)	11 (11.96%)	47 (11.78%)
k) Any other	12 (6.78%)	8 (6.15%)	7 (7.61%)	27 (6.77%)

In general, the majority of total respondents stated the reasons 'library does not have adequate collection' (62%), 'collection does not cover foreign publications' (38%) and 'library does not have Internet facility' (31%) respectively, for using other sources of information.

Number of Publications/ Contributions (Journal Articles/ Conference Papers/ Books/ Patents) During the Last Five Years

Concretized innovative ideas through research lead to patents. Further scientists, research students and faculty communicated their findings, opinion and ideas, in their subject of interest through the publication of books, articles in journals and conference papers. For this purpose, scientists, research students and faculty usually seek information from various sources. Here the library plays a significant role in supporting the activity of bringing out patents, books and papers by scientists, research students and faculty. For this purpose data on different types of contributions made during the last five years (1996-2001) was collected through the questionnaire.

Percentages are calculated only for those who have responded for this question.

Journal Articles

Agricultural scientists, research students and faculty members may have different contributions to their credit during their professional services. Contributions may be in the form of patents, books, papers, presented in seminar/ conferences and articles published in various periodicals. For the above contributions, there are ample chances of utilizing the library. To ascertain whether any relation exists between agricultural scientists, research students and faculty members & personal contributions and their library use, data regarding contributions in the last five years (1996-2001) were analyzed in the following Table 131.

Table 131
Publications-Journal Articles

No. of contributions	*Scientists (N = 143)*	*Faculty (N= 122)*	*Research students (N= 56)*	*Total (N= 321)*
Below 5	86 (60.14%)	54 (44.26%)	43 (76.79%)	183 (57.01%)
6-10	26 (18.18%)	27 (13.93%)	11 (19.64%)	32 (9.67%)
11-15	14 (9.79%)	17 (13.93%)	1 (1.79%)	32 (9.67%)
16-20	8 (5.59%)	8 (6.56%)	0 (0%)	16 (4.98%)
21-25	2 (1.40%)	5 (4.10%)	1 (1.79%)	8 (2.49%)
26 and above	7 (4.90%)	11 (9.01%)	0 (0.00%)	18 (5.61%)
Total (N=321)	143 (100%)	122 (100%)	56 (100%)	321 (100%)

The above table reveals that the majority of scientists (60%), faculty (44%) and research students (77%) wrote less than 5 articles in the last five years. Compared to other two categories more percent of faculty published 21 and above articles.

Number of Publications during the last 5 years – conference papers

Data has been gathered separately regarding the number of conference papers presented in the last five years. Percentages are calculated only for those who have answered this question.

Table 132
Publications-Conference Papers

Number of contributions	*Scientists (N= 84)*	*Research students (N=26)*	*Faculty (N=70)*	*Total (N=180)*
Below 5	50 (59.52%)	19 73.08%)	35 (50%)	104 (57.78%)
6-10	19 (22.62%)	5 (19.23%)	23 (32.86%)	47 (26.11%)
11-15	6 (7.14%)	0 (0%)	6 (8.57%)	12 (6.67%)
16-20	4 (4.76%)	1 (3.85%)	1 (1.43%)	6 (3.33%)
21-25	3 (3.57%)	1 (3.85%)	1 (1.43%)	5 (2.78%)
25 and above	2 (2.38%)	0 (0%)	4 (5.71%)	6 (3.33%)
Total (N=180)	84 (100%)	26 (100%)	70 (100%)	180 (100%)

Table 132 shows that the published scientists (60%) and faculty members (50%) and research students (73%) have presented below 5 conference papers during last five years the second highest percentage of them published articles ranging from 6 to 10. As the number of papers increase the number of users decreased showing more concentration in the first class. Very few of them found to be having 21 and above conference papers.

Number of publications during the last 5 years – Books

Response to this question is not encouraging. Only 23 percent, 4 percent and 21 percent of the scientists, research students and faculty respectively have responded. Those who gave response gave details about the number of books published. Following tables show these details.

Table 133
Publications—Books

Number of contributions	*Scientists (N = 42)*	*Faculty (N = 28)*	*Research students (N = 8)*	*Total (N =78)*
Below 5	37 (88.10%)	27 (96.43%)	3 (37.50%)	67 (85.90%)
5- 10	2 (4.76%)	1 (3.57%)	2 (25.00%)	5 (6.41%)
10-15	1 (2.38%)	0 (0%)	1 (12.50%)	2 (2.56%)
15-20	1 (2.38%)	0 (0%)	0 (0%)	1 (1.28%)
20-25	0 (0%)	0 (0%)	0 (0%)	0 (0%)
25 above	1 (2.38%)	0 (0.00%)	2 (25.00%)	3 (3.85%)
Total (N=78)	42 (100%)	28 (100%)	8 (100%)	78 (100%)

It may be seen from the Table 133 among those who have authored books that majority are wrote below 5 books (96 percent faculty, 88 percent scientists and 38 percent of students).

Number of publications during the last five years- Patents

Out of 411 scientists, only 11 and one each from the group of research students and faculty have responded to this question.

Table 134
Publications– Patents

No of Contributions	*Scientists (N = 11)*	*Faculty (N = 1)*	*Research students (N = 1)*	*Total (N = 13)*
Below 5	11 (100%)	1 (100%)	1 (100%)	13 (100%)
5- 10	0 (0%)	0 (0%)	0 (0%)	0 (0%)
10-15	0 (0%)	0 (0%)	0 (0%)	0 (0%)
15-20	0 (0%)	0 (0%)	0 (0%)	0 (0%)
20-25	0 (0%)	0 (0%)	0 (0%)	0 (0%)
25 above	0 (0%)	0 (0%)	0 (0%)	0 (0%)
Total (N=411)	11 (100%)	1 (100%)	1 (100%)	13 (100%)

Majority of the scientists reported that they have contribution of below 5 patents in the last five years. Only one research student and one faculty member reported having below 5 patents. None of the three group users found to be having patent rights of above 5 in the last five years.

Degree of Dependency on Library for Publication

Scientists, research students and faculty members may seek information for various reasons. Preliminary information is essential if a user who wants to be abreast of developments in his field. A particular piece of information may come to the aid of users in teaching, research and development activities responsible for innovations. Information may also be used by them while writing project reports, conference papers or articles for journals.

The extent of use of any information service by the user mostly depends upon its ability to match his information requirements. The form of presentations and extent of coverage of the required information are also important factors deciding the usefulness of the service to the user. All the services provided by the library may not be completely useful from the user point of view. An attempt has been made in Table-135 for the extent of dependency on library for preparing professional articles and papers.

Table 135

Extent of Dependency on Library for Publication Purposes

Extent of dependency	*Scientists (N = 184)*	*Faculty (N = 133)*	*Research Students (N = 94)*	*Total (N = 411)*
Greatly	40 (21.74%)	29 (21.80%)	23 (24.47%)	92 (22.38%)
Moderately	120 (65.22%)	90 (67.67%)	59 (62.77%)	269 (65.45%)
Scarcely	20 (10.87%)	13 (9.77%)	5 (5.32%)	38 (9.25%)
Not at all	4 (2.17%)	1 (0.75%)	7 (7.45%)	12 (2.92%)
Total (N=411)	184 (100%)	133 (100%)	94 (100%)	411 (100%)

Significant differences are not noticed in-terms of dependency on the library for publishing articles and papers among the three groups of users. Under each category as well as in general the same trend is noticed. Majority of the scientists (65%), research students (63%) and faculty (68%) are moderately dependent on the organization library. Second highest percent of these users (22%) are found to be depending greatly on the library for the sake of publications

All categories of purpose have same levels of dependence on libraries regarding their publications. A Chi-square test also supported the finding. (Calculated $\chi^2_{(4)}$=0.880, Table value $\chi^2_{(4)}$=9.49).

Frequency of Dependency on Other Sources of Information for Publishing Articles and Books

There are different sources from which users of agricultural information get the information's required by them. Library located in an agricultural organization may be one of them. Scientists, researchers and faculty members' access to different sources other than library may have effect on their use of the agricultural library. Tables in previous sections focused light on number of papers published in journals, conference papers, books and patent of different groups of users. For preparing and publishing them they might have depended on different sources of information.

Scientists, research students and faculty members may approach different sources like personal collection, (books, journals etc.), colleagues, other libraries, Internet, other institutions/ organizations and scientists working in other organizations. Some times they may gather information from more than one source. Hence, multiple responses were allowed and totals were not additive.

Further data showing use of different kinds of other sources for publishing purposes and frequency of use among three groups of users was given in the following Table 136. In this table, only the responses of those users who reported using one or more 'other sources' were considered for analysis. Hence 'N' changes for all the three groups of users.

Extent of Dependency on Personal Collections for Publication - Personal Collections

Among scientists majority (51%) found to be moderately dependent on their personal collections. Second highest percentages (39%) of them are depending greatly on personal collections. Slightly different trend is seen in the case of researchers and faculty. Highest percentages of them are greatly depending on personal collection. (55% faculty and 52% research students) Insignificant percent of the users stated that they are not at all depending on personal collections for publishing articles and books.

Table 136
Extent of Dependency on Personal Collection

Extent of dependency	*Scientists (N = 134)*	*Research Students (N = 66)*	*Faculty (N = 116)*	*Total (N = 316)*
Greatly	52 (38.81%)	34 (51.52%)	64 (55.17%)	150 (42.41%)
Moderately	68 (50.75%)	21 (31.82%)	45 (38.79%)	134 (47.47%)
Scarcely	13 (9.70%)	8 (12.12%)	5 (4.31%)	26 (8.23%)
Not at all	1 (0.75%)	3 (4.55%)	2 (1.72%)	6 (1.90%)
Total (N=316)	134 (100%)	66 (100%)	116 (100%)	316 (100%)

Extent of Dependence on Colleagues for Publication

Table 137

Extent of Dependency on Colleagues

Extent Dependency	*Scientists (N = 107)*	*Faculty (N = 93)*	*Researches Students (N = 42)*	*Total (N = 242)*
Greatly	14 (13.08%)	3 (7.14%)	7 (7.53%)	24 (9.92%)
Moderately	61 (57.01%)	15 (35.71%)	41 (44.09%)	117 (48.35%)
Scarcely	32 (29.91%)	24 (57.14%)	45 (48.39%)	101 (41.74%)
Total (N=242)	107 (100%)	42 (100%)	93 (100%)	242 (100%)

The analysis of data on dependency on colleagues for publication purpose reveals that the use of this source was predominant among scientists (57%); scarce in the case of research students (48%) and faculty (nearly 57%). Compared to scientists and faculty members, percentage of research students who never approached their colleagues to get required information is more. However 'greater' dependency on colleagues is prevalent only among 13 percent, 7 percent and 8 percent of the scientists, research students and faculty respectively.

General figures are also representing moderate dependency on colleagues by majority of the users (48%) followed by percentage of users depending on them scarcely (nearly 42%).

Extent of Dependency on Other Libraries for Publication

Table 138

Extent of Dependency on Other Libraries

Extent of Dependency	*Scientists (N = 114)*	*Faculty (N = 96)*	*Research Students (N = 64)*	*Total (N = 274)*
Greatly	14 (12.28%)	8 (8.33%)	7 (10.94%)	29 (10.58%)
Moderately	54 (47.37%)	43 (44.79%)	35 (54.69%)	132 (48.18%)
Scarcely	35 (36.70%)	35 (46.46%)	13 (20.31%)	83 (30.30%)
Not at all	11 (9.65%)	10 (10.42%)	9 (20.31%)	30 (10.95%)
Total (N=274)	114 (100%)	96 (100%)	64 (100%)	274 (100%)

Regarding extent of dependency on other libraries, much differences were not noticed among the three groups of users. Majority of scientists (47%), research students (55%) and faculty (45%) are found to be moderately depending on other libraries for publication purposes. Next highest percent of all the three groups of users viz. Scientists, research students and faculty (37%, 20% and 46% respectively) stated that they are scarcely dependent on other libraries. Nearly 10 percent of scientists, 20 percent of the research students and 10 percent of faculty members are not at all using the other libraries.

The majority of users (48%) among three categories i.e., scientists, research students and faculty members are depending moderately on other libraries Thirty percent of them are dependent of the other libraries scarcely.

Extent of Dependency on Internet for Publication

Table 139
Extent of Dependency on Internet

Extent of dependency	*Scientists (N = 99)*	*Faculty (N = 99)*	*Research Students (N = 60)*	*Total (N = 258)*
Greatly	10 (10.10%)	11 (11.11%)	5 (8.33%)	26 (10.08%)
Moderately	52 (52.53%)	58 (58.59%)	27 (45.00)	132 (51.16%)
Scarcely	39 (39.39%)	25 (25.25%)	15 (25.00%)	76 (29.46%)
Not at all	6 (6.06%)	5 (5.05%)	13 (21.67%)	24 (9.30%)
Total	99 (100%)	99 (100%)	60 (100%)	258 (100%)

The data in Table 139 shows the highest percentage of faculty members (59%) are depending moderately on Internet as source of information for publication. Further 25 percent of them scarcely, 11 percent of them greatly and 5 percent seldom dependent on Internet sources for writing articles and books. As many as (45%) research students are dependent on Internet moderately, 25 percent scarcely, 22 percent of them are not dependent on Internet and only 8 percent of them are dependent greatly on Internet. As many as 53 percent of scientists are moderately depending on Internet for publishing purposes.

The largest number of users among three groups i.e., scientists, research students and faculty members (51%) are moderately depending on internet as sources of information for publishing purpose. However 29 percent of them scarcely, 10percent of them greatly used, 9 percent of them seldom used the Internet for the same.

Extent of Dependency on Other Institutions or Organisations for Publication Purpose

The following table shows the degree of dependency of the users on other institutional libraries.

Table: 140
Extent of Dependence on Other Institutions/Organizations for Publication Purpose

Extent of dependency	*Scientists (N=99)*	*Faculty (N=99)*	*Research student (N=60)*	*Total (N=258)*
Greatly	10 (10.10%)	11 (11.11%)	5 (8.3%)	26 (10.08%)
Moderately	52 (52.53%)	58 (58.58%)	27 (45%)	132 (51.16%)
Scarcely	36 (36.36%)	25 (25.25%)	15 (25%)	76 (29.46%)
Not at all	1 (1.01%)	5 (5.05%)	13 (21.67%)	24 (9.03%)
Total (N=258)	99 (100%)	99 (100%)	60 (100%)	258 (100%)

Analysis of data shows that highest percent of all the three groups of users are depending moderately on other institutions/organizations for publication purpose (51%). Twenty percent of them found to be scarcely using them.

Group-wise analysis also reflects the same findings. Highest percent of scientists (53%), research students (45%) and faculty (59%) are depending moderately on other institutions and organization for publishing articles, conference papers, books etc.

Among those users depending scarcely on other institutions, scientists (36%) are more compared to faculty (25%) and research students (25%). Greater dependency was noticed among a few. Among those who seldom depended on other institutions or organizations researchers (22%) are comparatively more than scientists (1%) and faculty (5%).

Usefulness of Information Services

To obtain views of the scientists, faculty members and research students on the usefulness of different kinds of information services, the respondents were asked to give their views in terms of their usefulness. However, the responses indicate only general opinions of scientists, research students and faculty members about the thirteen information services like Current Awareness Services (CAS) and Selective Dissemination of Information (SDI); Information transfer service like Indexing and Abstracting; supporting services like Translation service and Photocopying service and Interlibrary Loan service and General Reference services like Literature Research Service and Bibliographics services.

The list of services has been prepared keeping in view the available library services in the organizations surveyed.

Table 141
Percentage Distribution to Scientists by Ranking of Usefulness of the Information Services (more than one)

	1	*2*	*3*	*4,5,6 & 7*	*8,9,10 & 11*	*12,13,14,15,16*	*No response*	*Total (N=184)*
a) Inter-library loan service	38 (20.65%)	17 (9.24%)	8 (4.35%)	15 (8.15%)	2 (1.09%)	0 (0%)	104 (56.52%)	184 (100%)
b) Photocopying service	55 (29.89)	24 (13.04%)	10 (5.43%)	19 (10.33%)	2 (1.09%)	0 (0%)	75 (40.76%)	184 (100%)
c) Translation service	0 (0%)	2 (1.09%)	3 (1.63%)	7 (3.80%)	0 (0%)	1 (0.54%)	171 (92.93%)	184 (100%)
d) Current awareness service	17 (9.24%)	10 (5.43%)	6 (3.26%)	20 (10.87%)	0 (0%)	0 (0%)	131 (71.20%)	184 (100%)
e) Selective Dissemination service	2 (1.09%)	8 (4.35%)	6 (3.26%)	9 (4.89%)	3 (1.63%)	0 (0%)	156 (84.78%)	184 (100%)
f) Bibliographies & reading lists	16 (8.70%)	24 (13.04%)	13 (7.06%)	25 (13.59%)	2 (1.09%)	0 (0%)	104 (56.52%)	157 (100%)
g) Indexing & Abstracting service	18 (9.78%)	14 (7.61%)	32 (17.39%)	29 (15.76%)	0 (0%)	0 (0%)	91 (49.46%)	184 (100%)
h) Reference service	12 (6.52%)	22 (11.96%)	19 (10.33%)	39 (21.20%)	7 (3.80%)	0 (0%)	85 (46.20%)	184 (100%)
i) Literature search service : (i) Manual	6 (3.26%)	9 (4.89%)	12 (6.52%)	28 (15.22%)	5 (2.72%)	0 (0%)	127 (69.02%)	184 (100%)
(ii) CD-ROM search	7 (3.80%)	8 (4.35%)	3 (1.63%)	32 (17.39%)	6 (3.26%)	1 (0.54%)	121 (65.76%)	184 (100%)

(Contd...)

	1	*2*	*3*	*4,5,6 & 7*	*8,9,10 & 11*	*12,13,14,15,16*	*No response*	*Total (N=184)*
(iii) Online database	0 (0%)	0 (0%)	0 (0%)	15 (8.15%)	5 (2.72%)	1 (0.54%)	163 (88.59%)	184 (100%)
(i) Internet	5 (2.72%)	3 (1.63%)	4 (2.17%)	35 (19.02%)	11 (5.78%)	0 (0%)	126 (68.98%)	184 (100%)
k) E-mail	0 (0%)	4 (2.17%)	2 (1.09%)	15 (8.15%)	13 (7.07%)	1 (0.54%)	149 (80.98%)	184 (100%)
l) Fax	0 (0%)	0 (0%)	1 (0.54%)	7 (3.80%)	4 (2.17%)	1 (0.54%)	171 (92.93%)	184 (100%)
m) Talex	0 (0%)	0 (0%)	0 (0%)	L (0.54%)	3 (1.63%)	1 (0.54%)	179 (97.28%)	184 (100%)
n) Another	0 (0%)	1 (0.54%)	0 (0%)	0 (0%)	0 (0%)	0 (0%)	183 (99.46%)	184 (100%)

Table 142
Percentage Distribution to Research Students by Ranking of Usefulness of Information Services (more than one)

	1	*2*	*3*	*4,5,6 & 7*	*8,9,10 & 11*	*12,13,14,15,16*	*No response*	*Total (N=94)*
a) Inter-library loan service	15 (15.96%)	1 (1.06%)	10 (10.64%)	2 (2.13%)	0 (0%)	1 (1.06%)	29 (30.85%)	94 (100%)
b) Photocopying service	40 (42.55%)	25 (26.60%)	6 (6.38%)	10 (10.64%)	0 (0%)	1 (1.06%)	82 (87.23%)	94 (100%)
c) Translation service	1 (1.06%)	1 (1.06%)	3 (3.19%)	5 (5.32%)	0 (0%)	0 (0%)	10 (10.64%)	94 (100%)
d) Current awareness service	9 (9.57%)	8 (8.51%)	3 (3.19%)	13 (13.83%)	1 (1.06%)	0 (0%)	34 (36.17%)	94 (100%)
e) Selective Dissemination service	2 (2.13%)	2 (2.13%)	6 (6.38%)	10 (10.64%)	3 (3.19%)	0 (0%)	23 (24.47%)	94 (100%)
f) Bibliographies & reading lists	7 (7.45%)	14 (4.89%)	15 (15.96%)	18 (19.15%)	3 (3.19%)	0 (0%)	57 (60.64%)	94 (100%)
g) Indexing & Abstracting service	1 (1.06%)	13 (13.83%)	16 (17.02%)	24 (25.53%)	2 (2.13%)	1 (1.06%)	57 (60.64%)	94 (100%)
h) Reference service	6 (6.38%)	8 (8.51%)	9 (9.57%)	32 (32.98%)	3 (3.19%)	3 (3.19%)	61 (64.89%)	94 (100%)
i) Literature search service - i) Manual	3 (3.19%)	1 (1.06%)	3 (3.19%)	13 (13.38%)	2 (2.13%)	3 (3.19%)	25 (26.60%)	94 (100%)
(ii) CD-ROM search	5 (5.32%)	8 (8.51%)	3 (3.19%)	21 (22.34%)	1 (1.06%)	3 (3.19%)	41 (43.62%)	94 (100%)

(Contd...)

	1	*2*	*3*	*4,5,6 & 7*	*8,9,10 & 11*	*12,13,14,15,16*	*No response*	*Total (N=94)*
(iii) on line database	1 (1.06%)	1 (1.06%)	1 (1.06%)	6 (6.38%)	3 (3.19%)	3 (3.19%)	15 (15.96%)	94 (100%)
j) Internet	2 (2.13%)	0 (0%)	0 (0%)	17 (18.09%)	6 (6.38%)	0 (0%)	25 (26.60%)	94 (100%)
k) E-mail	1 (1.06%)	0 (0%)	0 (0%)	6 (6.38%)	8 (8.51%)	10 (0%)	15 (15.96%)	94 (100%)
l) Fax	0 (0%)	0 (0%)	0 (0%)	1 (1.06%)	5 (5.32%)	1 (1.06%)	7 (7.45%)	94 (100%)
m) Taley	0 (0%)	0 (0%)	0 (0%)	0 (0%)	4 (4.26%)	0 (0%)	4 (4.26%)	94 (100%)
n) Another	0 (0%)	0 (0%)	0 (0%)	0 (0%)	0 (0%)	1 (1.06%)	1 (1.06%)	94 (100%)

Table 143
Percentage Distribution to Faculty by Ranking of Usefulness of Information Services (more than one)

	1	*2*	*3*	*4,5,6 & 7*	*8,9,10 & 11*	*12,13,14,15,16*	*No response*	*Total (N=133)*
a) Inter- library loan service	24 (18.05%)	6 (4.51%)	9 (6.77%)	10 (7.52%)	1 (0.75%)	0 (0%)	83 (62.40%)	133 (100%)
b) Photocopying service	59 (44.36%)	36 (27.07%)	10 (7.52%)	20 (15.04%)	2 (1.50%)	0 (0%)	6 (4.51%)	133 (100%)
c) Translation service	2 (1.50%)	0 (0%)	3 (2.26%)	9 (6.77%)	2 (1.50%)	0 (0%)	117 (87.97%)	133 (100%)
d) Current awareness	1 (0.75%)	8 (6.02%) service	10 (7.52%)	13 (9.77%)	1 (0.75%)	0 (0%)	118 (88.72%)	133 (100%)
e) Selective Dissemination service	9 (6.77%)	0 (0%)	2 (1.50%)	11 (8.27%)	1 (0.75%)	0 (0%)	100 (75.19%)	133 (100%)
f) Bibliographies & reading lists	1 (0.75%)	14 (10.53%)	19 (14.29%)	20 (15.04%)	3 (2.26%)	0 (0%)	68 (51.13%)	133 (100%)
g) Indexing & Abstracting service	12 (9.02%)	24 (18.05%)	21 (15.79%)	31 (23.30%)	2 (1.50%)	1 (0.75%)	53 (39.85%)	133 (100%)
h) Reference service	6 (4.51%)	17 (12.78%)	9 (6.77%)	38 (28.57%)	2 (1.50%)	1 (0.75%)	54 (40.60%)	133 (100%)
i) Literature search service: i) Manual	15 (11.28%)	7 (5.26%)	6 (4.51%)	15 (11.28%)	2 (1.50%)	1 (0.75%)	96 (72.18%)	133 (100%)
(ii) CD-ROM search	0 (0%)	6 (4.51%)	10 (7.52%)	24 (18.05%)	5 (3.76%)	0 (0%)	73 (54.88%)	133 (100%)

(Contd...)

	1	*2*	*3*	*4,5,6 & 7*	*8,9,10 & 11*	*12,13,14,15,16*	*No response*	*Total (N=133)*
(iii) on line database	2 (1.50%)	1 (0.75%)	2 (1.50%)	6 (4.51%)	4 (3.01%)	1 (0.75%)	120 (99.23%)	133 (100%)
j) Internet	0 (0%)	4 (3.01%)	5 (3.76%)	24 (18.05%)	9 (6.77%)	1 (0.75%)	88 (66.17%)	133 (100%)
k) E-mail	0 (0%)	1 (0.75%)	4 (3.01%)	14 (10.53%)	13 (9.77%)	2 (1.50%)	99 (74.44%)	133 (100%)
l) Fax	0 (0%)	0 (0%)	0 (0.00%)	2 (1.50%)	6 (4.51%)	3 (2.26%)	122 (91.73%)	133 (100%)
m) Telex	0 (0%)	0 (0%)	0 (0%)	2 (1.50%)	1 (0.75%)	5 (3.76%)	125 (93.98%)	133 (100%)
n) Another	0 (0%)	0 (0%)	0 (0%)	1 (0.75%)	0 (0%)	1 (0.75%)	131 (99.50%)	133 (100%)

But none of the libraries surveyed was offering all the services listed in the questionnaire. Therefore the preferences of scientists, research students and faculty members' for various services were obtained to make suggestions regarding those services they consider useful for them. Tables 141, 142 and 143 indicate ranking given by the three groups of users for various library and information services. Keeping in view of the decreasing importance of ranks, ranks beyond 3 were made into three groups.

Table 141 shows that highest percentage of scientists (30%) gave 1st and 2nd rank to photocopying services (13%) and 3rd to Indexing and Abstracting services (17%) respectively; 4th, 5th, 6th, and 7th to CD-ROM search; 8th, 9th, 10th and 11th to E-mail service.

Table-142. shows that highest percentage of research students (43%) gave first and second ranks to photocopying services, third to Indexing and Abstracting Services, 4th, 5th, 6th and 7th to reference service (33%) and 8th, 9th, 10th and 11th to E-mail service (9%).

Table 143 shows that highest percentage of faculty members (44%) gave 1st and 2nd (27%) ranks to photocopying service, 3rd rank to indexing and abstracting service.

In general, analysis of data reveals that majority of the users irrespective of their groups, have awarded 1st rank to photocopying service. 2nd rank was given to bibliography services by scientists where as it was again given to reprography services by researchers & faculty. 3rd rank was given to Indexing & Abstracting services by majority of the users.

Willingness to Pay for the Charged Services

Users may need a particular service whether it is charged or not. Especially for deciding the price of a service, it is required to know about the willingness of the user to pay for the service. The same aspect has been analyzed in the Table 144.

Table 144
Willingness to Pay for the Charged Services

Willingness	*Scientists (N = 184)*	*Faculty (N = 133)*	*Research students (N = 94)*	*Total (N = 411)*
Yes	150 (81.52%)	120 (90.23%)	71 (75.53%)	341 (82.97%)
No	34 (18.48%)	13 (9.77%)	23 (24.47%)	70 (17.03%)
Total (N=411)	184 (100%)	133 (100%)	94 (100%)	411 (100%)

Analysis of the opinions of users research a positive trend in the attitude or the users towards paying the priced services.

Majority of the faculty (90%), scientists (82%) and research students (76%) expressed their willingness to pay for the library services. Very few of them were not ready to pay for the services.

Purpose of Using the Services

Different services of the library are received differently by different users. The 'purpose' with which they are approaching the library is vital factor in deciding the relevance of service to him. The following are the reasons behind the use of various library services offered. Reasons with which the user may likely use service are grouped under nine headings. Users were asked to give their reasons the information services. There responses were analyzed in the following table. Sometimes the user may have more than one reason to give, the totals were not additive.

Table 145
Purpose of Using the Services (more than one)

Purpose	*Scientists (N = 184)*	*Faculty (N = 133)*	*Research students (N =94)*	*Total (N = 411)*
For teaching	28 (15.22%)	116 (87.22%)	4 (4.26%)	148 (38.05%)
For research	160 (86.96%)	92 (69.17%)	59 (62.77%)	311 (79.95%)
For guide the scholars	31 (16.85%)	74 (55.64%)	3 (3.19%)	108 (27.76%)
To keep abreast in the field	99 (53.80%)	60 (45.11%)	40 (42.55%)	199 (51.16%)
For writing journal article	123 (66.85%)	69 (51.88%)	40 (42.55%)	232 (59.64%)
For writing conference paper	70 (38.04%)	43 (32.33%)	13 (13.83%)	126 (32.39%)
For writing a book	18 (9.78%)	26 (19.55%)	3 (3.19%)	47 (12.08%)
For writing an examination	3 (1.63%)	9 (6.77%)	40 (42.55%)	52 (13.37%)
For preparing for an interview	19 (10.33%)	10 (7.52%)	25 (26.60%)	54 (13.88%)
Any other	3 (1.63%)	3 (2.2.6%)	4 (4.26%)	10 (2.57%)

Majority of the scientists (87%) and research students (63%) are using the services of the library for fulfilling their research information needs. As expected majority of the faculty (87%) stated that their main purpose of using the library services is teaching.

Second highest percentage of scientists (67%) are depending on library services for writing journal articles. 69 percent of faculty members are depending on the library for research. In the case of research students equal percentage of them (42%) are using the services for being upto date; for writing journal articles and for the purpose of preparing for examinations. Guiding the scholars is found to be the third important reason behind using library services in the case of faculty (56%).

In general, research found to be the main purpose of using library service (80%) followed by 'writing professional articles' (60%). Fifty one percent of the users are also depending on library services to keep themselves abreast of latest development in the field.

Three percent of the scientists, fellow research students and teaching faculty mentioned other reasons. Other reasons include mention about consultancy services preparing training manuals and translation work.

Preferences given for Different Categories of Documents by Ranking

One of the primary purposes of the library is to have collections or resources for answering bibliographical and factual enquiries. Collection of library materials should support the purposes of the user community. Library collections although they are ordinarily thought of in terms of books and serials, actually contain a very broad range of print and non-print materials. Each of them is a valuable source of information. The importance of each category of document/service to scientists, research student, and faculty members depends on its ability to meet their information requirements. To study the importance ascribed by the categories of them to each document category, they were asked to rank them (1 to 12) in terms of their usefulness 12 kinds of document are listed for ranking. Data in this regard is presented in Tables 146, 147 and 148. Ranks 4 and above were grouped into three groups, as ranks after four were considered to be not so important.

Information Sources-wise Analysis

Analysis also has been done considering each source separately to assess the importance given to them using ranks given by the individual users.

It may be seen from the Table 148 that highest percentage of research students (36%) gave first and second ranks to reference books (39%), third to periodicals (28%).In general, there is a significant variation between the three groups of users. Scientists and research students gave first rank to reference books whereas faculty members gave first rant to text books. An equal percent of scientists and faculty gave 2nd and 3rd ranks to theses/ dissertations respectively.

Opinion on Display of Materials in the Library

Knowing about the users' opinions on various aspects of the library and its services facilitates better planning of the library operations and services.

Table 146
Usefulness of the Information Sources- Ranking–Scientists (more than one)

	1	*2*	*3*	*4,5 & 6*	*7, 8,9*	*10,11&12*	*No response*	*Total (N=184)*
Text Books	25 (13.59%)	22 (11.96%)	36 (19.87%)	34 (18.48%)	5 (2.72%)	0 (0%)	62 (33.70%)	184 (100%)
Reference Books	36 (19.57%)	63 (34.24%)	37 (20.19%)	17 (9.24%)	0 (0%)	0 (0%)	21 (11.41%)	184 (100%)
Periodicals	67 (36.41%)	34 (18.48%)	27 (14.67%)	20 (10.87%)	1 (0.54%)	0 (0%)	39 (21.20%)	184 (100%)
Theses/Dissertations	1 (0.54%)	5 (2.72%)	17 (9.24%)	68 (37.00%)	6 (3.26%)	5 (2.72%)	82 (44.57%)	184 (100%)
Encyclopedias	2 (1.09%)	1 (0.54%)	3 (1.63%)	31 (16.85%)	31 (16.85%)	4 (2.17%)	112 (60.70%)	184 (100%)
Directories	1 (0.54%)	1 (.054%)	0 (0%)	15 (8.15%)	35 (19.02%)	10 (5.44%)	132 (71.74%)	184 (100%)
Govt. reports / new letters	2 (1.09%)	9 (4.89%)	11 (5.98%)	39 (21.20%)	24 (13.04%)	2 (1.09%)	97 (52.72%)	195 (100%)
Standards	0 (0%)	1 (0.54%)	2 (1.09%)	4 (2.17%)	31 (16.85%)	12 (6.52%)	134 (72.83%)	184 (100%)
Patents	0 (0%)	0 (0%)	0 (0%)	2 (1.09%)	11 (5.98%)	30 (16.30%)	141 (76.63%)	184 (100%)
Report literature	9 (4.89%)	10 (5.43%)	7 (3.80%)	44 (23.91%)	10 (5.44%)	5 (2.72%)	99 (53.80%)	184 (100%)
Abstracting and Indexing Journals	18 (9.78%)	12 (6.52%)	11 (5.98%)	33 (17.94%)	10 (5.44%)	15 (8.15%)	85 (46.20%)	184 (100%)
Any other	0 (0%)	0 (0%)	0 (0%)	1 (.054%)	0 (0%)	0 (0%)	183 (99.44%)	184 (100%)

Data from the Table 146 indicates that highest percentage of scientists (36%) gave first rank to periodicals and Indexing abstracting journals in terms of their usefulness, Second and third were given to reference books and the same rank is given (3rd) to text books and reference books.

Table 147

Usefulness of the Information Sources- Ranking – Faculty (more than one)

	1	*2*	*3*	*4,5,6 & 7*	*8,9,10 & 11*	*12,13,14,15 & 16*	*No response*	*Total (N=133)*
Text Books	73 (54.89%)	19 (14.29%)	12 (9.02%)	11 (8.27%)	3 (2.26%)	1 (0.75%)	14 (10.53%)	133 (100%)
Reference Books	31 (23.31%)	67 (50.38%)	12 (9.02%)	5 (3.76%)	3 (3.76%)	0 (0%)	15 (11.28%)	133 (100%)
Periodicals	14 (10.53%)	21 (15.79%)	54 (40.60%)	15 (11.28%)	3 (2.26%)	0 (0%)	26 (19.55%)	133 (100%)
Theses/ Dissertations	2 (1.50%)	9 (6.77%)	20 (15.04%)	45 (33.84%)	6 (4.51%)	1 (0.75%)	50 (37.5%)	133 (100%)
Encyclopedias	0 (0%)	1 (0.75%)	4 (3.01%)	42 (31.58%)	14 (10.53%)	2 (1.50%)	70 (52.63%)	133 (100%)
Directories	0 (0%)	0 (0%)	1 (0.75%)	25 (18.80%)	17 (12.78%)	7 (5.26%)	83 (62.41%)	133 (100%)
Govt. reports / new letters	1 (0.75%)	2 (1.50%)	5 (3.76%)	38 (28.57%)	23 (17.29%)	0 (0%)	64 (48.12%)	133 (100%)
Standards	0 (0%)	0 (0%)	0 (0%)	8 (6.02%)	14 (10.53%)	10 (7.52%)	101 (75.94%)	133 (100%)
Patents	0 (0%)	0 (0%)	0 (0%)	0 (0%)	13 (9.17%)	13 (9.17%)	97 (71.43%)	133 (100%)
Report literature	5 (3.76%)	1 (0.75%)	2 (1.50%)	24 (18.05%)	16 (12.03%)	5 (3.77%)	80 (60.15%)	133 (100%)
Abstracting and Indexing Journals	3 (2.26%)	4 (3.01%)	3 (2.26%)	26 (19.55%)	15 (11.28%)	10 (7.52%)	70 (52.63%)	133 (100%)
Any other	0 (0%)	0 (0%)	0 (0%)	1 (.75%)	0 (0%)	2 (1.50%)	130 (97.74%)	133 (100%)

The Table 147 shows that majority of the faculty members (55%) gave first rank to text books, second to reference books, third to periodicals.

Table: 148

Usefulness of the Information Sources- Ranking –Research Students (more than one)

	1	*2*	*3*	*4,5,6 & 7*	*8,9,10 & 11*	*12,13,14,15,& 16*	*No response*	*Total (N=94)*
Text Books	27 (28.72%)	14 (14.89%)	15 (15.96%)	14 (14.89%)	1 (1.06%)	0 (0%)	23 (24.47%)	94 (100%)
Reference Books	34 (36.17%)	37 (39.36%)	11 (11.90%)	2 (2.13%)	1 (1.06%)	0 (0%)	9 (9.58%)	94 (100%)
Periodicals	17 (18.09%)	21 (22.34%)	26 (27.66%)	14 (14.89%)	3 (3.19%)	0 (0%)	13 (13.83%)	94 (100%)
Theses/ Dissertations	4 (4.26%)	8 (8.51%)	12 (12.71%)	35 (37.23%)	6 (6.38%)	0 (0%)	29 (30.83%)	94 (100%)
Encyclopedias	1 (1.06%)	1 (1.06%)	7 (7.45%)	28 (29.79%)	11 (11.90%)	2 (2.13%)	44 (46.81%)	94 (100%)
Directories	0 (0%)	0 (0%)	0 (0%)	15 (15.96%)	14 (14.89%)	6 (6.38%)	59 (62.77%)	94 (100%)
Govt. reports / new letters	2 (2.13%)	4 (4.26%)	6 (6.38%)	21 (22.34%)	19 (20.2%)	2 (2.13%)	40 (42.55%)	94 (100%)
Standards	0 (0%)	0 (0%)	0 (0%)	7 (7.45%)	10 (10.64%)	4 (4.26%)	73 (77.66%)	94 (100%)
Patents	0 (0%)	1 (1.06%)	0 (0%)	2 (2.13%)	4 (4.26%)	9 (9.58%)	78 (82.98%)	94 (100%)
Report literature	4 (4.26%)	0 (0%)	2 (2.13%)	20 (21.28%)	10 (10.64%)	4 (4.26%)	54 (57.45%)	94 (100%)
Abstracting and Indexing Journals	2 (2.13%)	2 (2.13%)	4 (4.26%)	22 (23.40%)	10 (10.64%)	3 (3.19%)	51 (54.26%)	94 (100%)
Any other	0 (0%)	1 (1.06%)	0 (0%)	0 (0%)	1 (1.06%)	1 (1.06%)	81 (86.17%)	94 (100%)

Table 149
Opinion on Display of Materials

Opinion	*Scientists (N = 184)*	*Faculty (N = 133)*	*Research students (N = 94)*	*Total (N = 411)*
Satisfied	120 (65.22%)	92 (69.17%)	57 (60.64%)	269 (65.45%)
Not satisfied	64 (34.78%)	41 (30.83%)	37 (39.36%)	142 (34.55%)
Total (N=411)	184 (100%)	133 (100%)	94 (100%)	411 (100%)

It may be seen from Table-149 that highest percentage of faculty members (69%), scientists (65%) and research students (61%) are satisfied with the procedures followed by the library for displaying and organizing the materials.

All categories of users have same satisfaction levels i.e. the satisfaction level is independent of the user category. A Chi-square test at 5% level of significance shown the same fact. (calculated $\chi^2_{(1)}$=1.782, table $\chi^2_{(1)}$=3.84).

Opinion on Display of Materials – Reasons for not Satisfied

Table 150
Reasons for Dissatisfaction over the Display of Materials (more than one)

Reasons	*Scientists (N = 64)*	*Faculty (N = 41)*	*Research students (N = 37)*	*Total (N = 142)*
Scattering of related books	42 (65.62%)	30 (73.17%)	23 (62.16%)	45 (66.90%)
Difficult to remember class numbers	10 (15.62%)	9 (21.95%)	7 (18.92%)	26 (18.31%)
Inconvenient arrangements	28 (43.75%)	24 (58.54%)	11 (29.73%)	63 (44.37%)
The shelves are difficult to reach	24 (37.50%)	21 (51.22%)	11 (29.73%)	56 (39.44%)
Lack of bay guides	23 (35.94%)	11 (26.83%)	13 (35.13%)	47 (33.10%)
Sorting of used books not done regularly	33 (51.56%)	20 (48.78%)	15 (40.54%)	68 (47.89%)
Any other	10 (15.62%)	5 (12.19%)	2 (5.40%)	17 (11.97%)

Analysis of data related to dissatisfaction on the display of library materials reveals mainly three aspects of display – scattering of related books on one subject; incorrect arrangement and irregular sorting of used books.

Interms of problems with scattering of related books scientists, faculty members and research students expressed it as the primary reason (66%, 73% and 62% respectively). Second highest percentage of scientists and research students have complained against irregular sorting of used books causing waste of their time on searching for books on shelves on the other hand 58% of the faculty who are not satisfied have complained that the arrangement of books on shelves is incorrect. Difficulty in locating the books on shelves because of poor light was also a complaint made by 51 percent of the faculty. Significant percent of scientists (36%) and research students (35%) have also pointed out that lack of proper bay guides, shelves and rack guides are causing problems in locating required items. Twelve percent of the users mentioned other reasons like the library is very small, collections inadequate and lack of regular library staff.

Display of Periodicals

Periodicals, as sources of latest information, assume much significance in organizations where research is the major activity. Details about use of display racks for periodicals. The common method of exhibiting the periodicals in libraries is displaying them on slanted racks. Opinion of users about the usefulness of these racks were solicited through the questionnaire. Details are presented in Table 151.

Table: 151
Usefulness of Display Racks for Periodicals

Opinion	*Scientist (N= 184)*	*Faculty (N= 133)*	*Research student (N= 94)*	*Total (N= 411)*
Yes	135 (73.37%)	124 (93.23%)	87 (92.55%)	346 (84.18%)
No	49 (26.63%)	9 (6.77%)	7 (7.45%)	65 (15.82%)
Total	184 (100%)	133 (100%)	94 (100%)	411 (100%)

It is significant to note from the Table 151 that majority of faculty members (93%), research students (93%) and scientists (73%) stated that the libraries have display racks for periodicals.

Nearly 27 percent of scientists, 7 percent of research students and 7 percent of faculty stated that their library do not have separate, display racks for periodicals.

Satisfaction with the Present Arrangements of Periodicals

Convenience and ease of use are important aspects in deciding the display of materials in libraries. Display of latest issues and storage of unbound issues of periodicals, are important activities of periodical section. Standard racks with pigeon holes will serve both the purpose. Users opinions about the existing pattern of arrangement have been analyzed in Table 152.

Table 152
Opinion with Present Arrangements of Periodicals

Opinion	*Scientists (N= 184)*	*Faculty (N= 133)*	*Research students (N= 87)*	*Total (N= 411)*
Satisfied	130 (70.65%)	109 (81.95%)	68 (72.34%)	307 (74.70%)
Not satisfied	54 (29.35%)	24 (18.05%)	26 (27.66%)	104 (25.30%)
Total	184 (100%)	133 (100%)	94 (100%)	411 (100%)

It may be seen from Table 152 that the majority of the faculty members (82%), research students (72%) and scientists (71%) expressed their satisfaction regarding present arrangements of periodicals. Twenty nine percent of the scientists, Twenty eight percent of the research students and eighteen percent of the faculty members are not satisfied with present arrangements of periodicals.

Reasons for dissatisfaction

In continuation with the previous question users' who were not satisfied with the arrangement of periodicals were asked to state their reasons for their dissatisfaction.

Table 153
Reasons for Dissatisfaction about the Display of Periodicals (more than one)

Reason	*Scientists (N= 54)*	*Faculty (N= 24)*	*Research students (N= 26)*	*Total (N=104)*
Display of current issues is done not properly	28 (51.85%)	19 (79.17%)	13 (50%)	60 (57.69%)
Individual issues of journals are not systematically arranged	27 (50.00%)	16 (66.67%)	12 (46.15%)	55 (52.88%)
Issues are not available on shelves for months together	21 (38.89%)	11 (45.83%)	13 (50%)	45 (43.27%)
Back volumes of journals sent for binding are not available for years	17 (31.48%)	10 (41.67%)	12 (46.15%)	39 (37.50%)
Journal's catalogue is not maintained	17 (31.48%)	11 (45.83%)	4 (46.15%)	32 (30.77%)
Journal's catalogue is not up to date	20 (37.04%)	9 (37.50%)	11 (42.31%)	40 (38.46%)
Difficult to find information about missing issues	24 (44.44%)	12 (50%)	14 (53.85%)	50 (48.08%)
Any other	8 (14.81%)	1 (4.17%)	0 (0%)	9 (8.55%)

It may be seen majority of the faculty are with the view that the individual issues are not systematically arranged at present (79%), individual issues of journals are not properly displayed (67%), and difficult to find information about missing issues (50%).

Majority of the scientists stated that the display of current issues is done not properly (52%), individual issues of journals are not systematically arranged (50%), difficult to find information about missing issues.

Majority of the research students stated that it is difficult to find information about missing issues (44%), display of current issues is done not properly (50%), issues are not available on shelves for months together (50%).

Analysis of data shows that the majority of faculty (79%), scientists (52%) and research students (50%) are with the view that display of current issues is not done in a systematic way. Sixty seven percent of faculty, scientists (50%) and research students (46%) are with the view that individual issues of journals are not systematically arranged at present. Research students (50%), faculty (46%) and scientists (39%) are with the view that periodicals are not available on the shelves for months together.

Research students (46%), faculty (42%) and scientists (31%) are with the view that back volumes of journal sent for binding are not available for years. faculty (46%) scientists (31%) and Research students (46%) stated that separate journals catalogue is not mentioned.

Research students (42%), faculty (38%) and scientists (37%) stated the journals catalogue is not up to date at present. Research students (54%), faculty (50%) and scientists (44%) stated the difficult to find information about missing issues/ titles.

Reasons expressed for this dissatisfaction by users in general include improper display of periodicals issues (58%) and arrangement of individual issues of journals (53%); on shelves difficulty in tracing out the missing issues and titles (48%) and non availability of last issues of journals for longer periods (43%).

Library Catalogue and its Usefulness

Users' awareness about the available facilities in the library also influences their extent of use of these facilities.

Table 154
Maintain Library Catalogue

Opinion	*Scientists (N = 184)*	*Faculty (N= 133)*	*Research students (N= 94)*	*Total (N= 411)*
Yes	148 (80.44%)	123 (92.48%)	87 (92.55%)	358 (87.11%)
No	36 (19.57%)	10 (7.52%)	7 (7.45%)	53 (12.90%)
Total	184 (100%)	133 (100%)	94 (100%)	411 (100%)

Majority of research students (92%), faculty members (92%) and scientists (80%) stated that their libraries are maintaining library catalogue. Only 19 percent of scientists, 8 percent of faculty members and 7 percent of research students have stated that no library catalogue is maintained by the library.

Extent of Use of the Library Catalogue

The library catalogue is having a major role in bringing the user close to the collection. It facilitates the user to locate the material and asses their relevance of the material identified.

Table 155
Extent of Use of Library Catalogue

Opinion	*Scientists (N = 148)*	*Faculty (N = 123)*	*Research students (N = 81)*	*Total (N = 358)*
Frequently	35 (23.65%)	34 (27.64%)	28 (42.18%)	97 (27.10%)
Occasionally	93 (62.84%)	69 (56.10%)	39 (44.83%)	201 (56.15%)
Never	20 (13.51%)	20 (16.26%)	20 (22.99%)	60 (16.76%)
Total (N=358)	148 (100%)	123 (100%)	87 (100%)	358 (100%)

Occasional use of the catalogue is noticed among the majority of scientists (62.84%), faculty members (56%) and researchers (45%). Next highest percentages of all three groups of users (23% sciences, 42% research – and 27% the faculty) are referring to the catalogue frequently.

Compared to other two categories researchers are using the catalogue more frequently (42%),while majority of the scientists and faculty are using it occasionally.

Ways of Finding the Library Material

Scientists, research students and faculty members will try to get the required document/ information from the library through various means. For example they may consult the catalogue and locate the required document from the library's collection. Some times they themselves will scan the collection to locate the required item.

Through various means, the above three groups may try to get access to available information in the library. Their perception about the ease of access to the collection through different means may influence their extent of use of the library. The following table.shows different ways adopted by the users to locate and get the required information or document in the library.

Table 156
Ways of Getting Required Information from the Library

Ways	*Scientists (N = 184)*	*Faculty (N = 133)*	*Research students (N= 94)*	*Total (N = 411)*
a. Using a catalogue	99 (53.80%)	89 (66.92%)	52 (55.32%)	240 (58.39%)
b. Assistance of library staff	132 (71.74%)	90 (67.67%)	45 47.87%)	267 (67.96%)
c. Based on their own efforts	67 (36.41%)	58 (43.61%)	46 (48.94%)	171 (41.61%)
d. Assistance of others	1 (0.54%)	11 (8.27%)	4 (4.26%)	16 (3.89%)
e. Current Information service	8 (4.35%)	8 (6.02%)	6 (6.38%)	22 (5.35%)
f. Library orientations programmes	2 (1.09%)	1 (0.75%)	0 (0%)	3 (0.73%)
g. Any other	0 (0%)	0 (0%)	2 (2.13%)	2 (0.49%)

It is indicated through analysis that majority of the scientists (72%) and faculty members (68%) are taking the assistance of library staff to get the required information. Majority of the research students (55%) are using the library catalogue. Significant percent of scientists (36%), research students (49%) and faculty (44%) are found to be making their own efforts to find out required information from the library.

Awareness about Borrowing Privileges

As registered borrowers each group of users will have different borrowing privileges. To maintain discipline and control, these are to be understood and followed by the users properly. In order to make the users to follow and enjoy their respective privileges creating awareness among them is an important issue about them.

Table 157
Awareness about Borrowing Privileges

Awareness	*Scientists (N = 184)*	*Faculty (N = 133)*	*Research students (N = 94)*	*Total (N = 411)*
Yes	171 (92.94%)	127 (95.49%)	84 (84.36%)	382 (92.94%)
No	13 (7.07%)	6 (4.51%)	10 (10.64%)	29 (7.06%)
Total (N=411)	184 (100%)	133 (100%)	94 (100%)	411 (100%)

It is significant to note from above table that the large number of faculty members (95%), scientists (93%) and research students (84%) are aware about their borrowing privileges. Very few of them (research students 11%, Scientists 7%, faculty 4%) do not have knowledge about the borrowing privileges offered to them.

Opinion on Borrowing Privileges

Table: 158
Satisfaction on Borrowing Privileges

Satisfaction	*Scientists (N = 171)*	*Faculty (N = 127)*	*Research students (N = 84)*	*Total (N = 382)*
Yes	159 (92.98%)	115 (90.55%)	80 (95.24%)	354 (92.67%)
No	12 (7.02%)	12 (9.45%)	4 (4.76%)	28 (7.33%)
Total	171 (100%)	127 (100%)	84 (100%)	382 (100%)

It may be seen from Table-158 that highest percentage of research students (95%), scientists (93%) and faculty members (91%) are satisfied with the existing borrowing privileges given to them. Very few of them scientists (7%), faculty members (9%) and research students (5%) have reported that they are not satisfied with the borrowing privileges.

Opinion about the Existing Procedure of Issuing System

To evaluate the working of the existing procedures of issue/ returns of the libraries surveyed and their impact on the extent of use of library materials user's opinions have been ascertained on these activities.

Table 159
Opinion about the Existing Procedure of Issuing System

Opinion	*Scientists (N = 171)*	*Faculty (N = 127)*	*Research students (N = 84)*	*Total (N = 382)*
Simple	150 (87.71%)	109 (85.83%)	68 (80.95%)	327 (85.60%)
Complicated	2 (1.17%)	0 (0%)	5 (5.95%)	7 (1.83%)
Takes long time	3 (1.75%)	2 (1.57%)	1 (1.19%)	6 (1.57%)
Takes reasonable time	13 (7.60%)	12 (9.45%)	10 (11.90%)	35 (9.16%)
Any other	3 (1.75%)	0 (0%)	0 (0%)	3 (0.78%)
Total	171 (100%)	127 (100%)	84 (100%)	382 (100%)

It may be seen from Table 159. that the majority of the scientists (88%); faculty members (86%) and research students (81%) considered that existing issuing system as 'simple'. Next highest percentage of scientists (8%), research students (12%) and faculty members (9%) also felt that the present system of issue and returns takes reasonable time of the users. Very few of them described it as complicated that takes long time. Very few of the scientists (21%) felt the present staff of the library at circulation section is sufficient but they need trained staff.

Opinion about Library Staff

Staff of the library are key factors in creating good image about the library besides other factors. Their attitude and involvement in the profession undoubtedly reflects how they discharge their responsibilities and satisfy the users.

Scientists' Opinion about the Library Staff

The following table explains the opinion of scientists about the attitudes and behaviour of the library staff in different contexts.

Table 160
Opinion about Library Staff Scientists

Areas	*Helpful*	*Not helpful*	*Total (N=184)*
Finding and using the required material in the library	170 (92.39%)	14 (7.61%)	184 (100%)
Answering your queries	168 (91.30%)	16 (8.70%)	184 (100%)
Guiding you in the use of the library facilities.	162 (88.04%)	22 (11.96%)	184 (100%)

Regarding the three areas where library staff can play crucial role, almost above 88 percent of the scientists responded positively expressing faith and confidence in the library staff. However, 12 percent of them are not satisfied in-terms of the guidance in the use of library materials.

Faculty's Opinion about Library Staff

Library users very often will require the help and guidance of the staff in accessing the material and availing the library facilities and services. Data on opinions of the faculty about the attitudes and response of the library staff are presented in Table 161.

Table 161
Opinion about Library Staff – Faculty

Areas	*Helpful*	*Not helpful*	*Total (N=133)*
Finding and using the required material in the library	124 (93.23%)	9 (6.77%)	133 (100%)
Answering your queries	115 (86.47%)	18 (13.53%)	133 (100%)
Guiding you in the use of the library	114 (85.71%)	19 (14.29%)	133 (100%)

Majority of the faculty stated that the library staff is helpful in finding and using the required materials in the library (93%), answering their queries (86%) and guiding them in the use of library (86%). Very few of the faculty expressed negative opinion about the library ranging from 7 to 14 percent.

Research Students' Opinion about Library Staff

Table 162
Opinion about Library Staff – Research Students

Areas	*Helpful N=?*	*Not helpful*	*Total (N=94)*
Finding and using	88 (93.62%)	6 (6.38%)	94 (100%)
Answering your queries	84 (89.36%)	10 (10.64%)	94 (100%)
Guiding you in the use of library	79 (84.04%)	15 (15.96%)	94 (100%)

Majority of research students stated that the library staff are helpful in finding and using the required material in the library (94%); answering their queries (89%) and guiding them in the use of the library (84%). Negative opinion about the role of the library staff was expressed by few of them ranging from 6 to 16 percent.

In general, majority of the research students (94%), scientists (92%) and faculty members (93%) opined that the library staff is helpful in finding the required material, answering users' queries and guiding them in the use of library. However nearly 14 percent of them have expressed their opinion that they are not helpful in answering queries and guiding them in the use of the library.

Users' Opinion about Timings of Library

Table 163

Opinion about Timings of Library

Opinion	*Scientists (N = 184)*	*Faculty (N = 133)*	*Research students (N = 94)*	*Total (N = 411)*
Convenient	152 (82.61%)	99 (74.44%)	48 (51.06%)	299 (72.75%)
Not convenient	3 (1.63%)	2 (1.50%)	7 (7.45%)	12 (2.92%)
Needs modification	27 (14.67%)	29 (21.80%)	38 (40.43%)	94 (22.87%)
No idea	2 (1.09%)	3 (2.26%)	1 (1.06%)	6 (1.46%)
Total	184 (100%)	133 (100%)	94 (100%)	411 (100%)

From the Table 163 it is evident that highest percentage of scientists (nearly 83%), faculty members (74%) and research students (51%) reported that timings of the library are convenient.

However 22 percent of the users opined that there is a need to modify library timings. Compared to other two categories more number of research students (40%) have pointed out the need for modification.

Availability of Computers

Awareness about the existing equipment and infrastructure facilities among the users help them to avail all facilities and services of the libraries. Details pertaining to this aspect are shown in Table 164.

Table 164

Availability of Computers in Libraries

Availability	*Scientists (N = 184)*	*Faculty (N = 133)*	*Research students (N = 94)*	*Total (N = 411)*
Yes	100 (54.35%)	110 (82.71%)	74 (78.72%)	284 (69.10%)
No	84 (45.65%)	23 (17.29%)	20 (21.28%)	127 (30.90%)
Total	184 (100 %)	133 (100 %)	94 (100 %)	411 (100%)

Analysis of data reveals that larger number of faculty (83%); and research students (79%) and more than half of the scientists (54%) have reported that computers are available. However 46 percent of the scientists, 21 percent of the research students and 17 percent of the faculty members stated that their libraries do not have computers.

Computer skills of users

Users require basic knowledge and skills in the use of computer to avail computerized library operations and services. The basic objective of automating the library operation is to provide efficient services. The Table 165 gives details about the computer knowledge and skills of different groups of users.

Table 165
Knowledge of Computer Skills

Computer skills	*Scientists (N = 184)*	*Faculty (N = 133)*	*Research students (N = 94)*	*Total (N = 411)*
Yes	104 (56.52%)	106 (79.70%)	66 (70.21%)	276 (67.15%)
No	80 (43.48%)	27 (20.30%)	28 (29.79%)	135 (32.85%)
Total	184 (100%)	133 (100%)	94 (100%)	411 (100%)

Majority of the faculty members (80%), research students (70%) and scientists (57%) stated that they have computer skills to use the computers in the library. Among those who do not possesses any computer skills, scientists are more in number (43%) compared to research students (30%) and faculty (20%).

Training in the Use of Computers for Users by the Library

In order to fully exploit the advantages of automated services and facilities, users and staff require at least the minimum knowledge and skills in the use of computers. As part of their regular user training programme, libraries can organize courses to impart training in the use of computers, online catalogues and newly introduced services.

Table 166
Need to Conduct Training in Computers for Users by the Library

Need for Training	*Scientists (N = 184)*	*Faculty (N = 133)*	*Research students (N = 94)*	*Total (N = 411)*
Yes	115 (62.50%)	106 (79.70%)	66 (70.21%)	287 (69.83%)
No	69 (37.50%)	27 (20.30%)	28 (29.79%)	124 (30.17%)
Total	184 (100%)	133 (100 %)	94 (100%)	411 (100%)

To find out from the users whether they feel any need to have computer training organized by the library, data has been gathered. Majority of scientists (62%), research students (70%) and faculty (79%) expressed the need to organize training in the application of computers. Thirty percent of the users did not recognize the need for any such training.

Internet Facility in the Library

Libraries and information centers having internet connectivity will be in an advantageous position to provide access to their users to the information available globally.

Table 167
Internet Facility in the Library

Internet facility	*Scientists (N = 184)*	*Faculty (N = 133)*	*Research students (N = 94)*	*Total (N = 411)*
Yes	87 (47.28%)	75 (56.39%)	43 (45.74%)	205 (49.88%)
No	97 (52.72%)	58 (43.61%)	51 (54.26%)	206 (50.12%)
Total	184 (100%)	133 (100%)	94 (100%)	411 (100%)

It may be seen from the Table-167 that nearly 50 percent of the users stated that they have Internet facility in their libraries. The remaining half of the users indicated that they do not have Internet facility in their libraries.

Liberal Access to Internet Facility

Libraries and information centres need to incur a lot of expenditure to offer electronic information services. It may be the policy of the library whether to charge or not to charge these services. Data available from users in this regard has been analyzed and presented in the Table 168.

Table 168
Liberal Access to Internet Facility

Liberal Access to Internet facility	*Scientists (N = 87)*	*Faculty (N = 75)*	*Research students (N = 43)*	*Total (N = 205)*
Yes	37 (42.53%)	31 (41.33%)	20 (46.51%)	88 (42.93%)
No	50 (57.47%)	44 (58.67%)	23 (53.49%)	117 (57.07%)
Total	87 (100%)	75 (100%)	43 (100%)	205 (100%)

Analysis of responses on access to Internet facility indicates that majority of the users (57%) do not have liberal access to this facility. Only slight differences were seen among the three groups of users regarding this issue.

Charges by the Library for Internet Searching/ E-mail

Table 169
Charges for Internet Searching/ E-mail

Charges for Internet Searching by E-mail	*Scientists (N = 37)*	*Faculty (N = 31)*	*Research students (N = 20)*	*Total (N = 88)*
Yes	15 (40.54%)	20 (64.52%)	10 (50.00%)	45 (51.14%)
No	22 (59.46%)	11 (35.48%)	10 (50.00%)	43 (48.86%)
Total	37 (100%)	31 (100%)	20 (100%)	88 (100%)

In continuation to the previous question, users were asked to give details about the pricing of these services. It is found that even among those users reported to be having liberal access to internet, majority (51%) are not paying any charges for Internet and E-mail services. Among those paying for these services the percentage of faculty (64%) is more.

Awareness about Availability of CD-ROM Collection

Maintaining CD-ROM collections along with printed collection is a common feature of modern libraries & information centers. Users must be informed about them on par with printed collection. To know about users awareness and use of CD-ROM collection in the library, pertinent information was response were gathered from the users and shown in Table 170.

Table 170
Availability of CD-ROM Collection in the Library

Availability of CD-ROM collection	*Scientists (N=184) (N=94)*	*Faculty (N=133)*	*Research students*	*Total (N=411)*
Yes	74 (40.22%)	76 (57.14%)	52 (55.32%)	202 (49.15%)
No	92 (50%)	41 (30.83%)	34 (36.17%)	167 (40.63%)
No response	18 (9.78%)	16 (12.03%)	8 (8.51%)	42 (10.22%)
Total	184 (100%)	133 (100%)	94 (100%)	411 (100%)

It may be noted from Table 170 that 57 percent of the faculty, 55 percent of the research students and 40 percent of the scientists are stated that their libraries are having CD-ROM collections. A half (50%) of the scientists, 36 percent of the research students and 31 percent of the faculty have reporting that their libraries do not have CD-ROM collections.

Free Access to CD-ROM

To find out whether libraries surveyed are providing free and liberal access to CD-ROM collections, data is gathered from users and tabulated in the following table.

Table 171
Free Access to CD-ROM

Free access to CD-ROM	*Scientists (N = 74)*	*Faculty (N = 76)*	*Research students (N = 52)*	*Total (N = 202)*
Yes	44 (59.46%)	46 (60.53%)	26 (50%)	116 (57.43%)
No	30 (40.54%)	30 (39.47%)	26 (50%)	86 (42.57%)
Total	74 (100%)	76 (100%)	52 (100%)	202 (100%)

Analysis of data show that more than half of the users (57%) have free access to CD-ROM collection in their libraries. However nearly 43 percent of them also reported that they do not have free and liberal access to CD-ROM collection.

Availability and Use of Computers Outside the Library and at Home

Access to computers and Internet facility outside the library also influences the extent of use of library services and facilities. User may have Internet access at home or through commercial browsing centers. To ascertain the degree of user dependency on these facility out side the library ' Users' responses were gathered and analyzed in the following Tables.

Table 172
Availability of Computers at Home

Availability of computers at home	*Scientists (N = 184)*	*Faculty (N = 133)*	*Research students (N = 94)*	*Total (N = 411)*
Yes	47 (25.54%)	35 (26.32%)	17 (18.09%)	99 (24.09%)
No	129 (70.11%)	93 (69.92%)	76 (80.85%)	298 (72.51%)
No response	8 (4.35%)	5 (3.76%)	1 (1.06%)	14 (3.41%)
Total	184 (100%)	133 (100%)	94 (100%)	411 (100%)

Majority of the research students (81%), scientists (70%) and faculty (70%) do not have computers at home. However 26 percent of the faculty members, 26 percent of the scientists and 18 percent research students are found to be having computers at home.

Availability of Internet and E-mail Facility at Home

Only 24 percent of the users out of the total sample responded to this question. In order to find out the whether all of them have internet connectivity, data has been gathered.

Table 173
Internet/ E-mail Facility at Home

Internet/E-mail facility at home	*Scientists (N= 47)*	*Faculty (N= 35)*	*Research students (N= 17)*	*Total (N= 99)*
Yes	22 (46.81%)	21 (60%)	19 (76.47%)	56 (56.57%)
No	25 (53.19%)	14 (40%)	4 (23.53%)	43 (43.43%)
Total	47 (100%)	35 (100%)	17 (100%)	99 (100%)

Among the users having computer faciiity at home, only 57 percent have Internet connectivity even among those having the connectivity the percent of faculty found to be more compared to other two categories.

Table 174
Use of Internet Facility at Browsing centre

Use of Internet at browsing center	*Scientists (N = 184)*	*Faculty (N = 133)*	*Research students (N = 94)*	*Total (N = 411)*
Yes	42 (22.83%)	49 (36.84%)	55 (58.51%)	146 (35.52%)
No	142 (77.17%)	84 (63.16%)	39 (41.49%)	265 (64.68%)
Total	184 (100%)	133 (100%)	94 (100%)	411 (100%)

Analysis of data shows that only 35 percent of users are availing Internet facility through browsing center. Twenty three percent of scientists, 58 percent of research students and 37 percent of faculty are found to be approaching the browsing centers for Internet facility. Compared to scientists and faculty, research students are found to be using internet facility in the browsing centres is more.

Charges for using Internet Facility

Commercial browsing centers will charge the users for providing Internet services. The charge may vary from centre to centre. The charges are usually calculated on hourly basis. To know about the charges paid by users outside the library responses were gathered and analyzed.

Tables 175
Charges paid Outside the Library for Internet

Rates of Charge per hour	*Scientists (N=42)*	*Faculty (N=49)*	*Research students (N=55)*	*Total (N=146)*
Rs.20/ hr	36 (85.71%)	45 (91.84%)	31 (56.37%)	112 (76.74%)
Rs.25/hr	1 (2.38%)	1 (2.04%)	11 (20%)	13 (8.90%)
Rs.30/hr	3 (7.14%)	1 (2.04%)	8 (14.54%)	12 (8.22%)
Rs.35/hr	1 (2.38%)	1 (2.04%)	2 (3.64%)	4 (2.74%)
More than Rs.35/hr	1 (2.38%)	1 (2.04%)	3 (5.45%)	5 (3.42%)
Total	42 (100%)	49 (100%)	55 (100%)	146 (100%)

It may be seen from the above table that majority of faculty members (92%), research students (56%) and scientists (86%) are paying Rs.20 per hour for browsing the Internet outside the library.

Websites/ data bases frequently accessed by the users

Majority of the users access the following websites / databases frequently.

1. Some of the websites and home pages frequently accessed by the users are: the websites of www.icar.com; www.icrisat.Org; www.fors.org; www.larc.org; www.manage.gov.in; www.kiran.com; www.agriwater. com; www.nic.in. Most frequently used search engines are: altavista; google & yahoo.

Subscription/ Membership of Online Databases

To get access to majority of the online databases, users need to either subscribe or become registered members. In general these services are found to be expensive for individual subscribers. Institutional membership or subscription is more economical and convenient to access more number of databases which is otherwise a difficult task for the individual user.

Table 176
Subscription / Membership of Online Databases

Subscription / membership of online databases	*Scientists (N=184)*	*Faculty (N=133)*	*Research student (N=94)*	*Total (N=411)*
Yes	6 (3.26%)	3 (2.26%)	4 (4.26%)	13 (3.16%)
No	178 (96.74%)	130 (97.74%)	90 (95.74%)	398 (96.84%)
Total	184 (100%)	133 (100%)	94 (100%)	411 (100%)

Frequency of Use of Email Services

Table 177
Frequency of Use of E-mail Service

Frequency of use of E-mail service	*Scientists (N = 184)*	*Faculty (N = 133)*	*Research students (N = 94)*	*Total (N = 411)*
Very often	51 (27.72%)	35 (26.32%)	35 (37.23%)	121 (29.44%)
Occasionally	47 (25.54%)	49 (36.84%)	38 (40.43%)	134 (32.60%)
Never	28 (15.22%)	20 (15.04%)	8 (8.51%)	56 (13.63%)
No response	58 (31.52%)	29 (21.80%)	13 (13.83%)	100 (24.33%)
Total	184 (100%)	133 (100%)	94 (100%)	411 (100%)

Analysis of data revealed the expected findings. Only 3 percent of total number of users has registered membership to access online databases and online journals. Much variation is not seen among the three groups of users in this regard.

Though 24 percent of the users have not positively responded to this question, significant percentages of them are found to be using e-mail services occasionally (32%). Twenty eight percent of scientists, 37 percent of research students and 26 percent of the faculty are using it very often (frequently). Only 13 percent of the users stated that they never used the service before. Compared to other two groups highest percent of research students are found to be using E-mail services more frequently.

Purpose of using Computers Outside the Library (more than one)

Table 178
Purpose of Using Computers Outside the Library

Purpose	*Scientists (N=97)*	*Faculty (N=90)*	*Research students (N=58)*	*Total (N=245)*
Academic purpose	50 (51.56%)	67 (74.44%)	31 (53.45%)	148 (60.41%)
Research project	41 (42.27%)	49 (54.44%)	31 (53.45%)	121 (49.39%)
For personal work	68 (70.10%)	85 (94.44%)	48 (82.76%)	201 (82.04%)
Recreational purpose	20 (20.62%)	28 (31.11%)	13 (22.41%)	61 (24.90%)
Any other	0 (0%)	5 (5.56%)	0 (0%)	5 (2.04%)

Out of those users who have access to computer outside the library, majority (82%) stated that they are using them for personal work. Sixty percent and forty nine percent of them are using it for academic and research work respectively. About one quarter of them are also found to be using computer for recreational purpose.

Variations are seen among the three groups of users regarding the use of computers only in some of the aspects. For example compared to scientists (52%) and research students (53%), the percentage of faculty (74%) is more among those using computers for academic purpose.

Purpose of Using Internet/ E-mail

Internet is a wide source of global information. It not only stores lot of information on its www but also provides wide access to many online databases and services. Both general and specific sources of information available on Net are capable of satisfying different purposes of the users.

In general it is observed that majority of the users are found to be using Internet to maintain contacts with professional colleague followed by those who are using the Net for accessing databases (70%). All the research students are using Internet/ E-mail mainly for the purpose of maintaining contacts with colleagues and searching the databases. Majority of the faculty were also found to be using this facility with same purposes where as the priorities for scientists were found to be different. Database searching has been indicated as the main purpose followed by maintaining contacts with professional colleagues.

Purpose wise analysis shows that variations among the three groups. Internet was mainly used to access databases by more percent of scientists than other two groups. Among those using Internet the percent research students for knowing information on fourth coming conferences/ meeting is greater than faculty and scientists. To maintain contacts with professional colleagues, cent percent of the research students and faculty members are using the Internet/ E-mail at home.

Table 179

Purpose of using Internet/ E-mail Outside the Library (more than one)

Purpose	*Scientists (N=79)*	*Faculty (N=75)*	*Research students (N=48)*	*Total (N=202)*
Searching databases and other subject sources	50 (63.29%)	43 (57.33%)	48 (100%)	141 (69.80%)
For knowing information on forth coming conferences / meetings	29 (36.71%)	32 (42.67%)	29 (60.41%)	90 (44.55%)
To maintain contacts with professional colleagues	47 (59.49%)	43 (57.33%)	48 (100%)	138 (68.32%)
Sending articles/papers for publication / conferences	32 (40.51%)	39 (52%)	33 (68.75%)	101 (51.49%)
Links with professional associations	28 (35.44%)	25 (33.33%)	30 (62.50%)	83 (41.09%)
Any other	10 (12.66%)	11 (14.67%)	7 (14.58%)	28 (13.86%)

Among those using Internet for sending articles/ paper for publication/ conferences: majority of them are research students followed by faculty and scientists. In terms of maintaining contacts and link with professional associations more percent of research students are found to be using Internet / E-mail compared to other two categories.

Very few have stated other reasons for using Internet. They include reasons like entertainment, sending personal mails and maintaining contacts with others.

In general the use of Internet / E-mail facility was found to be mainly for two purposes viz. for maintaining contacts with the professional colleagues and searching the databases and other subject information sources on Net.

Suggestions from Users

If the library or information center wants to be more effective and user oriented it should try to know the feed back from the users. The feed back may be in the form of opinions. The last question is aimed at collecting suggestions from user regarding various aspects of the library.

Table: 180

Suggestions from Scientists, Faculty and Research Students (more than one)

Suggestions	*Scientists (N = 184)*	*Faculty (N = 133)*	*Research students (N = 94)*	*Total (N = 411)*
Collection/books & periodicals	133 (72.28%)	90 (67.67%)	66 (70.21%)	289 (70.32%)
Reading room/furniture	77 (41.85%)	52 (39.10%)	29 (30.85%)	158 (38.44%)
Staff	76 (41.30%)	54 (40.60%)	29 (30.85%)	159 (38.69%)
Library and inf. Service	74 (40.22%)	51 (38.35%)	27 (28.72%)	152 (36.98%)
Library automation	74 (40.22%)	53 (39.85%)	30 (31.91%)	157 (38.20%)
Internet/ E-mail	100 (54.35%)	75 (56.39%)	57 (60.64%)	23 (56.45%)
CD-ROM collections/ Databases	92 (50%)	43 (32.33%)	30 (31.91%)	165 (40.15%)
Issues and returns/ loan procedures	52 (28.26%)	26 (19.55%)	16 (17.02%)	94 (22.87%)
Physical facilities	63 (34.24%)	41 (30.83%)	21 (22.34%)	125 (30.41%)
User training/orientation program.	92 (50%)	57 (42.86%)	40 (42.55%)	189 (45.99%)
General	33 (17.93%)	9 (6.77%)	11 (11.70%)	53 (12.90%)

Suggestions were made by majority of the users from all the three user groups. Among various areas considered for suggestions, the first priority was given to library collection and second to Internet and E-mail facility. Third place was given to user-orientation programmes. However, 37-40 percent of the users also offered suggestions regarding CD-ROM collections, library staff, reading room facility, library automation and information services. They requested for improvement in the existing facilities and introduction of new services and facilities in libraries using the latest available technologies.

5

Conclusions and Suggestions

In the present chapter the findings of the study are consolidated and presented in two sections. While first section summarises the results gathered through the questionnaire survey of libraries while inferences drawn from user survey are presented in second section.

Library Survey

Library Survey Findings

The majority of the agricultural libraries in Andhra Pradesh are located in Agricultural Research Stations followed by those attached to ICAR Institutes. Agronomy and Plant breeding are found to be the areas on which the libraries focus their collection development.

Institution Budget

The Majority of the institutions to which the agricultural libraries are attached receive less than 10 lakhs budget every year.

Year of Establishment of Libraries

The majority of the agricultural libraries surveyed were established between 1981 and 1990. The oldest library covered in the survey was established in 1906 (i.e. Regional Agricultural Research Station (RARS), Lam, Guntur).

Library Budget

Majority of the libraries are receiving below Rs. 1 lakh yearly budget allocation. Among them many are receiving only upto rupees 25,000 per year. The budget of the academic libraries of the universities is found to be Rs. 50,00,000 and that for colleges is found to be below Rs. 1,20,000. It is also found that majority of the libraries are getting only below 0.5 percent of total budget of the institution. Provision of lumpsum budget allocation to the libraries is found to be the common practice among the agricultural libraries. Few librarians have responded to the question on item-wise expenditure in their libraries. Majority of them are found to be spending rupees 10,000 to 1,00,000 towards books and periodicals separately per year. Only one library spent Rs. 10,000 to 1,00,000 on electronic equipment in one year. Majority of the libraries are spending upto Rs.10,000 for office maintenance out of the expenditure on any other items. Upto Rs.10,000 was spent on an average per year on information services by majority of the libraries.

Library Staff

Most of the libraries have less than 10 staff members. Among them majority are manned by a single library staff.

Majority of the libraries are manned by incharge librarians who are non professionals. Nearly one quarter of the librarians are professionals with other BLISC or MLISC qualification. Majority of non professional librarians are found to be having agricultural science background. Expect two, all other librarians do not have knowledge in computer applications. Only one of them is a professional. Majority of the librarians have 21 years and above experience of service. Significant percentage of them also found to be having experience of below 5 years. Majority of the librarians stated that they have not published any articles or books. Among those published, majority have less than 5 publications to their credit. Majority of the librarians do not have knowledge in any of the foreign languages other than English and Telugu.

Users

Average number of postgraduate (PG) and undergraduate students (UG) served by the university and colleges is below 100 and 201 and above respectively where as the average number of research students served by majority of the libraries is below 100. On an average majority of the libraries are serving below 25 faculty and scientists.

Physical Facilities

More than ninety percent of the libraries surveyed do not have independent accommodation. The location of the library is found to be convenient to access for majority of the students. They have also expressed satisfaction regarding the lighting and ventilation in the library, scientists, faculty and research students are not fully satisfied with the existing accommodation.

Majority of the libraries are located in a plinth area of less than 150 sqmts. Majority of the libraries are not having separate space allocation for each facility and are facing the problem of inadequate space. Most of the libraries are able to provide seating or reading facility only for 1-15 readers at a time in the library.

Collection

More than 90 percent of the libraries are found to be possessing below 25,000 books.

Only one library has above 50,000 collection of books and it is the University library It has more than 75,000 books in its collection. Three fourth of the libraries surveyed are subscribing to less than 25 periodicals. Only 7 libraries are maintaining CD-ROM collections. Out of them, majority have less than 25 CD-ROMs in their collection. Only 3 libraries out of 46 found to be having micro form collections numbering below 500. Only 10 libraries (21.74%) are found to be maintaining collection in the form of thesis and dissertation. Nearly 43 percent of the libraries have pamphlets collections below 500 in number. None of the libraries provided information on report and trade literature collections.

Acquisition Procedures

Majority of the libraries are found to be acquiring books directly from publishers followed by local book sellers. The chief mode of periodical acquisition found among the libraries is through subscriptions. Even significant percent of libraries are receiving periodicals as gratis. Annual addition of books to the existing collection was found to be around 100 in the case of majority of the libraries. More than half were found to be subscribing annually to more than 21 and above periodical titles. Most of them are titles renewed every year for subscription.

Processing and Indexing of Library Materials

Majority of the libraries surveyed are not cataloguing the books. Among those doing cataloguing, majority are adopting dictionary catalogue. Remaining are simply maintaining accession wise lists of books. Even classification of library books is also seen only in limited number of libraries. Books are arranged in many libraries accession number wise. Majority of the libraries are classifying and accessing the periodicals just like books. Indexing of articles in periodicals is done by very few libraries.

Stock Verification and Weeding out

Stock verification is done by majority of the libraries, but occasionally. As a result weeding out of unused and mutilated books is not being done regularly.

Services

Reference service is found to be the most common service offered by the majority of the libraries surveyed followed by bibliographic services. Among various types of reference service short range service has been offered by most of the libraries. Bibliographies are compiled mainly based on user demand in majority of the libraries. However significant percent of the libraries are also offering this service in anticipation of the user needs. Per year on an average about 50 bibliographies are being compiled by majority of the libraries. Preparation of documentation lists on regular basis year wise has also been reported by majority of the libraries. Reprographic services are provided by only 30 percent of the libraries surveyed. Majority of the libraries are charging 0.50 paise per exposure. None of the libraries that have photo copying facility are offering this service free of cost to students or scholars. But only two libraries are offering this facility free of cost to teachers and scientists. Interlibrary loan services are not offered by majority of the libraries and out of those libraries offering the service only half are using union catalogues to facilitate location and exchange of items from other libraries. Majority are covering less than 10 other libraries for lending or loaning the items. Nearly one fourth of the libraries are found to be publishing one or other form of publications including brochures, pamphlets, newsletters and bulletins. Majority of the libraries do not have their own binding facility in the library.

Dependency on Other Sources

Among other libraries and institutions considered as sources of information ICAR libraries are found to be major sources upon which majority of the libraries are reported to be depending for information. Majority of the libraries surveyed stated that they are maintaining contacts or links with other libraries and sources for mutual benefit, Other libraries also include ICRISAT library, British Council Library, Acharya N.G. Ranga Agricultural University Library, Centre for Cellular and Molecular Biology (CCMB) library and Indian National Scientific and Documentation Centre (INSDOC) library. Nearly 9 libraries out of 46 surveyed are found to be having links with other libraries through internet and e-mail as well as offline modes.

Automation and Modernization

Out of 46 libraries surveyed only 13 libraries are found to be using computers for library housekeeping activities. Major areas where application of computers is seen are database creation and retrieval, information acquisition, services and circulation. Internet, E-mail and networking facilities are not available in most of the libraries. Only those libraries operating in and around cities found to be having these facilities. Services of the libraries are not charged in most of the libraries. Even among those libraries providing internet facility, only few are stated to be charging for browsing the net and using E-mail facility.

User Education

User education / training programmes are not conducted by majority of the libraries. Among those programmes conducted majority were meant for scientists and students.

Survey of User Information Needs

Prior survey and analysis of user's information needs was not done by majority of the libraries surveyed. Those libraries surveying their users are also doing it occasionally.

Problems

Though majority of the libraries have not responded to this question. Nearly 37 percent came out with many issues and problems mainly related to inadequate professional staff and finances.

Future Plans

Half of the librarians are found to be having plans to improve the prevailing conditions in their libraries. Most of these plans are concerned with library automation, subscription of new and more Journals, establishing LAN, Internet and E-mail facilities in libraries.

Suggestions

Majority of the librarians came forward to offer suggestions with a view to improve the existing conditions. According to them the libraries are badly in need of qualified trained staff. Giving training to the existing staff in computer applications and network management according to them should be taken up as the priority issue. Computerization of library activities and networking with other libraries in and outside the state are also recommended by the librarians. Provision of CAS and SDI services to users was also suggested. Need for independent and well planned library building with all facilities has also been pointed by many librarians.

User Survey Findings

The responses from users comprising of students, scientists, research students and faculty are condensed and presented in this section under various subheadings.

Extent of Use of the Library

Under graduate and Post graduate Students:

- Difference were noticed between undergraduate and post graduate students in terms of frequency of visits. Majority of PG students are visiting the library 'daily' and visiting the library 'once or twice a week' is found to be significant among undergraduate students.
- Compared to UG Students, PG students are spending more time in the library. Average number of hours used by P.G. and U.G students are 6-10 hrs and 5 or less hours per week respectively.
- Both UG and PG Students are visiting the library mainly to read books and journal. For this purpose they have suggested for extension of library working hours and improving the physical faculties in the library.
- Departments in the academic institutions are found to be taking more interest rather than the library in providing instruction and guidance to the students in the use of library resources.
- Differences were not noticed in terms of awareness about the ways of accessing information from the library between PG and UG students. Most of them seen to

be learnt how to use the library on their own. About one fourth of them took the guidance from their friends. They only considered library staff as third alternative in creating awareness and providing guidance in terms of use of the library. Teachers were remembered in this context only next to library staff.

- Regarding the possibility of getting required item from the library, majority of both UG and PG students stated though not always some times they could manage to get the required information.

Scientists, Faculty and Research Students

- Differences were not seen among the three groups of users (scientists, faculty and researchers) in terms of their frequency of visits to the library. Majority of them are found to be visiting the library 'twice a week' followed by 'daily'. However, compared to other two groups, more number of research students are found to be visiting library 'daily'.
- All the three groups of users visited the library mainly to read the material in the library. The main purpose for visiting the library as mentioned by the users is 'reading the library materials' second highest percent of them stated the reason 'borrowing books'. Third highest percent of them visited the library for 'borrowing journals'.
- Variations are noticed among the three groups, in terms of purposes of using the information. Majority of the scientists are using the information for writing research reports and for keeping themselves abreast of the latest developments in their concerned field of interest Research students are found to be using the information for study purpose and to be up-to-date in their field. Faculty have pointed out different other reasons. Since their main activity is teaching they are using the information they have gathered for teaching purpose. Second highest percent of them are seeking information to keep themselves current in their field of interest. All the three groups, though differ in terms of main purpose of using information, are found to be same in terms of the second reason they have indicated.

Dependency on Other Sources

Students

- Dependency on other sources and libraries for required information and books was noticed only among few students. The other sources include libraries of Universities, ICAR, Public libraries, British Council, DRR, DOR, NIRD, MANAGE, CRIDA, ICRISAT, NAARM etc. Degree of dependency on other sources was only moderate in the case of majority of those students approaching them.

Scientists

- Majority of the scientists and faculty were found to be depending on personal collections, other scientists and researchers as other sources of information. Other institutional libraries were approached for required information by most of the research students followed by other researchers and scientists. Personal collections were considered as third preference by researches students.

- Much differences were not observed among the three groups of users in terms of extent of dependency on other sources. All of them are moderately dependent on other sources for information.
- Majority of scientists, research students and faculty stated that due to lack of adequate and required items in the library collection, they were forced to approach sources other than the institution library. Second reason they mentioned is non availability by foreign books and journals in the library, for which they are depending on other sources.

Ways of getting Information

Students

- Differences were not noticed in terms of awareness about the ways of accessing information from the library between PG and UG students. Most of them seen to be learnt how to use the library on their own. About one fourth of them took the guidance from their friends. They only considered library staff as third alternative in creating awareness and providing guidance in terms of use of the library. Teachers were remembered in this context only next to library staff.
- Regarding the ways of finding required information majority of PG students approached the library catalogue where as UG students took the help of library staff.
- The library catalogue was considered to be useful by majority of both UG and PG students. But significant percent of UG students also found it not useful.
- Majority of them who are not satisfied with the catalogue and suggested for improving subject catalogue in the library.

Scientists

- Not much difference was seen between scientists and faculty in terms of ways of getting the required information or document from the library. The majority of them were found to be taking the assistance of the library staff. Dependency on library catalogue to locate required information was found to be more among the research students.

Library Services

Students

- *Awareness about services*: The survey reveals that majority of the students are aware about the services offered by their libraries. Reference service and photocopying are the services identified by students. Among various services offered by the library reference service is found to be the most popular service and used frequently by both UG and PG students. Among those services used occasionally current awareness service was found to be significant one. Among less used service inter library loan services and translation service.

- Majority of both PG and UG students found to be satisfied with reference service offered by their library. About usefulness of some of the services significant percent of the students, especially UG students could not express any opinions, which indicates two facts their non-availability and lack of awareness about them. Suggestions for improving reference service, bibliographic service, current awareness service (CAS), Inter library loan (ILL), literature search service with the help of trained library staff are made by significant percent of students. Among those students not satisfied with the existing photocopying facility are PG students.
- Regarding the willingness to pay for computerized services, majority of the students expressed willingness to pay for computerized services of the library.

Scientists

- Among the services offered by the library photocopying was considered to be the most useful service by all the three groups of users. Bibliographic service and Indexing and abstracting services were given second and third priority respectively. Scientists and research students are using the information services mainly to satisfy their research information needs. Where as faculty are utilizing them in support of their teaching and instructional purposes.
- Though the majority of the users are satisfied with the existing methods of display of materials, among those not satisfied, scattering of related books was found to be the major reason for their dissatisfaction.

Physical Facilities

Students

- Majority of the UG Students stated that they could manage to get the reading and seating space only sometimes. Whereas highest percent of PG students are always able to find the place for reading.
- The location of the library is found to be convenient for reach according majority of the students.
- According to the opinion of majority of the students the existing furniture is comfortable.
- Highest percent of UG and UG students were of the opinion that the lighting and ventilation in the library is satisfactory.

- Internal design of the library is found to be helpful and convenient for use according to majority of the students.
- Both PG and UG students who are not fully satisfied with the existing facilities offered suggestions regarding to location, size of the library building, furniture equipment, lighting and other physical facilities.

Scientists

- In their suggestions scientists, faculty and research students, faculty and research students expressed their dissatisfaction over the existing physical facilities. Especially they were particular about insufficient accommodation.

Library Procedures and Display and Organisation

Students

- In terms of making suggestions regarding the collection and its availability differences were noticed between UG and PG students. Highest percent of PG students are found to be active and made suggestions regarding the collection and its availability in the library. Majority of the UG students have not made suggestions on library collection.
- Majority of the students are offering the suggestions occasionally to the library.
- Majority of the students stated that the response from the library to their suggestions was positive and encouraging.
- It is found that three fourth of both PG & UG students were aware of library rules and regulations. About the borrowing privileges majority of the students are aware and at the same time they are satisfied with them. But students who are not satisfied with the existing system complained that number of books issued at a time to students and renewal of time are not enough and need to be increased. They also felt that rate of fine also should be reduced.
- Regarding the manual book issuing procedures, majority found them satisfied borrowing privileges of the library.
- Significant percent of both UG and PG also wanted to have free access to Internet, E-mail and CD-Rom search services. Second highest percent of them are demanded the extension of library working hours.

Scientists

- Though the majority of the users are satisfied with the existing methods of display of materials, among those not satisfied, scattering of related books was found to be the major reason for their dissatisfaction.

- A significant percentage of scientists also pointed out that irregular sorting of used books and incorrect arrangement of books on the shelves were creating problems for the users.
- The majority of the users expressed satisfaction over the display and arrangement of periodical publications. However among those not satisfied with existing practices the majority stated that display of current issues is not done properly. The second reason they have given is the difficulty they are facing in locating missing issues.
- A large number of scientists, faculty and research students are aware of the borrowing privileges.
- Library timings were found to be convenient for the majority of the users.

Types of documents preferred most

Students

- Among various types of documentary sources books, newspaper and periodicals are indicated as most useful sources in the order of priority for undergraduate students. Post graduate students considered periodicals as the most useful sources of information.

Scientists

- Periodicals especially Indexing and abstracting periodicals were considered as the most preferred items by the scientists, followed by reference books and text books. Reference books and text books were found to be the most useful items for research students and faculty respectively.

Knowledge about the Library and its Facilities

Students

- Departments in the academic institutions are found to be taking more interest rather than the library in providing instruction and guidance to the students in the use of library resources.
- Regarding the possibility of getting required item from the library, majority of both UG and PG students stated though not always some times they could manage to get the required information.
- Regarding the ways of finding required information majority of PG students approached the library catalogue where as UG students took the help of library staff.

- It is found that three fourth of both PG and UG students were aware of library rules and regulations. About the borrowing privileges majority of the students are aware and at the same time they are satisfied with them. But students who are not satisfied with the existing system complained that number of books issued at a time to students are less, time given for renewal of books is not enough and requested for change in these rules.

Scientists

- All the users expressed the opinion that library should take interest in organizing training programmes for them in the use of computers.

Response from the Library to the Suggestions made by Students

- Majority of the Post graduate students though occasionally took interest in making suggestions for improving library collection to the librarian. Most of them also stated that they have received a positive response.

Computers, Internet , E-mail and CD-ROMs

Students

- Majority of the UG and PG students stated that they do not have access to Internet, Email and CD-Rom databases. Majority of the libraries even do not have their own databases.
- Out of the students having access to Internet, highest percent have never used Internet, Email and CD-ROM databases. However significant percent of them are found to be occasionally using these facilities.
- Though majority of the users were not using the Internet regularly, they considered Internet as useful source of information.
- Those who are using Internet found to be using it for information on further studies / higher studies and to get information on subject of their interest.
- All the PG students used Internet for subject information where as UG students used this facility for information on further studies.
- Majority of the students were with the opinion that for effective use of automated library catalogue, training of users in its use is essential. The same opinion was expressed by majority of students when asked about the use of E-mail and Internet and searching of CD-ROM databases separately.
- Regarding the willingness to pay for computerized services, majority of the students expressed their willingness to pay for computerized services of the library.

Scientists

- Internet was used moderately as a source of information by the majority of the users.
- Most of the users reported that they have knowledge and skills in the use of computers.
- All the users felt that the library should take an interest in organizing training programmes for them in the use of computers.
- Non-availability of internet facility in the library was pointed out by the majority of the scientists and researchers. However, faculty stated that they have access to computers in their library.
- However access to Internet is restricted for the majority of the users in those libraries having internet facility. Internet services in most of these libraries though not charged are not available liberally for majority of them.
- Majority of the users do not have computers and Internet faculty at home. Most of them are approaching browsing center to use Internet.
- Some of the websites and home pages frequently accessed by the users are: the websites of www.icar.com; www.icrisat.Org; www.fors.org; www.larc.org; www.manage.gov.in; www.kiran.com; www.agriwater.com; www.nic.in. Most frequently used search engines are: altavista; google and yahoo.
- The majority of the users said they were paying Rs.20 per hour for internet outside the library.
- The majority of the users are aware of CD-ROM collections in their libraries. Moreover, access to these collections was found to be free and liberal in most of the cases.
- The majority of the users were found to be using the computers out side the library for personal and academic work.
- To maintain professional contacts and for searching the on-line data bases majority of the users are using Internet and E-mail facility.

Library Staff

Students

- Differences were not noticed in terms of awareness about the ways of accessing information from the library between PG and UG students. Most of them seen to be learnt how to use the library on their own. About one fourth of them took the guidance from their friends. They only considered library staff as third alternative for knowing about the use of the library. Teachers were remembered in this context only next to library staff. (TS).

- Regarding the ways of finding required information majority of PG students approached the library catalogue where as UG students took the help of library staff.
- Highest percent of students rated the behaviour of library staff working in different sections of the library as 'good' and considered them as helpful.

Scientists

- Library staff were considered by all the users as helpful and understanding.

Literary Productivity of Users and Dependence on the Library

- Majority of the scientists published articles in journals and presented conference papers in the last five years. But only 19 percent of them have published books and very few have 'patents' to their credit. Irrespective of their category all the three have published below 5 articles and conference papers in the last five years. Most of them are found to be moderately dependent on the institutional library for the purpose of writing articles, conference papers, books etc.

Discussion

1. Due to the intensive and sustained developments in the field of agriculture education period 1960-90 significant achievements have been made in different areas of agriculture in India. Achieving greater self- sufficiency in food production, dryland farming, social forestry etc. may be cited as examples.
2. Agriculture today has interdisciplinary relationship with basic science as well as several aspects of social sciences. There is a great need to develop effective bibliographic tools that facilitate location and access to available agricultural information.
3. The study of historical development reveals that while several colleges and research institutes in agriculture had been established before Independence, the real thrust in this direction however came only during the post-independence period.
4. The study of the developments of agriculture and agricultural libraries in India indicates that the history of agricultural libraries ran parallel to that of agricultural research and educational activities in the country. It is evident from the first chapter that for making agricultural sector more capable to meet the challenges posed by various demographic factors the Government of India has taken lot of steps.

5. It is found that many agricultural libraries in Andhra Pradesh attached to the Agricultural University, colleges and research institutes are managed by a single professional staff member. They provide services to their clintele mostly using manual methods. There is a scope for improvement and modernization of the existing information facility so as to meet the varied and specialized information needs of scientists, teachers, research students and students.
6. The developments in the publishing industry and intensified research and development activities created a challenge to the knowledge industry to develop a system of proper bibliographical control of published information in every country. It has further created the need for generous financial support for libraries. Since knowledge has no linguistic or national boundaries librarians certainly carry a heavy responsibility to select, acquire and provide all those documents published anywhere, in any language in any format which would be required by the users. This situation has however been further aggravated by the evincing cost of books, periodicals and other categories of documents with the result that the library budgets have greatly got shrunk in actual economic terms. In this respect the norms suggested by Radhakrishnan Report on Higher education (1949), Kothari Commission (1964), Indo-US survey teams and others for financial support ranging between 6.25% to 10% (depending on the stage of development of the library) of the total institutional budget can provide the minimum financial support for a library in a Agricultural University or a research institute. It is however found that in this respect the situation, as evident from the present study, is not quite satisfactory in most of the agricultural libraries. The share of agricultural libraries is only 0.5% of the total budget of the institution against the norms. To develop the libraries on modern lines the 6.25 percent as the norms suggested by the norms will not be sufficient. It is therefore essential to enhance this to 10% to 12% of the annual budget of the parent body. However situations such as the establishment of a new library, introduction of a new service, computerization of housekeeping operations, installation of CD-ROM workstations and others would always demand additional finances on non-recurring basis for items such as core document collection, hardware, software etc. The concerned authorities and funding agencies such as ICAR, UGC and others should therefore assess these requirements in an objective manner and provides financial support to meet them.

Library Staff

7. Competent staff are the backbone of the library. Quality of the service rendered by library indicates the efficiency of the functioning of the library. The two schools of library and information science (Department of library and information science, Banaras Hindu University and Delhi University) used to offer

specialization programme in Agricultural Librarianship and now no school in the country is offering formal education and training in the field of agricultural librarianship. Agricultural librianship should also receive its due share in the LIS programmes at the Masters Degree level of atleast some of the LIS schools in the country. So, that professionals with proper background and training are made available for positions in these libraries in the country. Intensive research programmes are also required at MPhil and PhD level to offer practical solutions to problems and find out new techniques and services beneficial for both agricultural librarians and their user communities.

8. In view of the rapid strides in the field of library and information profession to be successful LIS professional has to update his knowledge about latest trends. The study reveals that agricultural libraries in A.P. are beset with inadequate and ill-trained staff. Therefore, there is a need to organize refresher courses on latest trends in LIS field either by the Agricultural University libraries or professional associations like ILA, IASLIC or institutions like INSDOC / DRTC or academic departments in the Universities. Regarding the attitude and behaviour of library staff towards users, majority of the users expressed satisfaction. Positive attitude of the staff and his/her cordial relations with the users helps in improving the image of the library and the library profession. It develops a healthy rapport between the staff and the user which in turn positively influences the extent of use of the library and acts as a catalyst to convert potential user as a regular user. Because of prior knowledge and experience scientists, faculty, research students and PG students found to be less dependent on library staff where as undergraduate students who are new to the library seems to be taking the assistance of library straff more.

9. It is an established fact that unless libraries act as active and responsive organisations, their existence in the organisation may be in danger. In this context, every effort has to be made by the library staff to know, understand and assess the information needs of the users. The documentary resources and the services offered by the library must match with the changing and complex information needs of the users and the organisation. Services like Current Awareness Services (CAS), Selective Dissemination of Information (SDI), Repacking of Information, News clipping and Digest services have their genesis to meet the specific identified information needs of users. But surveying the needs of users was not given any attention by the libraries surveyed. This may be due to the age-old practices to assess the information needs through indirect methods or the ignorance of the staff about its importance in planning the library services or due to the passive attitude of the professionals. The library staff have to be educated in this regard. Marketing of information services and products is a management activity which necessitates research about the customer and his

requirements, needs and demands. The prime objective of information marketing is planning and offering the services and products to bring more satisfaction to users. Though it allows the pricing of the services, the main motto behind it is not to gain profit but to add more value to the product or service. Users are found to be willing to pay for the charged services. In a way it enables the library to generate resources on its own. Reprographic service, bibliographic and reference services are the services offered by majority of the libraries surveyed. Reference and bibliographic services are provided based on demand whereas reprographic service is a charged service for all the users. Since the libraries surveyed have the responsibility to support specific academic, research and extension needs of users, there is a need to offer even specialist services to the users at least for scientists and extension workers.

10. User education / training programmes will have lot of bearing in improving in the extent of use of the library and its resources. By making user more aware about various aspects of the facilities and their relevance for his / her purpose, the library can act as a catalyst in his academic and research pursuits. Little effort has been made in this regard by majority of the libraries surveyed. Lack of qualified and inadequate staff, finances and proper infrastructure may be the reasons for this. Established libraries like ANGRAU or ICRISAT or professional associated like AALDI or IASLIC or agencies like ICAR can take up this task and help the professionals.

11. The agricultural library system has a decentralized setup of libraries attached to the ANGRA University, its constituent colleges, research and extension centers. The geographic distribution and location of various libraries is dependent on their type and activities of the center to which they are attached. Majority of the agricultural libraries in Andhra Pradesh are serving the Agricultural Research stations and the institutions of Indian Council of Agricultural Research. Though research in the field of Agriculture and allied subjects is the main activity of most of these libraries. Agronomy and plant breeding are the thrust areas of research. Difference were noticed among these libraries interms of their location, objectives, basic infrastructure and functioning. However all of them are directly or indirectly involved in serving the three main objectives viz. agricultural education, research and extension. But the findings of the study indicate that in many aspects the libraries or information facility at the bottom level mostly working at village level in rural areas are lagging behind. They are deprived of minimum facilities like proper accommodation, trained staff and adequate collection in support of the services they have to offer to the extension officers and some times even to farmers at grass root level. On the other hand libraries in and around Hyderabad city and in some district headquarters are well developed. The present study projects the need for a well designed and

comprehensive plan for the development of an effective agricultural information facility in the state of Andhra Pradesh as a whole.

12. The library profiles indicate that though the origin of most of the libraries surveyed was between 1981 and 1990, regards the staff, budget, collection, services, automation and other physical facilities in the libraries, they are in bad shape. Most of these libraries are manned by non-professionals having qualifications in agricultural sciences.

13. Majority of the libraries are manned by only one person. Accomodation of these libraries, in most of the cases, is less than 150 sq.mts and as a part of another building. With this inadequate space, a large number of libraries are able to provide reading space only 1 to 15 users at a time. Within the same plinth area all the routine library activities including professional and office work are being performed by the library staff. Majority of them have to serve on an average 100 students and 25 faculty / scientists / research students per day. Inadequate space in the library is in fact not only a problem for the library staff but also for the users. Spacious accommodation provides proper ventilation and lighting with comfortable seating and reading facility. Library is a growing organism. New collection, new services and facilities definitely requires additional accommodation.

14. Libraries serving academic institutions are found to be possessing more books. Other libraries have collection of books below 25,000. Majority of these libraries are attached to Research Stations. Number of periodicals subscribed by the libraries are less than 25 titles. Few libraries have non-book materials like CD-ROMS; Microforms in their collection. The above figures on book collection though look sound users' opinion about them will help in evaluating the reasons for their dependency on other sources indicate the inadequacies in the collection. Users found to be coming regularly to the library mainly to read journal. Arrangement and display of books in majority of the libraries is done according to accession numbers. Catalogue is also not maintained by most of the libraries. Instead for locating required item from the collection they found to be using accession registers. It is because of these unscientific methods or organizing and retrieval of the library material, users of these libraries are facing problems in getting the required book from the collection. The possibility of locating the needed item may be restricted and users time getting wasted because of such outdated practices.

    However, the situation in libraries attached to the ANGRA University, its colleges and research stations are different. 13 .libraries are maintaining the library catalogue with classified arrangement of material on shelves. Threy have organised the collections according to prescribed standard. Majority of the students are satisfied with the existing library catalogue. As regards to the periodicals display and arrangement, scientists, faculty and research students pointed out the problems like improper arrangement; difficulty in locating the different issues of periodicals. Indexing of periodical articles subject-wise is not done by any of the libraries surveyed. The need for a mechanism for easy identification and location of the loose issues and current issues was felt by the users.

15. Scientists' and faculty's use of personal collections and fellow scientists' and research students and UG and PG students dependency on other libraries for required books and information clearly indicates the need to improve the existing collection in terms of quality and quantity and provision of access to various current information sources in the organisation libraries. For the sake of foreign journals and books and to refer latest reference sources dependency on other sources is noticed among the users. This shows one of the limitations of the existing collections in the library in terms of absence of latest additions issues books / periodicals. Latest information regarding scientific research in the field of agriculture to a maximum extent can be offered by providing access to CD-ROM, Online databases and Internet in the libraries. To overcome the burden of heavy costs, all the libraries can have cooperative arrangement to have access to electronic information sources through network facility. Internet can also act as a channel in this system facilitating easy flow of information. The survey also revealed that many of the users are not aware of the rich electronic sources available on Internet and through consortium approach. Internet acts as a platform changing research and academic information and building contacts with fellow researchers and academics. It widens, the knowledge and outlook of the user and makes him or her more confident and resourceful in his / her area of specialization.

16. The survey also presents some interesting findings on the information services front as in the case of majority of the special libraries in India. Agricultural libraries in AP are also providing services like answering users' queries, photocopying of documents and preparing list of references and subject bibliographies. As observed by many authors, the literature survey reveals that the literature in agricultural sciences and allied subjects is scattered in a wide variety of information sources that users may not find sufficient time for literature search and study. Further as they are engaged in teaching, research and extension activities, it is the responsibility of agricultural libraries to assist user, by providing the nascent, pertinent information in a form suitable for him/her availing all the possible traditional and electronic channels and sources. Moreover personalized services are the need of the user in the case of researchers and scientists. Adequate storage and access to latest information and necessary infrastructure if provided will enable the library to customize its services.

17. Availability of CD-ROM databases and access to internet sources, links with other sources made it possible, simple and easy to create local in-house services like monthly current awareness lists, abstracting and indexing of journal articles, list of conferences and events forthcoming. The location ordering and acquisition of latest electronic versions of indexing and abstracting periodicals demand adequate understanding and knowledge about the procedures, legal implication and technicalities involved on the part of the librarians.

18. User training and orientation programmes are essential to facilitate optimal utilization of the library and its resources. Majority of the libraries surveyed are not conducting such programmes. Majority of the students stated that they have come to know about the library and its procedures on their own. Some of them took the guidance from their friends. All the users need basic information and library skills and knowledge about the functional and structural aspects of the library. For introducing and implementing any new service and procedures successfully, the prerequisites is to create the conducive environment where the user will be made fully involved. Before introducing for the first time any computerized service, online access to databases; online public access catalogue, new software, Internet and E-mail facility, the end user needs relevant hands-on training to use the service with confidence and reap its benefits. Similar views were expressed by the users suggesting the organisation of training programmes in the use of computers, Internet and CD-ROM databases and to participate in the network environment.

19. The physical conditions of the library have impact on the functioning and extent of use of the library and information facility. Majority of the libraries surveyed do not have independent accommodation and are located in limited space. The routine work as well as provision of any services to the users will have implication because of this problem. It creates storage problems for growing collections unless stock verification and weeding out are done periodically.

20. It is not possible to think about library ergonomics in such conditions. User cannot spend more time in the library without proper and conducive environment. Further for installing new facilities like computers and other accessories, multimedia equipment, cubicles for internet and OPAC access, the existing accommodation of majority of the libraries may not be sufficient. Both the library professionals and users have pointed out the problems of inadequate accommodation and suggested for providing independent and larger accommodation for planning and giving better and advanced services. They have also indicated need for more space for creating pleasant and comfortable reading room facility.

21. Automation, as proved by many previous studies, is a boon to the agricultural libraries which are facing the problems of inadequate space and staff. But the study reveals that a little less than one quarter of the libraries surveyed are using computers for house-keeping operations. Majority do not have computers and consequently could not provide internet and E-mail facility. Majority are also not connected in any network activity. Libraries which are located in and around the cities and major towns are found to be using computers and having internet connectivity. The conditions in the other 33 libraries are not on par with them in terms of facilities and services. In this context it is relevant to examine the situation at the national level equipment, new requires in additional what is expected of the agricultural library facilities at the state level.

    The agriculture information handling activity at the international level is at advanced level involving efforts of many international organisations. Many national level agencies and authors associated with agriculture proposed the development of national information policy on agriculture, national Agricultural information system of all the agricultural libraries and information centers in India. Models were also suggested for developing the state level agricultural information systems and networks. But for implementing such plans, strengthening and modernizing the existing infrastructure facilities in the libraries is a must.

Suggestions

In keeping tune with current research and development in the field of Agricultural sciences, there has been realization of the importance and need for proper information support facilities at all levels. Library information centres attached to various agricultural institutions and organisations and R&D centres have a major role to play in the collection, and management of knowledge and data resources and in providing the scientists administrators, teachers, researchers and students and extension workers with appropriate information. The libraries of the various agricultural organisations and institutions must develop the capabilities and facilities to meet the continuously evolving needs of agricultural education, research and extension.

In India we find that most of the Government organisations and institutions, both Central and State connected with Agricultural sciences, have well developed libraries and information centers and facilities. In Andhra Pradesh the geographic area to which this study is confined, organisation like ICRISAT, NAARM, DOR, DRR, NRCOP, NRCS, NBPGR, NIRD MANAGE, CRIDA, NPPTI and Acharya N.G. Ranga Agricultural University are all located at Hyderabad and with liberal funds from the Indian Council of Agricultural Research. They have extremely good information systems. On the other hand, many of the research stations and extension centers located in the rural areas of

Andhra Pradesh have poor facilities in library and allied services. This is a situation which calls for remedial measurers because these are the centers which cater ultimately to the grass root levels where agricultural development is actually implemented.

Following are the specific recommendations made for enhancing the existing information facility in Andhra Pradesh.

1. To have proper control on the influx of information and documents produced in the field of agriculture, agricultural libraries and information facilities at all levels can take steps to automate their activities and services. Wider access to the world of agricultural information can be provided even in a remote center by providing network connectivity, and Internet access.
2. For maximum possible use of the resources, the agricultural libraries in the A.P. state can be connected to other libraries and institutions dealing with agriculture through inter-library loan facilities or resource sharing activities through networking.
3. Programmes of continuing education may be organized in the country for the benefit of the agricultural library professionals at the national as well as regional levels. Such programmes should include practical exposure to related technology combined with visits to specialized centers in the field, both in India and abroad.
4. Keeping in view different aspects such as increasing exchange rates of foreign currencies and steep rise in prices of journals and books, at least 8-10% of the recurring budget of the respective institute / university should be earmarked for the development of the library or information facility.
5. There is a need to develop a system of resource sharing among the libraries within a region so as to make the best possible use of their limited financial resources. At the national level the proposed National Agricultural Library should serve as an apex library for this purpose.
6. While recognizing the need for the requisite manpower for efficient and effective library services, it is suggested that libraries of the agricultural universities and research stations must be provided with library staff as per norms for staffing formula recommended by S.R. Banerji and others (1983) in consultation with the UGC norms and standards.
7. To make agricultural libraries more responsive and user-oriented conduct of user surveys periodically is essential to identify the information needs and requirements and plan the library services accordingly.
8. To ensure that the stock is upto date and free of unnecessary items and that there are no gaps in the collection, regular stock verification and rectification programme should be instituted in all the agricultural libraries surveyed.

9. To maximize utilization of library resources, the libraries of agricultural universities and institutes like Indian Council of Agricultural Research (ICAR) should take concrete steps to organize user education programmes on a regular basis.

10. Productivity of scientists, faculty and research students in terms of publications reveals that, research output is not so encouraging especially in the form of articles, books and patents. Information is essential in agricultural research for creativity. Useful scientific breakthroughs can be achieved earlier than expected if the right information is available and used at the right time. Hence it is the responsibility of the agricultural library to provide relevant and current information at the right time to the user.

11. Since information is a resource to be exploited and that if the organizations make better use of it, the research conducted there would be more innovative, more useful and would be adopted more quickly and more widely. It is suggested that there is an urgent need to improve the existing library and information facilities in Agricultural institutions to promote agricultural research.

12. All the libraries should be provided with computers to facilitate quick functioning in the matters of library technical work and services. In view of the growing frontiers of technical and scientific information and knowledge, establishment of databases may facilitate the work of library staff and users. By using computers, proper and regular documentation services can be offered by the library with minimum staff.

13. To further the professional development of the existing staff they should be encouraged to participate in seminars, conferences and workshops on professional subjects. They should also be encouraged to become members of the Association of Agricultural Librarians and Documentalists of India (AALDI).

14. To provide global access to information on agriculture, National Agricultural Information centres should be reorganized to liaison with international information systems and databases like AGRIS. Through this channel the state-wide information networks offer access to the local users located in different corners of the state.

15. A centralized system for procurement of foreign and electronic agricultural journals can be evolved through a consortium of agricultural libraries in a region with a view to minimizing the procurement cost and avoiding duplication of work in the present administrative framework.

16. Although a coordinated network of state and national level libraries would improve access to information, the lack of qualified and trained staff, under-development of technical infrastructure and financial constraints hamper the

progress of agricultural libraries. Hence to apply technology appropriately, the staff in agricultural libraries should have proper training and knowledge in the application of technology.

17. The traditional communication methods in dissemination of agricultural technologies have limitations in their outreach to a much wider range of extension workers working at rural and village level. Modern technology comes to the help of Krishi Vignana Kendras, DAATT centers and other agricultural research stations working in rural areas to establish better communication of required information.

18. There are different levels of user groups working in the agricultural institutions. Each group differs from the others in terms of its information requirements and approach. While planning the information services it is required to keep in view the distinct needs of each group to provide more valuable services to users.

19. The explosive growth of literature and knowledge makes it virtually impossible for researchers and scientists to satisfy their information needs without efficient use of modern technology. Automated library systems help these users to explore the in-house databases, CD-Rom databases and online databases for accessing information within no time and without much effort.

20. Before planning about automating or networking of Agricultural libraries attached to the research stations operating in rural areas, the first step to be taken is to improve the basic facilities in the library. Proper accommodation, qualified staff and minimum number of relevant books and periodicals, and computer system with network capabilities should be made available in the library.

21. In India, in the field of agricultural sciences there are no bibliographical sources worth mentioning either for books and periodicals or for non- conventional literature. It is , therefore recommended to start the bibliographical services for books published in agricultural and allied sciences in India.

22. The CD-ROMs have immense possibilities for developing countries like India, where the institutions cannot afford main frame or online services because of the enormous costs involved in telecommunications. Agricultural libraries in rural areas of AP can procure the CD-ROM databases in agricultural which are relatively cheaper than online databases.

Areas for Future Research

The present study is an attempt to study and evaluate the existing agricultural information facility in Andhra Pradesh, taking into consideration academic and research institutions and field stations catering to multi-level groups of users, comprising teachers, students, researchers, scientists and extension workers.

While the study has made an extensive coverage of the information needs of these users and the extent to which they are being met by the existing library and information services, it has not suggested a models for networking and for analyzing the economic viability of models as this area is not written in its scope.

However, earlier studies have suggested models of networks linking agricultural libraries nationwide, as well as networks connecting the states. while linking themselves to only a few libraries, no attempt has been made to work out the costs involved in setting up a network, and analyzing the layers and modes of the system in terms of financial requirements, staff patterns, documentary and electronic resources technical equipment including computers and IT training of staff, services that can be effected and the cost of such services and the communication links that are necessary, some of the models in practice in other developing countries may also be studied.

It is felt that this is an area that warrants further study and research, and proposing a viable model in the Indian context would be a major step forward for its agricultural information system.

Similarly, further study can be taken up of the base level agricultural stations located in remote areas and working under the age is of different government and non-government agencies such as RARS, ARS, DAATTCs, KVKs and extension services. At present there is no coordination in the work and activities of these organisations and an in depth study of their financial resources and actual facilities would help in achieving better cooperative effort and results.

It is felt that some of these areas can be taken up for more detailed studies in future. Limitations of time and costs have made this researcher confine herself to presenting a picture of the present situation with regard to agricultural information facilities for agricultural education, research and extension in Andhra Paradesh and offering suitable suggestions for improvement.

Marketing of agricultural information services and products is one technique that enables the management to offer value added services to the clientele. Revenue generation is also one of its objectives. This area also requires further study and research. The findings of such research will of immense help for planning information consultancy services and information brokering activities in the field of agriculture and allied subjects for Indian markets.

Survey of agricultural information needs of agro-based industries, Banks and other trade organisations may be planned to explore the possibilities of providing effective and market oriented information services.

Bibliography

Achrya NG Ranga Agricultural University, *Annual Report 1998-99.*

Addision, Chris and Cullen, Tim "Harvest from the NET: *Benefits of E-mail for disseminating Agricultural Information in the African Continet", IAALD/QBXLI* (2), 1996, p. 202-203.

Agriculture in Andhra Pradesh, Vol-1 (Resources) The Farmers Welfare Trust and the Society of Scientists for Advancement of Agriculture, 1982, Hyderabad – 500004.

Aguolu, I.E. "Agricultural Libraries and the Dissemination of Agricultural Informatin in Nigeria", *Annals of Library Science and Documentation*, 47 (3), 2000, p. 115-119.

Ahasan, Shoaib A and Mehla, R.D. "Problems, needs and approaches of users to information in agricultural sciences". *ILA Bulletin*, 22 (3-4), 1987, p. 120-140.

Ailin Ton, Isahak. "Addressing the information needs of farmers and the extension services: The Malaysian experience". *IAALD/QB XXXVI* (1-2), 1991, p. 36-39.

Aina, L.O. "Education and Training of Librarians for Agricultural Information work in Africa. Specialist Librarians for Agriculture can accelerate development", *IAALD QBXXXIV* (1), 1989 p. 23-26.

Aina, L.O. Provisions of Agricultural Information to farmers and extension officers; A catalyst in increased Agricultural Production in Africa, *IAALD/QBXXXVI* (1-2), 1991 p. 20-23.

Aina, L.O. The use of government documents by researchers in Agricultural Economics and agricultural extension in Nigeria: a research note, *Government Publication Review*. 15(1) Jan/Feb 1988, p. 61-64.

Ananda Parameswari, N. Extension Education through Village adoption, *University News*, 39 (46), Nov 12-18, 2001, p. 4-6.

Andre, Pamela, Q.J. Communicating Agricultural Information in remote places, *IAALD/QB XLI*, (1), 1998 p. 7-11.

Andre, Pamela Q.J. Optical technology: New Ways of providing information to the end user, *IAALD /QBXXXVI*, (1-2), 1991 p. 136-138.

Arunachalam, Subbiah and Umamani K. "Mapping Agricultural Research in India: A profile based on CAB Abstracts 1998", *Information Today and Tomorrow*, Vol.20, No4, 2001 p. 9-17.

Arunachalam, Subbiah. "National Mapping Science – India: Agricultural Sciences", *Information Today & Tomorrow,* Vol 19, No. 2, 2000 p. 13, 14,17.

Arun Kumar Chakrabarty. "National Policy for Agricultural Library in the persepective of Information Base for Agricultural Library". *National Policies and Programmes Seminar Papers XXXVII All India Library Conference IIT,* Madras, Dec 4-7, 1991, Indian Library Association p. 103-112.

Aswath, L. "University of Agricultural Sciences Library (GKVK) Bangalore : Structural evaluation of the library building", *Library Science with Documentation and Information Studies* 35 (1), Mar 1998, p. 47-58.

Attaullah and Johnson, Jane S. "From Camels to computers : The realities of increasing the flow of Agricultural Information in Pakistans North-West Frontier", *IAALD / QB XXXVI,* (1-2), 1991 p. 105-109.

AW, Samba. "Communication – Less Bases et Banques de Donnies Agricoles an Sahel : Analyse de le Situation, perspectives del Valorisation dans le cadre du Development durable et Integri de la sous-region". *IAALD/QBXLI,* (I),1996, p. 36-45.

Banerjee et al. "A study of S.I.U norms for Jobs in an agricultural library". *IJALIS,*11, 1983, p. 9-13.

Banerjee, S.R. Indian Agricultural Information System. In B.M. Gupta and others (Ed.), *Hand Book of Libraries, Archives and Information centers in India.* Vol. 3, New Delhi. Information Industry Publication. p. 75-88.

Bankapur, M.B. Need for National Agricultural Information Centre in India, *ILA Bulletin,* Vol XIII, No.1-4, Jan-Dec., 1977 p. 79-93.

Bankapur, M.B. and Mallinath Kumbar. Bibliometric and Scientometric tools for measurement of productivity in Agricultural Research, *IJALIS,* Vol 6, No.3-4, July-Dec 1993 p. 169-178.

Bankpur, M.B. and Tukaram, R. "Strategic issues in Agricultural Information Technology with special references to developing countries", *IJALIS,* V8, N3-4, July–Dec, 1995, p. 245-254.

Bankpur, M.B. and Varadraj, V. "Strategic issues in Agricultural Information Technology with special reference to developing countries", *IJALIS,* 17-1989, p.60-64.

Barile-Frias, Marina. "ALAP: A Government Partner in Agricultural Information Activities", *IAALD / QB XXXVI* (1-2), 1991 p. 94-96.

Baruah, Apurba. "Annual Report as a source of Information in Agricultural Science", *IJALIS* 22,-1994. p. 41-42.

Bay-Peterssen, Jan. "Equity for the Information poor: Marketing Information for Asian farmers in remote Areas", *IAALD/QB XLI* (1), 1996 p.87-91.

Beavers, Peggy.J., Russel, Keith W and Sibia, Ted S. "Supporting the information needs of Agricultural Research Scientists working in remote locations: Implecations of recent studies and changes in technology and delivery Mechanisms", *IAALD/QB XLI (2),* 1996 p. 204-209.

Beecher, John.W. "The United States Agricultural Information Network (USAIN): Providing information to the end user", *IAALD/QB XXXVI (1-2),* 1991 p. 59-61.

Bellomy, Margot. "Planning for sustainable Information System in the Electronic age: Tradition versus Tehcnology", *IAALD/QB XLI (1),* 1996 p. 47-51.

Beraho, Emmy, Sheahan, Basil and Reeves, Tim. "Opportunities and challenges for extension in rural areas. Experience from the Mukono district (Uganda) with the training and visit extension model", *IAALD/QB XLI (1),* 1996 p. 79-86.

Besemer, H and Veerman, I. "Agricultural Information on the Internet: What is out there and how to find it", *IAALD/QBXL (2-3),* 1995 p. 61-67.

Bharati, Tubachi and Stanley, M.K. "Evaluation of International Abstracting periodicals in their coverage of Indian literature.2. Field crops abstracts", *IJALIS-23,* 1993 p. 24-29.

Biradar, B.S. "Sources of information for farmers in Karnataka", *Annals of Library Science and Documentation 47,* 1, 2000 p. 17-22.

Bird, James E and Smith, Jessie C. "A Selected Annotated Bibliography of Agricultural information", *Library Trends,* Vol 38, No.3, winter 1990 p. 517-541.

Blanchard, J, "Agriculture", *Library Trends,* April 1967 p. 880-895.

Blanchard, J.R. "Agricultural libraries and collections". In A. Kent & H Lanour (Eds) *Encyclopedia of Library and Information Science,* Vol 1, 1968, p. 126-134, New York, Marcel Delcker Inc.

Blanchard, J.Richard, "The changing nature of librarianship: Observations and overview". *In International Librarianship: Continuity and Change,* West Port Connecticut (USA): Greenwood Press, 1979.

Blanchard, J.R. The history of agricultural libraries in the United States. In A.Fusonie and L.Morun (Eds), *Agricultural Literature; Proud Heritage, Future Promise,* Washington DC, Associates of the National Agricultural Library, Inc and the Graduate School Press, U.S. Department of Agriculture, 1977. p. 219 – 235.

Bloch, Thomas. "Agricultural libraries of Nepal". *IAALD/QBXXVI (3),* 1981 p. 85-88.

Bone, B.F. "The information service of the National Institute for Research in Dairying", *Aslib Proceedings,* 31(3), March 1979, p. 136-137.

Boraiyan, R. "Agircultural Research Information scene in India : An outlook", *IJALIS 20,* 1992, p. 1-63.

Boraiyan, R. "Atlases and maps as information sources in Agricultural research and development", *IASLIC Bulletin,* 39(4) 1994, p.165-169.

Boraiyan, R. "Changing nature of Agricultural Librarianship: Organisational and managerial aspects", *Indian Journal of Information Library and Society,* V5, N1-2, Jan-June, 1992, p. 79-87

Boraiyan, R. "Checks and Balance of a Librarian in an Agricultural University", *Indian Journal of Information Library and Society,* V8, N3-4, July-Dec, 1995, p. 229-240.

Boraiyan, R. "Computerised data bases in Agriculture: An outlook", *Indian Journal of Information Library and Society,* V6, 3-6 July- Dec, 1993.

Boraiyan, R. "Information sources in Agricultural research and Development", *Herald of Library Science,* 2:14 (J) : 55.2' N9, p. 16-22.

Boraiyan, R. "Organisation, Management and Administration of Research Libraries", *JALIS,* 19(1991), p. 53-58.

Boriayan, R. "Tamil Nadu Agricultural University Library: A Profile", *IJALIS-20,* 1992, p. 7-13.

Bose, P.C. "Agricultural Information Systems", *Annals of Library Science and Documentation 23(1),* Mar, 1976, p. 45-47.

Bose, P.C. "Application of Microcomputers in Agricultural Libraries", *IJALIS 17,*1989, p.1-5

Bose, P.C. "Information support for agricultural extension in India", *IJALIS,* 13-15, 1985-87.

Bose. P.C. "National Agricultural Research Information System". National Information Policies and progammes seminor papers, *XXXVII All India Library Conference IIT Madras,* Dec 4-7, 1991, Indian Library Association.

Brennen, Patrikw. "Documentation in the literature of tropical and subtropical Agriculture", *Special Libraries,* July 1974, p. 263-271.

Bretz, R.G. "The Agricultural Satellite Corporation: The start of a new demension for Agricultural education", *Journal of Agricultural & Food Information,* 1(3), 1993 p. 101-107.

Britton, C.J. "Agricultural Informtion via the Clevel and free-Net", *Journal of Agricultural & Food Information,* 3 (2) 1995, p. 49-56.

Burton, Hilary D. "Multi-Data base searching in agriculture – A Coperative, Computerized service", *Special Libraries,* July 1978 p. 244-249.

Bystrom, Marcia. "Agricultural Information : Can you find it with the index?" *Special Libraries,* Nov. 1968 p. 712-717.

Central Tobacco Research Institute – *Annual Report – 1999-2000.*

Chillag, John, "Non-Conventional literature in Agriculture – an overview", *IAALD/QB XXXII* (1), 1992, p. 2-7.

Chodhary & Suthar. *Agricultural Education & Career Opportunities.* 1996. Agro Botanical Publishers (INDIA), Bikaner.

Chottey Lal. "Growth of Agricultural Libraries in India in the Post-Independence Era", *DESIDOC Bulletin of Information Technology,* Vol 18, No.2, March 1998, p. 13-20.

Chottey Lal and Bhatia, S. "Adoption of information technology by Agricultural Libraries in India", *Annals of Library Science and Documentation,* 1993, 40 (1), p. 6-11.

Clark, K.A. "Internet resources for Agriculture", *College & Research Libraries News,* 57(6) June 1996, p.359-361-3.

Craig, Gillian. "A review of information research in agriculture". *Aslib proceedings, 3 (3),* March, 1979, p. 152-155.

Craig, Gillian M. "Information systems in UK Agriculture: Final Report of the Agriculture Information Review Committee", *ASLIB-Proceedings, 32 (5),* May, 1980, p.201-206.

Crowder, L.Van and Anderson, J. "Linking research, extension and education: Why is the problem so persistent and pervasive?", *Europeon Journal of Agricultural Education and Extension,* Vol. 3, No.4, 1997, p. 241-249.

Damodaran, T and V. Sambasiva Rao, "Growth of Doctoral dissertations in oilseeds in India: A study", *Library Science with a Slant to Documentation,* Vol 35,No. 4, 1998, Paper 2B, p. 227-235.

Darko - Ampem, K.O., "Needs Assessment of Researches carried out in Ghana and Nigeria", *Querterly Bulletin of the International Association of Agricultural Information Specialists. 40 (4),* 1995, p. 127.

Deshmukh, G.R. "Users survey of soil Conservation Research Institute Library", *Annals of Library Science and Documentation,* 1983, 30 (1), p. 31-34.

Deshmukh, G.R. and Despande, S.P. "Guidelines for cooperation and coordination for information network sytem among the four Agricultural University libraries of Maharashtra: A Model, *IJALIS,* 17, 1989, p. 52-58.

Deshmukh, P.P. "Planning and design of University Library Building", *IJALIS,* 21, 1993, p. 16-25.

Deshmukh, P.P. and Deshpande, S.P. "User Education: A challenge to Librarians to motivate students for effective and efficient use of libraries", *IJALIS* 19, 1991, p. 30-35.

Deshpande, S.P. and Deshmukh, G.R. "Role of Agricultural Libraries in Dissemination of agricultural information", *Herald of Library Scinece,* V 24, N 1-2 Jan. April; 1985, p. 18-22.

Devi, A.S. and Lahari, Ramamsu, "Information seaking behaviour of the agricultural scientists in Manipur", *Indian Journal Information Library and Society,* V10, N 1-2, Jan-June 1997, p. 62-67.

Deutsch, A.E. "How Agricultural Libraries can help fight a world- wide threat", *IAALD/QB XXVI (3),* 1981, p. 97-99.

Directorate of Oilseeds Research, *Annual Report, 1999-2000,* Rajendra Nagar, Hyderabad.

Directorate of Rice Research, *Annual Report. 1997-98,* Rajendra Nagar, Hyderabad.

Ditzler, Carolj, and others "Agricultural document delivery; Strategies for the future", *Library Trends,* Vol 38 No.3 winter, 1990, p. 376-396.

Dutta, S and Kumar, R.P. "SDI service of ICRISAT", *AALDI/QB X,* p. 12-15.

Ekpenyong, G.D. "Agricultural research in Nigeria: The role of Institutional libraries", *Information Development 17 (2),* Jun 2001, p. 118-122.

Elder, Nelda J et al. "Collection development, selection and acquisition of Agricultural materials", *Library Trends,* Vol 38, No.3, Winter 1990, p. 442-473.

Entsua-Mensah, Clement. "Linking Research and Extension services for sustainable food production in Ghana: Some options for achievement", *IAALD/QB XL,* 4, 1995, p. 121-125.

Eswara Reddy, D.B. "A study of the information sources of Agricultural Extension Officers with reference to technology transfer in agriculture". Ph.D. Thesis, Karnataka University, Dharwad, 1982. (unpublished)

Eswara Reddy, D.B. Cooperative storage library for less frequently used agricultural documents in Inda. In *ICAR-PAU Seminar on Agricultural in Librarianship and Documentation,* 2-5 Feb 1977.

Eswara Reddy, D.B. Cooperation and coordination among the agricultural libraries with reference to resource sharing. In ICAR Summer Institute on Information systems for Agricultural Sciences and Technology". 10-24 Dec, 1985, University library, PKV, Akola.

Eswara Reddy, D.B. Joint Agricultural Research libraries for multi institutional campuses– a note. In All India seminar on *Agricultural Library and Information Services,* Hyderabad, 29 Dce, 1980 -1 Jan, 1981.

Eswara Reddy, D.B. Recent developments in the transfer of Agricultural information in India. In ICAR summer Institute on "Information systems for Agricultural Sciences and Technology", 10-24 Dec, 1985, University Library, PKV, Akola.

Eswara Reddy, D.B. "Professional obsolescence of technology transfer agents and the need for information support – a note". In All India seminar on *Agricultural Library & Information Services,* Hyderabad, 29 Dec, 1980 – 1 Jan, 1981.

Fell, Elizabeth. "ARCIS : an agricultural research current information system", *Aslib Proceedings, 31 (3),* March 1979, p. 138-143.

Fisher Ritw C and kinch, Michael P. Agricultural reference services, Library Trends, vol 38, No.3, Winter 1990, p. 397-414.

French, Beverlee A User needs and Library services in Agricultural Services, *Library Trends,* Vol 38, No3, Winter, 1990, p, 415 – 441.

Frierson, Eleanor and Lindsey, George. Computers and Communication: Technologies for the Management of International Agricultural information, *Library Trends,* Vol 38, No.3, Winter, 1990 p.474-497.

Frierson, Elemor and Zoelick, Panline A. "Information Needs in Agriculture and Markets for CD-ROM Products: Results of a Joint market study", *IAALD/QB XXXVI (1-2),* 1991, p. 139-145.

Fusionie, A.M. *Heritage of American Agriculture: A Bibliography of Pre 1860 Imprints,* Beltville, MD: National Agricultural Library, 1975.

Gachie, Isabelle, "Producing and Disseminating Information to the Agricultural Producers of NIS Countries", *IAALD/QB XLI (1),* 1996.

Gaddagimath, R.B. "User Education Programe for the Agricultural Scientists: A model followed at the National Academy of Agricultural Research Management", *IJALIS,* 13-15, 1985-87, p. 31-41.

Gajendra Singh and Kushal Pal. "Agricultural Research Information System (ARIS) of ICAR". *DESIDOC Bulletin of Information Technology.* Vol 18, No.2, March, 1998, p. 5-12.

Garg, K.C. & Datt, B. Bibliometrics of Agricultural research in India, *QB IAAIS, 37 (3),* 1992, p.133-139.

Gaikwad, Bhaskar and Hendre, Purushottam. "Agriculture Communication through IT : A case study". Yojana, March, 2001, p. 27-30.

Gessesse, K and Mbwna, S.S. "Scientific literature service in Tanzania; Historical account", *Annals of Library Science and Documentation, 37(4)* Dec, 1990, p.121-124.

Giovannetti, Jean-Francois; Menou, J. Michel and Thorpe, Peter, "BABINET and the development of Micro computer based National Documentation Networks in the less developed countries", *IAALD/QBXXXVI,* 3,1991, p. 171-180.

Goldberg, E.D. "Information for research on sustainable agriculture in tropical America: A Collective Challenge", *QBIAAIS,* 41 (1) 1996, p.58-62.

Goyal, S.P. Sharing of Theses by Agricultural Universities in India: Case Study of Thesis Abstracts, *Herald of Library Science,* 18 (1-2) Jan-Apr 1979, p. 76-81.

Gras, Chris Le and Gardner, Howard. "CALM: An Adventure in Diffusion of Agricultural Communication Technology". *IAALD/QB XLI,* 1, 1996, p. 95-99.

Gray, D.E. and Johnston, Susan M. The use of Computer-based bibliographic information services in the ministry of Agriculture, Fisheries and Food, *Aslib Proceedings,* 31(3), March 1979, p.129-135.

Greorio, Leonar B and Sison, Josephine C. "Agricultural Information Provision in Developing Countries: Information Transfer is Still Inadequate in Rural Areas" *IAALD/QB XXXIV,* 1, 1989, p. 7-12.

Guha Roy, K.K. "Agricultural Research and Informational Service". *The Modern Librarian* Vol XI, oct-Dec, 1940, No.1, p.1-10.

Gunjal, S.R. "Application of Citation Analysis for Journal use Study in Agricultural Extension: A Case Study", *IASLIC conference,* (15) 1985, papers, p.117-120.

Gunjal, S.R. and Kumar, P.S.G. "Information Service for National Development. The Indian Context", *Herald of Library Science,* 23 (1-2), 1985 p.31.

Haavisto, Pekka and Ofuersten, Jukka. Agronet – A Business branch oriented network for the Agro-Industry. *IAALD/QB XLI* (1), 1996, p. 92-94.

Haendler, Harad and Paris Powell, Antoinette. IAALD : Forty Years of Progress, *IAALD/QB XI* (2-3), 1995, p. 68-74.

Handbook of Agricultural Education 1986. Association of Indian Universities, New Delhi.

Harris, Susan C. Agricultural Information in developing countries. *Library Trends,* Vol 38, No.3, Winter 1990, p. 578-634.

Haris, SusanC. Current Awareness methodologies for strengthening applied agricultural research in the tropics, *IAALD/QB XXX* (4), 1985, p. 101-107.

Hartevelt, J.H.W. Van. Introduction of CD-ROM technology in ACP countries; Report of a CTA Project, *IAALD/QB XXXVI* (1-2), 1991, p. 101-104.

Hauzner, I and Janvec, M. Knihouni ke a informcni Sluzby na Vysoke skole Zemedelske V Proze. [Library and Information services at the University of Agriculture in Prague] 1'92 *Casopis*, 34 (10) 1992, p. 246-247.

Hemasudar Naidu, G and Gunjal, S.R. Agricultural Library and Information services in Inda: Growth, development and contribution of Agricultural University libraries, *ILA Bulletin*. Vol XXIV, No.4, Jan-March 1989, p. 187-193.

Hemasundar Naidu, G and Gunjal, S.R. Agricultural Library buildings and their structure in India, *Herald of Library Science,* Vol 32, N3-4 July – Oct 1993, p.190-200.

Hema Sundar Naidu, G and Gunjal, S.R. *An Assessment of the Nature of Agricultural Information used by the Doctoral Students*. p. 233-246.

Hemasundar Naidu, G and Gunjal, S.R. "Collection tendency of Agricultural Libraries in India". *Herald of Library Science*. 24(J); 14.2' N9 V 31, N1-2 Jan-April 1992, p. 27-32.

Hemasundar Naidu, G. "Exchange of Publications in the Agricultural Libraries of India". *IASLIC Bulletin*. 34 (3), 1998, p. 137-139.

Hemasundar Naidu, G and Gunjal, S.R. "Inter-library loan service in Agircultural Libraries in India", *Annals of Library Science and Documentation,* 39 (4), 1992, p. 134-138.

Hemasundar Naidu, G and Gunjal, S.R. "Newspaper clippings in Agricultural sciences", *ILA Bulletion,* Vol.XXI NO.1-2 April-Sep 1985, p. 33-38.

Hemasudnar Naidu, G and Gunjal, S.R. "Organisation of document collection in Agricultural Libraries of India", *IJA LIS,* 17, 1989, p.65-72.

Herse, Edith. "Latin American Regional Initiatives in Agricultural Information". *IAALD/QB XLI,* 1, 1996 p.63-66.

Hirst, F.C. "UK liaison with international agricultural systems", *Aslib Proceedings* 31(3), March 1979, p.126-128.

Hittangi, N. Vasant Kumar and Kamalvijyan, D. "Academic librarianship as a career", *ALIS Bullition* 3(1), 1979, p. 39-40.

Howard, Isoseph, "Chief resource and service for agricultural information". *Herald of library Science*. 33 N3-4, July – Oct 1994. p.167-175.

Hutchinson, Barbara.S; Varady, Robert and Baldwin, Charlene. "Information Management projects in developing countries: The challenge of working with varying levels of Infrastructure", *IAALD / QB XXXVI* (1-2), 1991, p. 110-113.

Indian Council of Agricultural Research, *Agricultural Education in India*, 1960, New Delhi.

Indian Council of Agricultural Research, *Final Report on Research Institutes and Agricultural University Libraries*, New Delhi, ICAR, 1969, p. 29-30.

Indian Council of Agricultural Research: *Annual Report – 1997-98*, ICAR, New Delhi.

Jackson, George. "The scope of agricultural serials literature of the Science Reference library", *Aslib Proceedings,* 34 (4), April, 1982, p. 198-202.

Jehl, Maria-To see. The CTA and International Cooperation in the training of agricultural librarians and documentalists, *IAALD/ QB XXXVI* (1-2), 1991, p. 52-54.

Jhamtani, Anita. "Transfer of technology to farm Women". *Yojana,* Sep, 1995, p. 24-26.

John Newton. "Commonwealth Agricultural World Agricultural Information service", *Special Libraries,* July, 1978, p. 251-254.

Johnstone, A. "A system for the storage and retrieval of field trails data", *Aslib Proceedings,* 31(3), March 1979, p. 144-145.

Jones, Dougles, "Establishing an end user searcing service utilizing CD-ROM and low cost on-line systems. The changing role of the intermediaries in providing access to information", *IAALD /QB XXXVI* (1-2), 1991, p. 146-153.

Jones, Dougles E. "Sources of Agricultural Information", *Library Trends,* Vol 38, No.3, Winter, 1990, p. 498-516.

Joseph Howard. "Chief Resource and service for Agricultural Information". *Herald of Library Science,* V33 July-Oct 1994, p. 167-171.

Joshi, Y. "Rationalizing library acquisitions policy: A case study", *IAALD/QB XXX* (1), 1985, p. 7-13.

Judith Palmer. "Information services in a beleaguered agricultural industry". *Aslib Proceedings,* 38 (4), April, 1986, p. 101-113.

Kabir, H. "Citations in Indian Agricultural Research: An analysis", *Annals of Library Science and Documentation,* 37 (3) Sep, 1990, p. 102-109.

Kannappanavar, B.V. and Vijayakumar. "Use of IT in University of Agricultural Science libraries of Karnataka A comparative study". *DESIDOC Bulletin of Information Technology* 21 (1), Jan, 2001, p.21,

Kaur, Amritapal. "Restructuring education for Agricultural Information professionals in India". *Library Science with a Slant Documentation and Information Studies,* Vol.3, No.1, 1998 Paper B, p.21-24.

Kaur, Amritapal. "Use of Computer and CD-ROM in the libraries of Agricultural universities and Research institutes in the state of Punjab, Haryana and Himachal Pradesh: A study", *ILA Bulletin,* Vol XXXII, No.3-4 Oct 1996, March, 1997, p. 5-9.

Kaur Harpal, "The Relationship between the Academic Achievement and Library use Post-Graduate students in two Agricultural Universities". *IJALIS* 21, 1993, p. 33-39.

Kennedy-Olsen, Jan "Management of trends in Agricultural libraries", *Library Trends,* Vol. 38, No.3, Winter, 1990, p. 350-376.

Kotei, S.I.A. "Guiding Principles to evaluate special training programmes and packages for agricultural library and Information work", *IAALD/QB XXVIII* (3),1983,p. 110-125.

Kumar P.S.G. *Computerisation of Indian Libraries*, 1987, B.R. Publishing Corporation, New Delhi.

Kumar , P.S.G. "Agricultural Information services in India: An assessment", *IASLIC National Seminar* 10, 1982, p. 101-114.

Krieger, C and Schmid. The thesaurus implementation for AGRIS on CD-ROM. *IAAIS*, 38(4), 1993, p. 185-189.

Kumar, R.P. and Dutta. Selective Dissemination of Information (SDI). service of ICRISAT: An evaluation, *Iaslic National Seminar*, Kanpur (10), 1982, p. 59-65.

Kumar, R et al. Status report of Indian Scientific institutions/Universities in the field of agricultural sciences on the basis of Indian science Abstracts, *Information Services & Use*, 12 (92), 1992, p.119 – 124.

Lal, Arjun. "A trend in citation paltern in Agriculture Research in Bihar", *Iaslic Bulletin*, 34 (2) 1989, p.65-72.

Lal, Arjun "Book Bank Scheme: A case study of Rajendra Agricultural University Library, Pusa (Bihar)", *IJALIS*, 21, 1993, p. 41-45.

Lal, Arjun. "Citations in Agricultural Research", *IJALIS*, Vol 13, No.2, Dec 1988, p.175-183.

Lal, Arjun and Panda, K.C. "Channels of Scholory Communications of Plant Pathology literature": An evaluation, *Library Science with a Slant to Documentation and Information Studies*, Vol 35, No. 3, 1998, paper V, p. 179-188.

Lal, Arjun, "Staffing in Rajendra Agricultural University Library, Pusa: A case study". *IJALIS*, 22, 1994, p. 25-35.

Lal, S and Singh P. "Growth and development of agricultural University libraries in India: A case study of Haryana Agricultural University library", *Library Science with Slant to Documentation and Information Studies*, 32 (10), Mar. 1995, p. 41-55.

Lancaser, F.W. & Beecher, J.W. Agricultural librarianship and documentation as a profession. In Agriculture to hasten development (Proceedings of the VIth World Congress of IAALD. March 1980 Manila, Philippines) p. 197-210.

Los Banos, Laguna, *Philippines: Agricultural libraries Association of the Philippines* and Agricultural Information Bank for Asia.

Lazeaski, B. Internet resources in agriculture: favourite sources of an Internet trainer, *Journal of Agricultural & Food Information*, 3(2) 1995, p. 57-64.

Lenggang, Zainuddin H.R; Sirdi, Chan and Powell, A.P. "Management Techniques for developing libraries: Teaching library management techniques to Indonesian librarians", *IAALD/ QBXXXIV*, 4,1989, p. 167-170.

Le Gras, Chris and Garder, Howard. "CALM: An adventure in diffusion of agricultural communication technology", *IAALD /QBXLI*, 1, 1996, p. 95-99.

Lewis, D.A. "The future of Agricultural Information transfer: Technological and other aspects". *IAALD/QB XXVIII,* 3, 1983, p. 91-98.

Lilwall, N.B. "ESCA information awareness and retrieval service", *Aslib Proceedings,* 31(3), March 1979, p.146-147.

Livingston, E.D. "Agricultural University libraries in India", *Herald of Library Science,* 37(1-2) Jan-Apr 1998, p. 30-40.

Livingston, E.D. and Narasimha Raju, G.V.S.L. "Agricultural Library service in Guntur District: An Evaluation", *Iaslic Bulletin,* 37(2), 1992, p.67-72.

Livingston, E.D and Narasimha Raju, GVSL "Information needs of Agricultural Researchers – A Study", *IJA LIS,* 19, 1991, p. 14-21.

London-Lane, Chris. "Participatory Rural Appraisal Concepts applied to Agricultural extension: A case study in Sumatra", *IAALD / QBXLI* (1),1996, p.100-103.

Maheswarappa, B.S. and Trivedi, S.K. "Information needs of Indian food scientists A case study of C.F.T.R.I. Mysore", *Annals of Library Science and Documentation* 33(1-2), 1986, p.67-75.

Malhotra, H.K. "User studies in libraries of agricultural universities. 2 meeting information requirements of post graduate students" *Annals of Library Science and Documentation,* 37 (2) Jun, 1990, p. 59.62.

Mangla, P.B. "Library and Information Science Education in India". In *Handbook of Libraries, Archives and Information Centers in India,* Ed. By B.M. Gupta. et.al Vol 1, New Delhi, Information Industry Publications, 1985, p.237.

Mangla, P.B. "Agricultural libraries in India: An overall view—Key Note Address", *Journal of Library and Information Science.* Vol 13, No.2, Dec, 8, 1988, p. 97-108.

Maria-Josee Jehl. "The CTA and International Cooperation in the training of Agricultural librarians and Documentalists", *IAALD QB XXXVI,* (1-2), 1991, p. 52-54.

Manjunatha, K.K. "Sources of Agricultural Information", *Library Science,* 28, 1991, Paper U, p.150-159.

Mathiesen, Inger, "Ten years of agricultural documentation services in Denmark". *IAALD / QB XXXVI* (1-2), 1991 p. 41-43.

Martinelli, Monia Teresa Ronchi, "Education and Training for Agricultural Information Work", *Journal of Library and Information Science,* Vol. 8, No. 2, Dec-1983, p. 103-124.

Mbwana, S.S. "The role of Agricultural Information in research and training in Tanzania", *Journal of Library and Information Science,* Vol 12, Nov-June, 1987, p.38-45.

Mehla, R.D. "Publication Pattern of Indian Agricultural Theses", *Iaslic Bulletin* 32(2) 1987, p. 75-80.

Mehla, R.D and Singh, Prem. Agricultural data bases on CD-ROMs: Their relevance for libraries in developing countries, *IAALD/QBXL* (4), 1995, p. 144-150.

Metcalfe, J.R. and Cooper, S.E.V. "Non-Conventional Literature. The CAB View". *IAALD/ QBXXVII* (1), 1982, p.8-12.

Metcalfe, John R. "The CAB World Agricultural information service". *Aslib Proceedings,* 31 (3), March 1979, p.110-117.

Mohamadali, O.N. "Agricultural research and agricultural information services for East Africa", *Libri.* Vol 28.No.2: 1978, p.118-140.

Mohamadali, O.N. "Practical Agriculturists, Literacy and agricultural information in East Africa", *Libri.* Vol. 27, No.4; 1977, p. 341-351.

Mohan Surendra. "Agricultural Information network in India", *Annals of library and Documentation,* 1978 No. 25 (104), p. 110-114.

Mohan, Surendra. "Documentation services of the Commonwealth Agricultural Bureaux, U.K", *Annals of Library Science and Documentation.* Vol 19, No.3, Sept. 1972, p.146-154.

Mohan, Surendra. "Agricultural information systems and services". *Journal of Library and Information Science* 2(2) Dec, 1977, p.182-201.

Molster, H.C. "The integration of manual and computerized information services at the centre for Agricultural publishing and Documentation", *Aslib Proceedings,* 31(3), March, 1979, p.118-125.

Manasterios, I. "Evaluating AGRISEARCH: a database for Agricultural research Projects". *IAAIS/QB* 38 (4), 1993, p. 229-231.

Morton, Maragarat L. "Training for a changing environment : The challenges a decentralized system". *IAALD/QBXXXVI* (1-2), 1991, p. 133-135.

Mudannayake, Inangani. Information needs and Information practices of Agricultural Scientists in Srilanka edited by Y.D.A. Senanayake. Post Graduate Institute of Agriculture University of Pesadeniya. Sri Lanka 1989.

Musib, S.K. Production of journals in Agriculture, Agricultural Economics and Economics: Their country of origin frequency and agency of publication, *IJALIS,* Vol 9, No.2, Dec 1984, p.160-166.

Mully, M. Corn, "Cattle computers". *Scottish Libraries,* (55), Feb/Mar, 1996, p.16-17.

Margot Bellamy. "Planning for a sustainable information system in the electronic age: Tradition Versus technology", *IAALD / QB XLI,* 1, Jan 23-26, 1996, p. 47-51.

National Academy of Agricultural Research Management, *Annual Report, 1997-98,* Rajandra Nagar, Hyderabad.

National Institute of Rural Development, *Annual Report-1997-98,* Hyderabad

National Institute of Agricultural Extension Management, *Annual Report 1996-97,* Rajendra Nagar, Hyderabad.

National Plant protection Training Institute, *Annual Report 1997-98,* Hyderabad.

National Research center for Sorghum, *Annual Report 1996–97.* Rajendra Nagar, Hyderabad.

Ndicye. D. Sengal. Research and evaluation on the experience of training scientific and technical information to herds in Senegal? *Proceedings of the Seminar on Information Provision to Rural Communities in Africa,* Held in Gabarone, Botswana 22-25 June, 1994. p. 22-25

Newton, John. "Commonwealth Agricultural Bureau World Agricultural Information service", *Special Libraries,* July, 1978, p. 250-254.

Niang, Thiendou. "The role of CTA in Dissminating Agricultural Information in ACP Countries". *IAALD//Q BXLI,* 1,1996, p.12-16.

Ochs, Mary. "New Technologies for Document Delivery and the barriers to their use in the developing countries", *IAALD /QB XXXVI, 1-2,* 1991, p.118-121.

Ogbourne, C.Pand Ison, T. "International partnership his for improving access to Agricultural Information in the developing world: The role of CAB International". *IAALD/ QB XLI,* 1,1996, p. 18-25.

O'Hare, Margaret. "British Library supported research in agricultural, biological and medical information", *Aslib Proceedings,* 34(3), March 1982, p.141-150.

Olsen, Wallace C and Kennedy-Olsen, Jan. "Determining the current core Literature in the agricultural sciences", *IAALD / QB XXXVI* (1-2), 1991, p.122-126.

Oviss Oruma, B. "The problem of information management in Agriculture", *IAALD/QB XXIX,* 4,1984, p. 91-94.

Ozowa, Vincent N. Nature of agricultural information needs of small scale farmers in Africa: The Nigerian example, *Herald of Library Science,* Vol 34, N 1-2, Jan-April 1995, p. 3-9.

Pamela Q.J. Andre. "Optical Technology: New ways of providing information to the end user". *IAALD/QB XXXVI* (1-2), 1991, p. 136-138.

Pan Shuchun. "The Library of the Chinese Academy of Agricultural Sciences: Cooperation with other libraries important to CAAS Library". *IAALD/QBXXXIV,* (1), 1989, p. 19-22.

Peres, Fernando C; and others. "Agricultural science citation Index – IBCC Ag : Preliminary result", *IAALD/ QB XLI* (1),1996, p. 67-69.

Parker, Dorthy et. al. "Primer for agricultural libraries, Netherlands", *PUDOC for IAALD,* 1969, p.9.

Parker, Dorothy and Carabelli, Angelina. *Guide for an Agricultural Library Survey for Developing Countries*. 1970. The Scaregow Press, Inc. Metuchen..

Parikh, Ramlal. Agriculture for Rural development, *University News,* Vol XXXIV, No.23, June, 3, 1996. p. 1-5.

Paskoff, Bath M. "History and Characteristics of Agricultural Libraries and Information in the United States". *Library Trends,* Vol 38, No.3, Winter, 1990, p. 331-40.

Patil,Y.M. and Kumar, P.S.G. "Agricultural Information systems and services: Retrospect's and prospects", *Library Science with a Slant to Documentation and Information Studies,* Vol 35, No.1, March 1988 papers D, p.37-46.

Pavate, M.V., *Industrial Status for Agriculture*, Yojana, Dec, 1995. p. 27-28.

Perera, M.J.C. Development of Scientific information in Srilanka: a perspective with special reference to agriculture, *IAAIS,* 40 (4), 1995, p. 109-113.

Perumalsamy, K and Arunachalam N. "Evolution of Agricultural Education". *University News,* Vol. 39, No.52, Dec 24-30, 2001, p. 1-3.

Perumalsamy, K and Karunanidhi, R. "Modernisation of Agricultural University Libraries", *University News,* 40(5), Feb, 4-10, 2002, p.8-12.

Perumalsamy, K. "Role of Library in Agricultural Information System", *University News* 38(2), Jan 10,2000, p.6-9.

Phadnis, S.P. and Rajpal Sital. World Agricultural Information and availability to Indian Agricultural Scientists. *Annals of Library Science and Documentation,* Vol 21, No. 1-2 Mar-June 1974, p:32-53.

Phadnis, S.P. and Shoaib Ahasan, A. Training of Agricultural Scientists in information use. *Journal of Library and Information Science* 2 (2) Dec. 1977, p.151-181.

Pichappan, P. "Indian Agricultural Science Journals : A comparative study of the ranking list of Journals by citations, impact factor and discipline influence score", *IASLIC Bulletin, 35,(2)* Jun 1990, p. 83-86.

Pozdnjakov, V.G. The study of Information requests and forms of meeting them in Scientific Agricultural libraries of USSR, *IAALD/QB XXXVI,* 1-2, 1991, p.97-99.

Prabhakar, A.S. et al. "Higher Agricultural Education in Inda; thoughts for future planning". *University News,* 39 (24), June 11-17, 2001, p.7-9.

Parsher. R.G. Towards a better information service in agricultural libraries; proposal for postgraduate library course in agricultural and veterinary science. Paper submitted in ICAR, PAU seminar on agricultural librarianship and documentation at Ludhiana from Feb 2-5, 1977.

Prasher, R.G. Agricultural Libraries for Scientists and farmers, *IJALIS-21* (1993), p.1-8.

Prasher, R.G. *Managing University Libraries*. 1991. Today & Tomorrows Printers & Publishers, (India).

Prodhani, M.A. Press clipping service and its importance in agricultural research library. *Annals of Library Science and documentation.* Vol 29, No3, Sept.1982, p.135-137.

Quibo, Chen. A check on overlapping between AGRICOLA, AGRIS and CAB for Tropical Agricultural Records. *IAALO /QB XXXIV,* (2), 1989, p. 67-72.

Raina, Roshan Libraries in Agricultural Research Communication, *Lucknow Librarian,* 15 (2) 1983, p. 75-79.

Rajasekharan, K. Kerala Agricultural University Library system: A plan for action *ILA Bulletion,* Vol XX No1-2 April-Sept 1984, p. 29-37.

Rajasekahran, K. Librarian in an Agricultural College: A meaningful selection procedure, ILA Bulletin, Vol XXV, (1), April-June 1989, p.42-47.

Rajasekharan, K. "On information services in Agricultural Sciences", *Lucknow Librarian,* 18(3) July – Sept 1986, p.97-106.

Rajasekharan, K. "Certain issues associated with the computerization of an Agricultural Library", *IJALIS,* 18, 1990, p.17-20.

Rajasekharan, T.S. "Libraries and information centers in India". *In Encyclopedia of Library and Information Science* Ed by Allen Kent et al. New York. Marcel Dekar. Vol.27, p. 350-352.

Raju, K.A. "Rural development literature: Preliminary results of a Comparative study of three global Abstracting services". *IAALD / QB XXXVI (4) 1991,* p. 227-232.

Raman, K.V. National Agricultural Research Systems of the future. In Agricultural Research systems and Managemet in the 21st century. Ed. Raman, K.V., MM.Anwer M.M., Gaddagimath. R.B., Proceedings of the International Seminar, Dec. 8-10, 1987, NAARM, Hyderabad, p. 149-155.

Ramanna, B and Gopinath, M.V. "User studies in National information centre for food science and Technology (NICFOS)", *Iaslic National Seminar,* Kanpur (10), 1982, p. 1-8.

Rama Rao. D.Muralidhar, U. and Kalla, Jagadish C. *European Journal of Agricultural Education and Extension,* Vol 3, No2, 1996, p. 119-130.

Rama Rao, D, Mauralidhar, U. and Kalla, Jagadesh C. "Planning Agricultural Education in India". *Europeon Journal of Agricultural Education and Extension,* Vol 4, No.1, 1997, p. 67-80.

Rama Tirth Agricultural University Library Staff Norms, *IJALIS.* 11, 1983, p.16-18.

Ramesh, L.S.R. C.V. and Nagaraju, A.V.S.S. "Restructuring higher agricultural education for next millennium". *University News,* 37(18), May3, 1999, p.10-12.

Ranchi Martinalti, M.T. "Education and Training for the Agricultural information professionals", *IAALD / QBXXVIII,* 3, 1983, p. 126-151.

Ranganath, K.A., Geeta Seetaram Sangameswaram, S.V. and Narahari Rao, B.S. "Indian Information input to International food Information service". An Information Analysis. Case study. *Library Science,* 18, March, 1981, paper B, p.13-25.

Renuka, P. Specilization in Agricultural Librarianship: Some suggestions, Changing dimensions of LIS Education, seminar papers XVIII IATLIS National Seminar, Dept of Library and Information Science, Andhra University, Visakhapatnam. 12-14 Oct, 2001, p.247-253.

Ritzler, Claws, "Databases on CD-ROM: what can this technology mean for developing countries in the future?", *IAALD / QB XXXIV* (1), 1989, p.1-5.

Rolls, M.J. "Non-conventional literature in Agriculture". The Users view *IAALD / QB XXVII,* 1,1982, p. 25-29.

Rogers. A. Adult Education and Agricultural Extension : Some comparisons. *International Journal of Life-long Education,* Vol.12, No.3, 1993 p.

Roseboom, J. And Pardey, P.G. Measuring the Development of National Agricultural Research Systems. *Scientometrics*, 23(1), Jan 1992, p. 169-192.

Runcie, K.V. Agricultural and biological information-some remarks, *Aslib Proceedings*, 32 (5), May, 1980, p. 216-219.

Russel, Keith W. The "Information centre" concept as a fund-raising and Marketing tool for information organisations in developing countries, *IAALD VII World Congress* (1-2), 1991, p. 114-117.

Russel, Keith W. "The value of information in Agricultural research", *IAALD, QB XLI* (1) 314, 1997, p. 219-222.

Sanjeev, P. Research in Agriculture: A faceted analysis, *IJALIS-22*, 1994, p. 43-50.

Salman, S.C and Hansan, A.A. *Principles and Practice of Agricultural Research*, London: Leonard Hill, 1964.

Sengupta, I.N. Assessing information requirements of Scientists in a Research Institute. *Indian Journal of Information and Library Society*. Vol.3, No.3-4, Sep. Dec 1990, p. 1-15.

Shand, R.T. Approaches to farming systems Research. In Agricultural Systems Research for Developing Countries, Canberra, Australia : ACIAR, 1985.

Sharma, R.D. "Growth of Agricultural Journalism and Agriculture Research Information centre at ICAR", *DESIDOC Bulletin of Information Technology*, Vol 18, No 2, March 1998. p.21-30.

Sharma, V.P. and Murthy, L. User friendly and complete packaging: Consumer Orientation for marketing agricultural information, *International Information Communication & Education*, 14(2) Sep 1995, p. 173-178.

Shrimali, D.S. An Agricultural Library-its purpose and functions, *Indian Librarian* 33 (1), June, 1978, p.25-30.

Shuchun, Pan. The Library of the Chinese Academy of Agricultural Sciences: Cooperation with their Libraries important to CAAS Library. *IAALD/QB XXXIV*, 1, 1989, p. 19-21

Silk, J.K. Agricultural information services in ICI, *Aslib Proceedings, 31 (3),* March 1979, p. 148-151.

Singh, Prem and Mehla, R.D. Agricultural Databases on CD-ROMS their relevance for libraries in developing countries. *IAALD/QBXI(4),*1995, p.114-120

Singh, Virendra Prakash and Singh, Sanjay kumar Agricultural College Libraires in Bihar: A sample survey, *IJALIS,* 21, 1993, p. 56-61.

Singhvi, M.L. An Evaluation of the Biliography of agriculture from its user point of view, *IASLIC BULLETIN* Vol 9, No.2 June, 1964, p. 95-100.

Singhvi, M.L. Referece Material in Agricultural. *Indian Librarian,* Sep, 1964, p. 97-102.

Sittler, P.M. Liviathan: An extension service information server, *Journal of Agricultural and Food Information*, 3(2), 1995, p.83-90.

Siva Prasad, Y.V. and Gaddigamath, R.B. user Education Programme for agricultural scientists at the National Academy of Agricultural Research Management, *Indian Journal of Information Library & Society,* V9, N3-4 July-Dec,1996, p. 218-222.

Smith, Helen. "Agricultural Documents; Acquisition control", *Special Libraries Winter*, 1991, vol 82, No1, p.23-29.

Smith, H. and Martin, N.P. "Information service and delivery for agricultural extension agents". *Resource sharing & Information Networks,* 8 (2) 1993, p. 15-25.

Somashekar, K.T. "Development of Agricultural Education and Libraries: Indian scene". *IJALIS-21,* 1993, p. 9-15.

Somashekar, K.T. "Growth and development of agricultural education and libraries in India with special reference to Karnataka – A project report submitted to University of Mysore as a partial of specilization for M.Sc. 1973.

Somashekar, K.T. The need for co-operation among the agricultural University libraries: Some reflections. *IAALD/QBVIII,* 1980, p.5-8

Srinivas,S. and Venkatesan, V. Inpact of Semi-Arid Tropical Crops information services (SATCRIS) on Agricultural Scientists: Perspectives for the Next decade. *IAALD/QB (42),* 314, 1997, p. 157-162.

Stanley, M.K. Indian National Agricultural Library. *IJALIS –21,* 1993, p. 26-31.

Subbaiah, R. "Conceptual Framework for an Indian National Agricultural Information System". *(INAGRIS) Ph.D. Thesis submitted in Library and Information Science.* Department of Library and Information Science, University of Kerala, Trivandrum, 1985.

Subbaiah, R. *Agricultural Library Users*. New Delhi, 1989. Metropolitrn.

Subbaiah, R. "Bibliographical control of Indian Agro biological literature: An aim of National Agricultural information system". *IJALIS,* 12, 1984. p 21-22.

Subbaiah, R. *Agricultural Librarianship in India: An Overview*. Metropolitan New Delhi, 1988.

Subbaiah, R. A "Conceptual model for agricultural knowledge generation and transfer". *Annals of Library Science and Documentation.* Vol.32, No.3-4 Sep-Dec, 1985, p. 80-82.

Subbaiah, R. "Planning for Automation in Agricultural Libraries : A System approach", *IJALIS-17,* 1989, p. 40-47.

Subbaiah, R. "Towards bibliographical control of Indian agro-bilogical literature". *Annals of Library Science and Documentation.* 29 (1) Mar 1982, p. 12-15.

Subbiah, R. Organisational pattern of Indian Agrobiological literature based on user information needs; *Annals of Library Science and Documantaion.* 29, Vol.4, 1982, p. 187-192

Sugunavathy, C. Information Needs and Sources of Information of subject matter specialists in the Training and Visit system of Agricultural Extension. *Ph.D. thesis.* Department of Library and Information Science, Osmania University, Hyderabad, 1997.

Sugunavathy, C. "Partners in Communication of information", *IJALS,* 17 ,1989, p. 48-51.

Suryanarayana, Y.V. "Bibliometric analysis of publications of CTRI and its Research Stations". *IJALIS,* 23, 1995, p. 13-23

Sunyanarayana Y. V and Raman, M. "Library and Documentatin services at central Tobacco Research Institute", Rajahmundry, *IJALIS,* 20, 1992, p. 24-29.

Swaminathan, M.S. "Indian Agriculture: Looking back and forward", *Yojana,* Jan, 1997, p. 5-13.

Swaminathan, M.S." Shaping our agricultural future", *Hindu* 11th Jan, 2001.

Thomas, Bloch. "Agricultural Libraries in Nepal", *IAALD/QBXXVI* (3), p. 85-88.

Thomas, John. T. "Automation feasibility study of the North Cardina Agricultural & Technical State University Library". *Indian Librarian.* June, 1971. p. 5-12.

Thomas, Kurian K. "Evaluation of Indian Agrobiology – Journals. Coverage in Abstracting / Indexing services", *IAALD/QB XLI* (3/4), 1996, p. 245-250.

Thomas, Sarah E. "Bibliographic control and Agriculture", *Library Trends,* Vol 38, No.3, Winter, 1990, p 542-561.

Thomas, Sarah E. Improved access to Agricultural Literature through a comprehensive, detailed agricultureal Thesaurus. *IAALD/QB XXXVI* (1-2), 1991, p. 80-82

Thomas, Sarah E. United States Agricultural Information Network: Genesis of a cooperative Organisation, *Special Libraries,* Spring 1989, p. 113-117.

Thomas, Sarah E. Use of the CAB Thesaures at the National Agricultural Library, *IAALD/QB XXX* (3), 1985, p.61-65.

Thorpe, Peter Priorities in Information Management for strengthening National agricultural research *IAALD/QB XXX* (4), 1985, p. 77-84.

Ton, Isahak Allin. "Addressing the Information needs of farmers and the extension services: The Malaysian experience". *IAALD /QB XXXVI* (1-2), 1991, p. 36-39.

Uberoy, Asha "New technologies for Women in Agriculture"; *Yojana,* Sep 1995, p. 17-20.

UDO, Schutzsack, "Trends in agricultural information with reference to developing countires. The literature is growing, Financial resources are shrinking and technology is only one answer", *IAALD/QBXXXZV,* (2) 1989, p. 41-45.

Universities Hand Book, 28th Edition Association of Indian Universities AIU House, 16 Kotla Marg, New Delhi – 110002.

Van Crodor, L. and Anderson, J. Linking research, extension and education why is the problem so persist and perversive, *European Journal of Agricultural Education and Extension,* Vol3, NO.4, 1997, p.241 - 247

Van Hartevelt, J.H.W. "Introduction of CD-Rom Technology in ACP countries: Report of a CTA project". *IAALD/QB XXXIII* (1-2), 1991, p.101-104.

Vashishth, C.P. "Indian participation in INIS and AGRIS Global information systems". *ILA Bulletin,* Vol XV No. 3-4, July – Dec 1979, p. 77-93

Veeranjaneyulu, K. "A Study on Agricultural Information systems in Andhra pradesh (India)". *Doctoral thesis submitted to Department of Library and Information Science,* Sri Venkateswara University, Tirupathi 1997.

Veeranjaneyulu, K. "Library information services in Central Library, Acharya N.G. Ranga Agricultural University, Hyderabad, Library practices for effective management", *ILA Seminar Papers 47th All India Library Conference,* Warngal, 20-23-Dec, 2001, p. 29 -37.

Vijayalakshmi, N.R. "CD-ROM and its implications for agricultural information system in India". *IJALIS 17, 1989,* p. 25-28.

Walton, Peter. "Improving Agricultural Information services of small Island Nations in the pacific region". *IAALD/QB XXXIV* (2), 1989, p. 73-77.

Wyatt, HV. Information or Communicatin? *Aslib Proceedings,* 32 (5), May 1980, p. 207-210.

Widge, M.K. "Women in Agriculture", *Yojana,* Sep 1995, p. 21-26.

Xianfu, Wang; Kaiyang, Li and Shuchun, Pan. "Implementing results, roles and effects of the Chinese agricultural information services projects". *IAALD/QB XXXVI* (1-2), 1991, p. 128-132.

Yaikova, Antonia,T. "Fifty years of servicing the information needs of agricultural science and practical farming". *IAALD/QBXXVI* (2),1981, p. 47-53.

Zhang, Qiaoqiao. Agricultrual Library and information systems in China. *Journal of Informatin Science.* 17 (4) 1994. p. 235-245.

Zhang, Qiaoqiao. "Improving the accessibility and availability of information in the agricultural library and information system of China". *IAALD /QB XXXVI* (1-2), 1991, p. 55-58.

Index

■■■